The Reception of David Ricardo in Continental Europe and Japan

This book is a coherent and unique collection of chapters exploring the reception and diffusion of David Ricardo's writings in different languages. It highlights the similarities and differences between them and seeks to delineate the diffusion of Ricardo's theory in various parts of Europe and Japan. While there may have been case studies about the reception of Ricardo's thoughts for several countries, there has not yet been a systematic study of the diffusion process under consideration as a whole.

This book caters to all scholars dedicated to the history of economic thought and to students who are interested in learning about the peculiarities of the evolution of economic theories in different countries. This book is the first of its kind, with no known predecessor, and it aims to shed light on how and why some of Ricardo's writings were picked up and why others were not. Given Ricardo's importance in the field of economics, this book will be of interest to many.

Gilbert Faccarello is Professor at Université Panthéon-Assas, Paris, and a member of the research centre Triangle, École Normale Supérieure de Lyon and CNRS (UMR 5206), France. He is a co-founder and co-editor of *The European Journal of the History of Economic Thought* (London: Routledge) and at the time of writing is chairing the ESHET Council (European Society for the History of Economic Thought).

Masashi Izumo is Professor at Kanagawa University, Yokohama, Japan. He is a committee member of the Ricardo Society (Japan) and council member of the JSHET (Japanese Society for the History of Economic Thought).

The Reception of David Ricardo in Continental Europe and Japan

Edited by
Gilbert Faccarello and Masashi Izumo

Routledge
Taylor & Francis Group
LONDON AND NEW YORK

First published 2014
by Routledge
2 Park Square, Milton Park, Abingdon, Oxfordshire OX14 4RN

and by Routledge
711 Third Avenue, New York, NY 10017

First issued in paperback 2016

Routledge is an imprint of the Taylor & Francis Group, an informa business

British Library Cataloguing in Publication Data
A catalogue record for this book is available from the British Library

Library of Congress Cataloging-in-Publication Data
The reception of Ricardo in continental Europe and Japan / edited by Gilbert Faccarello, Masashi Izumo.
pages cm
Includes bibliographical references and index.
1. Ricardo, David, 1772-1823. 2. Economics--Europe--History.
3. Economics--Japan--History. I. Faccarello, Gilbert. II. Izumo, Masashi.
HB103.R5R43 2014
330.15'3094--dc23
2013029782

ISBN 13: 978-1-138-68557-4 (pbk)
ISBN 13: 978-0-415-82771-3 (hbk)

Typeset in Times New Roman
by Taylor & Francis Books

Contents

Contributors

Salvador Almenar is with the University of Valencia, Spain and a correspondent member of the Royal Academy of Moral and Political Sciences, Madrid.

Alain Béraud is with the University of Cergy-Pontoise, France, and THEMA, CNRS.

José Luís Cardoso is with the Institute of Social Sciences, University of Lisbon, Portugal.

Gilbert Faccarello is with Panthéon-Assas University, Paris, France, and Triangle, École Normale Supérieure de Lyon and CNRS.

Christian Gehrke is with Karl-Franzens University, Graz, Austria, and Graz Schumpeter Centre.

Masashi Izumo is with Kanagawa University, Yokohama, Japan.

Anna La Bruna is with the University of Catania, Italy.

Denis Melnik is with the National Research University Higher School of Economics, Moscow, Russia.

Annalisa Rosselli is with the University of Roma Tor Vergata, Rome, Italy.

Shigemasa Sato is with Onomichi City University, Japan.

Introduction

Ricardo's travels into several remote nations

Gilbert Faccarello and Masashi Izumo

It is always fascinating to see how the writings and ideas of authors – be they philosophers or scientists – are progressively taken into account, discussed, accepted or rejected in their own countries according to various historical intellectual circumstances. It is even more interesting to study how these writings and ideas cross borders and spread across nations and through time, being discussed, rejected or accepted anew in totally different environments to those prevailing in their home countries.

Yet this kind of inquiry, at least in the history of economic thought, is still in its infancy. While some one-off studies have been published in the past, large-scale research on the reception and dissemination of specific authors or doctrines is rare[1] and certainly needs to be developed. Not only does it shed new light on the works in question, but it is also a powerful aid to understanding the theories and contexts with which they often came into conflict. It highlights the fact that the history of economic thought is not only the logical analysis of certain corpuses, or the rigorous restatement of theoretical approaches, but also an account of the non-linear developments of concepts, ideas and policies according to the different national realities.

The present book is an attempt to go in this direction and to study the reception and dissemination of the works of David Ricardo in various European countries (French-speaking and German-speaking countries, Italy, Portugal, Spain and Russia) and in Japan, with the discourse being even wider if we take into account the role of some Latin American countries (Brazil, Argentina, Mexico) in the case of Portugal and Spain. The chapters collected here were presented at a conference organized in Kyoto by the Ricardo Society Japan in March 2012[2] – 'The reception and diffusion of Ricardo: an international comparison' – and rewritten for this publication.

The nature of the project

Two centuries after the publication of Ricardo's major works, and when so much has been written on the different elements of Ricardo's doctrine, it is high time that we had a precise idea of their effective reception. The case of Great Britain has been investigated while studying the important theoretical developments and controversies that took place there during the nineteenth century. But Britain attracted almost all the attention of scholars, and other countries have been largely neglected. Moreover, students of the history of economic thought were gradually taught a strange success story – the result of decades of retrospective illusions. As an example of such an account, let us refer to the introduction Paul Beauregard wrote in 1889 for the first – and unique – abridged edition of the French translation of Ricardo's *Principles of Political Economy and Taxation*.[3] After reassessing the main points of Ricardo's theory of value and distribution, he remarks:

> When the book was published in 1817 it was prodigiously successful. It was an event and it seemed that the science of economics was disclosed for the first time. Of course there was some resistance: Malthus had reservations and our J.-B. Say vigorously fought some of Ricardo's doctrines. But critiques remained few and went almost unnoticed amidst general applause […]. J. Mill and, after him, the main economists in England declared they were Ricardo's disciples. The doctrine became *orthodox* and they were tempted to despise those who dared oppose. This was no transient success: the work is still a classic and one can say that, from 1817 until today, the history of an important part of political economy has been the very history of Ricardo's book.
>
> (Beauregard 1889: xx–xxi)

Of course, this statement echoes the celebrated passage of the *Confessions of an English Opium-Eater* – quoted by Beauregard – where Thomas De Quincey describes how deeply he was impressed when he read Ricardo's *Principles* in 1818. But Beauregard generalized this reaction, making it appear to be the general opinion not only in Britain but also implicitly in France and Europe. Of course, he admitted, the interest in Ricardo's writings faded away over time because economists realized that some predictions, or rather alleged predictions – especially the evolution of the distribution of income between rent, profits and wages – had not been fulfilled, and also because, after the publication of *Das Kapital* by Karl Marx, Ricardo became the 'prisoner' of the socialists. But in the end, this qualification sounds minor and does not weaken the overall impression of the immediate success of Ricardo's approach and its triumphant march through most of the nineteenth century. While Beauregard's account may be highly sketchy, it was nevertheless shared afterwards in various forms by many scholars.

However, the studies collected in this book tell an entirely different story. The reception of Ricardo, at least in continental Europe – the case of Japan being more specific – had nothing of this triumphant march and the success, if any, was not immediate. Why this was so depended of course on the peculiar intellectual and political situation of each country. Our purpose is therefore to outline a much more exact picture of what actually happened.

The study of Ricardo's international reception first raises the question of the availability of his texts. His writings could of course be read in their original English versions. At the beginning of the nineteenth century, this was the case in Switzerland, and more precisely in Geneva, where the active group around the periodical *Bibliothèque Britannique* – then the *Bibliothèque Universelle* – paid great attention to everything that was published in Great Britain. This was also the case with Jean-Baptiste Say in France and some prominent Spanish and Portuguese *émigrés*: the best examples being those of the Portuguese intellectual Francisco Solano Constâncio, who translated Ricardo's *Principles* into French in 1819, and of the Spaniard Alvaro Flórez Estrada, who published his *Curso de economia política* in London in 1828. But those who could read the original versions of Ricardo's writings were in fact a tiny minority who had, moreover, some direct link with England. For wider diffusion, translations were needed.

The French translations were the first available and played an important role in the reception of Ricardo's ideas in Europe. As early as 1810, the French version of the third edition of *The High Price of Bullion* was published in three instalments in a newspaper, *La Gazette Nationale ou le Moniteur Universel*. In 1817 and 1818 excerpts from the first chapter of the *Principles* were inserted, with comments, in the Genevan *Bibliothèque Universelle* and, in 1819, the first edition of the book was published in French in Paris, with critical notes by Jean-Baptiste Say. Almost three decades later, in 1847, the translation was revised and republished, allegedly on the third edition, with many other works by Ricardo, under the title *Œuvres complètes de David Ricardo*.

Another case of early translation was the German version of the first edition of the *Principles*, published in 1821. The second edition was not translated until 1837, and the third in 1877. In the other countries studied in this book, the first translations of the full text of the *Principles* were slower to arrive: 1856 in Italian, 1873 in Russian, 1921 in Japanese, 1932 in Spanish and 1975 in Portuguese, although excerpts were published in 1848 in Spanish and in 1938 in Portuguese. There were also other ways to come into contact with the Ricardian approach, especially through the various translations of James Mill's *Elements of Political Economy*, John Ramsay McCulloch's *Principles of Political Economy* and, some decades later, John Stuart Mill's *Principles of Political Economy*, which were more adapted to a large audience than Ricardo's own works.

But the dates of the translations do not tell the whole story, and their late publication in most countries, while meaningful, is far from decisive. As a matter of fact, during a significant part of the nineteenth century, the French language was still dominant among cultivated people on the continent, and the French editions played an important role in the reception of Ricardo's ideas. As is stated clearly in the chapters on Portugal, Spain, Italy and Russia – but also that on Germany and Austria – the French editions circulated widely among economists in these countries.

The question of the first availability of translations inevitably raises the issue of their quality. We can easily imagine that at the beginning of the nineteenth century, with Smith's and Say's prose in mind, it was not easy to understand and translate Ricardo's much more precise and abstract developments. And on this point the picture is not rosy. While widely circulated and read, the French translations of some of Ricardo's works – especially the 1819–35 editions of the *Principes de l'économie politique et de l'impôt* – proved to be approximate and even defective, and it is likely that some important aspects of Ricardo's doctrines – the theory of rent for example – were misunderstood because of this. Unfortunately, the nineteenth-century German translations were apparently even worse, with the same consequences. German-speaking readers had to wait until 1905 to have an accurate version of the *Principles.*

If we discard this problem of accuracy, the reception of Ricardo also depended on the intellectual and political circumstances prevailing in the different countries. Ricardo's writings did not reach their readers in a vacuum: many currents of thought already occupied the space. Cameralism, for example, was still important in Austria. The so-called 'use-value school' developed in Germany, which later saw the emergence of the two German historical schools. In France, the works of Jean-Baptiste Say and his interpretation of Adam Smith were predominant and the writings of 'outsiders' such as Jean-Charles-Léonard Simonde de Sismondi also played an important role. This means that, generally speaking, Ricardo's ideas arrived in countries where a different approach to political economy predominated, roughly based on a supply and demand framework and thus a priori hostile to his doctrines of value and income distribution, although his view on money was generally considered more sympathetically.

In this theoretical landscape, Say's writings were central, and in particular the notes he appended to the French translation of the *Principles.* If we add the fact that, for the major part of the nineteenth century, Say and the French liberal economists exerted great intellectual influence abroad – through their many books and treatises but also, from the 1840s onwards, through the Société d'économie politique, the *Journal des économistes* and the *Dictionnaire de l'économie politique* – it is easy to understand that, for a time, their specific vision of Ricardo shaped his reception in other countries. Other French thinkers had also exerted some influence, to a lesser degree: Sismondi, for example, Jean-Paul Alban de Villeneuve-Bargemont and his Christian political economy, and some socialist writers. But they all held a critical attitude towards Ricardo. This does not mean that, in the different countries, one author or another did not adopt some of Ricardo's ideas. Nor does it mean that there were no Ricardians at all, but they almost always had some reservations, such as Pellegrino Rossi in France, Francesco Fuoco in Italy, or Karl Heinrich Rau in Germany. The case of Japan is particular, since the works of Ricardo were introduced there very late, when they were already considered part of the history of economic thought.

The history of the reception of Ricardo's writings concerns not only the geographical dissemination of his ideas, but also the positions the readers held in their own countries – were they teachers, journalists, politicians, etc.? – and, inextricably, time. In the different countries, the specific intellectual and political events during the nineteenth century and the beginning of the twentieth century played a part and most often dictated the choice of the topics which, in Ricardo's works, were to attract attention: the theory of rent, the inverse relation between wages and profits, money and banking, the theory of value and prices, etc. This is particularly true for Portugal and Spain, where the political turmoils and the sporadic emigration of intellectuals played an important role – some of them lived for many years in England or France and may have had direct knowledge of the writings published there and their authors. This is also striking for Italy where, in the late nineteenth century, almost only the monetary doctrines of Ricardo were of interest to the majority of economists. And for all the European countries – except perhaps France – and Japan at various moments in their nineteenth-century history, the critical attitude towards Ricardo's *Principles* was rooted in an awareness of the need to modernize their economy and to achieve important reforms for the sake of development. In these circumstances Ricardo's discourse seemed too theoretical and abstract, unable to suggest suitable policies to cope with such specific situations.

Last but not least, the consideration of time is obviously also important for understanding the Ricardo revival in the late-nineteenth and the twentieth century, before the important wave of studies generated by the Sraffa edition of the *Works and Correspondence of David Ricardo* – from 1951 on – and the publication of his own *Production of Commodities by Means of Commodities* in 1960. This first revival was due to Marx and the various Marxist currents of thought that followed, especially in Germany and Russia where their influence was strong. It presented two different aspects. On the one hand, some authors – such as Yuli Galaktionovich Zhukovsky, Vladimir Karpovich Dmitriev and Ladislaus von Bortkiewicz – were motivated by a genuine interest in Ricardo and published valuable analyzes which may have gone unnoticed at the time but were fortunately rediscovered later on. The best example is Dmitriev's *Economic Essays* (1904), which were only brought out of oblivion by their French translation in 1968. Although intellectually important, these authors were a minority. On the other hand, as time went by and especially after the 1917 Revolution in Russia, other authors read Ricardo more through Marxian spectacles and his theory of value and distribution was again studied in the perspective dictated by the new Bible, *Das Kapital*. Isaak Illich Rubin is certainly one of the most interesting of these authors. In a sense, Beauregard was not wrong when he wrote that they made Ricardo their prisoner – he could not have foreseen that, some decades later, a strange Italian *émigré* would set Ricardo free again.

The content of the book

The studies included in this book have been approximately ordered according to the chronology of the contact the different countries had with Ricardo's works.

Chapter 1, by Alain Béraud and Gilbert Faccarello, aims to provide a first precise picture of the French reception of Ricardo's works and ideas. Limiting the study to the first three-quarters of the nineteenth century, it concentrates on some of the most important debates in which Ricardo's ideas were discussed. After setting the stage and describing the intellectual context of this reception, the chapter presents the various translations and editions of Ricardo's writings in the French language. It then deals with some methodological aspects of Ricardo's approach to political economy – mainly his 'abstract' theoretical way of thinking – in general heavily criticized by the French authors. The following sections are devoted to more specific topics: value and wealth, rent, money and banking, and finally Say's law of markets and crises. On all these points, the reception was rather hostile and critical. On the whole, Ricardo's ideas were received in a theoretical context marked by Turgot and Say and a widely accepted French adaptation of Adam Smith's *Wealth of Nations* in a supply and demand framework. This does not mean that Ricardo was not influential in France, but his legacy was fragmented, and some economists only retained the aspects of Ricardo's doctrines that were of interest to them, discarding or criticizing the rest. Ricardo was also influential in another, more diffuse way. His writings obliged certain authors to react to and discuss his ideas, thereby also driving them to clarify and develop their own theories. This was obviously the case for Say and Sismondi who had, furthermore, the opportunity to discuss directly with the author of the *Principles.*

Chapter 2, by Christian Gehrke, reviews some of the more important German contributions to the development of the classical approach to value and distribution in the 100 or so years from the publication of Ricardo's *Principles* in 1817 to the beginning of the Great War in 1914. After providing an overview of the German editions and early book reviews of Ricardo's *Principles* and a summary account of the development of the German economic discourse in this period, the role of the German historical schools in the demise of Ricardian economics in the German-speaking countries is briefly discussed. Then two different lines in the further elaboration of Ricardo's approach to the theory of value and distribution are examined in greater detail, focusing on the contributions of F. B. W. Hermann and Johann-Carl Rodbertus. The final two sections offer a critical assessment of the contributions of Ladislaus von Bortkiewicz and Georg von Charasoff, and of their critique of Marx's attempt to elaborate on Ricardo's analysis of prices and income distribution.

Chapter 3, by José Luís Cardoso, is devoted to the diffusion and appropriation of Ricardo's thought in Portugal and explains why it was limited and confined to a small number of authors. After presenting a descriptive account of the reading of Ricardo during the period under analysis, the chapter emphasizes the role of Solano Constâncio, a Portuguese *émigré* who lived most of his active life in Paris and who translated Ricardo's *Principles* into French. However, Constâncio was also responsible for the spread, among

Portuguese readers, through his essays and reviews, of a critical view of the alleged universal and abstract principles of political economy usually associated with Ricardo and Ricardian economics, which may be considered one of the main causes of the limited influence of Ricardo in Portugal during the first half of the nineteenth century. This chapter also describes how, having lost the opportunity to be influential during the period of the hegemony of classical economics, Ricardo's thought and Ricardian economics alike have not attracted thorough and competent interpretation by Portuguese economists in more recent periods.

Chapter 4, by Salvador Almenar, examines the reception and dissemination of Ricardo's theories in Spain, distinguishing different channels, forms and degrees. It first deals with the period up to 1834. Ricardo was known in Spain through the French translation of the *Principles* and, above all, indirectly through authors such as James Mill, or the critical comments by Sismondi and Say. The chapter then examines the case of Alvaro Flórez Estrada (1766–1853), because of his singular reception and reformulation of the ideas of Ricardo, McCulloch and Mill in his *Curso de economía política* – which had seven editions between 1828 and 1853. Flórez accepted the Ricardian theories of distribution and development, but he modified the model by proposing a regular process of improvement in agriculture and by expanding the analysis of the incidence of a land tax. His influence in Spain and Latin America was important during the 1830s and 1840s. This chapter finally presents some other attitudes adopted by Spanish economists towards Ricardo between 1834 and 1868: simple ignorance, partial and explicit criticism, or systematic refutation.

Chapter 5, by Anna La Bruna and Annalisa Rosselli, enquires as to whether Ricardo's monetary thought and theory of value met with different fortunes in Italy in the nineteenth century. The authors argue that at the theoretical level it is legitimate to separate the destiny of Ricardo's ideas on money from that of his ideas on value and distribution. They show that Ricardo's views on money enjoyed a wider and more favourable reception than those on value and distribution, but ultimately they were no better understood or endorsed, since neither the historical situation nor the approach to economics favoured their acceptance. To support this conclusion, the authors outline the main monetary issues that were discussed in Italy subsequent to independence in 1861, the major laws proposed or approved to solve them, and the protagonists of the debates they entailed. After a summary of the main conclusions of Ricardo's theory that are relevant to the issues debated in Italy, the influence of Ricardo on the monetary debates in Italy in the nineteenth century is discussed, with particular focus on the controversy of the late 1870s. The authors show that, unlike Ricardo's approach, the Italian debate was developed at the micro-economic level: the differences between protagonists concerned the factors that affect the preferences of individual agents for different kinds of money.

Chapter 6, by Denis Melnik, reviews the three periods in the development of economic science in Russia during the last two centuries. For different reasons, these periods provided an unfavorable context for the reception of

Ricardo's economic ideas. In the first period, for about half of the nineteenth century, the name of Ricardo was not unknown, but his theory attracted no attention. In the second period, which started in the 1860s and ended with the Russian Revolution, the consensus towards Ricardo among the majority of Russian economists was based on a respectful distance. Still, there were some attempts to update the relevance of Ricardo's economics to Russia. Nikolai Ivanovich Sieber, the first translator of Ricardo into Russian, regarded his theory as a preceding stage to Marx's, while Yuli Galaktionovich Zhukovsky, who rejected Marxism from the very beginning, made an attempt to reformulate Ricardo's theory in terms not dissimilar to the later neoclassical interpretation. The subsequent rise of marginalism and the heated debates among Marxists at the turn of the twentieth century resulted in endeavours to 'synthesize' classical and marginalist approaches to value and distribution characteristic of a number of Russian economists: this was the background to Vladimir Karpovich Dmitriev's original interpretation. In the third period, during the Soviet era, the canonical version of the history of economic thought placed Ricardo as an immediate predecessor of Marx. By comparing the approaches to Ricardo's economics proposed by Isaak Illich Rubin and Piero Sraffa, the author outlines the difference between the two lines of development of the classical approach during the twentieth century.

Chapter 7, by Masashi Izumo and Shigemasa Sato, describes the reception and diffusion of Ricardo in Japan from 1869 to 2012. Although it cannot avoid being selective, it singles out those studies that best illustrate the reception of Ricardo's works and the main currents in Japanese Ricardo studies. The chapter deals with two distinct periods, each starting with a major event which had a deep impact on Japanese society: the Meiji Restoration and World War II. During the first period, i.e., during the late nineteenth and early twentieth century, a wide range of translations of Western economic writings played a significant role in advancing and developing economic thought in Japan. But, in this context, the introduction of Ricardo was late compared with J. S. Mill, Malthus, Smith, Say, Marshall, Jevons, List and Marx. It is shown how studies of Ricardo, both from the Marshallian and Marxian points of view, were introduced into Japan in the 1910s and then passed on to later generations of scholars. For the second period, i.e., from 1945 to the present, particular attention is paid to certain Japanese studies of some controversial interpretations of Ricardo – for example, Sraffa's interpretation of early Ricardo in terms of a 'corn-ratio theory', or the question of whether or not Ricardo's theory of money departs from the classical quantity theory – thus providing possible interesting comparisons with analogous debates abroad.

Notes

1 See for example Delmas, Demals and Steiner 1995 on the international dissemination of Physiocracy; Tribe 2002 on the reception of the works of Adam

Smith, and Kurz, Nishizawa and Tribe 2011 on more specific topics. For some general reflections on the international diffusion of economic thought, see Cardoso 2003 and the appended bibliography.

2 This conference is part of a series of seminars and meetings around David Ricardo and classical political economy financed, since April 2010 and for five years, by a Grant-in-Aid for Scientific Research (A) No. 22243019 of the Japanese Society for the Promotion of Sciences (JSPS). The authors of the chapters of the present book gratefully thank the organizers and the participants for helpful comments and discussions.

3 For the history of the French translations of the works of Ricardo, see Chapter 1. In general, for extensive developments of the topics alluded to in this introduction, please see each relevant chapter of this book.

References

Beauregard, Paul (1889). Introduction. In David Ricardo, *Rente, salaires et profits.* Paris: Guillaumin, pp. i–xxviii.

Cardoso, José Luís (2003). The international diffusion of economic thought. In Samuels, Warren, Biddle, Jeff and Davis, John (eds.), *A Companion to the History of Economic Thought*. Oxford and New York: Blackwell, pp. 622–33.

Delmas, Bernard, Thierry Demals and Philippe Steiner (eds.) (1995). *La diffusion internationale de la physiocratie (XVIIIe-XIXe)*. Grenoble: Presses Universitaires de Grenoble.

Kurz, Heinz D., Tamotsu Nishizawa and Keith Tribe (eds.) (2011). *The dissemination of economic ideas.* Cheltenham: Edward Elgar.

Tribe, Keith (ed.) (2002). *A critical bibliography of Adam Smith*. London: Pickering & Chatto.

1 'Nous marchons sur un autre terrain.' The reception of Ricardo in the French language

Episodes from a complex history

Alain Béraud and Gilbert Faccarello

> A journal (*Edinburgh Review*, n. 59, June 1818) […] announces [Ricardo's *Principles*] as having provoked, in political economy, the greatest step forward since Adam Smith. However, we feel so much that we are walking on a different ground [*nous marchons sur un autre terrain*] that we would hardly have had the occasion to quote this book […] were it not because its fame obliged us sometimes to do so. (Sismondi 1819, 1: 58–59)

> His [Ricardo's] writings might be found beautiful, but reading them without an authorized guide is perhaps no less dangerous for the scientific truth than, for the Catholic religion, reading the Bible without the commentaries of the Church. (Puynode 1866, III: 59)

On 4 September 1820, alluding to his *Principles of Political Economy and Taxation*, Ricardo wrote to Malthus that he 'did not expect' he 'had so many readers in France as the number of copies of the French translation which […] have been sold would seem to imply'. He was of course pleased, but without any illusions about the quality of the reception of his ideas. He thus added: 'I am not surprised that you found few who understood my theory correctly, and still fewer who were disposed to agree with me' (Ricardo 1951–73, 8: 227). Ricardo was not far from the truth, and the reception of his works in France does indeed present an intriguing and complex history. The two quotations with which this chapter is headed give some idea of the tone of some French reactions to the *Principles.*

This chapter aims to provide a first precise picture of the French reception of Ricardo's works and ideas. The subject is certainly wide and the authors to be taken into account are numerous. We therefore had to make a choice. While limiting our study to the nineteenth century – with some unavoidable references to later works – we have selected some periods, authors and themes that, we think, give a significant idea of debates of the time about the various aspects of Ricardo's theories.[1] Some topics had to be omitted, such as the discussions about machinery, wages and profits, and employment. Some other discussions too, about international trade or socialism, have been discarded: in these debates, Ricardo's works and ideas were not a main concern. On international trade, for example, the main question was free trade or protection, and the theory of comparative advantage, when it was correctly understood, was probably considered by most writers to be a simple extension of Smith's ideas.[2] And for the various socialist movements – outside the Marxist currents that developed late in the century – Ricardo was not a reference: it was Smith who was read and commented. Ironically enough, those who referred to Ricardo in relation to socialism were certain liberals frightened by the possible consequences of the Ricardian theory of rent.

This chapter is organized as follows. Section 1 sets the stage and briefly describes the context of this reception. Section 2 presents the various translations and editions of Ricardo's writings in the French language. Section 3 deals with some methodological aspects of Ricardo's approach to political economy. The following sections are devoted to more specific topics: value and wealth (section 4), rent (section 5), money and banking (section 6) and Say's law of markets and crises (section 7).

1. Ricardo: ' ... deadly boring for the reader'?

The reception of the works of David Ricardo in the French language stands in sharp contrast to what happened in England. Today, almost all Ricardo scholars have in mind the enthusiastic lines Thomas De Quincey wrote in his *Confessions of an English Opium Eater*, recalling his first reading of the *Principles of Political Economy and Taxation* and quoting the *Bible*, Books of Samuel: 'Thou art the man!'

> Had this profound work really been written in England during the nineteenth century? Was it possible? I supposed thinking had been extinct in England. Could it be that an Englishman, and he not in academic bowers [...] had accomplished what all the universities of Europe, and a century of thought, had failed even to advance by one hair's breadth? [...] Mr. Ricardo had deduced, *a priori*, from the understanding itself, laws which first gave a ray of light into the unwieldy chaos of materials, and had constructed what had been but a collection of tentative discussions into a science of regular proportions, now first standing on an eternal basis. (De Quincey 1863: 255)

A neo-Smithian context

To say that the French readers were less enthusiastic is certainly an understatement. Look at the press, for example, that shaped the opinion of the general learned public of the time. In 1819, *Le Journal des Débats* announced the publication of the translation of the first edition of Ricardo's *Principles* in the following terms:

> The book [...] that has just been published in French with notes by M. J.-B. Say incited us to read again Say's praised *Traité* and to make a

> comparison with the new English writer. This comparison fully confirms that […] when foreigners and French authors deal with the same subjects, the former can write a book in which there is some good stuff; but only the latter know how to write a good book […]. In sum, M. Ricardo's book is very useful while not always pleasant; but we do not need it. (12 February 1819: 3)

Three years later, in 1822, and while Ricardo was not the only target of the critique, the *Revue Encyclopédique* – despite being an open-minded periodical – was even more negative: 'MM. Ricardo, Malthus and others […] have written some books that are difficult to apply to the needs of life, and deadly boring for the reader' (XIII: 631), adding:

> French translations of the *Political Economy* of Ricardo and Malthus have been published; people we consulted on these books admitted that they were unable to read them to the end. (XIII: 631 n.1)

Of course, not all reactions were so negative, and some were also fortunately better documented, but these quotations nevertheless set the tone of many comments. They induced the reader to think, moreover, that there was an opposition between a French and an English political economy. In fact the situation was much more complex than seems at first sight, and Ricardo's theories, while not enthusiastically acclaimed and accepted, actually had a real influence on the evolution of French thought.

On the one hand, at the beginning of the nineteenth century, the writings of Ricardo, Malthus, McCulloch and others reached a French public influenced by the Physiocrats, Turgot and above all Say, and who had long since read, discussed and on the whole accepted *and adapted* the work of Adam Smith (the *Theory of Moral Sentiments* and the *Wealth of Nations*: see Faccarello and Steiner, 2002). At that time, the French public and authors were imbued with specific interpretations of the *Wealth of Nations* – by Germain Garnier, Jean-Baptiste Say, Antoine-Louis-Claude Destutt de Tracy and Jean-Charles Léonard Simonde de Sismondi for example – and could not accept without reluctance the new and so very different view of Ricardo: they were and they remained 'neo-Smithian' (Béraud, Gislain and Steiner, 2004). A passage from Auguste Walras's *Esquisse d'une théorie de la richesse* expresses this general attitude quite well:

> God forbid! We do not deny in Ricardo some interesting research and instructive observations; but in our view, his theories of value and rent are simply an exaggeration of the vice Adam Smith introduced in his system: ascribing to human labour alone the whole creation of social wealth […] Had it had some success, Ricardo's book would have caused a regression in political economy; but his theory was not successful […] Thus, until now, there are only two famous names in political economy […]: *François Quesnay* and *Adam Smith*. All political economy prior to

> *Adam Smith* comes under *Quesnay*. All modern political economy is tied up with *Adam Smith*. (1844: 437)

As stated eloquently by Sismondi in the first quotation heading this chapter, French economists were 'walking on a different ground'. This explains the critical tone of the reception of the works of Ricardo – in this respect Malthus was more fortunate with his *Essay on the Principle of Population* and his *Principles of Political Economy*, on many points closer to the French ideas and approaches.

However, this is not to say that the French reactions were only negative and without consequences on the evolution of French economic thought. Firstly because among the French-speaking economists, although none can be characterized as a disciple of Ricardo, some of them accepted certain specific Ricardian doctrines, either on the distribution of income or on monetary questions. And secondly because the discussions of Ricardo's theories often provoked the evolution and modification of their own points of view, forced as they were to delve deeper into the subjects under examination.

Before turning to some of the episodes in this complex reception of Ricardo's writings in the French language, however, we must set the stage more completely and some preliminary remarks are in order: firstly on the opinions expressed on Ricardo's personality; secondly on the many strands of literature to be taken into account; and thirdly on the fact that the inquiry must not be limited to France but extended to other French-speaking countries.

A positive opinion of Ricardo, the man

In the first place, it should be noted that Ricardo, the man, was respected by the French economists. In almost all their writings – there are only few and marginal exceptions – they stressed his intelligence, honesty and intellectual disinterestedness. 'Like his friend Jeremy Bentham, Ricardo only listened to advice from the general interest' (Comte 1833: 89–90). 'He was neither Whig nor radical. His tactic was that of his reason, and not of his ambition or the ambition of others' (Fonteyraud 1847: xlv). They noted the fact that he was a poor orator, quoting his own confession that, in the House of Commons, 'I have twice attempted to speak, but I proceed in the most embarrassed manner, and I have no hope of conquering the alarm with which I am assailed the moment I hear the sound of my own voice' (Ricardo to McCulloch, 7 April 1819, VIII: 21). His peculiar written style was also often highlighted and most of the time criticized as being too dense, highly theoretical and almost mathematical. 'Never was a man less possessed with the demon of dissertation' (Fonteyraud 1847: xv). Hence some rather embarrassed judgements, such as Joseph Garnier's in a note to his 'Ricardo' entry in the influential *Dictionnaire de l'économie politique*:

> As a thinker, Ricardo appears to be superior, original and profound; as a writer, he sometimes obscures his thought in abstract formulations, the rigour of which is only apparent – but we do not mean to say that he is mistaken when he is obscure. (Garnier 1853: 531 n3)

Finally, French authors were also fascinated by Ricardo's 'success story' as a broker and financier, permitted by his 'sound and cold capacity to judge, his penetrating sagacity' (Garnier 1853: 530). This certainly stood in sharp contrast to the poor entrepreneurial capacities of J.-B. Say, for example.

> As a broker at the London stock exchange, he acquired a vast fortune, further increased since then by some always judicious speculations and the greatest order in his business; so much that he was said to be in possession, when he died, of more than forty million in our currency. One might be tempted to say: '*who minds the millions?*' because he used his wealth in such an excellent way that they became respectable. (Comte 1833: 86)

The many receptions of Ricardo's writings

In the second place, and even limiting our inquiry to the nineteenth century, we have to deal with a huge set of literature of many theoretical origins. The various groups of liberal economists – Jean-Baptiste Say and his followers, the Doctrinaires, etc. – are of course the most directly concerned in this story. But the many 'associationist' or socialist writers are also part of the picture, and so are the various tendencies of the so-called Christian political economy, not to speak of some original and rather independent writers like Cournot and A. and L. Walras. Their evaluation of the works of Ricardo are far from homogeneous, and the positions evolved through time – sometimes because of the many political events that shook France during the century,[3] in which our protagonists often played a role. Moreover, their opinions varied greatly according to the different topics dealt with – method, value and prices, income distribution, money and banking, machinery and employment, pauperism, etc. – and it is also natural that the interest in some Ricardian themes faded away as the century progressed.

Broadly speaking and to greatly simplify the picture, three periods can be distinguished in the reception of Ricardo's writings.

The first covers the Napoleonic era and the Restoration, i.e., approximately, the early nineteenth century until the death of Say (1832), a period during which the many currents of the liberal school opposed the political regimes of the Empire, the Restoration and their economic policies. These eventful decades were indisputably dominated by the writings of Say and Sismondi. The neo-Smithian wisdom of our authors was challenged by Ricardo's writing, provoking a re-examination of many points of doctrine. As a consequence, almost all the theoretical themes were addressed and discussed – sometimes with Ricardo himself – and, a point of no mean importance, the technical vocabulary was also considered and fixed.

The second period includes the July Monarchy, the 1848 Revolution and the Second Republic. This period is also fertile in economic and political events. Certain liberal economists, the Doctrinaires, were in power: after J.-B. Say died in 1832, Guizot and the Duke of Broglie asked Pellegrino Rossi (who was much closer to Ricardo's ideas than Say was) to go to Paris and succeed him to the chair of Collège de France. Some other liberals, more radical – the so-called School of Paris, with many followers of Say – were heavily attacked from all corners and attempted to organize themselves to fight for their free market ideas; and this was the time of the emergence and affirmation, from the late 1820s and the early 1830s on, of new currents of thought who challenged the economic wisdom of Smith and Say: the many 'associationist', socialist and Christian schools. As time went by, the positions sharpened and, around 1848, on the occasion of the economic crisis and the revolutionary events, they crystallized into clear political and theoretical opposition. During this period, the perception of Ricardo changed markedly, becoming much more diverse even among the liberal authors: Bastiat, for example, moved away from both Say and Ricardo, while Dupuit and Molinari adopted some Ricardian themes.

The third period covers the Second Empire and the first decades of the Third Republic, during which the various schools developed their positions in sharp contrast to each other. It is striking to see how the figure of Ricardo progressively became a moment in the history of economic thought, and how his doctrines were less and less topical, except perhaps for certain socialist or Christian authors. He was, in a way, replaced by John Stuart Mill. However, for various reasons to be analyzed, he never disappeared from the debates within the liberal schools and was even the object of a kind of liberal rehabilitation, even on the subject of ground rent.

Perspectives from the French-speaking community

In the third place, we are concerned here with French-speaking countries in general, not just France. This involves firstly Switzerland (and more specifically Geneva), a point whose importance we must stress, and secondly Belgium, after its independence from the Low Countries in 1830.

There were significant links between Geneva and France during the first half of the century, thus continuing a tradition which, during the eighteenth and at the turn of the nineteenth century, was exemplified by Jean-Jacques Rousseau, Jean Herrenschwand, Jacques Necker, his daughter Germaine Necker de Staël, and Benjamin Constant. Some Genevan economists played a prominent role in relation to our subject: first and foremost Jean-Charles Léonard Simonde de Sismondi (1773–1842) and Antoine-Élisée Cherbuliez (1797–1869). We should not forget Bentham's friend Étienne Dumont, and remember that Say, although born in France, came from a Genevan family – 'our fellow citizen Say' (*Bibliothèque Universelle*, 1818:11) was always considered as an eminent member of the community by the other Genevan writers.

There are also less well-known figures who are important for the beginning of our story: Marc-Auguste Pictet (1752–1825), his brother Charles Pictet de Rochemont (1755–1824), Pierre Prévost (1751–1839) and his son Guillaume – respectively the brother-in-law and the nephew of Jane Marcet, herself of Swiss origin.[4] They were almost all scientists and philosophers and played a not unimportant part in the political life of the city. They also had family and intellectual links with Britain and were personally acquainted with English writers (Prévost knew Malthus well). Ricardo visited them during his 1822 travel on the continent. Napoleon spoke angrily of Geneva – a French 'département' during the Empire, the 'département du Léman' – as 'this town where people know far too much English'. Sismondi himself described Geneva as 'an English town on the Continent, an advanced post for political and religious enlightenment' (Sismondi 1814: 4), 'a town where people think and feel in English but speak and write in French' (Sismondi 1814: 7). As stated in 1816 in the first issue of the influential *Bibliothèque Universelle*:

> It is above all as thinkers and scholars that the English and Scottish men of letters appear in the great market for human knowledge. All that supposes long meditations, strength in the analysis and a logical sequence of ideas belong to them as their own. Their success in philosophical studies, the progress and dissemination of the best principles of political economy and legislation, depend on this faculty for reflection and great capacity for serious studies that distinguish them among all others. (*Bibliothèque Universelle*, 1816: 9)

M.-A. Pictet and P. Prévost introduced Sismondi and Cherbuliez to political economy, informing them of the English and Scottish authors in the field. Pellegrino Rossi, who also played an important role in the French debates, lived and taught for a time in Geneva and was acquainted with all of them.

They also had an intense editorial activity. In 1796, during the post-Thermidorian period and before the annexation of Geneva to France, the Pictets founded the *Bibliothèque Britannique* – called the *Bibliothèque Universelle* from 1816 onwards[5] – with a clear intellectual programme referring to the Scottish philosophy as an antidote to what they considered the foolish and dangerous ideas of the time.[6] In 1816, in the paper introducing the first issue of the new formula, the *Bibliothèque Universelle*, the discourse remained the same and the reader was reminded that one aim was 'to fight, with the weapon of reason, all kinds of subversive principles and their pernicious influence on the younger generation' (*Bibliothèque Universelle* 1816: 10).

The series 'Littérature' of the *Bibliothèque*, directed by P. Prévost from 1803 on, contained excerpts of English books and even full translations of some papers – some of them, for example, in the 1820s, were originally published in the *Edinburgh Review*. Charles Pictet also published separately a French translation of Henry Thornton's *Paper Credit* (1802).[7] Pierre Prévost translated works by Adam Smith,[8] Benjamin Bell,[9] Dugald Stewart,[10] Hugh Blair[11] and Malthus's *Essay on the Principle of Population* – first some excerpts from the second edition, in 1805 in the *Bibliothèque Britannique*, and then the entire third edition in 1809, the subsequent versions being revised by his son Guillaume. Guillaume Prévost also translated into French Jane Marcet's *Conversations sur l'économie politique* (1817), her *Conversations sur la philosophie naturelle* (1820) and J. R. McCulloch's *Discours sur l'origine, les progrès, les objets particuliers, et l'importance de l'économie politique* (1825), all published by J. J. Paschoud in Geneva. It is also interesting to note how quickly these translations were published after the publication of the original works in Britain.[12]

The case of Belgium after its independence in 1830 is no less important. A prominent and original liberal economist such as Gustave de Molinari (1819–1912) was Belgian, lived in Paris for a time and played a significant part in French intellectual life during his long life. Christian political economists also had very close ties with Belgium. Charles de Coux (1787–1864), one of the 'founding fathers' of the movement, though French, held the first chair of political economy at the new Catholic University of Malines (later to become the Catholic University of Louvain), and his Belgian disciple and successor at the chair, Charles Périn (1815–1905) – almost the exact contemporary as his liberal fellow countryman Molinari – played a prominent role in the French Catholic movement during the second part of the century.

2. The French translations of Ricardo's works

The first step in our inquiry is to note what among Ricardo's writings was translated, by whom and when. Appendix 1 recapitulates the various editions in the French language published during the nineteenth century. Those from the twentieth century, while not included in our period, are nevertheless listed in Appendix 2.

From Paris to Geneva: the first translations into the French language

Our story starts in Paris. The first work translated was the third edition of Ricardo's *High Price of Bullion*. It was published in September 1810 in the quasi-official *Gazette nationale, ou le Moniteur universel*, in three instalments. The occasion was the debate about the organization of the French banking system and the role of the Banque de France (founded in 1800). The problems of monetary circulation and its unification also created fear among the public – especially the fear of seeing the creation of paper money again after the disastrous collapse of the assignats system – and led to the monetary and then economic crisis of 1810–11. Ricardo's ideas on money and banking were thus quickly noticed and they were often referred to in the debates during the following decades. The subsequent publications by Ricardo, about the Corn

Laws and an economic and secure currency, were published after the fall of the Empire, when French people had many other concerns, and this might explain why they were relatively neglected at that time, together with the fact that the *Principles of Political Economy and Taxation* appeared soon afterwards.

To take this new element into account, we must cross the border to Geneva and the Pictet/Prévost group around the celebrated *Bibliothèque Britannique* (1796–1815), renamed *Bibliothèque Universelle* in 1816 to show that, while the British authors were still a major reference, the editors wanted to widen the horizons of their fellow citizens and draw their attention to other valuable intellectual productions. Immediately after the publication of the first edition of Ricardo's *Principles*, two excerpts were translated and published in the November 1817 and January 1818 issues of *Bibliothèque Universelle (Littérature)*. Both were drawn from the first chapter of the *Principles*. The first excerpt was the translation of pp. 1–11 of the first edition, i.e., the opening pages where Ricardo criticizes Adam Smith's theory of value. The second was the translation of some passages, together with the summary of certain developments, from the rest of Chapter 1: pp. 19, 21, 22, 23–25, 31–36, 41–42, 44–48 – the final pages of the chapter – of the 1817 edition of the *Principles*, mainly devoted to the influence of distribution on prices.

Each excerpt is followed by an unsigned commentary:[13] while the first is entitled 'Observations du traducteur' and the second, 'Observations du rédacteur', they are by the same author. The first commentary concludes with the remark that only the most important chapters of Ricardo's book will be analyzed. The second ends with the mention 'to be continued', but the table of contents of the issue indicates that this was the 'second and last excerpt' and, in fact, the following issues do not contain anything more. The publication thus stopped suddenly. The translation is unsigned as well, but some passages in the text indicate that the translation and the comments are by the same person, Pierre Prévost.[14] We know that he was interested in political economy[15] and a very active translator. Moreover, he was just back from a four-month stay in London (Cherbuliez 1839: 54) and at that time he was interested in income distribution: 'I would like some day to publish a book on political economy entitled *Of Labour*, in which I would show the necessity of raising wages', he wrote on 4 April 1817 in his diary. Ricardo's book, no doubt, challenged his Smithian ideas.

Back to Paris, via Lisbon

The next stage in the story deals with the publication of Ricardo's *Principles* in their entirety. This also happened quickly: the French translation of the first edition was published in Paris in 1819, in two volumes, by J.-P. Aillaud, a publisher who was later described as being partly specialized in Portuguese books. As a matter of fact, the translator was a cosmopolitan Portuguese intellectual, Francisco Solano Constâncio (1777–1846), who was active in Paris at that time as a kind of diplomatic agent and collaborated there, between 1818 and 1822, on a journal in Portuguese, *Anais das Ciências das Artes e das Letras por huma Sociedade de Portuguezes Residentes em Paris* (Annals of Science, Arts and Letters) published by A. Bobée.[16] He was interested in political economy and especially in the controversy between Malthus and Say about the possibility of general gluts. In addition to his translation of Ricardo's *Principles*, Constâncio also published with Aillaud a translation of Malthus's *Principles*[17] in 1820 and a French version of William Godwin's refutation of Malthus's *Essay on the Principle of Population* in 1821.[18]

Constâncio's translation of Ricardo is important because the French learned public could read the *Principles* in their own language as soon as 1819, because Ricardo's text was supplemented by a series of notes by J.-B. Say, and finally because this text, revised in 1847 by Alcide Fonteyraud (see below), formed the basis for most subsequent editions and remained the main reference in France for almost a whole century, until the new 1992 translation published by Flammarion (on all these points, see Appendices 1 and 2).[19] It was, however, defective, with many errors and approximations that obscured the meaning of some chapters – the chapter on rent in particular.

The 1819 translation was nevertheless republished twice in 1835. First by J.-P. Aillaud in Paris, in two volumes, and then in one volume by H. Dumont in Brussels (probably an unauthorized edition, Belgium being specialized in this kind of publishing during the nineteenth century). The Paris edition was misleadingly presented as the 'second edition', and the Brussels edition as the 'third edition', but both were in fact simply the republication of Constâncio's translation of the 1817 text. The notes by Say were also reprinted, and a preface was added: 'Notice sur la vie et les écrits de Ricardo, publiée par sa famille' (Memoir on the life and writings of Ricardo, published by his family). Despite what the French subtitle indicates, this Memoir is not the text published by Moses Ricardo in 1824, but the translation of McCulloch's eulogy first published in 1824 in *The Edinburgh annual register for 1823* and then independently, in 1825, as *Memoir of the life and writings of David Ricardo, Esq. M.P.* – although this text does, it is true, make extensive use of Moses's obituary.

The Fonteyraud edition in Guillaumin's 'Collection des principaux économistes'

The third stage in our story took place when the economists, for the most part liberal and followers of Jean-Baptiste Say, started to organize themselves to defend their ideas when, after the first modern economic crises, they were attacked from all corners on the question of pauperism and a number of important issues were being discussed – like free foreign trade, for example. One entrepreneur played an important part in this movement: Gilbert-Urbain Guillaumin (1801–64), a publisher. He started publishing the *Journal des économistes* in 1841 and before that, in 1840, the famous series 'Collection des principaux économistes', intended to present the most important texts in the recent history of economic theory. Fifteen thick volumes were published during the following decade. The 13th of the series, a tall 8° of more than 800 pages, was devoted to Ricardo and entitled *Œuvres complètes de David Ricardo* (1847).

The editor was a young liberal economist who was to die prematurely, Paul Henri Alcide Fonteyraud (1822–49). In the first part of the book, Fonteyraud republished Ricardo's *Principles.* He was supposed to revise Constâncio's translation and take into account the changes made by Ricardo in the third edition. However, the result is almost appalling: 'the version of the *Principles* which it presents is no better than a pastiche of the first and third original edition' (Sraffa in Ricardo 1951–73, 10: 375).

> The revision is superficial. While the new chapters of the third edition are translated, it is at the cost of many additional mistranslations […]; a certain number of new texts and notes inserted into the last English edition were omitted; and some passages of the first edition suppressed in the third were maintained. […] It thus happens that the 1847 Guillaumin edition […] is neither the translation of the first English edition nor of the third, but a kind of hybrid of the two. (Delmas et al., 1992: 11)

In the second part of the book – entitled 'Œuvres diverses relatives à des questions de monnaies, de banque, de finances et de liberté commerciale' – Fonteyraud published his translations of some other major publications by Ricardo: *The High Price of Bullion*, *Reply to Mr Bosanquet's Practical Observations*, the *Essay on Profits*, the *Proposals for an Economical and Secure Currency*, *On Protection to Agriculture*, the *Plan for the Establishment of a National Bank*, and 'Funding system'.[20] These translations also remained the reference in France for more than a century, the *Essay on Profits* only being retranslated in 1988, and some monetary writings (1809–11) in 1991. Fonteyraud, who contacted and visited Ricardo's family for this work, added a long and interesting introduction to this collection – on which more below – simply entitled 'Notice sur la vie et les écrits de David Ricardo' (Fonteyraud 1847). This 'Notice', declared Adolphe-Jérôme Blanqui in February 1848 at the Académie des Sciences Morales et Politiques, is 'the most perfect that has been written on any economist'.[21]

This volume of the 'Collection des principaux économistes' was republished in 1882 – a preface by Maurice Block being added – and again in 1966. Only two other minor publications are to be noted during the nineteenth century. In 1865, Ricardo's 1818 evidence on the usury laws was translated in Paul-Jacques Coullet and Clément Juglar's *Extraits des enquêtes parlementaires anglaises sur les questions de banque, de circulation monétaire et de crédit. Enquêtes de 1810, 1811, 1819, 1841*, together with his 1819 evidence on the resumption of cash payments. A few years later – in 1889 according to the catalogue of the Bibliothèque nationale de France – some excerpts from the *Principles* were edited by Paul Beauregard. They consisted of eight chapters of the book (see

Appendix 1). The Constâncio/Fonteyraud translation was used but revised by Charles Formentin. As for Ricardo's correspondence, only the letters to Say were translated and published twice, first in Say's *Mélanges et correspondance d'économie politique* (1833) and then in *Œuvres diverses* (1848).

3. Methodological approaches to political economy

Against abstract principles

It was Say's opinion – and most French economists shared this point of view – that one of Smith's greatest achievements had been to apply

> to political economy the new mode of scientific investigation, i.e., not looking abstractedly for principles but ascending instead from facts the most constantly observed to the general laws which govern them, thanks to a rigorous manner of reasoning and without relying on simple assumptions. (Say 1814: 34)

He criticized Ricardo for doing precisely the reverse: reasoning from abstract principles whereas political economy 'in order to be useful, should not teach […] what should *necessarily* happen, but show how what really happens is the consequence of another real fact' (Say 1819: 45). Discussions on abstractions are endless, useless and dangerous. People argue about words, the reader is bored and ends up believing that in political economy, authors are unable to agree on any truth (Say 1825: 270). Dismissing both the followers of Quesnay and those of Ricardo, he insisted again on the complexity of the reality:

> They keep on generalizing and I am afraid that they have all moved away from the path of nature that only shows us complicated phenomena – the result of several combined actions – and moves towards its goal in its own way and despite the rules that we wish to impose on it. (Say 1825: 270)

Pierre Prévost was of the same opinion. In his series of observations on Ricardo's *Principles*, he wrote: 'All is extreme in this system of thought. No consideration is paid to modifying circumstances, and consequences are inferred from each other with too much confidence' (P. Prévost 1818: 14).

François Ferrier, who did not share Say's liberal ideas, also stressed the same point. 'Would you like to know what Ricardo proved in his two volumes? Nothing […]. M. Ricardo usually reasons on hypotheses: *I suppose that …* ' (Ferrier 1822: xxix–xxx). The legitimacy of a deductive approach that draws all the consequences from a series of hypotheses is thus rejected. On this point, Sismondi's opinion is not different from Say's or Ferrier's and will also, with variations, be shared by some other currents of thought, like the Saint-Simonians for example.

> Adam Smith's followers moved away from his doctrine and still more from his way of searching for the truth. Adam Smith considered political economy as a science based on experience. His new disciples […] have thrown themselves into abstractions that make us absolutely lose sight of reality. In their hands, science is so speculative that it seems to be removed from any practice […]. We believe that in so doing, it has moved away from both truth and clarity. (Sismondi 1819, 1: 57)

This kind of criticism was in general accepted by a majority of authors and was repeated during the following decades. A liberal author, Gustave du Puynode, wrote for example half a century later: 'When dealing with the economic science, one has the impression that he [Ricardo] does not remember that it is a question of men and of societies; he only speaks of them as a mathematician facing rigorous and dry theorems' (Puynode 1866, III: 51). But there were also some dissenting voices that were more radical, either intensifying the critique of 'abstraction' or on the contrary opposing the usual wisdom and stressing the fact that Ricardo, in his attempt to reason in a rigorous way, did not go far enough.

A more radical view against abstraction

Among those who held a more radical position are a number of authors who, during the 1830s and 1840s, sought to develop a Christian critique of the new industrial society and of political economy. In their opinion, the massive phenomenon of pauperism and the first modern economic crises were due to the adoption of a new social system based on free markets and first advocated by the English political economists. From this point of view, Ricardo's theories represented the most perfect achievement of an approach that, basing its reasoning on abstractions – and here the words 'abstract' and 'abstraction' have a different and more aggressive meaning than in Say – lost sight of men and only focused on things, in other words they lost sight of the political, moral and religious principles and only focused on material interests and the economy. Let us note what two eminent Christian writers wrote at that time: first Jean-Paul Alban de Villeneuve-Bargemont, whose voluminous *Économie politique chrétienne* (1834) is a landmark in the field and, second, Eugène Buret, who unfortunately died at a young age after the publication of his celebrated *De la misère des classes laborieuses en Angleterre et en France* (1840). Moreover, Buret's book is an important step in the dissemination of Ricardo's works and ideas: Marx, when in Paris, first read Ricardo in Buret's book and the excerpts from Ricardo's *Principles* that are to be found in the celebrated 1844 *Manuscripts* are drawn from it (Hattori 1994, Vatin 2001–2, 2005).

One can mainly criticize Ricardo, Villeneuve-Bargemont stated, 'for having considered wealth in an abstract and absolute way, without consideration for the lot of the workers. Like most English economists, he was more concerned with the collective power of nations than with the individual well-being of their citizens, and very often he considered men as instruments instead of treating them with care as sensitive beings' (Villeneuve-Bargemont 1841, 2: 396). His attitude, like that of his followers, is 'the inflexible absolutism of the manufacturing system which consists in pushing the products and manhandling the producer, if not with indifference then at least through an abuse of principles' (1841, 2: 397). The 'exaggerated disciples of Smith', Villeneuve insisted, aimed at 'governing, settling everything'.

> Whenever one wants to fight one of their principles with moral or political arguments, they answer: 'You go beyond the limits of science, this is not our concern: our task is just to show how wealth is created.' That's a fine idea! But in this case allow us to neglect some economic considerations when it is the matter of the great interests of the morals and happiness of the people. Since the writings of Smith and MM. Say and Ricardo, one would not deny that political economy has the form and attributes of a real science. But in order for its principles be accepted as true and absolute, they still have to prove that they spread well-being in all the classes of the human society – and it is doubtful that they will ever succeed in doing this. (Villeneuve-Bargemont 1834, 1: 32)

It is interesting to note that the critique also concerned Jean-Baptiste Say and his followers, who were considered as bad as their British counterparts.

Buret made this critique his own and developed it in the long introduction to his *Misère des classes laborieuses.* Villeneuve-Bargemont was very critical of Smith: in his opinion, the evil started with the *Wealth of Nations*:

> It is certain that Smith almost always disregards moral and religious considerations: with the consequence that, basing the principle of work and civilisation on a continuous excitement of the needs, he founded the theory of the production of wealth on industrial monopoly, sensationist philosophy and the selfish morals of personal interest. (Villeneuve-Bargemont 1836, 87)

Buret partly saved Smith from this original sin: 'he is the least exclusive economist of his school' (Buret 1840, 1: 5). In his eyes, Smith did not limit himself to the study of the production of wealth but also dealt with some 'high questions of social philosophy' (Buret 1840, 1: 6). But after him political economy confined its field to the abstract theory of value and production, with no consideration of morals, religion and politics. 'Its aim is to be a fully positive science like mathematics, and in this perspective it claims for its principles the privilege of absolute certainty' (Buret 1840, 1: 7). The real culprit for this negative evolution was of course Ricardo, the 'ingenious metaphysician' of land rent: 'For M. Ricardo, men are nothing, products are all that matters' (1840, 1: 6n).

> The most complete and exaggerated expression of this political economy that we would call absolute, can be found in the books of M. Ricardo, the ingenious metaphysician of the 'fermage'. There all social tendencies have disappeared. Nations are now only considered as productive workshops; – man as a productive and consuming machine, and human life as a capital. – All is weighted and calculated, and economic laws inevitably govern the world.[22] (Buret 1840, 1: 6)

Unfortunately, a science that limits itself to studying the 'abstract phenomena of wealth' is an impossibility: 'It is much more difficult to separate the various branches of the social science than those of physical sciences: the tree of moral knowledge cannot be mutilated without danger' (Buret 1840: 12). The best proof of this is to look at the practical consequences of this 'science': pauperism and crises. 'We are not playing on words when we say that, opposite the picture of the wealth of nations must stand the picture of the poverty of nations' (1840, 1: 13). And he asked: 'Which man, which Christian would not recoil in front of the complete implementation of the economic system advocated by the books of the English school?' (Buret 1840, 1: 38–39).

From arithmetic to mathematics: hurrah for abstraction!

A few authors, however, were not afraid of abstraction – in yet another meaning of the word. Say and Sismondi rejected Ricardo's deductive methodology. They proposed an inductive reasoning, but they lacked any meaningful data as well as any adequate statistical method. Rossi, in his lectures, challenged this view: 'The science of political economy, to the extent that it concerns what is general and invariable', he wrote, 'is rather a science of reasoning than a science of observation' (Rossi 1836–38, 1: 32). It is 'speculative economics' and in his eyes it was important to distinguish 'rational political economy' from 'applied political economy' and 'social economics'.

Some authors also looked favourably on deduction and 'abstraction' in keeping with the French intellectual tradition of *mathématique sociale.* 'We must bind men to reason through the precision of ideas and the rigour of proofs, thus placing the truths out of reach of the eloquence of words or the sophism of interest' (Condorcet 1793: 109). The theory of value and prices must serve this purpose (1793: 166). Auguste Walras belonged to this tradition, as did Cournot. To prove a proposition, it is impossible to limit oneself to giving a numerical example that simply illustrates it. One must go further and use algebra, as he wrote in *Recherches sur les principes mathématiques de la théorie des richesses.* No elementary algebra like Ricardo, but arbitrary functions:

> Some authors, like Smith and Say, wrote on political economy while preserving in their style the amenities of a purely literary form; but others, like Ricardo, dealing with more abstract questions or in search of

> greater precision, could not avoid algebra but disguised it in the form of arithmetical calculations of a tiring prolixity. […] In this essay I intend to show that the answer to the general questions raised by the theory of wealth essentially depends, not on elementary algebra but on this branch of calculus that deals with arbitrary functions. (Cournot 1838: 4–5)

Cournot's position was odd in the French context. Even Auguste Walras declared he had 'never well understood' Cournot's 1838 book. And he added: 'but from what I could grasp, I suppose that M. Cournot translated into algebra the metaphysics of Ricardo' (Auguste to Léon Walras, 18 May 1861, in A. Walras 2005: 490). However, the idea that political economy should become a mathematical science, in order to acquire the rigour that Ricardo was aiming at, gradually spread.

4. Value and wealth

The French context

Value theory and the definitions of wealth and productivity were considered of the utmost importance among French economists, who realized that many problems in economics required the clarification of such basic concepts. This was not new: Turgot, for example, called for rigour and developed a fascinating subjective theory of value. But in the first half of the nineteenth century this was still a novelty and Ricardo and Say were often considered responsible for this evolution. 'All that pertains to the exchange value is fundamental in political economy. David Ricardo declared it and J.-B. Say repeated it after him' (A. Walras 1849: 505). But it was also obvious that there was, on the whole, little agreement on these topics on both sides of the Channel.

> Two main opinions on the origin of exchange value dominate the economic world today. We can call the first the opinion of the English economists: it is based on the authority of Smith, Ricardo and McCulloch. The second can be called the French doctrine, and is linked with the names of Condillac and J.-B. Say. (A. Walras 1849: 506)

At the beginning of the century, before the publication of Ricardo's *Principles*, Say, Sismondi and Destutt de Tracy had developed their own theories of value. We cannot of course enter into details and analyze the differences between these theories here. However, one common feature must be stressed: they all confer a fundamental role on utility and demand – the legacy of Turgot and Condillac. While not neglecting the cost of production, they thought that, in markets, it forms a kind of floor below which the price cannot permanently fall. But the effective price, the 'valeur vénale' of a commodity, is determined by demand and supply – again Turgot's legacy. On the whole, these authors used the idea of 'gravitation', first proposed by Turgot and developed by

Smith, but they adapted it to their purpose. For Say, for example, the market price is supposed to gravitate around a natural price[23] understood as the sum of the remuneration of the services of labour, capital and land; for Destutt, the cost of production is but a floor, the lower limit below which a price cannot remain for a long time. Moreover, Say and Destutt stressed again and again that production, through the transformation of things, is only the production of utility. Ricardo shared none of these points of view.

In this context, Destutt de Tracy's writings nevertheless attracted Ricardo's attention. Basing his analysis on the first edition of Say's *Traité*, powerfully developing the French sensationist tradition, this key figure among the Idéologues developed a political economy in the last part of his *Éléments d'idéologie* entitled *Traité de la volonté et de ses effets*, 1815, and his *Commentaire sur l'Esprit des lois de Montesquieu*.[24] Criticizing Say on this point, Destutt stressed that all wealth finds its origin solely in the use by men of their own faculties, thus advancing the paramount importance of labour activity and denying the existence of other factors of production such as land and capital – itself the product of labour:

> The old French economists […] have not then sufficiently studied the nature of man, and particularly his intellectual predispositions. They did not perceive that in our faculties and in the manner in which our will employs them, all our treasure consists, and that this employment, *labour*,[25] constitutes the only wealth that in itself has a natural and necessary primitive value, which it communicates to all things upon which it is employed, and which have not other. (1811: 185–86)

In the *Traité de la Volonté*, he specified:

> … as it is certain that our physical and moral faculties are alone our original riches, the employment of those faculties, labour of some kind, is our only original treasure, and that it is always from this employment, that all those things are created which we call riches […]. It is certain too, that all those things only represent the labour which has created them, and if they have a value, or even two distinct values, they can only derive them from that of the labour from which they emanate. (Destutt 1817: 64)

While Destutt's approach is not independent of his views on the determination of prices – fixed by the interaction of demand and supply, they measure 'the value of things, and of the labour which produces them' (1817: 31) – this and other aspects of his writings were obviously of interest to Ricardo, who referred to them in the paragraphs he inserted in 1821 in Chapter XX, 'Value and Riches, their Distinctive Properties', of the *Principles* (1817–21: 284–85). Ricardo met Destutt in Paris during his 1822 journey on the continent:

> M. Destutt Tracy [is] a very agreeable old gentleman, whose works I had read with pleasure. I do not entirely agree with him in his Political Economy,—he is one of Say's school:—there are nevertheless some points of difference between them. (Ricardo to Malthus, 16 December 1822, in 1951–73, 9: 248)[26]

Say was thus unfair – and inaccurate in his interpretation – when, after the death of Ricardo, reviewing Prévost's translation of McCulloch *Discourse*, he wrote:

> Not only has Ricardo's book been given an importance that I feel to be exaggerated; but it was also granted, with as little justification, the merit of originality and novelty. According to M. McCulloch, the publication of this book opens a *new and memorable era*, and it is stressed that he [Ricardo] discovered that all exchangeable values are but the price of labour, and land does not influence prices; but M. Destutt de Tracy, in his *Commentaire sur Montesquieu* – which, even before the 1814 events, had been translated into English by the renowned Jefferson, former President of the United States – had advanced the same principles that he repeated in his 1815 *Traité de la volonté*. (Say 1825: 275)

The first discussions

Say was in England from September to December 1814, sent by the French Government – he subsequently published *De l'Angleterre et des Anglais* in April 1815. There he met James Mill, Jeremy Bentham and David Ricardo. Say took the opportunity to send Ricardo a plan for a reform of the French currency system inspired by the Appendix of *The High Price of Bullion*. After his return to Paris, he sent him his *Cathéchisme d'économie politique*. Ricardo replied on 18 August 1815 and a correspondence started between them, mainly devoted to the discussion of Ricardo's critiques of Say's theory of value.

While at this time neither Ricardo's nor Say's approaches were fixed – and consequently the theoretical vocabulary was still vague and hesitant – this first debate before the publication of the *Principles* is important for understanding the nature of their divergence. It turned on the role of utility. Both admitted that utility is 'the foundation of value', but they did not give the same meaning to 'foundation'. Ricardo specified that 'a commodity must be useful to have value' (to Say, 18 August 1815, in Ricardo 1951–73, 6: 247). In his answer[27] (10 September 1815, ibid.: 270–73) Says asserted that Ricardo in fact shared his analysis of value, and that utility is not the sole but the primary cause of value. In order for a commodity to be produced:

> the price that its utility determines people to accept must be sufficient to repay the expenses incurred in its production […]. I thus say, like you, that these expenses of production determine the lowest limit for its price;

> but that they are not the primary cause of the price that people offer for it. (ibid.: 271)

In fact, Ricardo criticized Say on three points. First, he criticized him for having stated that utility is the measure of value: 'the degree of utility can never be the measure by which to estimate value' (ibid.: 247). Say denied having made such a statement: rather, value is the measure of the utility.[28]

Second, Ricardo criticized Say for having written that 'a man is superlatively rich, although he has few valuables, who can procure easily or for nothing those things which he wishes to consume' (ibid.: 248, cf. Say 1814: 1194 and 1815: 95). Ricardo took the example of a man who:

> may only wish to consume bread and water and may be able to procure no more. He cannot be so rich as his neighbour who has abundance of valuables which he can exchange for all the luxuries of life, which it is his desire to consume. (Ricardo 1951–73, 6: 248)

He concluded: 'Riches are measured by the quantity of valuables which a man possesses, not by the moderation of his wants' (ibid.). Say denied having said that a man is all the richer for having less desires, but repeated that a man is all the richer when he can satisfy his desires at a lower cost.

Third, Ricardo criticized Say for having stated that an entrepreneur 'must make an inventory of all that he possesses, valuing each commodity at its current price' (Ricardo ibid.: 248, cf. Say 1814: 184 and 1815: 21) in order to know whether his capital has increased: this is misleading, according to Ricardo, because the calculation will reflect the evolution of prices. Say replied that the value of money is assumed to be unchanged: to measure the increment of capital by its capacity to employ labour, as Ricardo suggests, is to return to Smith, which is unfortunate because the price of labour is more variable than the price of money.

Two problems emerged from this exchange. The first is the question of the link between utility and exchangeable value, considered here from the point of view of the measure. However, this debate came to a sudden end when Ricardo quoted the correct sentence from the second edition of Say's *Traité*: 'Price is the measure of the value of things, and their value is the measure of their utility' (Ricardo 1817–21: 282, cf. Say 1814: 83). He did not comment directly on this sentence but neither did he change his mind. Utility remained linked in his eyes with value in use. The last sentence of the *Principles* leaves no room for ambiguity: 'value in use cannot be measured by any known standard; it is differently estimated by different persons' (Ricardo 1817–21: 429).

The second problem is the question of the definition of wealth. Disregarding here the evolution of Say's thought on this point, it is enough to note that in the fourth edition of the *Traité*, wealth is defined as 'the things we possess and that can be used to satisfy our needs' (Say 1819: 1156). Say, however, while giving up the idea that 'the value of things measures the quantity of wealth' when two countries are compared, implicitly admitted that it is still possible to proceed in this way for two men living in the same place and facing the same price system. As for Ricardo, he ended the *Principles* with the assertion that, like for Smith, wealth or riches 'consist of the necessaries, conveniences, and enjoyments of human life. One set of necessaries and conveniences admits of no comparison with another set' (Ricardo 1817–21: 429). It is then impossible to consider riches as a sum of values, as Say did. 'Value [...] essentially differs from riches, for value depends not on abundance, but on the difficulty or facility of production' (Ricardo 1817–21: 273).

The subsequent debates: some examples

In spite of its importance in the French context, the controversies about the nature of wealth and how to measure it will be left aside here: the subsequent discussion between Say and Ricardo, and the reactions and developments it generated, especially from Pellegrino Rossi, Augustin Cournot and Jules Dupuit, are analyzed in a former paper (Béraud 2005). It should also be noted that many authors contested the fact that wealth was solely to be apprehended in purely economic and material terms: the emerging Christian political economy forcefully denounced this way of thinking – but so did some other authors independently of their political inclinations, the best example being the ultra-liberal Charles Dunoyer. The following will instead focus on the theories of value and prices.

We know how Ricardo, in the *Principles*, specified what he meant by value in use and value in exchange, and by reproducible or non-reproducible commodities, and how his theory of value worked in each case. It is also well-known that Say, especially in the notes he appended to the French translation of the *Principles*, rejected the idea that the value of a commodity is determined by the quantity of labour necessary for its production. In this context, one apparently insignificant assertion by Ricardo – namely, that the exchange value of a commodity rises with the quantity of labour spent in its production – generated a discussion and an evolution in Say's own conceptions.

To Ricardo's assertion, Say objected that the demand for that commodity must also increase in order for its value to rise with its cost of production. But, without entering into too much detail, Say's argument is puzzling. In fact Say faces two difficulties here. In the first place, the concept of demand is not clearly defined: is 'demand' the quantity demanded, or a relationship between this quantity and the price? In the second place, the idea that 'the value of every commodity always rises in direct ratio to the demand, and in inverse ratio to the supply' is, as Ricardo states (1817–21: 382–85), a source of error: it led Say to maintain wrongly that, in order for the price to rise with the costs, there must be an unchanged proportion of demand to supply. He wrote in his notes to Ricardo's *Principles*:

> When costs of production increase, it would be necessary for the proportion of demand to supply to remain the same for the price also to increase; it would be necessary for demand also to rise; but actually it decreases; and it is impossible, all circumstances being the same, for it not to decrease. Exchange value cannot rise like the costs of production. (1819, 1:10)

This proposition seems paradoxical and even absurd. It can be interpreted as follows. For a rise in the cost of production to be fully transferred to the current price, the demand must increase – more specifically, the demand price must increase like the supply price. However, Say's analysis of the determination of prices through the interaction of demand and supply remains too vague to form the basis for a theory of prices.

To answer Ricardo, Say was thus obliged firstly to explain what he meant by 'demand'. In his *Cours complet d'économie politique pratique*, he insisted both on the choice of individuals and on the role of income distribution. 'Men […] make a kind of classification of their needs according to the degree of importance they attach to the satisfaction of each of these needs' (Say, 1828–29, 1: 356). Each man, according to his income, satisfies the most urgent need first. When the price of a good is high, only the rich can afford it. If the price falls, it becomes accessible to a greater number. The notion of demand was thus clarified: it is the quantity of a commodity demanded by those who can pay for its costs of production.

In the second place, the shape of the relation was specified: when the price decreases, the demand increases because there are more buyers. Its shape can even be analyzed. Income distribution can be represented as a pyramid: the rich are fewer than the poor. In this perspective, a reduction in price affects the demand for a commodity all the more when the price was initially rather low, and the concentration of incomes influences the shape of the demand function. The idea that demand is a function of the price – in the mathematical meaning of the term – is not to be found in Say, but Cournot and Dupuit took inspiration from Say's text to formulate it. It is thus not unreasonable to think that the first attempts to build a demand function owed something to Ricardo. The influence was indirect: his criticism of Say induced a more accurate study of the concepts used in demand and supply analysis.

In the last editions of the *Traité*, Say re-examined the idea that the costs of production determine the value of products. He concluded that Ricardians were right to some extent:

> in that products never could be sold for a long time at a lower price than their costs of production; but when they said that the demand for these products does not influence their value, they were wrong […] because demand influences the value of the productive services. (Say, 1826a: 619)

Some other opinions

While Jean-Baptiste Say was certainly the prominent figure in this debate, some other writers held different views. Louis Say (Jean-Baptiste's brother), for example, put forward a very different opinion. In his 1822 book, *Considérations sur l'industrie et la législation*, Chapter 8 is devoted to an 'Examen de l'ouvrage de M. David Ricardo, intitulé: *Des Principes de l'économie politique*', in which his intention was to intervene in the controversy between Ricardo and his brother on value and wealth and state his own position (1822: 158–59). He rejected the Smithian opposition between value in use and value in exchange as well as the idea that the exchange value measures utility. Prices are important for an individual, but only the utilities that he can buy with his income really matter. 'If the word value has to be used in political economy, it can only be understood as the degree of utility possessed by things […]. It is this utility possessed by a thing which forms its real effective value' (L. Say 1822: 158). Louis Say thus agreed with Ricardo, against his brother: 'as M. Ricardo states rightly, exchangeable value is no measure of utility' (1822: 161). But the solution he proposed was of course totally different from that of Ricardo.

In the same perspective, some years later, Auguste Walras criticized Ricardo for having contrasted two kinds of commodities: those which are rare, and those of which the quantity can be increased through industry. But, Walras remarked, a commodity is always produced because it is rare. 'It is impossible to distinguish among the commodities […] between those that are rare and those that are not. All the goods that exist in limited quantities are rare; and only unlimited goods form an exception' (1831: 183). To make things more precise, A. Walras redefined certain concepts. According to him, scarcity is the relationship between demand and supply, but absolute demand and supply. Absolute demand is defined as the demand 'which is the expression of all the needs taken together […] disregarding the means men have to satisfy them' (1831: 235–36). The absolute demand for a thing is thus the quantity that would allow everyone to fully satisfy his need for it. Absolute supply is simply the quantity of a thing that exists at a given point in time. When the absolute demand for a good exceeds the absolute supply, it is said to exist in limited quantity. It is rare and its value is in proportion to its scarcity. While A. Walras gave 'scarcity' a meaning that is now ours, he had difficulty specifying the links between value and scarcity. As we know, his son took up the torch, with success: scarcity was defined as 'the intensity of the last need satisfied' and 'scarcity is the cause of exchangeable value' (Léon Walras 1874: 144, 145).

Finally, let us note two other important consequences from the debates generated by Ricardo. In the first place, Dupuit discarded Say's assertion that the prices of things measure their utility. He replaced it with the idea that 'the greatest sacrifice that we would be prepared to make to get a thing we desire, or the price at which you would decide to do without it, can act as a measure of utility' (Dupuit, 1849: 205). In the second place, Cournot, just like Ricardo, asserted that there is no fixed measure of the utility of things. But the he drew a different conclusion: he held that riches must be understood as the value of the products, not as their utility.

> We must totally identify the meaning of the word *riches* with that of these other words *exchangeable value* […]. We must accurately distinguish the abstract idea of riches […] from the secondary ideas of utility, scarcity, suitability to the needs and enjoyments of man, which the word riches still suggests in the ordinary language (1838: 8).

We must acknowledge that riches can vary without affecting the public utility or the general well-being: it is also possible for riches to increase while well-being decreases. In any variation of income, it is thus necessary to distinguish the real and the nominal variations. Cournot showed that to measure the real increment of riches, it is necessary to reason, as we now do, with constant prices.

As for Pellegrino Rossi – certainly the most Ricardian of the writers of the time in France – his analysis is mainly grounded on a theory of value based on the costs of production. No doubt demand and supply, he argued, play an important role in the true explanation of the determination and variations of prices. But these concepts are difficult to understand and to work analytically with them is almost impossible. This is the reason why economists should resort to another law, a kind of approximation and certainly a better analytical tool, the determination of the value of commodities by the quantity of labour necessary for their production (Rossi 1836–38, 1: 89–90). From the quantity of labour he then moved on to costs of production in general, including the profits of the entrepreneurs but not the rent of land: like Ricardo, he thought that rent is a consequence of prices and not an element of cost.

News from the Genevan Front

Many other aspects of Ricardo's theory of value and prices were discussed, especially during the first half of the century. Without entering here into too much detail, some other important points are to be noted: they came from Switzerland, from the group of authors around the *Bibliothèque Universelle*.

Pierre Prévost's commentaries (1817, 1818) on the first chapter of the *Principles* are not really developed but are interesting because they show, more clearly than the case of Say, for example, the reactions of a Smithian reader to Ricardo's attacks in the field of the theory of value and prices. He raised two main criticisms. In the first place, and with great clarity, Prévost defended Smith's 'adding-up' theory and the measure of value through the labour a commodity can command. It is not true, he wrote, that Smith is inconsequent, as Ricardo affirmed. He does not have two theories of values, one for the rude and primitive state of society and another for the commercial society with private land property and accumulation of capital. Labour commanded is the measure of value in both societies.

> When Smith said 'The real price of every thing […] is the toil and trouble of acquiring it', he was establishing his doctrine of the measure of value. We known that the basis of this doctrine is the labour that a commodity commands. But when he said 'In that early and rude state of society […] the proportion between the quantities of labour necessary for acquiring different objects seems to be the only circumstance which can afford any rule for exchanging them for one another',[29] he was dealing with the distinction between the component parts of a price, and his aim was to dissipate a cloud that could rise on this discussion. He remarked in consequence that there is a stage, in social life, when these two measures – the labour that a commodity commands and the labour spent in his production – are almost the same, and when consequently the distinction is not really necessary. (Prévost 1817: 217–18)

So Ricardo was not a good reader, and Smith was not inconsequent. In the second place, Ricardo was accused of introducing new and unclear definitions for concepts that were defined by Smith in an appropriate way – the distinction between fixed and circulating capital, for example (Prévost 1818: 12–13) – and thus creating a lot of confusion. But Prévost simply did not understand the pages where Ricardo discusses the influence of a change of income distribution on relative prices and the relationship between wages and the rate of profits – that was, in his eyes, incomprehensible because he stuck to an 'adding-up' theory of value – and his criticism petered out.

Another interesting criticism came from Sismondi, because he simply did not accept Ricardo's process of economic adjustment through the mobility of capital and labour. 'M. Ricardo does not leave the abstractions on which he founded his system, and it is difficult to bring them closer to the facts' (1819, 2: 215), he wrote in the *Nouveaux Principes d'Économie Politique*. After some perturbation in the economy, it is not true that things return easily to equilibrium, simply because it is not correct to consider capital and labour as mobile.

> Let us beware of this dangerous theory of an equilibrium that restores itself! […] Some equilibrium, it is true, is again reached in the end, but through incredible suffering. One can take it as certain that capital only leaves an industry through the bankruptcy of the owner, and men only leave a job through the death of the worker: all those who find a job or move more easily must be seen as the exception and not the rule. (1819, 2: 217)

Some other reasons – a long apprenticeship or experience necessary for the production, the investment of an important amount of fixed capital – explain the relative immobility of factors of production. With the notable consequence that there is no uniformity in wages and in the profit rates among the different sectors.

> we do not admit the foundations of M. Ricardo's reasoning or a continuous equilibrium of profits in all industries. We believe instead that, because it is impossible for the owners of fixed capital to withdraw it and invest it elsewhere, they keep this capital in the same industry for a long time after it has started to yield a much lower income than all others. Their persistence in the same industries is also strongly augmented by their reluctance to loose the skilfulness they have acquired in them, and their incapacity to embrace another vocation. (1819, 1: 277–78)

It is however worth noting that Sismondi – like Say, as we will show below – somewhat misinterprets Ricardo on this point, insisting on short-term difficulties. In Chapter IV of the *Principles*, 'On Natural and Market Price', Ricardo actually describes a more complex process of readjustment, introducing finance capital into the picture. And, at the beginning of Chapter XIII 'On Taxes on Gold' and extensively in Chapter XIX 'On Sudden Changes in the Channels of Trade', he insists on the fact that a reallocation of capital between industries could take a long time, be difficult and entail important negative consequences in the short term.

5. The nature and evolution of rent

Setting the stage

Even more than the theory of value, the question of the nature and evolution of ground rent remained topical among French-speaking economists during almost the entire century. It was, of course, the theory of income distribution that continuously raised lively discussions, especially around the question of pauperism – later the 'social question'. But it went much further: the problem of rent considered as a monopoly income challenged firstly the legitimacy of the status of the landowner, and secondly, over and above the question of land property, the legitimacy of private property. This was of course the danger, as stated by Hippolyte Passy in his entry 'Rente du sol' in the *Dictionnaire de l'économie politique*:

> For some authors, rent is a monopoly that forces those who do not possess land to pay a greater price for their subsistence than it really costs to those who possess it; for others, it is, using Scrope's phrase, a limitation to the enjoyment of the gifts that God gave to men for the satisfaction of their needs. From these opinions to the celebrated axiom: *La propriété, c'est le vol*,[30] there is only one step that was quickly made. (Passy 1853: 518)

Some decades later, the same problem was still topical.

> Ricardo's theory, well stated by Rossi in France and J. Stuart Mill in England […] was accepted by the economists when the 1848 Revolution happened and socialism came openly to the light. Ricardo said: 'a part only of the money paid to the landlord is paid for the use of the original and indestructible powers of the soil'.[31] Proudhon and the German refugees in Paris took over this idea not only to attack land property but property in general. (Courcelle-Seneuil 1892: 711)

The most varied opinions were thus expressed on rent and the discussions went well beyond economic theory. But the economists were of course standing on the front line, and the subject was often discussed at the Société d'économie politique and in the *Journal des économistes* – so much that some readers of the *Journal* complained.[32] In the 1850s, a number of books were still published on the question, either in favour of Ricardo's theory, like Mathieu Wolkoff's *Opuscules sur la rente foncière* (1854), or to criticize it, for example along the lines developed by Bastiat just before his death, as in Roger de Fontenay's *Du revenu foncier* (1854). The Académie des science morales et politiques of the Institut launched a competition on the theory of rent three times, the prize being eventually awarded to Auguste Boutron, who later published his book on the subject: *Théorie de la rente foncière* (1867). The report on this competition, by Hippolyte Passy, was published in 1858 in the *Journal des économistes* (Passy 1858). In 1866, the Société d'économie politique, at the suggestion of Frédéric Passy, organized one more discussion on the theory of rent, with this question: 'Is ground rent different from interest on capital?' (*Journal des économistes*, June 1866: 447–67).

Before examining the positions developed during these controversies, three remarks are in order.

In the first place, and contrary to a generally accepted opinion, Ricardo's theory of rent, while having faced strong criticism, also had influential advocates *within* the liberal current of thought and not only among its opponents. The case of Pellegrino Rossi (Rossi 1836–38) is well-known. But Antoine-Élisée Cherbuliez (on whom more below) is also a central figure in this story, as well as the uncompromising liberal Gustave de Molinari. The case of Charles Coquelin is worth citing. The following is a testimony by Molinari taken from the 'Notice biographique sur Charles Coquelin' he wrote for the second (posthumous) edition of Coquelin's *Du crédit et des banques*, entitled *Le Crédit et les banques* (1859):

> He came across Ricardo only later; but Coquelin had already found by himself […] this ingenious theory of rent which is one of the main claims to fame of the renowned English economist. He later said to his friends how much he was surprised – and up to a point frustrated – when he found in Ricardo's writings what he thought his own discovery. This

> incident, during his first studies of political economy, explains the enthusiasm with which he defended the theory of rent when it was challenged by M. Carey and […] Bastiat. Charles Coquelin considered more or less Ricardo's theory as his own. (Molinari 1859: 7)

A similar acceptation also came unexpectedly from one of the main authors who developed Catholic Christian political economy during the second half of the century and inspired the so-called social doctrine of the Church (as promulgated by Pope Leo XIII in his 1891 encyclical letter *Rerum Novarum*), namely the Belgian economist Charles Périn. He was the successor to the Frenchman Charles de Coux – the co-founder, even before Villeneuve-Bargemont, of this current of thought – at the chair of political economy at the Université Catholique de Louvain. Villeneuve-Bargemont accused the 'English school' in general, and Ricardo specifically, of having only developed the laws of the production of wealth, and neglected its distribution. Périn stressed instead the progress made by Ricardo in distribution theory.

> In Ricardo's view, the main problem in political economy is the determination of the laws of the distribution of wealth. Unfortunately, the nature of his mind was fond of abstraction and he lost the fruit of this genuine conception of the economic science. (1880: 66)

In particular, too much emphasis was placed on the theory of value: 'Contrary to what was alleged, all political economy does not lie in the theory of value' (1880: 67). In spite of this, Ricardo is granted 'the merit of having, the first, laid the foundations for a theory of the distribution of wealth' (1880: 68). The positive point is his conception of rent, which Périn himself used in his writings together with Malthus's principle of population.

Second, the vocabulary employed by Smith and Ricardo raised a problem for French-speaking economists. The word 'rente' was already widely used in the French language to designate something that has nothing to do with ground rent: it referred mainly to the constitution of life annuities. To translate 'rent', many French writers thus used the word 'fermage' but also progressively adopted 'rente' to this context. The reluctance to call the revenue of the landowner 'rent' also had theoretical bases. For Say, for example, the global revenue of the landowner is the 'fermage' which includes the profits on the capital he invested in the land and the 'profits of the land', i.e., the bare income from property – what Ricardo calls rent.[33]

What is ground rent? asked Hippolyte Passy in the *Dictionnaire de l'économie politique*: 'It is the share of property. It must not however be confused with "fermage", although it is one element thereof. Any "fermage" […] includes an additional part: the payment to the landowners because of their spending, at different times, with a view to facilitating labour or multiplying the product' (Passy 1853: 509), in other words because of the capital landowners themselves invested in the land. Some other writers included both elements – the property income and the remuneration of the capital invested – under the same term of 'rente'.

The problem was raised very early on. F. S. Constâncio, the translator of the first edition of the *Principles*, translated the title of the chapter 'On Rent' by 'Du fermage ou profit des terres' (Ricardo 1819, 1: 63), i.e., 'Of "fermage" or profit of land.' In the text, he sometimes used 'fermage', sometimes 'profit des fonds de terre' because, as he explained in a footnote (in Ricardo 1819, 1: 64), they have different meanings, while his translation of the title of the chapter makes them appear to be equivalent!

> I thus was obliged to translate the very vague English word 'rent' sometimes by *profit des fonds de terre*, and sometimes by *fermage*, which are two things that the author does not distinguish enough: the first refers to the profit that land gives to the cultivator, the second to the rent [*loyer*] that the farmer pays to the landowner who does not himself farm his property. (Constâncio, in Ricardo 1819, 1: 64n)

Constâncio's comment shows that he did not understand Ricardo properly, and we can imagine what the French readers might have understood during 30 years whenever they did not have access to the English text. This question induced Alcide Fonteyraud, in 1847, to add a long footnote at the beginning of the Chaper 'On Rent' of his revised translation of the *Principles.* He rightly chose to adopt the term 'rente' everywhere.

> We did not hesitate to substitute […] the word 'rente' for the word 'fermage' which most writers used to translate the English 'rent'. Before us, people were afraid to introduce an uncommon term into the scientific nomenclature […] [but] every new idea in science […] brings its form, its expressions. (1847: 38)

The word 'fermage' was also to be rejected for a theoretical reason: 'This is something more than a mere lexicographic rectification, this is above all a scientific rectification' (1847: 39) because otherwise Ricardo's theory appears absurd and incomprehensible.

> In political economy, what do we mean by the word 'fermage'? It is the sum paid by the cultivator […] to the landowner. Now what do we mean by '*rente*'? Following the very definition of Ricardo, it is that portion of the produce of the earth, which is paid to the landlord for the use of *the original and indestructible powers of the soil*. The difference is here obvious, essential […] and the author dedicated a series of arguments to making it stand out. Moreover, after having well established that the portion of the produce given to the owner for the interest on the capital he devoted to the betterment of land […] etc, cannot be called rent, he […] says that *in popular language the term is*

> *applied to whatever is annually paid by a farmer to his landlord, and that Adam Smith often conformed to this mistake made by most writers.* Rent is thus a fee attached to the ground itself, to property rights (1847: 38).

In the third place, for sake of brevity, some comments on the origin of the theory of rent – concerning Anderson, West, and Malthus – will be omitted here. French authors at least agree on one point: Ricardo's version is the most rigorous statement of it. Some other criticisms must also be omitted, though they were heavily debated at the time, such as, for example, the problem of the order in which different plots of land are cultivated – some authors contesting that the most fertile are cultivated first. We also exclude the interesting point that the order of fertility is not a physical property given once for all but can change according to the techniques employed by the farmers, as well as the possibility and consequences of technical progress in agriculture – on all this see for example Fonteyraud (1847) and G. du Puynode (1866) as well as the above-quoted books on rent.

Say's critique

What characterises Say's views on rent is twofold – two consequences, probably, of his faithfulness to Smith's analysis: rent enters into the formation of prices, and intensive rent is disregarded.

> My argument respecting rent, profit and taxes – Ricardo wrote to Say – is founded on a supposition that there is land in every country which pays no rent, or that there is capital employed on land before in cultivation for which no rent is paid. You answer to the first proposition, but you take no notice of the second. The admission of either will answer my purpose. (Ricardo to Say, 11 January 1820, in 1951–73, t. 8: 149–50)

Hence an interesting debate with Ricardo which provoked, significantly, an evolution in both positions: Say was led to accept, in some specific cases, the existence of a marginal land deprived of rent as well as the existence of an intensive rent; and Ricardo admitted that, in some specific cases also, an absolute rent can arise.

For Say, 'fermage' is a component part of the prices of commodities. It remunerates the productive capacity of the land and the capital irreversibly invested in it. Rent thus includes a kind of monopoly income because land is limited in quantity and private property of it is socially and economically useful – an argument which was of course taken up and developed by the liberal economists. 'Were the landowner not certain of enjoying his fruits, who would accept to advance the labour and money necessary for its cultivation?' he wrote in his notes to Ricardo's *Principles* (Say 1819b: 83). A social convention – land property – increases productivity. 'This is why land could supply a quantity of products useful to men ten times, a hundred times, superior' (1819b: 83). Could not we say, he insisted, 'that the owner fulfils a productive function because without it [private property] production would not take place?' (1819b: 92). Say thus accepted the existence of an absolute rent on land. In the same notes to the *Principles*, he wrote that, 'in populous and productive countries, the pieces of land of worst quality, from the moment they are cultivated, always yield some *fermage* and consequently some income from land property' (Say 1819b, 1: 95).

At the same time, however, Say recognized that in some situations, a marginal piece of land may not yield any rent to its owner. In his marginal notes to the *Wealth of Nations*, he remarked that 'plots of land which are not worth being cultivated' can exist (in Hashimoto 1980: 77) and the income of the owner be nil. This idea is picked up in slightly different forms in the successive editions of the *Traité*. In the fifth edition, for example, he wrote:

> a plot of land which does not yield any profit can still be cultivated provided that the cultivator can find compensation for the capital and labour invested. As it is impossible to find a farmer for such a piece of land, it is usually cultivated by its owner. (Say 1826a: 805–7)[34]

But this is, in his eyes, an exceptional case. Disregarding the possibility of increasing corn production through the adoption of more intensive techniques, Say's normal situation is the following. In rich countries where agricultural production reaches its limits, where the demand for agricultural products is high and exceeds production, the price of corn – fixed by the interaction of demand and supply – is always a monopoly price in excess of the cost of production on marginal land. It generates an income for its owner, i.e., a rent on the marginal land.

Ricardo, for his part, was willing to accept this possibility. But, in his opinion, the situation judged normal by Say was instead exceptional:

> The corn and raw produce of a country may, indeed, for a time sell at a monopoly price; but they can do so permanently only when no more capital can be profitably employed on the lands, and when, therefore, their produce cannot be increased. (Ricardo 1817–21: 250–51)

At the end of his life, Say somewhat reconsidered his analysis of 'fermage' in the fifth edition of his *Traité* and in his *Cours complet d'économie politique pratique* (1828–29). It is likely that the evolution of his thought was due to his past debate with Ricardo.

On three points he appeared to have moved closer to Ricardo. First, he accepted in the fifth edition of the *Traité* that some marginal land, when cultivated by its owner, may not yield any rent (Say 1826a: 805, see above). Second, he acknowledged that:

> the supply of the produce of land is not limited as long as there remains some uncultivated land on our earth; if demand goes on increasing when Beauce is totally cultivated, there is still some land in Berry that is not yet under cultivation.[35] (Say 1828–29, 2: 96)

Of course, the costs increase when the product comes from a more distant place: but this last remark matches Ricardo's theory. Thus the idea of a normal case with a limited supply and a rent on the marginal land faded away in *Cours complet*.

Finally, when criticizing the notes McCulloch appended to his edition of the *Wealth of Nations*, Say seemed to acknowledge the existence of an intensive rent: 'on the entire capital employed in agriculture, a portion of it does not give any profit for the land [*profit foncier*]' (McCulloch, quoted by Say 1828–29, 2: 111). But he did not think that it brought a new element to the discussion. This gave him instead the opportunity to reaffirm his approach – and implicitly that of Ricardo. McCulloch realized, Say stressed, 'that the idea which considers the land of bad quality as the cause of the profit on the land of better quality is ridiculous', and this is the reason why he switched to the other formulation (just cited above). Quoting Malthus instead of Ricardo,[36] Say insisted that the cultivation of land of bad quality and the increase in 'fermages' are the consequence, and not the cause, of the rise in agricultural prices. And he added:

> the theory of rent did not introduce any new truth into the science of political economy and […] does not explain any phenomenon that cannot be more naturally explained by the already established truths. I shall refrain from any supplementary discussion on that topic, to avoid the reproach levelled at the debates that have taken place hitherto, i.e., of being incredibly boring and of having put many people right off a study [of political economy] so attractive because of its applications and its influence on the lot of mankind. (1828–29, 2: 111–12)[37]

Fundamentally, Say's approach remained the same in spite of some specific developments. Agricultural products should be dealt with in the same way as the other products, and land like the other factors of production. On the one hand, land generates a productive service that, like any other productive service, is bought by the entrepreneur. And the productive service of land is the basis of 'fermage'. 'Fermage' can differ according to the fertility and the location of land. This is a general phenomenon: the price that an entrepreneur is willing to pay for a productive service depends on the importance of its contribution to production. On the other hand, agricultural products behave in the same way as other commodities. Whenever the demand for corn increases, plots of land of bad quality will be cultivated and costs and prices will increase. This happens for all kinds of products.

> The products cost more as they come from farther afield […]. If the producers who are closer do not produce enough for the needs of society, the price of the product in demand increases and is then sufficient to pay for the production costs of the quantity one is obliged to bring from a more distant place. When a manufacturer succeeds in enjoying a specific advantage, as a more favourable location, he earns more than the one who necessarily incurs higher costs of production (Say 1828–29: 109).

More on the French theoretical landscape

We know that Pellegrino Rossi, who succeeded Say to the chair of political economy at the College de France, was in favour of Ricardo's theory of rent and stated this in his lectures (Rossi 1836–38). While modifying Ricardo on some points – it was his opinion that rent also depends on the 'absolute' and not only comparative productive power of land – he basically accepted his theory. He criticized Say for supposing that the supply of agricultural products could meet a limit and for denying that the marginal capital invested in land yields no rent: to Rossi's mind, Say does not understand that the fact that no land remains without rent is no proof of his denial, simply because rent is not only extensive but also intensive. A land can thus on the whole yield a rent while the last portion of capital invested in it only produces the usual rate of profit and no rent.

We also know that Coquelin and Molinari accepted Ricardo's theory of rent. But between the time of Say and the Second Republic, other economists developed different opinions. Let us briefly mention two of them: Adrien de Gasparin and Frédéric Bastiat.

Gaparin was a friend of François Guizot and thus probably close to Rossi too. The theory of rent was important in his view because he was mainly interested in agricultural economics and legislation. In his 1829 *Guide des propriétaires des biens ruraux affermés*, he wrote that Ricardo's theory of rent was certainly the most satisfactory but he also confessed that, in the end, he did not see much difference between Ricardo's and Say's ideas.

> Ricardo's theory is […] identical to M. Say's. As a matter of fact, the more land is in demand and the more plots of land of inferior quality are cultivated, the more the rent increases on land of better quality […] and this demand will always stop, in both cases, at the point where land only pays for the costs of production (1829: 46).

Gasparin tried to reformulate some points in Ricardo's theories of value and rent but, using odd definitions and vocabulary, he eventually ended with the same results. More polemical, but incomplete because of his death, is Bastiat's attempt to reformulate the question of rent.

Bastiat wrote his pamphlets on land property and rent at the time of the 1848 Revolution during which the liberal camp took a tougher stand against the various socialist movements. These essays, together with others, already published or not, were included in his posthumous *Harmonies Économiques* (1850, with a second enlarged edition in 1851). Bastiat's position was radical – like that of Henry Charles Carey at that time, who accused Bastiat of plagiarism. In order to fight the socialists, Bastiat simply denied that rent resulted from a monopoly power, linked to property rights and not corresponding to any human service or labour: 'The theory of rent is an illusion.' According to Bastiat, what is called rent is nothing other than the just remuneration of the capital and labour invested by landowners to make land suitable for cultivation. Hippolyte Passy summed up Bastiat's arguments well:

> Now M. Bastiat acknowledges that rent may well rise without the landowner having to make any sacrifice to benefit from this increment; but this case, he remarks, is not specific to land property. What creates the value of any service rendered by human industry […] is not only the effort incurred by the producer, but also the effort spared to the consumer: any time his needs increase, the latter pays more for the service he buys, which spares him the more important efforts he would have been obliged to make to get it himself. (H. Passy 1853: 510)

Now the liberal economists were aware of the fragility of this thesis. 'It is unfortunate', H. Passy went on, 'that his death did not give M. Bastiat enough time to specify and coordinate his ideas more rigorously' (H. Passy 1853: 510).

To have an idea of the last step in the evolution of the debates on rent, let us jump to the *Nouveau dictionnaire d'économie politique*, edited by Léon Say (Jean-Baptiste's grandson) and Joseph Chailley, published in 1891–92 with Guillaumin. The author of the entry 'Rente (loi de la)' was Jean-Gustave Courcelle-Seneuil, already active for some decades and the translator of John Stuart Mill's *Principles.* His text shows how the liberal discourse changed during these decades. Courcelle-Seneuil's is a defence of the theory of rent which, he said, although forcefully accepted or attacked in the past, was never properly understood. The law of rent, he argued, is in fact more general than initially thought by Ricardo. Some authors, however, generalized it too much: after von Thünen, for example, who enlarged its purpose, 'it was thought that the law of rent was not specific to agriculture, mining industries or locations; it was claimed that it was general and was felt in all branches of industry, including trade' (1892: 713).

But this evolution is questionable, Courcelle-Seneuil claimed, because in this way the law loses any precision. He preferred another, more usual perspective. Referring to the production of all kinds of agricultural products and raw materials, he reformulated the law in the following way: 'As the number of men rises and want to satisfy new needs, they consume in greater quantities the raw products supplied by nature, the quantities of which are limited' (1892: 715). This formulation simply refers to industries that produce with increasing costs. Thus understood in a rather loose way, the law of rent is opposed to the 'law of markets' interpreted as a law of increasing returns experienced in the other industries and in trade. While the old names of 'law of rent' and 'law of markets' are still retained and used, Courcelle-Seneuil noted, it is also possible 'to speak, like some English authors, of a "law of decreasing returns" for the first, and a "law of increasing returns" for the second' (1892: 717). He was, however, using the new phrases with reluctance. 'We do not think that these new names must be preferred to the old ones: the latter have the advantage of reminding us of the works of Ricardo and Jean-Baptiste Say' (ibid.). With one important qualification: the law of diminishing returns is not an inevitability, thanks to science and technical progress.

Back to Geneva

In Geneva, the Ricardian theory of rent was immediately received as an important development in economic theory, all the more so since one of the origins of Ricardo's ideas was Malthus. In the December 1824 issue of *Bibliothèque Universelle*, Charles Pictet (Pictet 1824) commented on a review – translated from the *Edinburgh Review*[38] – of a book by John Cazenove on the accumulation of capital and its effects on prices. He explained Ricardo's views on rent quite accurately, but the paper itself – a discussion of the possible consequences of an abolition of the corn laws – did not go deep into the subject: Pictet in fact could not fully understand Ricardo because he could not get rid of the idea that prices are determined by adding up wages, profits and rent. Guillaume Prévost also discussed briefly the Ricardian principle of rent in the 'Réflexions du traducteur sur le système de Ricardo' he appended to his translation of McCulloch's *Discourse* (G. Prévost 1825b). He developed an idea similar to that of Say, that rent affects the price of commodities because, due to the institution of private property, there is no land that does not pay any rent. Referring to James Mill's defence of Ricardo's principle in his *Elements of Political Economy* (Chapter 2, section 1 on rent), he accepted that the rent on marginal land could be very small, even negligible, as Mill wrote,[39]but it nevertheless exists (G. Prévost 1825b: 172–75).

A radically different picture is given by Sismondi's writings. In his 1803 *De la richesse commerciale*, Sismondi used Smith to reject the Physiocratic propositions. Rent, he wrote, is a mixed income that partly remunerates property rights on uncultivated land, and partly the labour accumulated on that land in order to make it suitable for cultivation. This part of the rent which is not the counterpart of human labour:

> results from a kind of monopoly that landowners enjoy against their fellow citizens […]. It is the sole part of the product of labour that is purely nominal, and does not correspond to anything real; it is in fact the result of the increase in price that a seller obtains because of his privilege, though the thing which is sold is not worth more. (Sismondi 1803, 1: 49)

However, like Say, he qualified this heretical assertion by stressing the fact that the monopoly of the landowners is useful to society, because only privately appropriated land can be properly cultivated.

When dealing with the Ricardian theory of rent, in the *Nouveaux principes*, he limited himself to referring to Say's notes, which he found excellent. He still thought that rent ['fermage'][40] is a monopoly income but, to clarify this opinion he had to analyze the determination of the price of the product and the way in which the net product is shared between the farmer and the landlord. In this perspective, he used his own theory of prices and his rejection of the hypothesis of mobility of capital and labour. His starting point is the idea – later attributed to Ricardo by Sraffa – that in agriculture the product and the means of production are homogeneous (Sismondi 1819, 1: 279–82), viewed here from the perspective that agriculture can form a vertically integrated sector where labour is the sole primary input.

> As farming is the only work that meets [the needs of] life, it is also the only work that can be appreciated without any exchange. Land can provide a man with all the necessaries of life if he cultivates it. If he clothes himself in the skins of his sheep, as he eats their meat and the seeds he harvests, and builds his hut from the wood of his forests, he can compare directly the quantity produced by his labour with the quantity used during his work, and he can thus see that the latter is smaller than the former. He sees with his own eyes the emergence of a net product […], absolutely free of any competition, any market demand, any value against which he might exchange this product. (Sismondi 1819, 1: 282)

The farmer thus knows the physical size of the surplus. If we assume a gross product of 25 sacks of wheat, the means of production (seeds) requiring five sacks and his own consumption another five sacks, then he can immediately see that the net product amounts to 15 bags (Sismondi 1819, 1: 281–82). But sharing this surplus depends on the relative price of the agricultural product and the relative bargaining powers of the landlord and the farmer. The price of wheat depends on the supply and demand for it in the *local* market. If this market is in excess demand, the farmer raises his price and the equilibrium is reached when the price allows 'the producer the most distant from this market to sell in it although he spent as much to produce the wheat and incurred the additional cost of bringing it from his distant fields'. After having negotiated the price under these conditions, the farmer has to negotiate the amount of rent he must pay the landlord, and in this process he must be aware of the competition of other farmers wishing to rent the same land. In spite of its lack of precision, Sismondi's discourse is clear. The general result depends on the relative bargaining powers of the participants – the consumer, the landlord and the farmer – and what each of them gets of the surplus can vary greatly:

> the mercantile value [of the *produit net*] can be determined through a double or triple struggle [*lutte*] so that, according to circumstances, it will sometimes entirely go to the landowner […]; sometimes it will partly go to the farmer […]; and the consumer will also often benefit from it. (Sismondi 1819, 1: 284–85)

In this process, however, the landowner has a prominent role that ensures the positivity of the rent and of the price of wheat:

> Property rights, or the monopoly warranted by society, that any landowner has against two classes of people – those who demand foodstuffs [the consumers] and those who offer labour to produce them [the farmers] – prevent the price of 'fermage' on the one hand, and that of foodstuffs ['denrées'] on the other hand, from being too much reduced in value. (Sismondi 1819, 1: 286)

What about the circumstances that Ricardo proposed to explain the existence and level of the differential rent? They are, Sismondi stated, of secondary importance. 'It is only after these three causes worked with infinite variations and according to the circumstances, that the other causes acknowledged by M. Ricardo are felt' (1819, 1: 286). From this point of view, part of the criticism raised later by A. Walras is formulated along the same lines:

> Malthus' and Ricardo's doctrine to explain the origin of 'fermage' is certainly most ingenious but it is wrong. To explain the origin of 'fermage' by the inequality of land is like explaining wages by the unequal capacities of workers. The inequality of the workers explains the inequality of wages, just as inequality of land explains the inequality of 'fermages'. But the origin of 'fermage' and the origin of wages, considered in themselves independently of their levels, comes from another source than the inequality that can be found between one worker and another or one plot of land and another. (A. Walras 1830: 16)

Finally, yet another different point of view on rent was advanced by Antoine-Élisée Cherbuliez, a renowned utilitarian politician and intellectual, and a collaborator of the *Bibliothèque Universelle* – now *Bibliothèque Universelle de Genève* – who was to play an important part in the group of liberal economists in France. He was already the celebrated author of the *Théorie des garanties constitutionnelles* (1838), was teaching at the Genevan Académie and was a member of the Conseil Représentatif de Genève. Drawing some inspiration from ideas expressed by P. Prévost and Sismondi, he published a book entitled *Riche ou pauvrre, exposition succincte des causes et des effets de la distribution actuelle des richesses sociales* (Cherbuliez 1840) which was an acute analysis of the economic and social consequences – unequal distribution of income, insecure condition of the workers and pauperism, etc. – of the new industrial order. Contrary to Ch. Pictet and G. Prévost, he understood perfectly the Ricardian theory of rent – intensive[41] as well as extensive – and accepted it. His conclusions, however, were radical and, like Ricardo, he affirmed the conflicting interests between the landowners and the other classes in society. He heavily stressed that, while landowners can also marginally accumulate capital on land and earn a profit from it, rent is an income they get without any labour or activity of their own. This income, moreover, was steadily increasing with population growth and accumulation of capital, thus favouring the 'interests of the past' – the landowner's – against those of the dynamic elements of the new economic and social order: the capitalists and the workers.

> These are men who receive an ever-increasing part of the social income, without doing any physical or intellectual activity, without incurring any risk, without making any sacrifice, solely by virtue of a right that the law confers on them over the [...] territory of their nation. (Cherbuliez 1840: 163)

> Landowners are idle persons kept at the expense of the public without any advantage for either industry or the general welfare of society. They form a powerful class, an unavoidable aristocracy whose interests are isolated and distinct from the interests of the other members of the association. (Cherbuliez 1840: 205)

To remedy this damaging situation and referring to the Physiocratic single tax project, Cherbuliez imagined a tax on rent – he rejected the idea of a land tax levied on landowners independently of the fertility of their property – which would replace all existing taxes and thus suppress their negative impact on the accumulation of capital, while allowing the the State to finance its expenditure. The consequences on the economy would be positive because the landowners are generally not inclined to save and accumulate from their income, and because they would be unable to transfer the new tax onto any other social group (Cherbuliez 1840: 203–4). It is, however, Cherbuliez's opinion that this scheme, although just, could not be implemented for practical reasons:

> Unfortunately, it is impossible to levy a tax on rent and rent alone; because while it is already difficult, for the land exploited under the regime of farming leases, to know which portion of 'fermage' corresponds to the rent itself – i.e., which does not represent the profit of any portion of agricultural capital – this difficulty turns into an absolute impossibility for the plots of land exploited by their owners. (Cherbuliez 1840: 204)

The only solution, then, is more radical: 'why should we not go one step further and abolish the private appropriation of land?' (Cherbuliez 1840: 205).

The State should replace private landowners. It would not cultivate the land itself, but rent it out to farmers.

> The abolition of the private ownership of land would not change anything in the causes that give rise to the rent, and this rent would still exist. But if would be received by the State […] and land would be leased to individuals in possession of sufficient amounts of capital to exploit it. […] The State would find in this revenue the means, first to supply the ordinary needs of the administration, and then to cover the country with canals and roads and create all kinds of establishments favourable to industry and to the increase of the general welfare. All direct and indirect taxes would be suppressed […]. Finally, industry, emancipated and unfettered, would expand in an unprecedented manner, while the cultivation of land, under free competition, would rapidly go from progress to progress! (Cherbuliez 1840: 206–7)

Needless to say, *Riche ou Pauvre* caused a huge scandal in Geneva. But it was read with interest in France where an edition – probably unauthorised – was published in Paris in 1841 under a slightly different title, *Richesse et pauvreté*, on the initiative of a confidential social Christian movement named the 'Solidairunis'.[42] A preface was added and signed P. G.-B.,[43] entitled: 'Résumé de la doctrine des Solidairunis', stating that while Cherbuliez's analysis was right, he hardly proposed anything to remedy the dramatic situation of the workers. But the book was on the whole well received, even outside the 'leftist' circles of the time.

Contemporaries could see an heir to Cherbuliez's 1840 ideas, or an echo of them, in Auguste and Léon Walras' well-known proposal for the nationalization of land. However, it should be noted that Auguste Walras – with, strikingly, almost the same phrases as those employed by Cherbuliez – had already formulated his proposal in a manuscript entitled 'De l'abolissement de l'impôt et de l'établissement de la loi agraire, telle qu'elle peut être conçue et pratiquée au XIXe siècle', written ten years *before* the publication of Cherbuliez's book (A. Walras 1830). This is all the more interesting since A. Walras' theoretical background was different: and this shows how Ricardo's assertion that landowners benefited from the situation and threatened capital accumulation and economic growth caught the imagination of his readers.

As for Cherbuliez, he later repudiated his former ideas and, in his *Précis de la science économique et de ses principales applications* (Cherbuliez 1862), while still sticking to the Ricardian theory, defended the institution of private land ownership.

6. Money and banking

Ricardo's ideas on money and banking, developed in his monetary pamphlets and in the *Principles*, were received by the French economists with both interest and reluctance. They all stressed the great expertise of Ricardo in the field, and respected his rigour and action during and after the Bullion controversy. Some of them even considered that the originality and importance of Ricardo in the post-Smithian debates lay precisely in his theory of money and banking:

> there we find all that most entitles him to the admiration of the economists. It is strange that the relative merits of his works have been so misjudged and that his entire glory usually rests on the theory of rent. (Fonteyraud 1847: xxvi)

Say's opinion was not different (below). Whatever their opinions on this point, however, French economists mainly considered Ricardo's monetary doctrines with the greatest suspicion. From Ricardo's chapter on money and banking in the *Principles*, the majority of French economists retained three intertwined propositions: (i) the quantity of paper money determines its value; (ii) the convertibility of the paper money is not necessary to preserve its gold parity; and (iii) the most perfect currency is made of paper.

The first proposition was in tune with the most generally accepted theory of value which, with variations from one author to another, conferred an important role on the interaction between supply and demand. It was nevertheless widely discussed (see below the remarks on the definition of paper money and the need to distinguish it from money proper and bank notes). In addition, disregarding the coherence of Ricardo's assertions in the field, many authors jumped at the opportunity of accusing him of inconsistency. In their eyes, the role of the quantity of money in the determination of its value was in total contradiction to his general theory of value. Say, for whom the debate about value was of paramount importance, was only too willing to take this opportunity:

> It is amusing to see – he wrote – that Ricardo's doctrine in this field is precisely grounded on the principle of the proportion between the quantities supplied and demanded – principle the influence of which he refuses to acknowledge. He irrefutably proves that the medium of exchange is a commodity of the same nature as any other, and he denies that the others are subject to the same influences. (Say 1825: 278)

The denunciation of this alleged inconsistency was subsequently repeated by French authors. Auguste Walras, for example:

> Had gold and silver a value proportionate to the quantity of labour employed in their production, one should not say that the value of money is regulated by its quantity; and were the quantity of money existing in a country the real rule for its value, one should give up stating that the value of money stems from the quantity of labour used in the production of gold and silver. (A. Walras 1831: 179)

The second and third above-mentioned propositions were in general opposed. The fact that Ricardo was in favour of a paper currency raised serious doubts about the pertinence of his theory: as a matter of historical fact, John Law's bankruptcy and the recent disaster of the assignats were still very much present in French minds. Consider the opinions expressed by some of them in the 1820s: Charles Ganilh, François Ferrier, Isaac Péreire and Louis Say, for example. They did not go deep into theoretical investigations nor analyze the historical experience from which Ricardo's proposal stemmed: their reaction was instinctive. Some other French economists – in fact, the majority – developed a more documented position. They opposed Ricardian ideas because they were attached to a theory of commodity money: money can only be made out of a commodity which, also serving for other purposes, has its own value. Finally, the reception of Ricardo's monetary theory also depended in France on the debate between central banking and free banking.

Reactions against paper money

To explain how an object without intrinsic value could act as money, Ricardo used the quantity theory. He first explained that, provided the State has the monopoly of coinage, a limitation on the quantity of coins could raise their value to any level so that the seigniorage could increase without limit. He then asserted that this principle regulates the circulation of paper money. With this conclusion: 'though it has no intrinsic value, yet, by limiting its quantity, its value in exchange is as great as an equal denomination of coins, or of bullion in that coin' (Ricardo 1817–21: 353). Ganilh exclaimed: 'What! Paper money has a value provided that its quantity is limited to the needs of the circulation!' (Ganilh 1821, 2: 137). He did not deny that an object deprived of any intrinsic value could theoretically act as a means of payment, but he thought that, if such money were issued by a Government, citizens would think that it was risky to accept it. They would prefer to hold commodities rather than money and would accept the latter only when they could not do otherwise. Trade would quickly decline. It is certainly possible to imagine theoretically how paper money could circulate, but this circulation would be impossible in practice.

Moreover, contrary to Smith, Ricardo asserted that:

> it is not necessary that paper money should be payable in specie to secure its value; it is only necessary that its quantity should be regulated according to the value of the metal which is declared to be the standard. (1817–21: 354)

Ganilh was puzzled. He admitted he did not understand this theory and reasserted the traditional analysis that opposes the banknote to paper money. The former, at least, is convertible. 'The former is guaranteed by all the commercial values that it circulates […], the latter depends solely on public trust ['foi publique'] which is rarely well kept' (1821, 2: 142).

Ricardo also concluded that 'a currency is in its most perfect state when it consists wholly of paper money, but of paper money of an equal value with the gold which it professes to represent' (Ricardo 1817–21: 361). Ferrier (1822: 205) feared the worst and prayed God that France would avoid a third experience of paper money. Isaac Péreire was puzzled and cautious. He warned his audience: 'You all still have in mind the disorders that paper money has provoked' (Péreire 1832: 16). As for Louis Say, Ricardo's formulation was a *non sequitur* because paper money has no value in the Ricardian sense of the word (L. Say 1822: 229). One should speak of its purchasing power [*capacité acquisitive*]. Ricardo should have written that the most perfect money is a paper the purchasing power of which is equal to that of the gold it represents. L. Say seems to play on words, but his acceptation of Ricardo's opinion is not evident. When Ricardo asserted that a perfectly safe paper redeemable in 15 years is of equal value to a paper redeemable on request (Ricardo 1817–21: 356), L. Say disagreed. People are cautious, he argued, and would always prefer the latter: 'they would get more cheaply what they acquire with a paper redeemable on request than with a paper redeemable in fifteen years' (L. Say 1822: 230).

Say's dissenting voice

In the 1820s, surrounded by this chorus of criticism, Say's voice is resolutely out of tune. He supported Ricardo's ideas and made them his own. In a review of G. Prévost's translation of McCulloch's *Discourse*, he did not hesitate to write: 'To come back to Ricardo, I think that his only claim to fame is his doctrine on money' (Say 1825: 278).

His position was not new. Ten years before, his reading of *The High Price of Bullion* led him to reconsider the analysis of paper money he had proposed in the first edition of his *Traité* (1803). His opinion, at that time, was not clear. On the one hand, he stressed that 'money is a commodity having its own value' (1803: 456), this value being determined, like that of any other commodity, by supply and demand: with the consequence that 'the adoption of a commodity as money considerably increases its intrinsic value' (1803: 458). But, on the other hand, he acknowledged that a commodity deprived of any utility – he gave the example of the cowry – could also act as money. The problem was then for him to explain the value of paper money defined as notes 'that do not oblige the issuing authority to reimburse them, at least not immediately' (1803: 502). In 1803 and in the second edition in 1814, Say maintained that such a money deprived of intrinsic value can nevertheless have a value for three reasons: (i) it can be used to pay taxes; (ii) it can be used to buy commodities at given prices, because the Government 'obliges the producers not to refuse to give such quantity of goods in exchange for this quantity of paper money' (1803: 504); and (iii) people's need to use money can give paper some of the value that its role as medium of exchange confers on metal. Say's ambiguity lies in the fact that it is not clear whether this third reason is sufficient per se.

Say's journey to England during the last months of 1814 gave him the opportunity to reconsider the question. His analysis of the British monetary problems and his reading of Ricardo's *High Price of Bullion* prompted a change in his thinking. He probably evoked this development in a letter to James Mill, who in turn referred to it in a letter to Ricardo dated 9 November 1815:

> I have a long letter from our Parisian friend [...]. He says he is rectifying his chapters on money to a conformity with your ideas, for the third edition of his book, which will probably appear next year. (Ricardo 1951–73, 6: 321)

In 1815, Say stated clearly that the value of the notes issued by the Bank of England did not depend on the flimsy hope for future convertibility into gold: it was only determined by their quantity.

> It is [...] the proportion of notes and not the discredit that influences their value; discredit, whatever it can be, does not possess the least influence on that value [...]. Were I asked what time I believe the Bank of England would repay its bank notes on demand, I would answer that I do not know [...] and that my answer would also be of no importance. (Say 1815: 75)

The Bank of England, he added, can control the value of its notes. To restore them to par, it is sufficient to reduce the amount of discounted paper in order to diminish their quantity.

In 1814, before returning to the continent, Say wrote down a plan for the reorganization of the banking system in France. He sent it to Ricardo who replied that it was similar to the proposals he himself had made for the Bank of England as set out in the 1811 Appendix to the *High Price of Bullion* (Ricardo to Say, 24 December 1814, in 1951–73, 6: 165). The only difference, stressed by Ricardo himself, was that in Say's plan the Government was supposed to be the issuer of the notes. Ricardo thought that this clause was dangerous because no Government could resist the temptation of misusing this power.

Say subsequently[44] showed some interest in Ricardo's plan to reform the English banking system set out in his 1816 *Proposals for an Economic and Secure Currency*. He made them his own in the third edition of the *Traité*:

> The extraordinary circumstances that have occurred in England in respect to money [...] have given a decisive proof, that the mere want of a medium of exchange [...] is sufficient to support the value of a paper money destitute of security for its convertibility, provided it is limited in

> amount to the actual needs of circulation. Whence some English writers […] have been led to conclude, that […] it was possible to use, for that purpose, some substance less costly than the precious metals: paper, for instance, due attention being paid to keep the amount of the paper money within the needs of the circulation. The celebrated Ricardo has, with this object, proposed an ingenious plan, making the Bank or corporate body invested with the privilege of issuing the paper-money, liable to pay in bullion for its notes on demand. (Say 1817: 555)

He repeated his approval in his 1819 notes to the French translation of the *Principles* (Say 1819b, 2: 236–37). He justified his position by referring anew to the English experience and to the fact that, when the war against France was over, the inconvertible notes of the Bank of England were again at par. This appreciation of the notes, he stressed, was not caused by trust but by the fact that the quantity of circulating notes corresponded to the needs.

However, Say's approval faded away. The above quotation from the *Traité* no longer appeared in the fifth and sixth editions. Obviously Say – who, at the end of his life, wanted to stand apart from Ricardo – became increasingly sceptical and eventually accepted the common monetary wisdom of the time. In 1826, in the fifth edition of the *Traité*, he reconsidered the question. He maintained, it is true, that Ricardo's proposal was clever but specified that its implementation supposed 'a Government that could offer all the desirable guarantees, together with an independent bank' (Say 1826a: 513). While he was not explicit on this point, it is not difficult to imagine that in his eyes, these conditions were not fulfilled in France. He quoted Smith's celebrated phrase on the 'Daedalian wings of paper money' (1776: 321) and eventually accepted Tooke's cautious attitude: even if the convertibility into coins is more expensive than the convertibility into bullion, it is safer and should therefore be preferred.

Central or free banking?

The reaction of most French economists against paper money has been noted above. Their own ideas must be briefly stated at this point because the name of Ricardo was used during the controversies that raged between them about the best way to organize a monetary and banking system.

Basically, most liberal economists were of the opinion that money should be made of a commodity having a value of its own. In a traditional way, they thought that the choice of the commodity to act as money was a practical choice based on the physical properties of the good. The other forms of medium of exchange – bills of exchange or any paper that circulates through endorsement, bank notes, or the most modern form at that time: cheques – result from operations of credit and are not money as such. Bank notes, for example, are just a different and more developed form of bills of exchange, an evolution permitted by the creation of modern banking institutions. The banker substitutes his signature for that of the issuer of the bill, and himself issues another bill – his bank note – which, contrary to the original commercial paper, circulates without endorsement, does not entail any redemption date but is instead redeemable to the bearer on demand. Hence, obviously, the importance of the convertibility into money, i.e., in specie or bullion.

This scheme was reassessed several times (see for example Charles Coquelin 1842, 1848, 1852a and b, 1859, or Michel Chevalier 1850, 1853) especially against the many projects that, during the century, aimed at reorganizing the monetary and banking system along the most diverse lines of thought. In this perspective, French liberals insisted on the fact that bank notes are not money. To state that notes replace money is 'a fatal doctrine […], the poisonous source of all wrong systems' (Coquelin 1848: 46).

> All these bonds and credit instruments are substitutes for money – Chevalier stressed – but none of them is money, and it is impossible to deny their difference without important risks. This would be the same kind of mistake as mixing a portrait with the original or the shadow with the substance. (Chevalier 1853: 216)

Along the same lines, they warned that bank notes should not be confused with paper money. The latter is an inconvertible paper issued by the State, generally through a bank granted with a monopoly of issue: 'it is the creation of the political power […]; the bearer of paper money has no right to any exchange against specie' (Courcelle-Seneuil 1853: 316).

In this perspective, how was it possible to organize the monetary system in an efficient way? Roughly speaking, discarding the idea of the establishment of paper money, two broad solutions were possible: a system with a central bank, i.e., a convertible but monopolized bank note – sometimes called paper money by its opponents – or free banking. The historical context in France favoured the debates: it witnessed the development of the Banque de France, created in 1800 and progressively transformed during the century into a monopolized institution with the privilege of issue on the entire territory.

At first sight, Ricardo's writings – his 1816 *Proposals* and especially the 1824 *Plan for the Establishment of a National Bank* – together with his widely discussed assertion that the most perfect currency is made of paper, could be interpreted as supporting the first system. It was the opinion of most French liberal economists that Ricardo's plans were adopted in Great Britain in 1844, even if there were some differences that they considered minor (Fonteyraud 1847: xxvii–xxviii, Courcelle-Seneuil 1857: 545–47). Some supporters of the Central bank system only criticized Ricardo for having limited the convertibility of notes to bullion alone. Alfred Sudre, for example, thought that this measure was intended to avoid runs, the depletion of the Bank of England's gold reserves and the contraction of the level of activity, and asserted that it would be ineffective against these evils.

> Finally, we must remember that the celebrated economist Ricardo had outlined a plan for a bank the notes of which would have been redeemed […] in bullion […]. This plan, rather unworthy of the reputation of its author, could only hinder the demands for reimbursement of small holders of banknotes – these mass panics called *runs* by our neighbours. But these panics have not recurred since half a century, and experience shows that the cause of the demands for precious metals that assail banks at the time of commercial crises does not lie in the fears of the notes-holders but solely in the deterioration of the exchange and in the needs of the commercial world [*haut commerce*] for exportation. Now, the reimbursement in bullion at a fixed rate would not have any effect in this case, because the bankers and the tradesmen can export ingots as well as species. […] Ricardo's *Bullion system* would be powerless to protect the reserves of the banks and to avoid a rise in the discount rate and the contraction of circulation, all measures taken by these institutions in time of crisis. (Sudre 1865: 18–19)

Faced with Ricardo's authority, which they also respected, supporters of the free banking idea reacted in various but converging ways. Gustave du Puynode, who published a series of three papers on Ricardo (Puynode 1866) in the *Journal des Économistes*, again accused him of inconsistency: while advocating free trade everywhere, he was favouring monopoly in the banking sector.

> Who has ever studied in a better way than him the questions of money and credit? And after having stated so many profound and ingenious considerations on these questions, does he not end with the iniquitous and the impossible, with the monopoly of credit and the sole circulation of paper? (Puynode 1866, I: 12)

In addition, Ricardo was accused of imagining 'that banks could arbitrarily decide on their issues without any need to adjust them to the demands of trade' (Puynode 1866, I: 12), i.e., of not understanding how strong the free banking approach is and how dangerous a national bank. Finally, he was accused – and this may be the source of all his mistakes – on confusing bank notes with paper money (Puynode 1866, II: 14): he did not pay sufficient attention to the question of credit, and left it unsolved (Fonteyraud 1847: xxviii–xxix).

> In our opinion, the problem [the question of the 'science of credit'] slipped out of Ricardo's hands without having been solved, and this because of two distinct reasons. In the first place, he did not reach, in his skilful analyses, the very sources of the circulation; – in the second place, he did not acknowledge the check and regulatory power that credit exercises on itself, so that he was led to seek aid and assistance from the State, and to

> see in illusory regulations an equilibrium that would naturally ensue from a regime of liberty. (Fonteyraud 1847: xxix)

Finally, some authors tried to explain what Ricardo really meant by his assertion that the most perfect currency is made of paper. They interpreted it by referring to a basic idea of Ricardo's plan: the currency had to be economical.

> A Bank has fulfilled all its useful functions when it has substituted paper in the circulation for gold; when it has enabled us to carry on our commerce with a cheap currency, and to employ the valuable one which it supplants productively. (Ricardo 1822: 233–34)

Ricardo added: 'provided it fulfils this object it is of little importance at what rate of interest it lends its money' (Ricardo 1822: 234). He was speaking of 'a Bank' with a capital B, i.e., the Bank of England or its equivalent, any Central Bank in modern parlance. In the French translation, however, 'a bank' is written without the capital B, implicitly generalizing the assertion to all kinds of bank, and this may have been a source of confusion.

As a matter of fact, Chevalier noted, the development of notes brought about an important saving in the cost of circulation. But this saving, he stressed, was somewhat limited for a time, because people still needed specie whenever a bank note was of too high a denomination. The development of commercial accounting, clearing houses, cheques and bank transfers, while greatly favouring economic activity, allowed further reduction in the metallic circulation (see also Puynode 1866, II: 15 & sq), thus fulfilling Ricardo's prediction. At that time, at least in Great Britain and the United States, Chevalier insisted, the quantity of specie and even of banknotes was very small compared to the mass of other instruments used for the same purpose, and this is the real meaning of Ricardo's famous assertion.

> It is in this sense, and not literally and in an absolute meaning, that Ricardo's expression – so widely discussed but distorted because of exaggeration – must be understood: the most perfect state of money is to be made of paper (Chevalier 1853: 216).

But while admitting that a saving in the cost of circulation is not to be neglected, and disregarding the fact that Ricardo was speaking of a Central Bank, Coquelin disapproved of Ricardo's assertion. In his view, the function of a bank is not primarily to issue notes in that purpose, but to develop credit, i.e., to advance money to entrepreneurs and to incite them, simply by their presence and function, to grant credit to each other (1848: 316).

At this point, of course, the positions could not be reconciled. 'Our utopia', Fonteyraud wrote, would be to see a strong monetary circulation based on precious metals and on credit made by free banks whose accounts and situation are permanently in public view; a flexible and secure circulation that would give life to economic activity and resist, because of its flexibility, the most important shocks; a 'democracy of credit' replacing the oligarchy that governs the stock exchanges. In essence: 'by dint of freedom and publicity, we would join the interest of the banks with that of the population' (Fonteyraud 1847: xxxv). With this parable as a conclusion and a warning:

> A nice legend […] says that a saint, who took refuge in a poor cottage in Brittany, took off his wet coat […] and, not finding any coat-peg, hung it on a sunbeam. The circulation of paper such as the alleged economists of the day would like it, exactly represents this sunbeam: and this is, we think, a far too fragile support to entrust to its care the wealth of a whole generation. Freedom alone has foundations wide enough to resist shocks, and were Ricardo alive now […], he would not hesitate to seek in freedom, like us, the true solution of credit. (Fonteyraud 1847: xxxvi–xxxvii)

7. Say's law and crises

One point is expected a priori to be unproblematic: the question of the 'loi des débouchés' – Say's law. We know that Ricardo accepted this law, and the majority of French economists who dissented on this point criticized primarily Say and his followers, not Ricardo. However, things did not happen exactly in this way, and there are some marked differences between Say and Ricardo on this topic as well. This is all the more interesting since, in dealing with this point, we will again meet the question of money.

Is Say inconsequent?

Acknowledging the importance of the chapter on 'débouchés' in Say's *Traité d'économie politique*, Ricardo wrote, in his preface to the *Principles*, that 'it contains […] some very important principles, which I believe were first explained by this distinguished writer' (1817–21: 7). Further on in the book, he explained his opinion:

> M. Say has, however, most satisfactory shewn, that there is no amount of capital which may not be employed in a country, because demand is only limited by production. No man produces, but with a view to consume or sell, and he never sells, but with an intention to purchase some other commodity, which may be immediately useful to him, or may contribute to future production. By producing, then, he necessarily becomes either the consumer of his own goods, or the purchaser and consumer of the goods of some other person. (1817–21: 290)

At the same time, however, he criticized the way in which Say analyzed the effects of the accumulation of capital on the evolution of profits. Later, when reading Say's letters to Malthus, he thought that Say 'has said a great deal for the right cause, but not all what could be said' (Ricardo to Malthus, 4 September 1820, in 1951–73, VIII: 227). It is therefore questionable to suppose that Say and Ricardo had the same conception of the law of markets (Forget 2003, Gehrke and Kurz 2003). In the discussions in this field, it is legitimate to ask to what extent the critical remarks of Ricardo influenced Say's thought.

When Say examined the determination of the interest rate, he asserted that 'the greater the abundance of capital in proportion to the extent of its employment, the lower the interest on the capital that is lent' (1814: 765). He also specified that only the available capital – still in circulation and not yet invested – influences the rate of interest. To put it briefly, he maintained that the rate of interest is determined on the loanable funds market. Ricardo thought this proposition to be incompatible with the law of markets. 'If capital to any extent can be employed by a country', he wrote, 'how can it be said abundant, compared with the extent of employment for it?' (1817–21: 290). In a note to the *Principles*,[45] Say seemed at first to accept the criticism:

> From the principle established in my *Traité*, M. Ricardo infers here a perfectly correct consequence. He explains satisfactorily the decrease in the capital-profits, or interest, with the increase in capital while the occasions to use it multiplies with it. It is also certain that I was wrong when I said that capital can be more or less abundant compared with its employments because I proved elsewhere that these employments multiply in proportion to the abundance of capital. (Say 1819b, 2: 107)

Did Say change his mind after this self-criticism? Surprisingly, he did not. Moreover, the passage criticized by Ricardo is one of the few that remained unchanged throughout the various editions of the *Traité*. Why? Two reasons may explain this fact.

A question of definition

The first reason has something to do with the subject of the analysis. In Chapter XXI of the *Principles* to which this note is appended, Ricardo dealt with the 'Effects of Accumulation on Profits and Interest'. In his opinion, the accumulation of capital only provokes a lasting fall in profits if wages rise, and he criticized Smith's assertion that the fall in profits can be due to capital competition resulting from accumulation:

> The increase of stock, which raises wages, tends to lower profit. When the stocks of many rich merchants are turned into the same trade, their mutual competition naturally tends to lower its profit: and when there is a like increase of stock in all the different trades carried on in the same society, the same competition must produce the same effect in them all. (Smith, 1776: 105)

For Ricardo, the evolution of profits determines that of interest. If demand is only limited by production, competition in the goods market cannot explain the fall in profits when accumulation increases. He did not understand how Say could speak of an abundance of capital compared with its employments while asserting that 'a product is no sooner created than, from that very moment, it affords a market for other products to the full extent of its own value' (Say 1814: 250).

In Say's opinion, Smith and Ricardo, under the term 'profit', confused 'the income that the entrepreneur gets from his industry, his talent, and the income coming from his instrument, his capital' (1826a: 691). The nature and evolution of these two kinds of income are different. When Say referred to capital competition, he examined how the interest rate is determined. The capital he referred to is the available capital – the loanable funds. The interest rate is determined by supply and demand for these funds. When supply increases – when a greater amount of capital is available – the rate of interest decreases. This evolution does not imply that capital accumulation entails greater competition in the goods market. In Say's view, there is no conflict between the law of market and the proposition that an increase in the capital available provokes a fall in the interest rate. On this point, Ricardo's criticism did not incite him to change the view he advanced in the second edition of the *Traité*. But he had to make his point clearer.

The nature of adjustment

There is also a second reason why Say did not change his mind. In the first edition of the *Traité*, Say maintained that 'when a nation has too many products of one kind, the way to sell them is to create products of another kind' (Say 1803: 246). It is the lack of counterpart that explains the glut in some markets.

> It is because the production of the *lacking commodities* suffered that the *superabundant commodities* cannot be sold and their value falls. To use a more hackneyed phrase, many people have bought less, because they have earned less; and they have earned less, either because they have had difficulty in the employment of their means of production, or because these means have themselves been deficient. (Say 1814: 252–53)

He explained that 'when crops are deficient, *manufactured products* do not sell well, because part of these *manufactured products* is bought with the product of crops' (Say 1814: 1104). On this point, it seems that Say's analysis conflicted with that of Ricardo, who explained that crises were due to 'sudden changes in the channels of trade' and the mistakes of capitalists when choosing the activities in which to invest their capital.

Say subsequently reformulated his opinion and wrote that 'one can only speak of a complete production when all the services needed for it are paid with the value of the product' (1827, in 1833: 309–10). This new formulation of the law of market has been considered as inadequate (Baumol 1977: 159). But the problem is real. It is perfectly possible that entrepreneurs made wrong choices and that their production cannot be sold at a high enough price to cover their costs. The supply of such goods cannot finance the purchases and there is no reason to think that, in the budget constraint of the firms, the products must be valued according to their costs of production. Say always accepted that an unfortunate allocation of capital could provoke an overproduction of some commodities and, as a consequence, some disequilibrium in other markets. The law of markets does not deny the possibility of such crises: it dismisses the idea that economic growth cannot be sustainable because of insufficient consumption.

Ricardo and Say agreed on this point. But what is at issue, and a subject of controversy between them, is the process of adjustment. While Ricardo suggested that equilibrium is restored through a reallocation of the means of production, Say's opinion was that the readjustment necessitates an increase in the production of the commodities in excess of demand. Say wrote to Malthus:

> I uphold that, whenever there is a glut, a superabundance of some kinds of commodities, it is because some other commodities are not produced in amounts sufficient to be exchanged with the former; if their producers could produce more […] then the former could find the sales they are lacking. (Say 1820: 227)

Ricardo disagreed:

> In one point I think he [Say] falls into the same error as Torrens in his article in the *Edinburgh Review*. They both appear to think that stagnation in commerce arises from a counter set of commodities not being produced with which the commodities on sale are to be purchased, and they seem to infer that the evil will not be removed till such other commodities are in the market. But surely the true remedy is in regulating future production, – if there is a glut of one commodity produce less of that and more of another but do not let the glut continue till the purchaser chuses to produce the commodity which is more wanted. (Ricardo to Malthus, 4 September 1820, in 1951–73, t. 8: 227–28)

However, while Say proposed the development of the activities where supply was falling short, he did not explicitly exclude a transfer of means of production from the branches where they are superabundant to those where they are lacking. But there are obstacles. Some of them are purely political or pertain to a wrong economic policy:

> Major causes […] like natural or political disasters, the greediness or incompetence of Governments, necessarily maintain somewhere this

> shortage that creates a glut elsewhere. Whenever this political disease stops, the means of production go where production is insufficient; and, in this way, they favour the progress of production in all other branches. A kind of production would seldom be in excess, and its product seldom depreciated if they all would enjoy an entire liberty. (Say 1826a: 253)

The analysis of the effects of taxation raised a similar debate. Say thought that 'a tax on a commodity does not raise its price by the whole amount of the tax' (1814: 1018) because, if that were the case, this would mean that the demand for it remains the same – which is impossible because any increase in the price of a commodity reduces the number of buyers. Ricardo, on the contrary, asserted that the price of the commodity would rise by the amount of the tax because if the price of the commodity 'did not rise by a sum equal to the tax, it would not give the same profit to the producer which he had before, and he would remove his capital to some other employment' (Ricardo 1817–21: 243). But Say rejected this hypothesis and, on this point, his arguments are similar to those advanced by Sismondi (see above) when he objected to the process of gravitation:

> […] M. Ricardo, too generally and without restriction, admits that capital and industry leave a production that does not generate profits equal to those of other trades. In almost all kinds of industry, there are stocks so completely invested that it is impossible to withdraw them from their employment without considerably damaging their value. Talents and industrial labour themselves do not change object without serious disadvantages. People prefer working in an activity that is less remunerative because they would incur greater losses if they changed; and this effect lasts sometimes for half a century. (Say 1819b, 2: 3)

And he added:

> It is impossible to neglect the circumstances that influence so powerfully the results; there is a great risk of being mistaken when one's attention is only focused on some great principles, the modifications they receive from some other secondary considerations being neglected. Circumstances act following principles that are equally undisputable. (Say 1819b, 2: 3–4)

In conclusion, like Sismondi, Say disagreed with Ricardo on the pertinence of a seemingly 'empirical' hypothesis. If the structure of demand changes, it was Ricardo's opinion that the allocation of the existing capital would be modified in consequence. By contrast, in Say's view, the allocation would not be modified and the adjustment would only take place through new investment. Of course Say's judgment – like that of Sismondi – in part reflects an incomplete understanding of Ricardo's position, as already noted above.

Money and crises

From the first edition of the *Traité* onwards, Say stressed the beneficial effects of the active circulation of money and commodities: the more rapidly a commodity is produced and sold, the more swiftly the stock immobilized can be devoted to a new productive employment. There is no opposition here between money and goods: both ready cash and stored commodities are idle capital. In order to lose as little as possible on the interest on the invested capital, entrepreneurs accelerate the turnover of their capital. Interest influences the velocity of the circulation of money. The latter is slow in periods of fear and uncertainty; it accelerates in the event of inflation.

> When money […] depreciates, people try to exchange it, to get rid of it by all means. This is the reason why there was such prodigious circulation when the discredit of the assignats was increasing. Everyone endeavoured to find an employment for paper money of which the value was vanishing every hour: one only received it to employ it immediately; it seemed to be burning everyone who touched it (Say 1826a: 268).

This implicitly acknowledges that money can be hoarded. In his *Lettres à Malthus*, Say explicitly admitted this point. He criticized Ricardo for his assertion that 'all saved capital is always employed […]. On the contrary, many savings cannot be placed during hard times' (Say 1820: 272). Money is hoarded during a crisis and, in this case, a general glut can occur: but hoarding is a consequence, not a cause, of the crisis.

In 1826, Say analyzed the commercial crisis in England in a paper published in the *Revue Encyclopédique*: 'De la crise commerciale en Angleterre'. Against Sismondi, he developed a monetary theory of crises.[46] He explained that an excessive issue of banknotes greatly encouraged speculation because anybody who wanted to create or develop a business could obtain the required amount of money.

> What happened? The abundance of the medium of exchange (coins and banknotes) caused its depreciation with respect to bullion; and from the moment a gold coin was no longer equal in value to an ingot of the same weight, people ran to the bank to convert banknotes into gold coins, and gold coins into ingots […]. As a consequence […] the banks, obliged to convert their banknotes and being incapable of issuing new ones, could no longer discount the bills of exchange presented by entrepreneurs […]. Obliged to pay their liabilities, and having no real capital, entrepreneurs went bankrupt after having turned everything into cash and sold their commodities for next to nothing. (1826b: 241)

What is puzzling is that Say argued that the commercial crisis could be explained according to Ricardo's principles concerning money, although

Ricardo never stated a monetary theory of crises in this way. Say probably wanted to assert that his analysis followed logically from Ricardo's theory of money, and especially from the idea that the quantity of banknotes 'is necessarily limited by the needs of circulation […] [and cannot] without danger exceed this amount' (1826b: 241).

Sismondi's critique: back to the adjustment process

At first sight, it seems paradoxical that Ricardo could influence Sismondi's theory of crises, since their opinions on that topic are supposed to be radically different. But the question deserves closer examination.

As early as 1815, in his entry 'Political Economy' of the *Edinburgh Encyclopaedia*, Sismondi asserted that

> surely none will maintain that it can be advantageous to substitute a machine for a man, if this man cannot find work elsewhere; or that it is not better to have the population composed of citizens than of steam-engines, even though the cotton cloth of the first should be a little dearer than that of the second. (1815: 76)

In his *Nouveaux principes d'économie politique*, he developed this thesis, basing his arguments on four ideas.

(i) An increase in production leads to a general glut whenever it is not caused by an increase in income and demand but by the accumulation of capital (Sismondi 1827, 2: 398).

(ii) The knowledge that entrepreneurs obtain of the market for their product, through prices, is too patchy to guide their decisions in an efficient way.

> Someone who lives from commercial wealth depends on a metaphysical public, on an invisible and unknown power; he must satisfy its needs, anticipate its tastes […]; he must guess without it speaking, and he cannot allow himself to misunderstand it without risking his subsistence because of a miscalculation. (Sismondi 1819, 1: 301)

(iii) The mobility of the means of production is low: 'Workers can seldom do another job […]. Fixed capital cannot be employed for another use […]. Finally the manufacturer himself needs his industry to get his living, and he does not abandon it easily' (Sismondi 1819, 1: 308–9).

(iv) the introduction of new techniques of production does not necessarily have a positive result, since it can destroy employment.

> Whenever the discovery cannot increase the number of consumers, while serving them more cheaply, either because they are all already provided with the commodity or because they do not need it, whatever its price, the discovery becomes a calamity. (Sismondi 1819, 1: 321)

Sismondi answered Torrens and Say, but he did not comment on the chapters of Ricardo's *Principles* that analyzed the phenomena he was trying to understand: the consequences of a misallocation of resources and of the introduction of machines. However, he reported three times (1824: 264–98; 1827: 408–58; 1837: 81–91) the discussions he had with Ricardo when the latter visited him in Geneva during his journey to the continent in 1822.

They assumed a closed economy with three sectors: agriculture (wheat), manufactured necessities and luxury goods. They also typically abstracted from *numéraire* and thus from the role of money in crises. The model is characterized by the fact that consumption of commodities produced in the first two sectors cannot be increased. They further assumed a discovery that allows a 50 per cent increase in the agricultural product. The consumption of wheat being fixed, two situations can be envisaged: in the first, the number of workers in agriculture is reduced; in the second, nobody is sacked but wages decrease. In both cases, the demand of the agricultural workers for manufactured products diminishes, which causes a diminution of the level of employment and output in that sector. The landowner, however, has a surplus in wheat that he wishes to exchange for luxury goods. For Ricardo, the solution lies in the transfer of some means of production to the third sector: not only will the workers who had become redundant in agriculture be employed there, but it will also be possible to employ new workers. Sismondi stressed that this solution was difficult to implement. It would be necessary to extend the factory that produces luxury goods or build a new one, train the workers to their new jobs, build machines, etc. He concluded:

> When a discovery in the productive powers of labour is applied to agriculture without having been required by a previous demand for labour; when, moreover, a single man is the owner and all others supply their labour to get their living, a single one benefits from the discovery suggested by the progress of sciences; stocks, materials, men, industry, all are lacking to put the rest of society in equilibrium with the too rapid pace of agriculture. (Sismondi 1824: 279)

Ricardo's influence is manifest but very specific. Sismondi accepted neither his opinions nor the law of markets. But using a scheme of Ricardian flavour, he tried to show how the introduction of machines can reduce employment, and – as before in his critique of the hypothesis of the mobility of the factors of production – stressed the complexity of the adjustment process that would be necessary to reach a new equilibrium.

8. Conclusion

Even though this chapter has been limited to the first three quarters of the nineteenth century and to some main topics which generated lively debates (method, value and wealth, rent, money and banking, Say's law of markets and crises) it shows how the reception of the works and ideas of Ricardo among French-speaking economists was complex. Ricardo the man, no doubt, was highly appreciated and respected, and even admired for the financial skills that allowed him to build up a sizeable fortune. His writings, however, were received in a theoretical context marked by Turgot's writings and a widely accepted French adaptation and development of Adam Smith's *Wealth of Nations* by Jean-Baptiste Say which, among other things, emphasised a theory of value and distribution based on supply and demand.

At the beginning of the nineteenth century, the French approach to political economy was also in a sense the result of severe traumas that had affected the country in the more or less recent past: the bankruptcy of John Law's system at the beginning of the eighteenth century, for example, but first and foremost the French Revolution with its erratic economic policy and the dramatic monetary episode of the assignats. It is therefore not surprising, in this context, to see most of the French economists mistrusting abstract principles and asking for concrete and practical reasoning – thus paving the way for a suspicious and even hostile reception of Ricardo's writings. If we add their selective reading of the *Principles*, according to their immediate preoccupations, and the poor translation of some strategic chapters – like the chapter on rent – we can understand why no French economist could be considered as a Ricardian, except perhaps Pellegrino Rossi, and then with qualifications. The first economic crises of the industrial age and the appalling development of pauperism also generated deep mistrust of what was called 'English' political economy, of which Ricardo was the main representative.

However, this does not mean that Ricardo was not influential in France. Quite the contrary. But his legacy was fragmented, and French-speaking economists only retained the aspects of Ricardo's doctrines that were of interest to them, discarding or criticizing the rest.

One of the best examples is certainly Ricardo's theory of rent: it was accepted by some liberal writers such as Rossi, Cherbuliez and Molinari and inspired some doctrines that other writers (Léon Walras, for example) made their own and developed afterwards. Other examples can also be advanced. There is no doubt that Cournot was positively struck by Ricardo's abstract way of reasoning, which might have strengthened his project to develop a mathematical theory of market forms. Rossi also, while rejecting or neglecting some important aspects of Ricardo's doctrines, developed some interesting points out of the *Principles*: his concept of 'rational economics' was subsequently taken up and developed by Léon Walras, and his rehabilitation of the opposition between use value and exchangeable value – questioned by most of the other French economists – was probably a source of inspiration for Dupuit.

But Ricardo was also influential in another, more diffuse way. His writings obliged some authors to react to and discuss his ideas, thereby also driving them to clarify and develop their own theories. This was obviously the case for Say and Sismondi – who had furthermore the opportunity to discuss directly with the author of the *Principles*.

Last but not least, the French reception of Ricardo's ideas and doctrines was of the utmost importance on the continent. As time went by, and for the major part of the century, Say and the French economists exerted a great intellectual influence abroad – first through their writings and then, from the 1840s on, through the Société d'Économie Politique and the *Journal des Économistes*. In this way, they also shaped, for a time, the reception of Ricardo on the continent, as the following chapters show.

Appendix 1

Publications of the works of David Ricardo in the French language during the nineteenth century

(1810). Le haut prix de l'or et de l'argent, considéré comme une preuve de la dépréciation des billets de banque. Troisième édition revue et augmentée. *Gazette nationale, ou Le moniteur universel*, 24, 25 and 26 September: 1050–52, 1054–56, 1058–60. [Translation of the third edition of *The High Price of Bullion, a Proof of the Depreciation of Bank Notes*.]

(1817). *On the Principles, etc.* C'est-à-dire, *Des principes de l'économie politique et des taxes; par D. Ricardo*. Londres, 1817. Un vol. in-8° de 600 pages. (Premier extrait.) *Bibliothèque Universelle. Littérature*. VI(3), November: 207–15. [Translation of some excerpts from Chapter I of the *Principles*.]

(1818). *On the Principles, etc.* C'est-à-dire, *Des principes de l'économie politique et des taxes; par D. Ricardo*. Londres, 1817. Un vol. in-8° de 600 pages. (Deuxième extrait.) *Bibliothèque Universelle. Littérature*. VII(1), January: 1–11. [Translation of some excerpts from Chapter I of the *Principles* (continued).]

(1819). *Des Principes de l'économie politique et de l'impôt*, par David Ricardo, traduit de l'anglais par F.-S. Constancio, avec des notes explicatives et critiques par J.-B. Say. Paris: J.-P. Aillaud. 2 vols.

(1833). Correspondence with Ricardo, in Jean-Baptiste Say, *Mélanges et correspondance d'économie politique, ouvrage posthume […] publié par Charles Comte*. 92–136. Paris. Chamerot.

(1835). *Des Principes de l'économie politique et de l'impôt*, par David Ricardo. Traduit de l'anglais par F.-S. Constancio, D. M., etc., avec des notes explicatives et critiques par J.-B. Say […]. Deuxième édition, revue, corrigée et augmentée d'une notice sur la vie et les écrits de Ricardo, publiée par sa famille. Paris: J.-P. Aillaud. 2 vols. [Misleadingly indicated as 'deuxième édition' (second edition).]

(1835). *Des Principes de l'économie politique et de l'impôt*, par David Ricardo. Traduit de l'anglais par F.-S. Constancio, D. M., etc., avec des notes explicatives et critiques par J.-B. Say […]. Deuxième édition, revue, corrigée et augmentée d'une notice sur la vie et les écrits de Ricardo, publiée par sa famille. Bruxelles: H. Dumont. 1 vol. [Misleadingly indicated as 'troisième édition' (third edition).]

(1847). *Œuvres complètes de David Ricardo*, traduites en français, par MM. Constancio et Alc. Fonteyraud, augmentées de notes de Jean-Baptiste Say, de nouvelles notes et de commentaires par Malthus, Sismondi, MM. Rossi, Blanqui, etc., et précédées d'une notice par M. Alcide Fonteyraud. Paris: Guillaumin. [Volume XIII of the Collection des principaux économistes.]

(1848). Correspondence with Ricardo, in Jean-Baptiste Say, *Œuvres diverses*: 406–29. Paris: Guillaumin.

(1865). (a) Enquête sur les lois qui limitent le taux d'intérêt. Déposition de M. Ricardo. Séance du 30 avril 1818: 69–76. (b) Enquête sur la reprise des paiements en espèces. Déposition de M. Ricardo. Séance du jeudi 4 mars 1819: 188–205. (c) Deuxième déposition de M. Ricardo. Séance du vendredi 19 mars 1819: 205–16. In Coullet, Paul-Jacques and Clément Juglar (eds). *Extraits des enquêtes parlementaires anglaises sur les questions de banque, de circulation monétaire et de crédit. Enquêtes de 1810, 1811, 1819, 1841. Bullion report. Intérêt de l'argent. Paiements en espèces.* Paris: Furne & Guillaumin.

(1882). *Œuvres complètes de David Ricardo*, trad. en français par MM. Constancio et Alc. Fonteyraud; augm. de notes de J.-B. Say, Malthus, Sismondi … [et al.]; précédées d'une notice biographique sur la vie et les travaux de l'auteur par M. Alcide Fonteyraud; et d'une préface par M. Maurice Block. Paris: Guillaumin. (*Collection des principaux économistes*)

(1889). *Ricardo: rentes, salaires et profits*, éd. par Paul Beauregard; trad. revue par M. [Charles] Formentin. Paris: Guillaumin. *Petite bibliothèque économique française et étrangère.* [A selection of 8 chapters from the *Principles*, under 4 headings: Value (chapters I ant IV), Rent (chapters II, XXIV and XXXII), Wages (chapter V) and Profits (chapters VI and XXI). The Constâncio-Fonteyraud translation is revised by Formentin.]

Appendix 2

Publications of the works of David Ricardo in the French language during the twentieth century

(1933–34). *Principes de l'économie politique et de l'impôt*. Avec introduction, notes et appendices de E. C. K. Gonner. Traduit de l'anglais par C. Debyser. Paris: A. Costes. 2 vol. [This translation was made on the Gonner 1891 English edition of the *Principles.* It borrowed in fact a lot from the former translations, even reproducing some of their mistranslations and errors.]

(1966). *Œuvres complètes de David Ricardo*, trad. en français par MM. Constancio et Alc. Fonteyraud; augm. des notes de Jean-Baptiste Say; de nouvelles notes et de commentaires par Malthus, Sismondi, MM. Rossi, Blanqui, etc.; et précédées d'une notice biographique sur la vie et les travaux de l'auteur par M. Alcide Fonteyraud. Osnabrück: Otto Zeller. (*Collection des principaux économistes*, vol. 13.) [This is the facsimile of the 1847 edition.]

(1971). *Principes de l'économie politique et de l'impôt*. Préface de Christian Schmidt. Paris: Calmann-Levy. [Republication of the 1933–34 Debyser translation in the series 'Perspectives de l'économique. Les Fondateurs de l'économie'.]

(1971). *Des Principes de l'économie politique et de l'impôt*, introd. de Pierre Dockès; trad. de P. Constancio et A. [Alcide] Fonteyraud. Paris: Flammarion. [Republication of the 1847 Constâncio-Fonteyraud translation in the series 'Sciences'. Republished in 1977 and afterwards in the series 'Champs'.]

(1973). *Croissance et progrès?* textes [de] Jean-Baptiste Say, David Ricardo, John Stuart Mill, Karl Marx ... [et al.]; réunis et présentés par J.-Marie Hervé. Tours: Mame. [Some texts by Ricardo, included in a book of readings.]

(1988). *Essai sur l'influence d'un bas prix du blé sur les profits*, [trad.,] présentation et comment. de M.-F. Jarret et F.-R. Mahieu. Paris: Economica.

(1991). *Écrits monétaires, 1809–1811*, édités sous la direction de Bernard Courbis et Jean-Michel Servet. Lyon: Association des amis du Musée de l'imprimerie et de la banque. [Translation of Ricardo's letters to the *Morning Chronicle*, 1809 and 1810, of the fourth edition of *The High Price of Bullion, a Proof of the Depreciation of Bank Notes*, 1811, and of the *Reply to M. Bosanquet's Practical Observations on the Report of the Bullion Committee*, 1811.]

(1992). *Des principes de l'économie politique et de l'impôt*, traduction par Cécile Soudan en collaboration avec B. Delmas, T. Demals, F.-R. Mahieu, H. Philipson et F. Vandevelde; présentation de François-Régis Mahieu. Paris: Flammarion. (*Classiques de l'économie politique*.)

Notes

1 Some very partial studies are, however, available: see for example Gehrke and Kurz on Say and Ricardo (2001, 2003) and Kurz and Salvadori on Walras and Ricardo (2002).

2 See for example Bloomfield 1989. Is should also be stressed that, in England, Ricardo's theory of comparative advantage had to wait for John Stuart Mill's publications in the 1840s to be fully understood.

3 1789: French Revolution. 1804: First Empire. 1814 and 1815: fall of the Empire, the *Cent Jours* and the Restoration of the Bourbon dynasty. 1830: July Revolution. 1848: February Revolution and Second Republic. 1852: Putsch by the President of the Republic, Louis-Napoléon Bonaparte, and Second Empire. 1870: fall of the Empire. 1871: Civil War of the Paris *Commune*. 1875: Third Republic.

4 Her father, Antoine François Haldimand, was Swiss. In 1799, she married Alexandre John Gaspard Marcet, himself Swiss, who was banned from Geneva in 1794 and became a British citizen in 1800. Pierre Prévost married two of Alexandre's sisters successively: Louise in 1788, who died the same year, and Jeanne in 1795.

5 *Bibliothèque Universelle des Sciences, Belles-Lettres et Arts, faisant suite à la Bibliothèque Britannique, rédigée à Genève par les auteurs de ce dernier recueil.*

6 'There is a science, the principles of which we particularly wish to propagate: the books of the English and Scottish moralists contain its precious lessons. No one, better than these philosophers, ever knew how to develop and cultivate this instinct of justice and guide this passionate and blind desire of happiness to which all the secret workings of the human heart tend. The moral doctrine of these writers is luminous and pure, its colours pleasant and attractive. Never the mistakes of a wrong philosophy and the evils that are overwhelming mankind ever made this antidote more necessary' (*Bibliothèque Britannique*, 1796, 1, Préface: 6–7).

7 *Recherches sur la nature et les effets du crédit du papier dans la Grande Bretagne*, Geneva: Imprimerie de la Bibliothèque Britannique, 1803. The quality of this translation is questionable.

8 *Essais de philosophie, précédés d'un Précis historique sur sa vie par Dugald Stewart*, Paris: Agasse, 1797.

9 *De la disette.* Geneva: Imprimerie de la Bibliothèque Britannique, 1804.

10 For example Stewart's *Éléments de la philosophie de l'esprit humain*, Geneva: Paschoud, 1808.

11 *Cours de rhétorique et de Belles lettres*, Geneva: Manget et Cherbuliez, 1808.

12 The 1825 translation of McCulloch's *Discourse*, made on the first edition (1824) also contains the additions McCulloch introduced for the second edition (1825).

13 Guillaume Prévost referred to them in his 1825 remarks on McCulloch's *Discourse.* There he notes, in relation to the idea that the capital could be evaluated by the labour which was necessary to produce it: 'We see this idea already stated by the author of three articles on Ricardo's book in the *Bibliothèque Universelle*, vol. 6 and 7, *Littér.* 1817, 1818.' (G. Prévost 1825: 183 n. 2). Guillaume mentions three papers, but only two were published.

14 The first commentary ends with a note signed 'P.P.p.' and, in the second commentary, the commentator refers to one of his previous papers, published in the *Bibliothèque Britannique* and also signed in the same way. From some publications in *Bibliothèque Britannique*, and from the tables of this journal, it appears that 'P.P.p.' means 'Pierre Prévost prof.' (Professor Pierre Prévost) – Pierre Prévost was teaching at the Genevan Académie.

15 In 1783, when he was in Berlin at the Academy of Sciences, Pierre Prévost published an essay entitled *De l'économie des anciens gouvernements comparée à celle des gouvernements modernes. Mémoire lu dans l'Assemblée publique de l'Académie royale des sciences et belles-lettres de Prusse du 5 juin 1783*. Berlin: G.-J. Decker.

16 On Constâncio, see Cardoso (1999, 2009) and Chapter 3 of the present book.

17 *Principes d'économie politique, considérés sous le rapport de leur application pratique.* Paris: Aillaud, two volumes.

18 *Recherches sur la population et sur la faculté d'accroissement de l'espèce humaine, contenant une réfutation des doctrines de M. Malthus sur cette matière.* Paris: Aillaud, two volumes.

19 Some excerpts of the Constâncio/Fonteyraud translation were revised and published in 1889 with Guillaumin and the entire translation was still republished in 1971 with Flammarion. An alleged new translation by Charles Debyser was published in 1933–1934 – and also republished in 1971 with Calmann-Lévy – but it borrowed in fact a lot from the former ones, even reproducing some of their mistranslations and errors.

20 As Sraffa remarked, the Fonteyraud volume contains all the works published by McCulloch in his 1846 edition of the works of Ricardo 'with the exception of the two papers on Paliamentary Reform': 'Observations on Parliamentary Reform' and 'Speech on Voting by Ballot' (in Ricardo 1951–1973, 10: 375).

21 *Séances et travaux de l'Académie des sciences morales et politiques*, vol. 13, 1848: 211.

22 On the word 'fermage', see below, section 5.

23 'I do not like the expression *natural price*, because this rate at which the commodity is not sold is no price' (Say, marginal note to the *Wealth of Nations*, in Hashimoto 1980: 70).

24 The *Traité de la volonté* was published in English in 1817 as *A Treatise on Political Economy*, the translation being revised by Thomas Jefferson (Destutt de Tracy 1817). As for the *Commentaire*, its American translation by Jefferson – *A Commetary and Review of Montesquieu's Spirit of the Laws*, 1811 – was published long before the French original text in 1819 (Destutt de Tracy 1811, 1819). It is also to be noted that, in France, an unauthorized and anonymous edition of the French version was published in 1817.

25 Jefferson's 1811 translation reads here 'this employment of nature' instead of 'this employment, *labour*' in the French edition (Destutt's italics, 1819: 282). It is not clear, however, whether this difference comes from a change later made by Destutt for the French edition of his *Commentaire.*

26 Ricardo was obviously also interested in the idea Destutt stated, after Turgot, that to measure a thing, we must compare it to another thing of the same kind. And he contrasted Destutt with Say on this point. 'I cannot agree with M. Say – he wrote in the third edition of the Principles (1951, 1: 284) – in estimating the value of a commodity, by the abundance of other commodities for which it will exchange; I am of the opinion of a very distinguished writer, M. Destutt de Tracy, who says that "To measure any one thing is to compare it with a determinate quantity of that same thing which we take for a standard of comparison, for unity. To measure, then to ascertain a length, a weight, a value, is to find how many times they contain metres, grammes, francs, in a word, unities of the same description." A franc is not a measure of value for any thing, but for a quantity of the same metal of which francs are made, unless francs, and the thing to be measured, can be referred to some other measure which is common to both. This, I think, they can be, for they are both the result of labour; and, therefore, labour is a common measure, by which their real as well as their relative value may be estimated. This also, I am happy to say, appears to be M. Destutt de Tracy's opinion.' Ricardo is, however, certainly deluding himself about the degree of agreement between his approach and that of Destutt.

27 Curiously, the text of Say's letters to Ricardo is different in the edition of Charles Comte (Say 1833) and in that of Sraffa. In the present case, the letter found in Ricardo's papers was dated 10 September, but that of the 1833 edition is dated 2 December. Sraffa suggests that Say forgot his first answer and wrote a second letter that he did not send when he realized his mistake.

28 This assertion appears in the letter dated 2 December, but not in the letter Ricardo received (see the previous note).

29 The original quotation is here restored. Prévost wrote a summary – 'à l'origine des sociétés, le travail dont une marchandise est chargée, le travail nécessaire pour la produire, est la mesure de la valeur' – because the full quotation was written some pages before as quoted by Ricardo in Chapter 1 of the *Principles* (P. Prévost 1817: 217 n. 2).

30 'Property is theft.' Passy is alluding here to Proudhon.

31 Courcelle-Seneuil is obviously misquoting Ricardo here. Ricardo wrote: 'Rent is that portion of the produce of the earth, which is paid to the landlord for the use of the original and indestructible powers of the soil' (Ricardo 1817–1821: 67).

32 'Some readers criticized us […] for having devoted too much space to the question of the rent; but some also levelled the opposite complaint' (*Journal des économistes*, 15 April 1854: 128).

33 Moreover, for Say, because of the old French meaning, 'rente' designates a ratio: the ratio of the income from land ownership to the price of land.

34 Hollander considers that this is 'an instance of *silent adherence* to Ricardo's position' (2005: 56).

35 Beauce and Berry are two French provinces. Beauce, a very fertile and rich province, is traditionally called the granary of France.

36 Say (1826a: 808) attributed also this proposition to Ricardo. But it seems that Ricardo never advanced such an assertion.

37 Fonteyraud also wrote that the doctrine of the rent 'has only been an opportunity to argue endlessly and to practice high scholastics' (1847: xliii).

38 'Considerations on the accumulations, etc. Considérations sur l'accumulation des capitaux, et sur ses effets relativement aux valeurs échangeables.' *Edinburgh Review*, March 1824, *Bibliothèque Universelle*, October and November 1824. The name of John Cazenove was not mentioned.

39 ' … the rent paid for the barren mountains of Scotland is anything but a trifle' (J. Mill 1824: 35). It is to be noted that Mill only accepted this idea temporarily in order to dismiss the objections made to Ricardo's theory and to restate it.

40 It is interesting to note that while Sismondi, in 1803, used the French word 'rente' [rent], this is no longer the case in 1819 where he employs the word 'fermage'. On this question of vocabulary, see above.

41 An unusual fact at the time. Cherbuliez started with intensive rent and addressed extensive rent after that.

42 'Solidairunis' is the contraction of 'solidaires' (people showing solidarity with each other) and 'unis' (united).

43 Probably a physician, the doctor P. Gallier-Boissière according to Charles Louandre and Félix Bourquelot, *La littérature française contemporaine*, Paris: Félix Daguin, 1846 – 'The "solidairunis" are a kind of communists; the author of the Résumé is M. Gallier-Boissière, physician in Paris' (2: 617).

44 In the Bibliothèque Nationale de France in Paris, there is a 'Plan d'une nouvelle monnaie dans le genre de Ricardo' – "Plan for a new money in Ricardo's style"' – (manuscript 11 739: 66–68; the reference is indicated by Jacoud 2010: 29 n. 58 and translated in Say 2013: 237–239; see also Jacoud 2013). This paper is going to be published in one of the forthcoming volumes of Say's *Œuvres complètes* (Paris: Économica). The manuscript is undated. It is not clear whether it is a re-elaboration of the plan Say sent to Ricardo, nor when it was rewritten.

45 There is a problem of interpretation here. Hollander (2005: 65) stresses the fact that Say did not indicate precisely where his note was to be placed. In the 1819 edition, the publisher placed the note in such a way that it seems to refer to the law of markets. In a more recent edition, however (Ricardo 1992: 303), the note seems to refer to Smith's analysis of the decline of profits in Holland. The principle to which Say is thought to have alluded would have been the idea that a rise in wages reduces profits. The first interpretation seems more adequate. But the fact that Say left unchanged the passage of the *Traité* where he analyzes the influence of the abundance of available capital on the rate of interest is an argument in favour of the second.

46 Say repeated this analysis in his paper 'Économie politique' (1826b: 251) published in Guizot's *Encyclopédie progressive*, and in his *Cours complet* (1828–29, 1: 474).

References

Bastiat, Frédéric (1850a). Propriété foncière. In *Œuvres complètes de Frédéric Bastiat*. Paris: Guillaumin, 1870, VI (*Harmonies économiques*): 297–348.

——(1850b) De la rente. In *Œuvres complètes de Frédéric Bastiat*. Paris: Guillaumin, 1870, VI (*Harmonies économiques*): 430–36.

Baumol, William J. (1977) Say's (at least) eight laws, or what Say and James Mill may really have meant. *Economica*, 44 (74): 145–61.

Béraud, Alain (2005) Richesse et valeur: la contribution des économistes français au début du 19e siècle. *Économies et Sociétés, Cahiers de l'ISMEA*, 39 (6), série *Œconomia*, PE 36: 1009–32.

Béraud, Alain, Jean-Jacques Gislain and Philippe Steiner (2004). L'économie politique néo-smithienne continentale. *Économies et Sociétés, Cahiers de l'ISMEA*, 38 (2), série *Œconomia*, PE 34: 325–418.

Bloomfield, Arthur I. (1989) Aspects of the Theory of International Trade in France: 1800–1914. *Oxford Economic Papers*, New Series, 41(3): 619–39.

Breton, Yves (1984) Les économistes français et la rente foncière entre 1830 et 1870. *Économie rurale*, 161, May–June: 10–14.

Buret, Eugène (1840) *De la misère des classes laborieuses en Angleterre et en France; de la nature de la misère, de son existence, de ses effets, de ses causes, et de l'insuffisance des remèdes qu'on lui a opposés jusqu'ici; avec l'indication des moyens propres à en affranchir les sociétés.* Paris: Paulin.

Cardoso, Josè Luis (1999) The road to heterodoxy: F. S. Constâncio and the critical acceptance of classical political economy. *History of Political Economy*, 31(3): 473–92.

——(2009) F. Solano Constâncio on political economy: A 'science of proportions'. *History of European Ideas*, 35: 227–35.

Cherbuliez, Antoine-Élisée (1839) *Discours sur la vie et les travaux de feu Pierre Prévost*. Genève Ferdinand Ramboz.

——(1840) *Riche ou pauvre. Exposition succincte des causes et des effets de la distribution actuelle des richessses sociales.* Paris and Geneva: Librairie d'Abel Cherbuliez.

——(1862) *Précis de la science économique et de ses principales applications.* Paris: Guillaumin.

Chevalier, Michel (1850) *Cours d'économie politique au Collège de France. III. La monnaie.* Paris: Capelle.

——(1853) *Monnaie.* In Coquelin and Guillaumin, 1852–53, II: 200–219.

Comte, Charles (1833) Notice sur Ricardo. In Say 1833:86–91.

Condorcet, Jean-Antoine and Nicolas de Caritat (1793) Tableau général de la science qui a pour objet l'application du calcul aux sciences politiques et morales. *Journal d'instruction sociale*, n. 4: 105–28, n. 6: 166–84.

Coquelin, Charles (1842) Du crédit et des banques dans l'industrie. *Revue des Deux Mondes*, July–August: 776–827.

——(1848) *Du crédit et des banques.* Paris: Guillaumin.

——(1852a) Banque. In Coquelin and Guillaumin, 1852–53, I: 107–45.

——(1852b) Billet de banque. In Coquelin and Guillaumin, 1852–53, I: 177–78.

——(1859) *Le crédit et les banques.* Paris: Guillaumin.

Coquelin, Charles and Gilbert-Urbain Guillaumin (eds.). (1852–53) *Dictionnaire de l'économie politique.* Paris: Guillaumin.

Courcelle-Seneuil, Jean-Gustave (1853). *Papier-monnaie.* In Coquelin and Guillaumin, 1852–53, II: 316–23.

——(1857) *Traité théorique et pratique des opérations de banque*, 3rd edn. Paris: Guillaumin.

——(1892) Rente (Loi de la). In Say and Chailley 1891–92, II: 711–17.

Cournot, Antoine-Augustin (1838) *Recherches les principes mathématiques de la théorie des richesses.* Paris: Hachette. As in *Œuvres complètes de A. A. Cournot*, Paris: Librairie Vrin, tome VIII: 1980.

De Quincey, Thomas (1863) *Confessions of an English Opium Eater.* In *The Works of Thomas De Quincey.* Edinburgh: Adam and Charles Black.

Delmas, B., T. Demals, F.-R. Mahieu, H. Philipson, C. Soudan and F. Vandevelde (1992) Note sur la présente édition et la nouvelle traduction. In Ricardo 1992: 7–15.

Destutt de Tracy, Antoine-Louis-Claude (1804) *Élémens d'idéologie. Première partie. Idéologie proprement dite*, 2nd edn. Paris: Courcier.

——(1811) *A Commentary and Review of Montesquieu's Spirit of the Law,* trans. Thomas Jefferson. Philadelphia: William Duane.

——(1815) *Éléments d'idéologie: Traité de la volonté et de ses effets.* Quatrième partie des *Éléments d'idéologie*, 2nd edn. Paris: Vve Courcier, 1818.

——(1817) *A Treatise on Political Economy, to which is prefixed a Supplement to a preceding work on the understanding or Elements of Ideology.* Georgetown: Joseph Milligan.

——(1819) *Commentaire sur l'Esprit des lois de Montesquieu.* Paris: Théodore Desoer.

Dupuit, Jules (1849) De l'influence des péages sur l'utilité des voies de communication. *Annales des Ponts et Chaussées*, Mémoires et documents, n° 207: 217–31, as in Yves Breton and Gérard Klotz (eds.), *Jules Dupuit, Œuvres Complètes*, 1: 243–308.

Faccarello, Gilbert and Philippe Steiner (2002) The Diffusion of the Work of Adam Smith in the French Language: An Outline History. In Keith Tribe (ed.), *A Critical Bibliography of Adam Smith*, London: Pickering and Chatto, 61–119.

Ferrier, François L. A. (1822) *Du gouvernement considéré dans ses rapports avec le commerce ou de l'administration commerciale opposée aux économistes du 19ème siècle*, 3rd edn. Paris and Lille: Pelicier and Danel.

Fonteyraud, Paul Henri Alcide (1847) Notice sur la vie et les écrits de David Ricardo. In Ricardo 1847: v–xlviii.

Forget, Evelyn L. (2003) Jean-Baptiste Say and the law of markets: entrepreneurial decision-making in the real world. In Stevens Kates (ed.), *Two Hundred Years of Say's Law.* Cheltenham: Edward Elgar.

Ganilh, Charles (1821) *Des systèmes d'économie politique, de la valeur comparative de leurs doctrines et de celle qui paraît la plus favorable au progrès de la richesse*, 2nd edn. Paris: Treuttel et Würtz.

Garnier, Germain (1802) *Recherches sur la nature et les causes de la richesse des nations, par Adam Smith. Traduction nouvelle avec des notes et observations par Germain Garnier.* Paris: H. Agasse.

——(1822) *Recherches sur la nature et les causes de la richesse des nations, par Adam Smith. Seconde édition avec des notes et des observations nouvelles, par le marquis Garnier.* Paris: Agasse.

Gasparin, Adrien de (1829) *Recueil de mémoires d'agriculturre et d'économie rurale. Guide des propriétaires des biens ruraux affermés.* Paris: Huzard.

Gehrke, Christian and Heinz D. Kurz (2001) Say and Ricardo on value and distribution. *The European Journal of the History of Economic Thought*, 8 (4): 449–86.

——(2003) Say et Ricardo. In Jean-Pierre Potier and André Tiran (eds.), *Jean-Baptiste Say: nouveaux regards sur son œuvre.* Paris: Économica, 215–63.

Hashimoto, Hitoshi (1980) Notes inédites de J.-B. Say qui couvrent les marges de la *Richesse des Nations* et qui la critiquent. *KSU Economic and Business Review*, 7: 53–81.

——(1982) Notes inédites de J.-B. Say qui couvrent les marges de la *Richesse des Nations* et qui la résument. *KSU Economic and Business Review*, 9: 31–134.

Hattori, Fumio (1994) Marx und Buret. *Mega Studien*, 1: 142–47.

Hollander, Samuel (2005) *Jean-Baptiste Say and classical canon in economics, The British connection in French classicism*. London and New York: Routledge.

Jacoud, Gilles (2010) *Political economy and industrialism: Banks in Saint-Simonian economic thought*. London: Routledge.

——(2013) Introduction. In Say 2013: 1–22.

Kurz, Heinz D. and Neri Salvadori (2002) One theory or two? Walras's critique of Ricardo. *History of Political Economy*, 34(2): 365–98.

McCulloch, John Ramsey (1825) *Discours sur l'origine, les progrès, les objets particuliers, et l'importance de l'économie politique. Traduit de l'anglais par G.^{me} Prévost*. Geneva: J.-J. Paschoud.

Molinari, Gustave de (1859) Notice biographique sur Charles Coquelin. In Coquelin 1859: v–xii.

Passy, Hippolyte (1853) Rente du sol. In Coquelin and Guillaumin, 1852–53, II: 509–20.

——(1858) Rapport sur le concours ouvert au sujet de la rente des terres. *Journal des économistes*, June: 405–25.

Péreire, Isaac (1832) *Leçons sur l'industrie et les finances*. Paris: Au Bureau du Globe.

Périn, Charles (1880) *Les doctrines économiques depuis un siècle*. Paris: Librairie Victor Lecoffre.

Pictet de Rochemont, Charles (1824) Observations sur le morceau contenu dans les cahiers d'octobre et de novembre, concernant l'accumulation des capitaux, et ses effets sur les valeurs échangeables. *Bibliothèque Universelle, Littérature*, December: 313–40.

Potier, Jean-Pierre (2003) Quelques remarques sur l'évolution des idées de Jean-Baptiste Say au sujet de la valeur et des prix. In Jean-Pierre Potier and André Tiran (eds.), *Jean-Baptiste Say, Nouveaux regards sur son œuvre*. Paris: Economica.

Prévost, Pierre (1817) Observations du traducteur. *Bibliothèque Universelle. Littérature*, VI(3), November: 215–21.

——(1818) Observations du rédacteur. *Bibliothèque Universelle. Littérature*, VII(1), January: 11–16.

Prévost, Guillaume (1825a) Préface du traducteur. In McCulloch 1825: i–xiii.

——(1825b) Réflexions du traducteur sur le système de Ricardo, contenant l'exposé et la discussion sommaires des principes et des conséquences de ce système. In McCulloch 1825: 155–204.

Puynode, Gustave du (1866) Étude sur les divers systèmes d'économie politique et sur les principaux économistes. Ricardo. *Journal des Économistes*, I. April: 5–29, II. July: 12–33, III. October: 39–60.

Ricardo, David (1810) *The High Price of Bullion, a Proof of the Depreciation of Bank Notes*. London: John Murray, in *The Works and Correspondence of David Ricardo*, vol. 3, Piero Sraffa (ed.). Cambridge: Cambridge University Press, 1951.

——(1816) *Proposals for an Economical and Secure Currency with Observations on the Profits of theBbank of England as They Regard the Public and the Proprietors of Bank Stock*. London: John Murray, in *The Works and Correspondence of David Ricardo*, vol. 4, Piero Sraffa (ed.). Cambridge: Cambridge University Press, 1951.

——(1817) *On the Principles of Political Economy and Taxation*. London: John Murray.

——(1817–21). *On the Principles of Political Economy and Taxation*. In *The Works and Correspondence of David Ricardo*, vol. 1, Piero Sraffa (ed.). Cambridge: Cambridge University Press, 1951.

——(1819) *Des Principes de l'Économie Politique et de l'Impôt*, trans. F. S. Constâncio with 'Notes explicatives et critiques' by J.-B. Say. Paris: Aillaud.

——(1822) *On Protection to Agriculture.* London: John Murray, in *The Works and Correspondence of David Ricardo*, vol. 4, Piero Sraffa (ed.). Cambridge: Cambridge University Press, 1951: 207–70.

——(1951–73) *Correspondence.* In *The Works and Correspondence of David Ricardo*, Piero Sraffa (ed.). Cambridge: Cambridge University Press.

——(1992) *Des principes de l'économie politique et de l'impôt.* French translation. Paris: GF/Flammarion.

Rossi, Pellegrino (1836–38) *Cours d'économie politique*, 4th edn. Paris: Guillaumin.

Say, Jean-Baptiste (1803) *Traité d'économie politique ou simple exposition de la manière dont se forment, se distribuent, et se consomment les richesses*, in Say 2006.

——(1814) *Traité d'économie politique*, 2nd edn. Paris: Renouard, in Say 2006.

——(1815) *De l'Angleterre et des Anglais.* Paris: Bertrand. New ed. in *Jean-Baptiste Say, Cours d'économie politique,* Paris: GF-Flammarion, 1996.

——(1815b) *Catéchisme d'économie politique, ou Instruction familière qui montre de quelle façon les richesses sont produites, distribuées et consommées dans la société.* Paris: Crapelet.

——(1817) *Traité d'économie politique*, 3rd edn, in Say (2006).

——(1819) *Traité d'économie politique.* 4th edn, in Say (2006).

——(1819b) *Notes explicatives et critiques.* In Ricardo 1819.

——(1820) *Lettres à M. Malthus sur différents sujets d'économie politique, notamment sur les causes de la stagnation générale du commerce.* Paris: Bosange, reproduit in *Cours d'économie politique et autres essais.* Paris: GF-Flammarion, 1996.

——(1821) *Catéchisme d'économie politique ou instruction familière qui montre comment les richesses sont produites, distribuées et consommées dans la société*, 2nd edn. Paris: Bossange.

——(1825) Examen critique du discours de M. McCulloch sur l'économie politique. *Revue Encyclopédique*, March. As in Say 1848: 261–79.

——(1826a) *Traité d'économie politique*, 5th edn. Paris: Rapilly, in Say (2006).

——(1826b).Économie politique. In François Guizot (ed.), *Encyclopédie progressive.* Paris: Aux bureaux de l'Encyclopédie progressive.

——(1826c) De la crise commerciale de l'Angleterre. *Revue Encyclopédique,* 32: 40–45.

——(1828–29) *Cours complet d'économie politique pratique.* Paris: Rappily, 3rd edn with notes by Horace Say, Paris: Guillaumin, 1852.

——(1833) *Mélanges et correspondance d'économie politique, ouvrage posthume de J.-B. Say publié par Charles Comte, son gendre.* Paris: Chamerot.

——(1848) *Œuvres diverses.* In Collection des principaux économistes, vol. 12. Paris: Guillaumin.

——(2003) *Politique pratique.* In *Jean-Baptiste Say, Œuvres complètes*, vol. 5, *Œuvres morales et politiques.* Paris: Economica.

——(2006) *Traité d'économie politique.* Variorum edn of the six editions, edited by Claude Mouchot, in *Œuvres complètes de Jean-Baptiste Say*, vol. 1. Paris: Economica.

——(2013) *Money and banking in Jean-Baptiste Say's economic thought.* Ed. Gilles Jacoud. London: Routledge.

Say, Léon, and Joseph Chailley (1891–92) *Nouveau dictionnaire d'économie politique.* Paris: Guillaumin.

Say, Louis (1822) *Considérations sur l'industrie et la législation sous le rapport de leur influence sur la richesse des États et examen critique des principaux ouvrages qui ont paru sur l'économie politique.* Paris: Aillaud.

——(1827) *Traité élémentaire de la richesse individuelle et de la richesse publique et éclaircissements sur les principales questions de l'économie politique.* Paris: P. Mongie. [Simonde de Sismondi: cf. Sismondi.].

Sismondi, Jean-Charles Léonard Simonde de (1803) *De la Richesse nationale ou principes d'économie politique appliqués à la législation du commerce.* Geneva: Paschoud.

——(1814) *Considérations sur Genève dans ses rapports avec l'Angleterre et les États protestants, suivies d'un Discours, prononcé à Genève, sur la philosophie de l'histoire.* London: John Murray.

——(1815) Political Economy. In Brewster (ed.) *Edinburgh Encyclopedia*, Edinburgh: Blackwood and Vaugh, London: Murray, Baldwin & Cradock, Richardson: Vol. XVIII of the 1830 edn: 37–80.

——(1819) *Nouveaux Principes d'économie politique*, 1st edn. Paris: Delaunay and Treuttel and Wurtz.

——(1824) Sur la balance des consommations avec la production. *Revue Encyclopédique*, 22(04): 264–98.

——(1827) *Nouveaux Principes d'économie politique*, 2nd edn. Paris: Delaunay.

——(1837) *Études sur l'économie politique.* Paris: Treuttel et Würtz.

Senior, Nassau W. (1836) *An Outline of the Science of Political Economy.* London: W. Clowes & Sons.

Smith, Adam (1776) *An Inquiry into the Nature and Causes of the Wealth of Nations.* London: Strahan and Cadell. As in *The Glasgow edition of the works and correspondence of Adam Smith*, vol. 1. Oxford: Clarendon Press, 1979.

Tooke, Thomas (1826) *Considerations on the state of the currency.* London: John Murray.

Vatin, François (2001–2) Le travail, la servitude et la vie. Avant Marx et Polanyi: Eugène Buret. *Revue du MAUSS*, 18: 237–80.

——(2005) *Trois essais sur le genèse de la pensée sociologique.* Paris: La Découverte.

Villeneuve-Bargemont, Jean-Paul-Alban de (1834) *Économie politique chrétienne ou Recherche sur la nature et les causes du paupérisme en France et en Europe et sur les moyens de la soulager et de le prévenir.* Paris: Paulin.

——(1836) Cours sur l'histoire de l'économie politique: Introduction. *L'Université catholique*, I(1): 82–90.

——(1841) *Histoire de l'économie politique, ou études historiques, philosophiques et religieuses sur l'économie politique des peuples anciens et modernes.* Paris: Guillaumin.

Walras, Auguste (1830) De l'abolissement de l'impôt et de l'établissement de la loi agraire, telle qu'elle peut être conçue et pratiquée au XIXe siècle. In A. Walras, *Richesse, Liberté et société*, Paris: Économica, 1990: 7–20.

——(1831) *De la nature de la richesse et de l'origine de la valeur.* Paris: Johanneau. As in A. Walras, *Richesse, Liberté et société*, Paris: Economica, 1990: 47–233.

——(1844) Esquisse d'une théorie de la richesse. *Revue de Caen* and *Recueil des travaux de la société libre d'Agriculture, Sciences, Arts et Belles-Lettres de l'Eure.* As in A. Walras, *Richesse, Liberté et société*, Paris: Économica, 1990: 427–42.

——(1849) Mémoire sur l'origine de la valeur d'échange ou exposition critique et réfutation des opinions les plus accréditées, chez les économistes, sur cette question. *Séances et travaux de l'Académie des sciences morales et politiques*, 2nd series, VI: 201–33. As in A. Walras, *La vérité sociale*, Paris: Économica, 1997: 505–27.

——(2005) *Correspondance.* Paris: Économica.

Walras, Léon (1874) *Éléments d'économie politique pure ou théorie de la richesse sociale.* Lausanne: Corbaz, Paris: Guillaumin, Bâle: Georg. As in *Œuvres Économiques Complètes d'Auguste et Léon Walras*, Paris: Économica, 1988.

2 The reception and further elaboration of Ricardo's theory of value and distribution in the German-speaking countries, 1817–1914

Christian Gehrke

1. Introduction

This article reviews some of the more important German contributions to the development of the classical approach to value and distribution in the century spanning from the publication of Ricardo's *Principles* in 1817 up to the beginning of the Great War in 1914. It is part of a larger project, which aims at reconstructing the early reception of Ricardo's *Principles* in the German-speaking countries and the dissemination and further elaboration of Ricardo's ideas in the course of the nineteenth century.[1] But since this is of course much too large a field to be properly discussed within the confines of a short chapter, the following discussion will be much more restricted in several respects. First, the chapter will be exclusively concerned with the theory of value and distribution. Second, with regard to Ricardo's theory of distribution, a disproportionate amount of space will be devoted to the analysis of rent. Third, and most importantly, the contributions of only five authors (Hermann, Rodbertus, von Bortkiewicz, von Charasoff, and, indirectly, Marx) will be examined in somewhat greater detail in this chapter. This is of course a rather severe restriction, which is mainly motivated by limitations of time and space.

The chapter is organized as follows. Section 2 informs briefly about German translations and early German book reviews of Ricardo's *Principles.* Section 3 provides an overview of the state of economics in the German-speaking countries at turn of the nineteenth century, in order to explain the background and inherited traditions against which the diffusion of Ricardo's theory of value and distribution took place. In addition, this section also contains a discussion of some specific characteristics of the German economic discourse in the nineteenth century and of the role of the historical school in the demise of Ricardian economic theory. In Sections 4 and 5, two different lines in the further development of Ricardo's theory of value and distribution in the first half of the nineteenth century are then examined in somewhat more detail: F. B. W. Hermann's *Staatswirthschaftliche Untersuchungen* (1832), which ultimately led to marginal productivity theory (Section 4), and Johann-Carl Rodbertus' *Zur Erkenntnis unserer staatswirtschaftlichen Zustände* (1842), which aimed at a critical elaboration on the surplus approach to value and distribution (Section 5). Section 6 contains a critical assessment of the contributions of Ladislaus von Bortkiewicz (1906/07, 1907, 1910/11) and Georg von Charasoff (1909, 1910) and their critique of Marx's attempt to elaborate on Ricardo's analysis of prices and income distribution.

2. Early German translations and book reviews of Ricardo's *Principles*

2.1 German editions of the Principles

The first German edition of Ricardo's *Principles*, entitled *Die Grundsätze der Politischen Ökonomie oder der Staatswirtschaft und der Besteuerung* (Ricardo 1821), was published in Weimar in 1821. The editor and translator of this edition was Christian August Schmidt. Apparently, the print run of the edition was rather small and the book did not circulate widely. Schmidt's translation was based on the first English edition of 1817, and it was complemented by a German translation of (some of) the 'notes explicatives et critiques', which Jean-Baptiste Say had appended to the first French edition of Ricardo's *Principles* (cf. Say in Ricardo 1819b). According to an anonymous reviewer in the *Leipziger Literatur Zeitung*, the French translation by Constâncio was much to be preferred over Schmidt's German one ([Anonymous] 1821: column 2293). An anonymous reviewer in the periodical *Hermes* likewise suggested that readers would be much better off using the French edition, because Schmidt's translation suffered not only from 'very poor style' but also from 'grave misunderstandings' with regard to both Ricardo's original text and Say's explanatory notes.[2] Moreover, Schmidt's edition omitted several important passages from Ricardo's text (and also from Say's notes), so that Ricardo's ideas were transmitted to the German readers in a somewhat diluted and partly even incomprehensible form ([Anonymous (C.E.M.)] 1821: 176–7). As German and Austrian intellectuals generally had a good knowledge of French then (which was often preferred by them over English), readers in the German-speaking countries would very often have learned of the ideas which Ricardo had expounded in his *Principles* through the first French edition – and thus would have been exposed immediately to Jean-Baptiste Say's critical commentaries on Ricardo's work.

In 1837, a new German translation of Ricardo's *Principles* was published by Eduard Baumstark under the title *David Ricardo's Grundsätze der Volkswirthschaft und der Besteuerung* (Ricardo 1837). It was based on the second English edition (1819), because the editor, 'despite all efforts, had been unable to obtain a copy of the third edition in either England or Germany' (Baumstark 1837: iv). In the following year, Baumstark supplemented his translation of the *Principles* with a companion volume with 'explanatory notes' of just over 800 pages (Baumstark 1838). According to Wilhelm Roscher,

> Baumstark deserves credit for truly having introduced Ricardo's powerful mind into German political economy for the first time: and not only through his splendid translation, but also through his eleven commentaries in the second volume. (Roscher 1874: 909)

In fact, Baumstark's extensive commentaries are partly unrelated to Ricardo's text and also exhibit a number of serious misunderstandings with regard to his theoretical propositions. Although Baumstark's translation was also favourably received by several other commentators, including Rodbertus, it is in fact not reliable. As both Karl Kautsky (1905: xvii) and Ladislaus von Bortkiewicz (1910/11: 20–21) have pointed out, the sense of Ricardo's statements has been missed or distorted in several passages; in some places it has even been turned into the exact opposite of what Ricardo had written. As von Bortkiewicz demonstrated with regard to various passages in Baumstark's 'explanatory notes', the errors in the translation can be traced back to incomprehension of Ricardo's argument on Baumstark's part. Referring to some false interpretative statements in Baumstark's commentary (regarding Sections IV and V in Chapter I of the *Principles*), von Bortkiewicz concluded:

> From these statements it is evident that in the case of Baumstark the great admiration which he expressed for Ricardo went hand in hand with a rarely to be observed incomprehension of the master's doctrines on his part. (1910/11: 20)

A German translation of the third English edition of Ricardo's *Principles* was not available until 1877, when Baumstark published a 'second edition' of his earlier translation, which incorporated the changes and alterations that Ricardo had introduced in his text in the third edition (Ricardo 1877). Baumstark's companion volume was not reprinted on this occasion.

In 1905, Professor Heinrich Waentig of the University of Halle edited a new German translation, which had been carried out by Ottomar Thiele, of the third English edition. Waentig's edition, which was entitled *Grundsätze der Volkswirtschaft und Besteuerung* (Ricardo 1905), was supplemented by an extensive commentary by Karl Diehl, who was then one of the leading 'Ricardians' in the German-speaking countries. Diehl's *Sozialwissenschaftliche Erläuterungen zu David Ricardo's Grundgesetzen der Volkswirtschaft und Besteuerung* (in two volumes, 1905) show a much better understanding of Ricardo's principal propositions on value and distribution than Baumstark's earlier treatise. (A 'second edition' of Waentig's *Grundsätze*, which was published in 1921, must in fact be regarded as a new edition, because the editor had 'deemed it necessary to correct and revise Thiele's translation so thoroughly' that he felt it was now appropriate for him 'to assume full responsibility not only for the edition but also for the German translation' (Waentig 1921, vii). A third edition with further revisions was published in 1923.)

While the first German translation of the *Principles* was thus published as early as 1821, it was only with Baumstark's edition of 1837 that Ricardo's *Grundsätze* became readily available to German-speaking readers, and it was only with Waentig's edition of 1905 that it became first available in a reasonably good translation. It should be noted, however, that in the nineteenth century it was still common for German academics to read not only German, but also French, Italian, and (less frequently) English. Accordingly, the major sources for the dissemination of Ricardo's doctrines in the nineteenth century seem to have been the original English versions of the *Principles* and, in particular, the French translation of 1819 with J. B. Say's 'explanatory notes'.[3] Moreover, it must be recognized that Ricardo's *Principles*, in either the original English version(s) or in the French and German translations, were not the only sources for the popularization of Ricardo's economic ideas in the German-speaking countries. Early on there were German translations of James Mill's *Elements* and of John R. McCulloch's *Principles*, as well as several translations of the popular writings of Harriet Martineau and Jane Marcet.[4] However, these sources would presumably have been more important for the dissemination of Ricardo's doctrines among students and laymen than among academics.

2.2 Early German book reviews of Ricardo's **Principles**

The first book review of Ricardo's *Principles* that was published in the German-speaking countries was a German translation of McCulloch's enthusiastic review in the *Edinburgh Review*.[5] It was published in 1819 in the first issue of the newly founded German periodical *Hermes*, which was a combined literary, political and economic journal. The first *original* German book review of the *Principles* was a long and highly favourable review article by Georg Sartorius, a Professor at the University of Göttingen, who had done much to popularize Adam Smith's ideas in the German-speaking world. In his review article, published in April 1820 in the *Göttingische Gelehrte Anzeigen*, Sartorius jointly reviewed the second English edition of Ricardo's *Principles* (1819a) and the first French edition (1819b). Sartorius was full of praise for Ricardo's treatise and opened his review article with the remark:

> The great importance of the book under consideration will sufficiently justify that the reviewer has claimed a space for his review which […] can be reserved only for books that considerably advance the frontiers of scientific knowledge. […] But even the largest possible space which might legitimately be claimed for such a review would not be sufficient to inform the reader about all the new and original ideas which are contained in this book. (1820: 682)

In his review article Sartorius provided a neat summary account of the book's contents and its main propositions, followed by some moderate criticisms in the final section. To Ricardo's theory of value Sartorius objected that the use values of commodities are generally taken to be given and immutable, whereas in fact 'the perception of a commodity's utility is volatile and changing, and therefore relevant for its exchangeable value' (1820: 699). Sartorius also put forward some shallow criticisms of Ricardo's theory of rent. His first objection is that the extension of cultivation to less fertile plots of land is generally considered by Ricardo as the *effect* of an increase in population, whereas it might equally well be regarded as a *cause* of the latter. Second, Sartorius took Ricardo to task for having maintained, wrongly, that land can only be rent-bearing when labour has been expended on it. As a counter example, Sartorius referred to a stone mine which is located close to a large town. Third, he considered his observation that 'equally fertile or even less fertile plots of land in the proximity of a large town often yield a higher rent than more fertile, but less favourably situated plots of land' as a serious objection to Ricardo's theory of rent (Sartorius 1820: 702).

In 1821 the literary periodical *Hermes*, which had already carried McCulloch's review in a German translation in 1819, published a further review of Ricardo's *Principles* which was signed by 'C.E.M.', which presumably refers to one C.E. Morstadt. It was a joint review article of the second English edition (1819a), the first French edition (1819b), and the first German edition by C. A. Schmidt (Ricardo 1821). Morstadt's review was much less favourable than those of McCulloch and Sartorius. Referring to England's economic problems, Morstadt opened his review with the remark that Ricardo's treatise had been awaited by his fellow countrymen with very high expectations, but that their hopes had been disappointed. Ricardo's treatise is said to be 'extremely difficult to understand', and to contain 'dark' and 'mysterious' passages. According to Morstadt, these difficulties are not caused by stylistic deficiencies, but are rather due to 'a complete lack of systematic order'. He also lamented the fact that Ricardo occasionally 'uses some well-established notions of political economy in a totally unusual way' ([Anonymous (C.E.M.)] 1821: 160–1). As an example, Morstadt referred to Ricardo's novel conceptualization of income distribution in terms of 'proportions', and accused Ricardo of having introduced 'linguistic and conceptual confusion' [Sprach- und Begriffsverwirrung] (1821: 161).[6] Morstadt claims that Ricardo's treatise is on the whole rather unoriginal, because 'his *general* propositions on the nature, formation, and consumption of riches are fully in line with those of Smith, Buchanan, Say, Malthus, Storch, Kraus and many of the other major political economists' (1821: 162). As compared to the works of the authors mentioned, Ricardo's *Principles* are in fact said to fall behind because of five major errors or shortcomings. First, Ricardo has 'completely disregarded or even denied the well-established truth that exchangeable values are regulated by the relation between supply and demand' (1821: 164–5). Second, he 'commits the great error to believe that labour is the only productive service, or more precisely, that also the profits of capital and land, considered in the light, are nothing but labour wages' (1821: 166). Since in Ricardo's view differential rent is 'nothing but the remuneration of the larger or smaller amounts of labour which are *saved* on the more fertile plots of land, in relation to the least fertile one, […] rent is in essence the remuneration for 'saved labour' (1821: 167). Third, Ricardo's distinction between values and riches (in Chapter 20) is 'a glaring heresy'. Fourth, Ricardo is taken to task for having 'completely disregarded Say's notion of the entrepreneur, and for making no use of it' (1821: 169–70). Fifth, Ricardo is said to have unduly neglected Say's distinction between entrepreneurial remuneration and profit on capital (1812: 170). Morstadt's overall assessment is summed up in the pun that in Ricardo's *Principles* 'everything that is new is not correct and everything that is correct is not new' (1821: 175).

An anonymous reviewer in the November 1821 issue of the *Leipziger Literatur-Zeitung* arrived at a similar conclusion:

> Readers who are sufficiently familiar with the current state of Political Economy will not find in this book any real and true enrichment of their science, or a more accurate discussion or delineation of their field. The praise which has been showered on Ricardo's treatise in England, and partly also in France, can only be explained by the fact that the scholars in those countries, and particularly in England, are not yet familiar enough with the advances which Political Economy has recently made on the Continent, and particularly in Germany. ([Anonymous] 1821: column 2277)

This anonymous joint review of the French edition of 1819 and of Schmidt's German edition of 1821 is written in a highly polemical tone – and full of elementary errors and misunderstandings. The author rejects almost all the main propositions of Ricardo. Ricardo's views on the theory of value and distribution, foreign trade, and taxation are dismissed as 'unrealistic' and 'erroneous'. Ricardo's theory of rent is said to be 'unmistakably wrong', because 'it is not primarily the natural fertility of the land […] but rather the supply and demand of land which determines the *real* rent' (Anonymous, 1821: columns 2283–4). The rent which is obtained from a given plot of land is said to depend

> not at all on the returns of other plots of land which are cultivated in the same way, but only on the individual fertility of this plot of land. […] The better plot of land yields a higher rent *not* because it is more fertile than the less fertile ones, but only because it is *good*. (1821: column 2284)

Moreover, the reviewer argues that the extension of cultivation to less fertile land will not raise the rents obtained on lands of better quality but, on the contrary, will lower them. The reason given is that the associated increase in the supply of raw produce must lower its price, and therefore also the rent (ibid.).

Our brief perusal of the early German book reviews confirms what has emerged also from the discussion of the first German editions, and what has also been pointed out by some commentators in the secondary literature that will be discussed in the following section: the early reception of Ricardo's *Principles* in the German-speaking countries was not only shaped by specific national traditions, such as the 'German use value school' and the inherited cameralistic habits of thought, but was also strongly influenced by Jean-Baptiste Say's doctrines and his critical commentaries on Ricardo's treatise.

3. Some characteristic features of the economic discourse in the German-speaking countries in the nineteenth century

Broadly speaking, two phases can be discerned in the nineteenth century with regard to the reception and further elaboration of classical economic thought in the German-speaking countries (Kurz 1989, 1998a; see also Scherf 1986, Brandt 1992). In the first half of the nineteenth century, up to c.1850, the doctrines of Adam Smith, and to a lesser extent also those of Ricardo, diffused quickly into the German economic literature, but they were amalgamated with the existing tradition of cameralistic thinking and with the ideas of Jean-Baptiste Say, who exerted a considerable influence on continental economic thought.[7] From the middle of the nineteenth century onwards, with the rise of the historical school and because of the widespread association of Ricardian economics with the ideas of socialist writers, classical economic theory rapidly lost support among German academics. It was only at the beginning of the twentieth century that some authors, mostly from non-German countries, revived the interest in the classical approach to value and distribution, and also made important contributions to its further development.

3.1 Specific characteristics of the economic discourse in the German-speaking countries

With regard to the first phase, some specific characteristics of the economic discourse in Austria, as opposed to that in the German Reich, must be briefly mentioned. Although one of the first chairs in economics was created in Austria (in 1763, for Joseph von Sonnenfels), 'economics as it was taught in Austria was for a long time notable only for its mediocrity' (Hennings 1997: 44). The dissemination of the new, liberal ideas of Smith and Ricardo took place much more slowly, and it was only with Joseph Kudler's textbook entitled *Grundlehren der Volkswirthschaft* (1846) that the prevailing cameralistic habits of thought in Austria gradually began to be displaced, and 'a standard similar to that in Germany was reached' (Hennings 1997: 52; see also Roscher 1874: 907–8).

The German economic literature of the first quarter of the nineteenth century was characterized not only by remnants of cameralistic thinking, but there was also a strong subjectivist tradition, which was associated with the works of authors such as von Jakob, Hufeland, Lotz, von Soden, and Thomas. This group of writers, the so-called 'German use value school', placed special emphasis on the role of the use value of a commodity and on the subjective evaluations of it by individuals. While they adopted main elements of Smith's doctrine, they generally rejected his labour theory of value, his emphasis on costs of production of reproducible commodities (to the neglect of scarce and non-reproducible goods), and also (with the exception of Lotz) his plea for free international trade. They also considered unsatisfactory Smith's treatment of entrepreneurial activities, and emphasized the productiveness of services and their positive contribution to the increase of individual and collective wealth (and power). The same holds true for the so-called 'German-Russian school', with von Schlözer and Storch as main representatives, which combined Smithian ideas (as presented by Say) with more subjectivist elements. According to Hennings (1997: 27), there was a distinctive 'continental tradition' that can be briefly characterized as follows. While Smith's *WN* was as successful in the German-speaking countries as it was in Britain, particularly after the turn of the century, and enthusiastically accepted by academic economists as well as public administrators, classical ideas were taken up mainly to serve as political weapons against the dominance of the French, and the French revolution in particular. In Hennings' view, this political bias in the acceptance of classical political economy prevented classical economic thought from completely replacing earlier forms of theorizing. While elements of 'pure' classical theory were accepted and taken on board, classical policy prescriptions were often tempered by cameralistic wisdom. These modifications took two forms. First, translations of foreign works were often heavily annotated, and therefore not allowed to speak for themselves. Second, the actual 'synthesis' of classical and cameralistic economic thought (if there was one) was then effected in textbooks such as Karl-Heinrich Rau's *Grundsätze*:

> The net result of these modifications was to add cautious riders to what Adam Smith had to say, and even more cautious ones to Ricardo's *Principles* and other writings of the Ricardian school. Indeed, several of the so-called anti-Ricardians (Lauderdale, Bailey, Read, Scrope and others) were given an often much more sympathetic hearing by German-speaking economists than was accorded to Ricardo. This was due partly at least to the fact that most Continental theorizing was heavily indebted to J.B. Say. Indeed the continental tradition can be said to be based on Say to the same extent that the Ricardian tradition in England was based on Ricardo and James Mill. (Hennings, 1997: 27)

In his entry for Max Weber's *Grundriß der Sozialökonomik*, entitled *Epochen der Dogmen- und Methodengeschichte* (1914), Joseph A. Schumpeter remarked about the German economic literature in the period from 1820 to 1850:

> About this there is little to be said. It is not that only little was written; and it is not that there are not some good ideas contained in it. It is rather that these books are totally uninspired, and we must understand that the general public and particularly the most spirited heads were

> repelled by this kind of science. Deeply stepped in the tradition of cameralism, these authors moved, as regards their purely scientific reasoning, under the influence of the easily accessible Smith. (1914: 55–6)

With regard to the theory of distribution, Schumpeter made out two main lines in the development of classical economic theory after Smith: the first line, which he associates with Say, von Jakob, Hufeland and Hermann, is the 'three factors of production (land, labour, capital)/three productivities' line, which ultimately led to the formulation of the marginal productivity theory of distribution. The second line, which Schumpeter associates with Ricardo, Mill, McCulloch, Torrens, and De Quincey in England, and with Rodbertus and Marx in Germany, is the surplus approach to value and distribution. Among the nineteenth-century German economic theorists, Schumpeter considers only four as noteworthy followers of Ricardo: von Thünen, Hermann, Rodbertus and Marx. But in Schumpeter's judgement neither Ricardo's English 'disciples' (i.e., McCulloch and James and John Stuart Mill) nor his German followers

> were up to the task that needed to be accomplished; they did not understand him in some points, and were even less capable of building up from him. Therefore, classical economics sank down in England and even more so in Germany, and on the infelicitous epigones a wave of hostility poured out (1914: 59).

Following Schumpeter's lead, the contributions of Hermann and Rodbertus will be discussed in Section 4 of this chapter, while Marx's contribution will be discussed indirectly in Section 6 (in connection with the contributions of von Bortkiewicz and von Charasoff). The only excuse that can be offered for not examining Johann Heinrich von Thünen's contribution is that the first part of Thünen's *Der isolirte Staat* (1826), which deals with the spatial allocation of economic activities and the problem of diminishing returns, was written in ignorance of Ricardo's *Principles*, and that the second part, published in 1850, mainly dealt with 'natural wages' along non-classical lines.

In the second half of the nineteenth century, Karl Marx clearly stands out as the major contributor to the further development of classical political economy. But when the first two volumes of *Das Kapital* appeared in 1867 and 1884, the majority of the economics profession in the German-speaking countries had already turned in a different direction and the classical approach to value and distribution had been submerged by analyses rich with concepts that pointed towards the 'marginal revolution'. Moreover, Smith and Ricardo had been scolded, particularly by some members of the younger historical school, for their alleged advocacy of 'Manchester liberalism'. (On the other hand, it was also recognized, particularly after the publication of Rodbertus's *Sociale Briefe* and the first volumes of Marx's *Kapital*, that Ricardo's theory of value and distribution could lend support to socialist and communist ideas.)

The main academic adherents of Ricardian economics in the last quarter of the nineteenth century were Karl Diehl, Heinrich Dietzel, Wilhelm Lexis and, to some extent, also Adolph Wagner and Adolf Weber. However, apart from Lexis, who anticipated some of the findings of Ladislaus von Bortkiewicz (which will be discussed in Section 6 below), none of them made a significant contribution to the further development of Ricardo's theory of value and distribution. Nevertheless, in the 1890s Karl Diehl and Heinrich Dietzel were widely considered as the leading 'Ricardians', and Diehl's *Sozialwissenschaftliche Erläuterungen zu D. Ricardos Grundgesetzen der Volkswirtschaft und Besteuerung* (1905) is a noteworthy contribution to Ricardian scholarship. Adolph Wagner also considered himself a Ricardian, but was mainly responsible, together with Ferdinand Lassalle, for the popularization of Rodbertus's ideas in the 1870s and 1880s. Heinrich Dietzel was involved in a debate with Eugen von Böhm-Bawerk in the early 1890s, which was triggered by the publication of Böhm-Bawerk's essay 'Grundzüge der Theorie des wirtschaftlichen Güterwerts', which was published (in two instalments) in the *Jahrbücher für Nationalökonomie und Statistik* in 1886/87. Dietzel's reply, entitled 'Die klassische Werttheorie und die Theorie vom Grenznutzen' (1890), drew a lengthy response from Böhm-Bawerk (1890, 1892), and several comments from other adherents of marginal utility theory. In this debate Dietzel rejected the view of the advocates of marginal utility theory that the development of the latter had been necessary because of the existence of 'unsolved riddles' in value theory. Dietzel contended that Ricardo's theory of value left nothing to be desired:

> The polemic of the marginal value theorists against the classical theory of value is mistaken; the dichotomy of the law of value at which the older theory arrives on the basis of the insight that there exist two categories of goods which need to be treated differently, is unimpeachable [unantastbar]. […] I can see in it [i.e., the new doctrine] solely retrogression and not an "epoch-making" discovery (1890: 606).

For a detailed summary assessment, see Kurz (1989, 1995).

In the 1890s, with the publication of vol. 3 of *Das Kapital* in 1894, the debates over the classical theory of value and distribution shifted to Marx and the labour theory of value. From the rather extensive literature triggered by it,[8] we can only discuss some selected writings that contributed to the clarification of the relationship between Marx's and Ricardo's approach to the theory of value and distribution: von Bortkiewicz's two essays (1906/07, 1907) and von Charasoff's two books (1909, 1910) on Marx's theory of value. When Kautsky edited Marx's economic manuscripts of 1861–63 (for the projected vol. 4 of *Das Kapital*) under the title *Theorien über den Mehrwert* in 1905–10, the immediate impact on the discussion of Ricardo's economics was rather limited (although Schumpeter made good use of it in his *Epochen der*

Dogmen- und Methodengeschichte (1914)). An important exception is Ladislaus von Bortkiewicz's essay 'Die Rodbertus'sche Grundrententheorie und die Marxsche Lehre von der absoluten Grundrente' (1910/11), which was based on a thorough study of Kautsky's edition. It will also be discussed in Section 6 below.

Some of the major neoclassical theorists in the German-speaking countries showed great admiration for Ricardo, and adopted certain concepts and analytical devices which he had first introduced. Amongst the advocates of the marginalist approach to the theory of value and distribution, Eugen von Böhm-Bawerk and Knut Wicksell came closest to elaborating on some genuinely Ricardian ideas. Böhm-Bawerk, in his critical discussion of Ricardo's theory of profit in his *Geschichte und Kritik der Kapitalzinstheorien* (1884), criticized Ricardo for his asymmetrical treatment of the distributive variables: 'If we take out the kernel from this theory, then Ricardo explains the level of capital interest from the level of the wage rate: the latter is the cause, and the level of profits is the effect' ([1884] 1921: 80). While Böhm-Bawerk considers it to be 'quite correct that wage, profit and output – after the deduction possibly of ground rent – must stand in a fixed relation', he contends that 'it is wrong to interpret this relation in the way that the level of output and the level of wages are the determining variables, and the level of interest is merely the determined variable' ([1884] 1921: 80). With the same right one could start from a given rate of interest and determine the level of wages residually. Ricardo did not do this, Böhm-Bawerk contends,

> because he rightly recognized that the level of the wage rate is determined by independent causes peculiar to the factor labour. But what Ricardo recognized for the wage rate, he overlooked for capital interest. Capital interest also has determinants of its level which arise from its own peculiar circumstances. It does not just take what is left over, but knows how to extort an appropriate share for itself. […] But a treatment of these specific causes of capital interest is completely absent in Ricardo. […] *The capital profit is based on no less independent causes than is the wage. To have completely neglected those independent causes is Ricardo's principal error.* ([1884] 1921: 81 and 83; emphasis added)

But in spite of Böhm-Bawerk's firm rejection of Ricardo's theory of profit and his asymmetric treatment of the distributive variables, there is nevertheless some truth in Schumpeter's observation that 'there is […] a Ricardian root to Böhm-Bawerk's achievement though he was entirely unaware of it' (1954: 846). This observation is correct inasmuch as Böhm-Bawerk adopted the classical long-period method of economic analysis and also took up certain Ricardian ideas regarding the structure of production. Böhm-Bawerk's concept of hierarchically ordered production stages is clearly related to Ricardo, who in Chapter 1 of his *Principles*, when explaining the role of compound interest for the determination of relative prices, typically disregarded circular production relations and focused attention on unidirectional production processes, in which commodities are produced by a finite stream of dated labour inputs (*flow input – point output* processes in 'Austrian' terminology).[9] However, Böhm-Bawerk's theory of interest is of course substantially different from the classical surplus approach, with its asymmetric treatment of the distributive variables, and rather belongs to the neoclassical approach, starting as it does from given endowments of labour, capital, and land.

One of Ricardo's greatest admirers amongst the marginalist writers was Knut Wicksell. In his *Über Wert, Kapital und Rente nach den neueren nationalökonomischen Theorien* (1893), he delivered the following comment on Ricardo:

> At a time when it has almost become a fashion to speak of Ricardo in disparaging terms, it may be permissible to emphasize once again the unquestionable merits of this acute thinker. I can by no means share Wieser's opinion, that Ricardo's works exhibit 'the great youth of economic science.' On the contrary; as I see it, his presentation, compared with the vagueness of many later schools, the superficiality of a Carey or a Bastiat and the 'Hegelian' darkness – and conceit – of Karl Marx, is distinguished by what I should choose to call its masculine features. He appeals to the understanding of his readers instead of to their emotions. […] The way in which Ricardo develops his argument – totally free from the fantastic ideas and dialectic leaps of many of the later schools – is a model of strictly logical reasoning about a subject which seems, at first glance, to admit of so little precision. (Wicksell [1893] 1954: 17 and 35)

Like Böhm-Bawerk, Wicksell also showed a clear grasp of the asymmetrical treatment of the distributive variables in the classical surplus approach when he remarked with regard to Ricardo's theory of profit:

> Since, according to Ricardo, wages represent a magnitude fixed from the beginning, and since – as he later shows – the level of rent is also determined by independent causes, the cause of capital profit is already settled. It is neither possible nor necessary to explain capital profit in other ways, if the other assumptions are sound. (Wicksell [1893] 1954: 37)

3.2 On the role of the German historical school in the demise of Ricardian economics

The idea that the German historical school was the dominant strand of thought in economics for most of the nineteenth century in Germany and that its adherents were completely averse to theoretical argument is now generally agreed to be ill-founded. Therefore, Friedrich A. Hayek's contention that the German historical school must be held responsible for the demise of Ricardian economics in Germany cannot be sustained:

> Nowhere was the decline of the classical school of economics as rapid and complete as in Germany. Under the attacks of the historical school the classical theories were not only abandoned – in fact they had never really taken roots in this part of the world – but any attempt at a theoretical analysis was regarded with deep suspicion. (Hayek 1968: viii)

Hayek's statement is certainly not applicable to the older historical school, that is, to Roscher, Knies and Hildebrand, and it seems insufficient as a characterization of the attitude of the younger historical school as well. The major exponents of the older historical school still combined a vigorous interest in economic theory with a concern for both historical research and practical questions of economic policy. And all of them held Ricardo in high esteem. In his *Geschichte der National-Oekonomik in Deutschland*, Wilhelm Roscher characterized Ricardo as

> in many ways the direct opposite of Malthus, but no less great. A system-builder of the first rank, who abstracts from all differences among the people and from all practical difficulties in the same way as Malthus takes them into consideration. But precisely because of this strict abstraction and the almost faultless logic of his thinking he was able to erect a solid and closely interwoven piece of art, designated to displace the learned monograph of Smith and the detailed descriptions of Malthus. His greatest achievements often concern the most intricate problems, like the theory of ground-rent, the international trade balance, and the incidence of taxes. (Roscher 1874: 652)[10]

In his review of Baumstark's German edition of the *Principles*, Roscher even defended Ricardo against some of his critics by arguing that his abstract theoretical approach to political economy is 'as necessary in one half of political economy as it is insufficient in the other' (1878: 21). He added that a close study of the *Principles* was 'all the more important today as (let us face up to it) both of the dominating schools, the historico-statistical and the practico-political, only too often tend towards a certain wooliness in their theoretical analyses' (ibid.; quoted from Hennings 1997: 39). Thus the German historical school, at least up to 1870, was not a major hindrance for the diffusion of Ricardian theory in the German-speaking countries.

The members of the younger historical school, most notably Gustav Schmoller and Lujo Brentano, clearly displayed a somewhat different attitude towards Ricardo. They were decidedly opposed to the abstract, axiomatic-deductive approach of the classical political economists, and in particular of Ricardo (and also, it must be noted, of the then emerging marginalist school). Lujo Brentano, a disciple of Hermann, was originally an adherent of classical theory but later became a staunch advocate of the historical method. In his Inaugural Lecture at the University of Vienna he argued that the classical approach to economic theory, which culminated in Ricardo's *Principles*, had led into a *cul de sac* because of its reliance on too abstract and unrealistic premises:

> This necessarily implies that for the time being the special or practical political economy must be given centre stage, whereas the general or theoretical political economy must be confined to the background. There simply are no general principles in economics […] For this reason there was a predominance of work in the so-called 'practical political economy' in the last few decades in Germany. This did not emerge from a disregard for theoretical political economy, but because only in this way could the foundations for a new construction be laid. (1888: 28–9)

Brentano also pointed out that Ricardo must be held responsible for the introduction of socialist ideas, including central planning. The former adherent of Ricardo's economic theory (in the form it had been given by Hermann) now exclaimed:

> It is hardly believable what devastation has been caused by this theory! The social democrats are completely right when they depict the doctrines and demands of Rodbertus and Marx as their logical implications, and it is remarkable in this regard that in the recently published letters of Ricardo to Malthus one finds indeed anticipations of those demands.[11] But also in the opposite direction have these doctrines been misused. In the 1860s and even in the 1870s essays and newspaper articles were still published, in which the workers' unions were advised, with reference to the universal laws of economics, of the impossibility of wage increases. (1888: 9–10)

The head of the younger historical school, Gustav Schmoller, commented on Ricardo in a few short passages in his voluminous *Grundriss der allgemeinen Volkswirtschaftslehre* (published, in two parts, in 1900 and 1904). After some honeyed words, he reproached him for having failed to contribute with his theories 'to the solution of the enormous and ever more pressing social problems' (1900: 122). According to Schmoller, the deeper reason for this failure derives from the fact that

> Ricardo lacks any historical learning; he schematizes and searches for simple axioms of natural law, which he then applies mechanically. […] Because of the unruffled exposition and his seemingly infallible logic it was for a long time not realized what contradictions were hidden in his theory of wages, and how little it was capable of doing justice to the broader historical and geographical reality. (Schmoller 1904: 342)

The cloth-and-wine example, by means of which Ricardo illustrated the theory of comparative advantage, is ridiculed by Schmoller as 'utterly misleading', because it disguises the real conditions, that is, 'the oppression and exploitation of the less developed regions, from whom agricultural and mining products are cheaply obtained in order to furnish them in return with English manufactures at the highest possible price' (1904: 699–700). The free trade doctrine of Smith and Ricardo is scolded as 'unhistorical', because it 'presumes a set of individuals which are all equal, and a set of nations that are similarly all equal'. But this abstract theoretical setting disregards 'the existence of nation states with their national interests, their national organisation, and their national egoisms' (ibid.). The classical economists, by making use of the concept of self-interested individuals, are said to have underestimated the role of the centralised nation state for the taming and balancing of individual interests and for the enhancement of the economic and social development. On the other hand, however, Schmoller defended Ricardo's 'law of production costs' against 'the onslaught of Macleod, Jevons and in its aftermath the school of the Austrian value theorists' (Schmoller 1904: 158–9). Heinrich Waentig was probably referring implicitly to accusations like Brentano's and Schmoller's, when he observed on the occasion of a new German edition of Ricardo's *Principles* in 1905:

> A period of blind glorification was followed particularly in Germany by a time of harsh criticism, which, operating partly with substantial arguments and partly by means of moral indignation, has exceeded by far the legitimate extent. (Waentig 1905: VII)

4. The reception and further elaboration of Ricardo's theory of value and distribution: Friedrich Benedikt Wilhelm Hermann

We now turn to the contributions of two authors who can be regarded as exemplary cases for two different lines of development in the early reception and further elaboration of Ricardo's theory of value and distribution in the German-speaking countries. Both authors considered themselves as critical followers of Ricardo, but they developed his ideas in rather different directions. In this section, which draws very heavily on Kurz (1998b), the contribution of F.B.W. Hermann will be discussed, while the following section is devoted to a critical appraisal of the contribution of Johann-Carl Rodbertus.

4.1 F. B. W. Hermann's Staatswirthschaftliche Untersuchungen *(1832)*

The most important economic theorist in the German-speaking countries in the first half of the nineteenth century, apart from Johann Heinrich von Thünen, was F.B.W. Hermann, who taught at the University of Munich. His main work, the *Staatswirthschaftliche Untersuchungen*, was first published in 1832. A trained mathematician with wide-ranging intellectual interests, Hermann was remarkably well-read in the contemporary economic literature.

There can be no doubt that Hermann regarded Ricardo's *Principles* as the main challenge for any economic theorist. While Paul Mombert's characterization of Hermann as the 'German Ricardo' (cf. Schachtschabel 1971: 78) is perhaps too strong, Mark Blaug's opinion that the *Staatswirthschaftliche Untersuchungen* 'owed much to the *Wealth of Nations* but little to the writings of either Malthus or Ricardo' (1987: 639) can easily be shown to be far off the mark. According to one of his students, Hermann considered himself as someone 'who continued and completed Ricardo's system' (cf. Weinberger 1925: 466 n.).

Hermann's approach to the theory of value

After defining a 'good' as anything 'that satisfies some want of man', Hermann introduces the distinction between 'economic goods', which have both use value and exchange value, and 'free goods', which lack exchange value (1832: 1, 3–4). While the idea that goods which are in excess supply assume a zero price is, of course, not new, but is already encountered, for instance, in Ricardo's chapter 'On Rent' with regard to 'air', 'water' and particular qualities of land, Hermann can be credited with having provided a more general definition by applying it to services of factors in general.

In Hermann's view, the main shortcoming of Ricardo's theory of value consists in the fact,

> that the price of those commodities which are regularly brought to the market in any desired quantity is not determined by cost alone, as Ricardo and his disciples contend. In any case, the primary and most important factor in the determination of price is rather demand, which springs from the use value of the good and from the purchasing power of the buyers. From demand and from what those who desire the good are willing to abstain derives the cost of the least efficient production that can be undertaken to satisfy the demand. (1832: 95)

Hermann placed much emphasis on the factors that affect the demand for commodities, and consequently also the derived demand for factor services, but he did not develop the concept of a 'demand function'. While he stressed over and over again the subjective element of valuation, and particularly emphasized the role of consumers' evaluations in the determination of prices, his argument remained confined to the use of the phrase 'supply and demand'.[12] In particular, there is no trace of the concept of 'marginal utility' in his writings. Therefore, Schumpeter was correct when he noted:

> As in France, perhaps in part under French influence, a utility-theory tradition had developed in Germany. But it was equally inoperative: it stopped at recognitions of the utility element that are difficult to distinguish from the Ricardian way of assigning to utility the role of a condition of

> value. Hermann went further than others but he also confined himself substantially to working with supply and demand. (1954: 600)

In parts of his analysis, Hermann adopted the classical concept of long-period normal prices (or 'natural prices'), which obtain in conditions of universal free competition characterized by a uniform rate of profits across sectors. He pointed out that the full working of the competitive process, and hence the formation of normal prices, could be prevented by either natural or legal circumstances: 'rare paintings' which require exceptional artistic talents are a typical example of the former, 'new products protected by patents and trade monopolies' of the latter. Setting aside such natural or legal constraints, Hermann advocated a 'cost of production' theory of value:

> It can thus be said in all brevity that the costs of a product are equal to the sum of the values of all capitals passed on to the product [i.e., circulating capital] plus the value of the services of all capitals employed in production. Calling A the circulating capital, which passes on to the product, and B the fixed capital, which is employed in production, and assuming that the value of the capital service is on average $\frac{p}{100}$ of the capital, then costs equal: $A + (A + B)\frac{p}{100}$. (1832: 79–80)

This is a 'price equals cost' equation. Let p_i $(i = 1, 2, ..., n)$ denote the normal price of commodity i and r the general rate of profit. Adding subscripts to the symbols Hermann introduced for the two kinds of capital, we have

$$(1 + r)A_i + rB_i = p_i \qquad (i = 1, 2, ..., n).$$

Hermann was one of the first authors in the German-speaking countries to envisage the interdependence of prices in a circular production system and to hint at the possibility of studying this interdependence in terms of systems of simultaneous equations. In his discussion of the impact of changes in one of the determinants of supply and demand on the price of a commodity he sought to take into account the repercussions which accrue from the impact exerted by this price change on the prices of other commodities that enter into the production of the commodity under consideration as inputs. In the context of this analysis, Hermann extended the law of diminishing returns, which Ricardo had confined to the agricultural sector and to mineral deposits, to all productive activities in the economy. He stressed that in a long-period competitive equilibrium the price of a commodity equals its marginal cost (including profits on capital at the normal rate). The price will always rise or fall to that level of costs, 'below which that part of the total quantity demanded which is provided by the least effective means of production cannot be supplied' (1832: 84). Hermann thus hinted at the idea (later to be encountered in Marshall) of long-run rising supply functions, but he did not provide an analytical formulation of it.

Of particular interest is Hermann's discussion of the choice-of-technique of cost-minimizing producers, which was clearly inspired by Ricardo's analysis of the conditions in which (new) improved machinery can be profitably introduced in competitive conditions. Hermann approached this problem in terms of *inequalities*, in the same way as (but apparently independently of) the Cambridge philosopher and mathematician William Whewell (1831), who attempted to put some of the arguments in Ricardo's *Principles* into a mathematical form.[13] According to Hermann, unit costs can inter alia be reduced by 'a change in the composition of costs, especially by replacing circulating capital by fixed capital' (1832: 87). The question is under what conditions a newly invented machine which replaces labour can be profitably introduced, i.e., under what conditions an invention becomes an innovation. Hermann's analysis starts from a situation in which the above price equation applies. Now suppose an invention is made, which allows to save a part of the circulating capital, a, by employing a machine, whose value is given by B', and whose annual wear and tear amounts to b. Then, Hermann argues,

> the new costs are $A - a + b + (A - a + b + B + B')\frac{p}{100}$ and these must be smaller than the previous costs, i.e.
>
> $$b + (B' + b)\frac{p}{100} < a + a\frac{p}{100}$$
>
> The change is advantageous, if
>
> $$p < \frac{100(a - b)}{B' + b - a}$$
>
> or $$b < \frac{a(100 + p) - B'p}{100 + p}$$
>
> or $$a > \frac{b(100 + p) + B'p}{100 + p}$$
>
> or $$B' < \frac{(a - b)(100 + p)}{p}$$
>
> It can be seen […] that this kind of cost reduction depends on the rate of profit and is the more effective, the lower are the ordinary profits. It is therefore indeed seen to be carried out mostly in countries in which the rate of profit is low relative to the wage rate. (1832: 87–8)

Hermann's finding not only confirms Ricardo's proposition that the choice of technique in general cannot be decided independently of income distribution but also corroborates his further proposition (which, however, can be shown to be *not* generally true)[14] that the introduction of machinery is facilitated by a fall of the general rate of profit (cf. Ricardo [1821] 1951–73, I: 395). The inequality provides a comparison between the profitability of the old and the new method of production, and thus informs about whether the new method of production is able to pay extra-profits or incurs extra-costs.

Hermann's treatment of capital and profits

In the *Preface* of his treatise, Hermann stressed:

> The most intricate problem in political economy is presumably the question what determines the level of profits and how profits and wages react upon each other. The first more exact investigation of this problem has been undertaken by Ricardo; however, since he does not proceed in a sufficiently general way, his results are often only valid under restrictions, which deprive them of almost any truth value. (1832: V)

With regard to the theory of capital and profits, Hermann's analysis is basically a re-combination of ideas which he derived from Torrens and Say. In fact, Hermann explicitly subscribed to Torrens's dictum that the articles produced by capitals of the same magnitude, together with the residues of the capitals, have the same value (cf. Torrens [1820] 1826: 71). Let K_i denote the capital advanced in industry i, $(i = 1, 2, ..., n)$ at the beginning of the period of production, Y_i the value of the product, R_i the value of the 'residue of capital', and r the (uniform) rate of profit, then we have

$$(1 + r)K_i = Y_i + R_i \qquad (i = 1, 2, ..., n).$$

Hermann was apparently impressed by Torrens's argument, which he takes to have overthrown Ricardo's labour-based approach to the explanation of exchange value. He explicitly credits Torrens with having developed 'the more correct rule' that after the separation of worker and capitalist commodities exchange in relation to 'the quantities of capital employed' (1832: 134 n.). However, Hermann contends that it is a major shortcoming of Torrens's formulation that he failed to consider 'the *capital services* [*Kapitalnutzung*] as an independent element of the products'; and he adds: 'As far as I can see, this is the main achievement in political economy we owe J.B. Say' (1832: 31–2 n.; cf. also 270 n.).

The existence of 'capital services' as an independent element in the formation of value is explained by way of a criticism of Ricardo's concept of value. Hermann points out that 'goods commonly buy more labour or the produce of more labour than has been necessary in their production; without this surplus the capitalist would have no profit and would refrain from advancing his capital' (1932: 132). He seems to think that the fact that the amount of 'labour commanded' by a commodity exceeds the amount of 'labour embodied' in it contradicts Ricardo's labour theory of value, and that it shows 'that in addition to labour another element is necessary in order to produce the good, namely the services of capitals'. Accordingly, Hermann concludes: 'If the good has an exchange value that is larger than the amount of labour it contains, then this shows precisely that these services not only have use value, but also exchange value' (ibid.). Obviously, Hermann's argument is premised on a misconception, because the existence of a difference between 'labour commanded' and 'labour embodied' is merely an expression of the existence of profits, and perfectly compatible with the explanation of relative prices in terms of relative embodied labour quantities. (However, with positive profits the labour theory of value is generally invalidated by the existence of differing capital-labour ratios across sectors.)

In addition, Hermann also denies that commodities cost only labour, because the role of durable capital in the form of tools and machines (as opposed to circulating capital, such as raw materials), cannot be reduced to the transfer of the labour embodied in it in proportion to its wear and tear:

> Although the machine itself contains labour, this labour is totally different from the labour contained in the material that enters the product; only to the extent to which the machine is consumed does it behave like material; the works and services combined in it, taken as a whole, do not enter into circulation, but are only the *basis* of a service which then becomes an element of the product. (1832: 133)

With regard to the problem of the determination of the level of the rate of profit, Hermann's discussion starts by taking issue with Ricardo's concept of an inverse relationship between the real wage rate and the rate of profit. In his view there is no such relationship: at any moment of time there is rather a particular constellation of the wage rate and the rate of profit which is compatible with the 'givens' of the economic system; that is, the needs and wants of consumers, the endowment of the economy with labour and capital, and the technical conditions of production. Hermann abandoned the asymmetric treatment of the distributive variables advocated by Ricardo, which implies that all shares of income other than wages are considered residual claims to the social product. He rather advocated the idea that wages, profits, and rents ought to be explained symmetrically in terms of the 'supply and demand' for the services of labour, capital and land.

Hermann's treatment of rent

The discussion of the theory of the rent of land is mainly contained in Chapter V, 'On Profits', and in particular in Section I, entitled 'Laws of the determination and equilibration of profits of the different types of capital', of Hermann's *Staatswirthschaftliche Untersuchungen* (1832: 145–99). The reason for this unusual treatment is easily explained. Hermann considers land as a particular species of fixed capital:

> Having conceived of the *source of a permanent service* as capital, the remuneration of all such services appears as a profit. This made it necessary to enlarge the principles of the determination and equilibration of profits in such a way that they now encompass much that formerly has been treated separately. […] The theory of the rent of land, for instance, could then only be treated as a particular case in the exposition of the principles according to which the profits on fixed capital are determined in general. (1832: v)

According to Hermann, there is no need for the elaboration of a separate theory of the rent of land, besides the theory of the profits of capital, as Smith and his followers, including Ricardo, had done:

> Smith's doctrine of capital, while correct in its distinctions of the basic concepts, nevertheless suffers from contradictions and shortcomings […]. Particularly suspicious is that he does not reckon land among the capital. (1832: 48)

With regard to the pricing of land and its remuneration, Hermann argues, two cases must be clearly distinguished:

> Land […] considered merely as a capital asset, differs in no way from other fixed capitals; it is evaluated, like these, in proportion to its return; and competition is thus always involved in the determination of its price; land, on the other hand, which is demanded because of specific peculiarities, may obtain a monopoly price. (1832: 75)

The latter case applies, for instance, to plots of land which are exceptionally well suited for the growing of particular grapes of wine. Hermann claims that productivity increases that result from agricultural improvements on plots of land which exhibit specific qualities must raise the prices of those plots: 'Profit increases which cannot be levelled out by competition are smudged over or removed by the market, to the advantage of the holder of that capital asset which gave rise to them' (1832: 153).

However, in general, land with no specific characteristics can be considered as a capital asset like any other, and its price must therefore be determined according to the principle of the equalisation of the rate of profit: 'The ownership of land thus becomes the source of a permanent rent income, and land becomes a fixed capital asset, the exchangeable value of which is conditioned by this rent' (1832: 169). Let us consider Hermann's treatment of land as a species of fixed capital in somewhat more detail. Is this treatment compatible with his approval of Ricardo's theory of differential rent? Let σ_j denote the rent per acre of a given quality j of land, π_j the price of land of that quality per acre, and r the general rate of profits, then the expression for a perpetual rent is $\pi_j = \frac{\sigma_j}{r}$. Following Hermann's suggestion, land can now be treated as a fixed capital good that must be advanced at the beginning of the production period. Assuming for simplicity that there is no durable capital other than land, and that land is not subject to qualitative change in the course of the production process, the following price equation for product *i* produced by means of land of quality *j* obtains:

$$(1+r)(A_i + \pi_j b_{ij}) = p_i + \pi_j b_{ij} \ ,$$

where A_i gives the value of the circulating capital per unit of output and the b_{ij} amount of land of quality *j* per unit of output. Clearly, this equation can be rewritten as

$$(1+r)A_i + \sigma_j b_{ij} = p_i \ .$$

While the first equation may be said to reflect the situation of a producer who has himself acquired the land, the second one could be said to reflect the situation where he rents it. This shows that Hermann's treatment of land as a fixed capital good does not constitute a departure from the classical theory of differential rent. In a long-period framework it is indeed of no importance whether the phenomenon of rent is made explicit in the *price* of the land or in its annual return: Rent does not vanish as a component of the functional distribution of income merely by treating land as a marketable commodity or capital asset.

Hermann emphasizes that the marginal plot of land, which pays no rent, must be considered a 'free good' (1832: 168). Ricardo was therefore justified in his criticism of Adam Smith's view that rent *always* forms a component part of the price of corn. However, he disagrees with Ricardo's statement that rent is *never* a component part of the price of corn: 'It is, but not for each individual part of the supply' (1832: 164). Moreover, he observes that the marginal land often obtains the character of a produced means of production, that is, it can often be used only after some capital investment has been undertaken to make it suitable for cultivation. Land which has been thus 'enriched', even if marginal, will obtain a 'rent', in proportion to the amount of capital investment that has been undertaken. Hermann notes:

> It is strange that the English writers take pains to demonstrate that in all countries the worst land that is least taken into cultivation never attains any part of the product for itself, while this is in fact of no importance for the theory of rent. (1832: 170)

Unlike Ricardo, Hermann also provided a rudimentary discussion of the problem of rent when multiple agricultural products can be raised on land of the same quality:

> If land and fixed capital assets exist only in limited amounts which are equally well suited for the production or obtainment of different products, then they cannot yield a higher profit in one of their uses than in any of the others. But for an increase in their profitability it is not necessary that the prices of all the commodities in the production of which they are required rise simultaneously. If the price of only one of the products rises, many producers will divert the required fixed capital good from other uses, and place it in the more profitable line of production. But this will immediately lower the supply of the other commodities produced by it, and thus force the buyers to accept prices that also allow for the higher profit which the fixed capital good yields in this other use. (1832: 153)

In his further exposition, Hermann presents an example in which commodities of varying qualities, for instance grapes, are produced on different types of land (1832: 153–4). The upshot of his argument is that the price of a better wine, and hence also the rent that is obtained from the land on which it is grown, need not necessarily fall when the supply of lower quality wines is increased.

Hermann also generalized the principle of extensive differential rent to all kinds of resources for which well-defined property rights exist and the supply of which cannot be increased for either natural or legal reasons: workers who possess special talents or exceptional abilities and producers who possess private knowledge about production methods or trade channels will earn differential rents (1832: 154). Moreover, Hermann showed that the principle of differential rent is also applicable to (economically) obsolete means of production, like old machines, which are reactivated when they can be profitably employed due to an increase in the price of the product (1832: 187–8). Hermann thus clearly anticipated the concept of 'quasi-rents', which was later introduced by Alfred Marshall.

Hermann then analysed the effects of rising product prices, which are taken to result from a permanent increase in the demand for the respective product, on the (quasi-) rents that are obtained from the fixed capital goods – including land – which are used in the production of those commodities. Hermann's analysis is a curious mixture of partial and total analysis, of short- and long-period analysis, and of static and dynamic aspects of the theory of rent. He starts by distinguishing two cases: (i) the supply of the fixed capital good that is involved in the production of the commodity *cannot* be increased; and (ii) its supply *can* be increased. With regard to the latter case, Hermann further distinguishes between the following three sub-cases: additional amounts of the fixed capital good under consideration – including land – can yield either constant (ii.a), increasing (ii.b), or decreasing returns (ii.c). Obviously, Hermann's case (i) is the typical case of a given amount of land of a certain quality, in which the theory of intensive rent applies, while case (ii.c) is the typical case of extensive rent. By applying those two cases to fixed capital items like machines, rather than to land, and by considering in addition also the cases (ii.a) and (ii.b), Hermann obviously hinted at the possibility of formulating supply functions with rising, falling, and constant costs (as they are later encountered in Marshall).

Hermann provided no proper discussion of Ricardo's analysis of the effects of improvements in agriculture. He argued, however, that in the course of the accumulation process new and better methods of cultivation are developed which increase the produce per acre and diminish unit costs. With regard to Ricardo's explanation of a tendency of the general rate of profits to fall he observed that it could be checked by improvements in both agriculture and manufacturing. His argument is that with a rising price of corn (because of deteriorating production conditions in agriculture) and improvements in manufacturing, money wages need not necessarily rise in order to prevent a fall of real wages, because the industrial commodities that enter in the workers' wage basket will become cheaper (1832: 261–3).

In his treatment of the rent of mines, Hermann follows Ricardo (and Smith) in arguing that the theory of ground-rent is also applicable to mineral deposits – and thus in failing to distinguish properly between *renewable* and *exhaustible* resources. However, in one respect Hermann's analysis of the rent of mines can be said to go beyond the analyses of his predecessors, because he points out that in the case of multiple agricultural products the prices of the various products and the rents must be determined simultaneously:

> Deposits of coal and peat only become exploitable when the price of wood has risen by so much that many consumers disregard the discomfort that is associated with those means of heating. If there is no other use for the land, then the coal and the peat can be brought to the market by their owners as soon as their prices cover only the current expenses plus ordinary profits on the circulating capital and on the entire capital that had to be advanced at the start of the business. But a further rise of the price of wood, and thus a further reduction in the demand for it in favour of an increased demand for coal and peat will raise their prices, and thus provide a rent to the coal mines and peat bogs that were first opened or are more favourably situated, which in turn gives capital value to the deposits themselves. At the same time it may now also become profitable to exploit less favourably situated deposits. Mineral deposits of differing qualities follow precisely the same principles with regard to their profitability (1832: 182–3).

Whereas Hermann thus clearly failed to distinguish between exhaustible and renewable resources, he showed a clear grasp of interdependencies in the economic system as a whole: he noticed that the rents of lands (or mines) of different quality and location depend not only on the prices of the commodities that can be produced on those lands (or obtained from those mines), but also on the demand for, and hence the prices of, commodities which are close substitutes for them.

To sum up, Hermann's treatment of rent incorporates elements of the classical conceptualization of rent and combines them with anticipations of conceptualizations that only became dominant with the advent of the marginalist approach to economic theory. Hermann fully endorsed Ricardo's theory of differential rent and clearly abandoned the physiocratic idea, which to some extent had still been present in Smith, of rent as a pure gift of nature. However, he also introduced some elements that are incompatible with Ricardo's conceptualization of rent. By treating land as a capital asset, Hermann conceived of the rent of land as a 'remuneration of a productive service', which is proportioned to the investment that has been necessary to render this factor service. This different conceptualization of rent comes to the fore in Hermann's concept of 'quasi-rents': according to Hermann, it is a characteristic feature of a 'quasi-rent', as opposed to a 'true rent', that the respective 'factor of production' receives a return that is *independent* of the expenses which have been incurred in order to provide the respective factor service (that is, independent of the investment outlays which have been 'sunk' in the fixed capital items). Finally, Hermann's suggestion of the applicability of the concept of differential rent to the explanation of remunerations which are received for natural talents or special abilities is a double-edged innovation: on the one hand, it can be regarded as a valid generalization of the concept of differential rent from land (and mines) to all kinds of scarce, non-reproducible resources which are in fixed supply. On the other hand, however, it could also be said to entail a return to the pre-Ricardian conceptualization of rent as a 'gift of nature'.

A summary assessment of Hermann's contribution

Hermann contributed to the gradual abandonment of the classical approach as much as to its further elaboration. By generalizing the principle of extensive and intensive diminishing returns, which Ricardo had confined to land and other scarce natural resources, to all factors of production alike, including a factor called 'capital', he contributed to the development of marginal productivity theory. From the idea that capital provides specific 'services' – over and above its wear and tear – he developed his own theory of profits, which emphasizes the productivity-enhancing effects of capital accumulation. Moreover, he also advocated a shift away from the long-period method of Smith and Ricardo to some kind of short-period method, in which 'demand and supply' are invoked in the determination of prices. In the context of his short-run analysis, Hermann anticipated Marshall's concept of 'quasi-rents'. On the other hand, however, he also contributed to the further elaboration of certain analytical concepts and ideas that were first developed by Ricardo. Thus he provided a precise definition of the notion of a 'free good' which Ricardo had employed in his analysis of extensive rent. In the analysis of prices, he made some attempts to take production interdependencies into account and hinted at the possibility of using simultaneous systems of equations. He formalized the choice of technique problem facing producers to whom machine-using and labour-using methods present themselves as technical alternatives. In this analysis he made use of inequalities, in terms of which the concepts of 'extra-costs' and 'extra-profits' are defined. In his theory of rent, Hermann grappled with the problem of analysing the case of a multiplicity of agricultural products.

Curiously enough, Hermann did not have many followers: 'He was much praised, but his views were rarely taken up' (Hennings, 1997: 35). But importantly, some of Hermann's ideas were taken on board by Karl Heinrich Rau, who is generally considered as the main figure for the dissemination of classical economics in the German-speaking countries in the first half of the nineteenth century. Similar to the role of Say in France, he was responsible for the systematic exposition and dissemination of the ideas of Smith, Ricardo and Malthus and their amalgamation with German contributions. The author of a highly influential compendium that went through several editions (first ed. 1826–27), he 'considered himself a follower of Smith and Ricardo, but was an eclectic, who abandoned main pillars of the classical edifice' (Kurz 1998a: 130).[15]

5. The reception and further elaboration of Ricardo's theory of value and distribution: the contribution of Johann-Carl Rodbertus

Johann-Carl Rodbertus[16] has been praised by Ferdinand Lassalle as 'the greatest German economist' and Adolph Wagner has called him 'the Ricardo of Socialism', a designation that was later adopted also by Gide and Rist (1923: 458).[17] While Rodbertus' first publications in economic theory, which already contained all his main ideas, date from 1837 and 1842, he only gained academic recognition and, indeed, also some popularity with the general public, in the 1860s and 1870s, largely through the praise that was showered on him by Lassalle. As is well-known, Marx studied Rodbertus' writings carefully and devoted several manuscripts to a critique of his views.[18] Böhm-Bawerk likewise devoted a long section of his *History and Critique* to a refutation of Rodbertus' theory of profits.[19] Strictly speaking, it was Rodbertus' theory of 'rents' that both criticized, since Rodbertus renamed profits as 'rent of capital', because he intended to provide a unified treatment of the 'rents' of capital and of land. In the last decades of the nineteenth century, Rodbertus' 'theory of rent' was in fact also critically discussed by several other economists, so much so 'that a refutation of Rodbertus's views on rent may well be said to have been an ingredient of the Continental tradition' (Hennings 1997: 38). According to Schumpeter, Rodbertus' overall analytical scheme can be described most briefly, and at the same time most tellingly, in the following way:

> Fundamentally, and in the same sense as Marx, he was a Ricardian. His analytic effort was an effort to develop Ricardian doctrine in a certain direction and was in essentials parallel to, though different from, Marx's

> effort. According to dates of publication, Marx could have derived inspiration from Rodbertus, particularly as regards the unitary conception of all non-wage incomes – Marx's surplus value and Rodbertus' 'rent' – which is a feature of both schemata. In the main, however, Rodbertus' example can at best have taught Marx how not to go about his task and how to avoid the grossest errors. (Schumpeter 1954: 506)

The following discussion will confirm this assessment.

5.1 Rodbertus' Zur Erkenntnis unserer staatswirtschaftlichen Zustände *(1842)*

Rodbertus' concern for the social question found its first expression in the essay *Die Forderungen der arbeitenden Klassen*, which he submitted in 1837 to the *Augsburger Allgemeine Zeitung* – which, however, refused to publish it.[20] Many of his statements in this essay, as well as in his later writings, show that Rodbertus regarded himself as a follower of Ricardo, who critically elaborated on the latter's approach. *Die Forderungen der arbeitenden Klassen* contains a remarkable passage on the post-Smithian developments in the theory of value and distribution, in which Rodbertus compared the development in England, where the surplus approach had been further elaborated by Ricardo, Mill and McCulloch, with the parallel developments in France and Germany, where this approach had been corrupted:

> One knows how Smith's theory was welcomed particularly in Germany; and how it was mainly the principle of labour as the cause and measure of value that found universal approval. And it will be remembered that Kraus even went so far as to compare this newly discovered principle to the great discovery of Galileo. But one also knows how much the unclear hints which this great Scotsman had given in this regard were misinterpreted, or differently interpreted, until finally in France and Germany, mainly through Say, that theory of value was completely abandoned and in its stead a different one was created from the empirical standpoint of the modern enterprise. And alongside it, and again mainly through Say, there developed a different theory of the cause and nature of rents, supplementing and glossing over the original one, in which the unnecessary and superfluous notion of 'productive services' helped to close off a return to the correct track.
>
> But the English school, under Ricardo and McCulloch, pursued further the line initiated by Adam Smith, remained faithful to the principle of labour, and developed on this basis a theory of value that belongs to the most profound insights ever discovered by the human mind […]. And it is this theory of Ricardo, which however must be corrected and complemented with regard to the theory of the rent of capital and land,

> which must be regarded as the tip-off of modern science. (Rodbertus [1837] 1972: 28)[21]

In 1842, Rodbertus published his second treatise, *Zur Erkenntnis unserer staatswirtschaftlichen Zustände*, in which he further elaborated on the theme of his first essay. As he explained in the Preface to his best-known publication, the *Sociale Briefe an von Kirchmann* (1850-4), the ideas which form the core of his theoretical system had been fully developed in 1842, and the *Briefe an von Kirchmann* are for the most part only a more detailed restatement of his earlier ideas (Rodbertus [1850] 1972: 233).[22] Accordingly, Rodbertus' treatise of 1842 will serve as the main source for the following discussion of his critical elaboration on Ricardo's theory of value and distribution.[23]

5.2 Rodbertus' critique of Ricardo's theory of value and distribution

In his essay of 1842 Rodbertus presented his ideas in the form of 'five theorems'. To the discussion of each 'theorem' he devoted a separate section, in which he attempted to provide a (verbal) 'proof' of the proposition under consideration. The five 'theorems' or propositions are:

> I. All economic goods cost labour, and cost only labour.
> II. If the value of the goods would always equal their costs reckoned in terms of labour, then labour would be an ideal 'measure of value'.
> III. The total rent is divided into the rent of land and the rent of capital. Both arise from the same principle. Given the existence of a separate class of capitalists and a sufficient value of raw produce, the rent of land derives from the common mode of calculation of the rent of capital.
> IV. Even if the values of the commodities were indeed equal to their costs in terms of labour, the value would in general still comprise both the rent of land and the rent of capital – provided the productivity of labour is at all sufficient for rents to exist.
> V. In a state in which the values of goods were always equal to their costs in terms of labour, a new money could be created that would fulfil all the requirements of a proper 'means of circulation' and a 'measure of prices', but which is neither a material good nor related, like the current paper money, to any material or metallic money. (Rodbertus [1842] 1972: 7–8)

According to Rodbertus, the first theorem can be 'proved' as follows. In order to obtain material goods which are suitable to satisfy human needs and wants it is necessary to use materials and tools and to expend (direct) labour. But the costs of the materials, which he takes to have been produced on a previous 'stage' of the production process, can be fully reduced to previously expended labour. In this argument, Rodbertus implicitly presumes a hierarchical structure of production, in which the first stage of the production process consists of agriculture/mining, where raw materials are obtained by 'unassisted labour' alone, that is, without using any tools or material inputs.[24] According to Rodbertus, the total amount of embodied labour in a commodity can be ascertained as follows:

> It is = the amount of labour which, as a part of the total amount of labour that has been expended in the production of the tool, is proportional to the used-up part of it. If a tool, for example, has cost n units of labour and is used for producing o goods x, each with m units of direct labour, then a unit of good x costs $x = m + \frac{n}{o}$ units of labour. ([1842] 1972: 12)

Rodbertus' treatment of the wear and tear of fixed capital is obviously rather primitive and clearly involves a retrogression with regard to Ricardo's more sophisticated one. More importantly, Rodbertus also fails to improve on Ricardo's neglect of circular production relations in his theory of value and distribution. However, a novel element is introduced by him with regard to the conceptualization of the workers' wages, which in Rodbertus' view should not be treated as advanced capital but as part of the net income of society, on the same footing as the rents of capital and land. He motivates this by arguing that

> there is no reason why the workers should still be diminished in political economy, so that their life and their pleasures count for nothing, and their only role consists in the production of pleasures for the rent income earners. It is easily recognized that this treatment [of wages in terms of capital advances covering subsistence requirements] implicitly presumes the existence of slavery. But then the workers are perfect machines, and their means of subsistence cease to be consumption goods or income, but are similar to the feed of the labouring cattle or the coal that feeds the machines. ([1842] 1972: 22)

Rodbertus stressed that this novel treatment of wages would imply that workers participate in the sharing out of the social surplus and that (money) wages are dissociated from any pre-specified fund of wage goods, and become mere 'entitlements' to a part of the social product. While Rodbertus thus criticized Ricardo for his treatment of wages as being strictly confined to subsistence, he then nevertheless adopted the same conceptualization in the remainder of his essay.

According to Rodbertus, it is a major advantage of the labour-based approach to the determination of exchange values that it allows to express prices and costs in objectively measurable terms:

> If it is true, then, that goods cost nothing but labour, then [labour] time gives a measure, in which the costs of each good can be exactly expressed.

> Accordingly, the usual time measurements give the units in terms of which the amount of cost for each good can be calculated and the amounts of costs for different goods can be compared. ([1842] 1972: 33–4)

Rodbertus' 'proof' of his second theorem consists of a rather muddled and inconclusive discussion of the problem of an invariable measure of value. The upshot of his argument appears to be this: if it could be presumed that commodities exchange in proportion to the amounts of labour embodied, then labour would provide an invariable measure of value 'at the same time and place', i.e., with given labour productivity, whereas with varying labour productivity no invariable measure of value is said to exist.

In the discussion of his first two theorems Rodbertus repeatedly claims (and this he then repeats over and over again in the following sections, and also in his later writings),[25] that Ricardo had maintained that 'commodities exchange in accordance with the amounts of embodied labour', and that he had failed to perceive that the 'law of normal value' (which is Rodbertus's term for the labour theory of value), 'is modified by the principle of equal profits' ([1842] 1972: 34). He also contends that it was part of Ricardo's doctrine that market prices gravitate towards, or oscillate around, labour values rather than production prices ([1842] 1972: 49). Rodbertus apparently had omitted to study carefully, or else had failed to understand, Ricardo's argument in the concluding four sections of Chapter 1 of the *Principles.*

Of particular interest in the present context is Rodbertus' discussion of his third 'theorem', which contains his ideas on the determination of the 'rents' of capital and land. As has already been mentioned, Rodbertus advocates a unified treatment of all non-wage incomes, and accordingly applies the term 'rent' to cover both the rent of land and the profits of capital. This he does because in his view

> a rent, both of land and of capital, is only possible when the productivity is so high that more goods are produced than the workers engaged in their production require for their subsistence; in other words, the basis of all rents is a sufficient productivity of labour. ([1842] 1972: 67)

Rodbertus contends that Ricardo had been unable to put forward such a unified treatment because he had failed to perceive the importance of the distinction between the *economic* and the *legal* conditions for the emergence of the two forms of 'rents'. *Economically,* both types of income derive from the same source, namely from the existence of a surplus over and above the subsistence requirements of the workers and the requirements for the reproduction of the social capital. Their *legal* foundation, however, is the existence of the legal instrument of private property. In Rodbertus' view, Ricardo's failure to distinguish properly between these two conditions is a source of erroneous opinions with regard to the determination of the level of the rent of land (ibid.).

Given the existence of a surplus – what determines its distribution, that is – how are the proportional shares of the proprietors of land and of capital determined? Rodbertus argues that historically the entire surplus has at first been distributed to the landowners alone. It is only when

> a separate class of capitalists has emerged besides the class of landowners, [that] the total rent will be divided among those two classes, and this distribution will be determined by the relation between the value of the raw produce and the value of the produce in manufacturing and transportation. With a sufficiently high value of the raw produce a rent of land must always exist: This emerges from the mode of calculation of the rent of capital. ([1842] 1972: 75)

According to Rodbertus, the distribution of the total surplus between the agricultural and the manufacturing sector depends on the relative values (that is, the relative labour contents) of the agricultural produce and the produce of the manufacturing sector, respectively. The general rate of profits is determined in the manufacturing sector alone, by simply dividing the (labour) value of this sector's total production by the (labour) value of the advanced capital. The resulting rate of profit is then multiplied with the amount of capital (in terms of labour) that is employed in the agricultural sector in order to calculate the total profit which accrues in agriculture. When the latter is deducted from the share of the agricultural sector in the total surplus, a residue remains, and

> this residue is the rent of land. This given, the land is capitalized, that is, by taking the rent as the interest payment, and applying the ordinary rate of interest, the proportional capital value of the land is determined. ([1842] 1972: 81)

Rodbertus accordingly suggests, like Hermann, that the price of land is determined by $\pi = \frac{\sigma}{i}$, where π is the price of land (per acre), σ the annual rent (per acre), and i the common rate of interest. He also suggests that with i different qualities of land the rents that accrue on the individual plots of land (the σ_i's) are determined according to Ricardo's theory of differential rent. Rodbertus raised no objections to Ricardo's theory of differential rent as such,[26] but contended that differences in fertility or location cannot explain the *origin* of ground-rent. Such differences merely explain differences in the levels of rents on the intra-marginal lands, but not the existence of ground-rent as such: even if all the land was equally fertile and equally well situated, rent would still exist, and with land of unequal fertility and location, also the marginal land would still yield a rent.

The fact that a residue remains, which can be distributed as rent to the landowners, when the rent of capital has been deducted from the total surplus value of the agricultural sector, is explained by Rodbertus in the following way. The determination of the rate of profit in the manufacturing sector (which is then also used for the calculation of profits in agriculture) is based on the value of the capital which is employed in manufacturing, which includes the value of the raw materials which the manufacturing sector has received from the agricultural sector. In the agricultural sector there is no analogous part of capital advances for raw materials, and therefore a part of the total surplus generated in agriculture cannot be attributed to a corresponding capital element: this part is the rent of land. Rodbertus claims that his theory demonstrates in one stroke the errors of both the French Physiocrats and of Ricardo ([1842] 1872: 86). The Physiocrats attributed the rent of land to the productivity of the soil, because they committed the error of basing their reasoning on a state of society in which the entire surplus is appropriated by the landowner and a separate class of capitalists did not yet exist. According to Rodbertus,

> Ricardo falls into the opposite error. He starts out from the state of new colonies founded by old nations which, because of the separation of landowner and capitalist, already know the notion of a capital rent […] but in which at the same time free, un-appropriated land is available in abundance. ([1842] 1972: 88)

Ricardo's theory of rent, and particularly his proposition that the marginal land yields no rent, is said to apply only to such 'new colonies', while it is inapplicable to 'old nations', where, historically, the exhaustion of free, unappropriated land has preceded the separation of landowner and capitalist. Rodbertus' critique of Ricardo's theory of rent culminates in the assertion:

> This theory basically is no theory of rent at all. For it does not explain the emergence of rent as such, but only its distribution among the individual landowners (under the condition of unequal qualities of land), that is, it only explains the differences of the particular individual rents. ([1842] 1972: 89)

Rodbertus' 'law of the tendency of the rate of profits to fall'

On the basis of his theory of 'rents', Rodbertus put forward an explanation of the proportional distribution of income, and its development over time, that starts out from the following idea:

> Since the productivity [of labour] is the most important regulator of the value of the products, it is also the ultimate regulator of the level of the rents, and since an increase in productivity causes a decrease in value, the levels of rent and the productivities are inversely related. ([1842] 1972: 94)

Rodbertus thus supposed that reductions in labour values, which result from productivity increases, must be associated with lower 'rents' of capital and land. From this false premise he then sought to deduce a 'law of motion' for the proportional distribution of income over time. Because he considers the general rate of profit as being determined in the manufacturing sector alone, he contends that the proportional shares of the rent of land and of the rent of capital (or their development over time) must depend on the *relative* productivities (or on the *development* of the *relative* productivities) in agriculture and in manufacturing, respectively:

> The more the productivity in manufacturing and transportation increases relatively to that of the labour employed in agriculture, the more will the rent of capital and the rate of interest fall and the rent of land correspondingly rise; and the more the productivity in agriculture falls (or merely fails to increase in proportion) relatively to that in manufacturing and transportation, the more will the rent of land increase and correspondingly the rent of capital and the rate of interest fall. ([1842] 1972: 94)

Rodbertus then goes on to suggest that for various reasons the productivity in manufacturing must indeed generally rise faster than in agriculture, and accordingly he arrives, like Smith, Ricardo, and Marx, at a 'law of a tendency towards a falling rate of profit' ([1842] 1972: 107). To Ricardo's different explanation of this tendency he objects that

> it is the rent of land much more than the wages of labour which mainly causes the fall of the capital rent. […] For, if the proportional wages rise because of the increase in the value of the raw produce, then the relative share of the produce that goes to the landlord must increase even more, for the latter is determined by the value of the raw produce *alone*, while the wages of labour comprise, besides the products of agriculture, also those of the ever more productive branches of manufacturing and transportation. It is therefore impossible to conceive of a rise in the wages of labour, and an associated fall in capital rent, and not *at the same time*, and even in larger measure, of a rise in the rent of land and a corresponding fall in the rent of capital. ([1842] 1972: 107)

In the section devoted to his fourth theorem Rodbertus does not arrive at any new findings, although he tends to present his propositions as criticisms of Ricardo (and McCulloch). Thus he claims novelty status for the following proposition: 'The statement that values are regulated by the quantities of embodied labour is only valid 'in general', whereas with regard to individual commodities values deviate from embodied labour' ([1842] 1972: 110). These deviations are said to be caused by two factors (and, again, Rodbertus claims that Ricardo had not noticed this): first, they arise from the competitive tendency towards a uniform rate of profit on the advanced capital; and, secondly, from the fact that the value is determined by the production conditions of those commodities which are produced under the worst conditions. In view of Ricardo's disquisitions on the modifications of the labour theory of value in the final sections of the chapter 'On Value' it is difficult to see how Rodbertus could have arrived at this view. (Rodbertus' 'proof' of his fifth theorem contains nothing of interest for the purposes of this essay.)

6. The contributions of Ladislaus von Bortkiewicz and Georg von Charasoff to the modern reformulation of the classical approach to value and distribution

In 1906 Ladislaus von Bortkiewicz[27] published the first instalment of his three-part essay 'Wertrechnung und Preisrechnung im Marxschen System'; the two further instalments followed in 1907 (cf. von Bortkiewicz 1906/07, I-III). In 1907 he then published his famous article 'Zur Berichtigung der grundlegenden theoretischen Konstruktion von Marx im 3. Band des Kapital' (cf. von Bortkiewicz 1907). In 1910/11 followed von Bortkiewicz's essay 'Die Rodbertus'sche Grundrententheorie und die Marx'sche Lehre von der absoluten Grundrente' (in two instalments), in which he critically examined the contributions of Rodbertus and Marx to the theory of rent (cf. von Bortkiewicz 1910/11). The three essays mark a milestone in the critical works on Ricardo and Marx and contributed significantly to the understanding of both the achievements and the deficiencies of Rodbertus' and Marx's elaboration on the classical approach to value and distribution.

6.1 Von Bortkiewicz's critique of Marx's elaboration on Ricardo's theory of value and distribution

In the first part of his 1906/07 essay von Bortkiewicz provides a summary assessment of the debate on Marx's theory of value and distribution by critically examining the contributions of Böhm-Bawerk, Hilferding, Diehl, Tugan-Baranowsky, and Lexis. He rejects the idea, which had been advanced, amongst others, by Böhm-Bawerk in his influential 1896 critique 'Zum Abschluß des Marxschen Systems', that there is an 'irreconcilable contradiction' between the first and the third volume of *Das Kapital*. However, he likewise dismisses the arguments that were put forward by Hilferding and others in defence of Marx's construction. According to von Bortkiewicz, neither the critics nor the defenders of Marx's theory have succeeded in providing a proper assessment of Marx's theoretical achievements vis-à-vis Ricardo's contribution to the analysis of prices and income distribution. Such an assessment he attempts to provide in the remaining two parts and in his 1907 article. His second aim is to reformulate the 'objectivist' approach to the theory of value and distribution of the classical economists and Marx in a form that is logically unassailable. For this purpose he makes use of some analytical concepts that were first developed by Vladimir K. Dmitriev in his

1898 reformulation of Ricardo's theory (cf. Dmitriev [1898] 1974, first essay).[28] Von Bortkiewicz is keen to show that Ricardo's theory is superior to Marx's in several respects, so that Marx must be held responsible for a number of 'unpardonable retrogressions' from the level of knowledge achieved by his great precursor. According to von Bortkiewicz, it is in one regard only that Marx's analysis may perhaps be said to be superior to Ricardo's: 'This concerns the doctrine of the *origin of profits*' (Bortkiewicz, 1906/07, III: 472, emphasis in original).

The main points of von Bortkiewicz's contributions of 1906/07 and 1907 can be briefly summarized as follows. First, he shows that Marx's 'successivist' theoretical construction for the determination of prices and the general rate of profits is fallacious. Second, he is concerned with demonstrating that the labour theory of value is not necessary in order to arrive at a consistent theory of the rate of profit and the prices of production. Third, he wants to show that the latter magnitudes can be related to value and surplus value magnitudes in a way which is logically impeccable. As the title of his second paper indicates, von Bortkiewicz aimed at the 'correction', rather than the refutation, of Marx's theoretical construction.

According to the approach adopted by Marx, which von Bortkiewicz calls 'successivist' (1906/07, II: 38), the determination of the general rate of profit and prices of production proceeds in two consecutive steps: first, the general rate of profit is ascertained on the basis of labour values as a ratio between total surplus value and the value of the total social capital. It is here that the labour theory of value is considered indispensable, because it allows the determination of the rate of profit as a ratio between two magnitudes which are independent of the variables to be ascertained. In a second step, this 'value rate of profit' is then used to calculate prices, starting from labour values, i.e., it is used for the 'transformation' of labour values into prices of production. However, Marx's 'successivist approach' is generally not tenable, because it cannot be presumed that the 'price rate of profit', which is obtained from calculating the ratio between the social surplus and the social capital evaluated in price terms, equals the value rate of profit. Confirming a finding by Dmitriev, von Bortkiewicz's conclusion is that the general rate of profit and the prices must be determined *simultaneously* (1906/07, II: 37–8):

> In this construction […] the technical conditions of production of commodities, including the technical conditions of production of the commodity labour power, which, in turn, are expressed in a given real wage, emerge as the ultimate and exclusive factors determining prices. (Bortkiewicz, 1906/07, II: 35)

Von Bortkiewicz stressed that the data from which the classical approach to the theory of value and distribution starts are sufficient to determine the rate of profit and relative prices; no additional data are needed to determine these variables. Von Bortkiewicz demonstrates this both for the case of a system of unidirectional or 'Austrian' production processes and for a system with circular production relations. In the first case, by tracing back the production of a commodity to the preceding 'stages', one arrives at a stage on which only direct labour without any means of production – Ricardo's 'unassisted labour' – is used, while in the second case this is not possible. In the *Principles*, and in particular in the chapter 'On Value', Ricardo had frequently employed the simplifying assumption of unidirectional production processes, in which commodities are obtained by a *finite* stream of labour inputs. In his 1906/07 paper, von Bortkiewicz develops his argument in terms of such an 'Austrian' approach, while in his 1907 paper he assumes circular production relations, in accordance with Marx's discussion of the transformation problem. Following Dmitriev ([1898] 1974), whom he praises for his innovative work (Bortkiewicz, 1906/07, II: 34–9), von Bortkiewicz presents his argument in algebraic form. Considering the set of price equations associated with a given system of production with n commodities, von Bortkiewicz points out that the number of unknowns exceeds the number of equations by two: there are $n+2$ unknowns (n prices, the nominal wage rate w and the rate of profit r) and n equations. Fixing a numéraire and given the real wage rate (or the proportional wage), one gets two additional equations (and no extra unknowns) and the system can be solved for the rate of profit and the prices in terms of the numéraire.

With regard to the treatment of fixed capital, von Bortkiewicz demonstrates that: (i) the annual charge of a fixed capital good which operates with constant efficiency is equal to a fixed annuity (1906/07, II: 29–32); and (ii) also in the case of fixed capital there exists a formula for the reduction to dated quantities of labour. In addition, von Bortkiewicz also demonstrates, contrary to Marx's opinion and in agreement with Ricardo's, that the general rate of profit depends exclusively on the conditions of production in the wage goods industries and in those industries that directly or indirectly provide them with means of production. As von Bortkiewicz stressed, the correct view fits much better with Marx's ideas on the origin of profits: 'If it is true that the level of the rate of profits in no way depends on the conditions of production of those commodities which do not enter wages, then it should be fairly clear that the origin of profits is to be sought in the wage relation and not in the positive impact of capital on productivity' (1906/07, III: 446). Von Bortkiewicz explains:

> For if this ability were relevant here, it would be inexplicable why certain spheres of production should become irrelevant for the problem of the level of profit. In other words, much better than Marx's contrary view, does Ricardo's thesis fit into that theory of profit which regards profit as a withholding of some of the produce of labour, i.e. into the 'Withholding Theory' (as I should like to call it instead of 'Exploitation Theory'). Compared with Ricardo's standpoint, Marx's view represents a decided retrogression. (1906/07: III, 446–7)[29]

The rate of profit as well as the respective prices are determined exclusively by the price equations of the industries producing the wage goods and the means of production used, directly or indirectly, in the production of wage goods – independently from the rest of the system. This implies that from this part of the price equation system one can also obtain one of the key concepts in Ricardo's theory: the inverse relationship between the rate of profit r and the 'proportional wage' w. As von Bortkiewicz rightly emphasizes, 'in Ricardo's oft-repeated phrase that every rise in wages must necessarily be accompanied by a fall in profits, and vice versa, one must understand by wages neither money wages, nor real wages, but that amount of labour which is needed to produce the complex of goods forming real wages. In Marxian phraseology, this is the (absolute) value of labour power' (1906/07, III: 448). If the total annual labour is given by L, and the amount of labour that is necessary to produce the wages of this labour is given by V, then proportional wages are given by $\frac{V}{L}$, or, in Marx's terminology, by $\frac{V}{S+V} = \frac{1}{S/V+1}$.[30]

This leads us to von Bortkiewicz's critique of Marx's infamous 'law of the tendency of the rate of profit to fall'. Again, Marx's argument does not pass von Bortkiewicz's test of logical consistency. As is well-known, Marx rejected Ricardo's explanation of this tendency in terms of the 'niggardliness of nature', which leads to a rise in the proportional wage because recourse must be had to less and less productive soils or methods of land cultivation. 'Nothing is more silly', Marx contended, 'than to explain the fall of the rate of profit by the rise in the rate of wages' (Marx, [1894] 1959: 258). According to Marx, the reason is rather to be found in the introduction of new production methods, i.e., the substitution of machinery for living labour and the associated rise in the organic composition of capital. Marx is confronted with the problem to explain how the decisions of individually rational capitalists can bring about a result which is detrimental to the class of capitalists as a whole. His answer is that the introduction of a new method will first give rise to extra-profits that can be pocketed by the innovator, but that the general adoption of the new production method will then generate a competitive tendency to reduce the price of the product, which in turn generates a falling rate of profit.

According to von Bortkiewicz, this argument is fundamentally flawed. With a *constant* real wage rate, technical change cannot possibly lower the rate of profit. The latter can either remain the same, and this is the case if the technical change concerns luxury goods, or else it must rise, and this must be the case if the technical change affects a necessary commodity. In this argument von Bortkiewicz assumes that the choice among alternative methods of production is based on cost-minimization. Hence a new method will only be adopted if at the currently prevailing prices the unit costs of the product can be reduced by it. With the further diffusion of the new method the extra-profits earned by the innovator who first introduced the new method will be wiped out by competition, but the new general rate of profit corresponding to the new prices of production cannot be smaller than the previously prevailing one. In addition, he points out that Marx's attempt to explain the fall in the rate of profit through changing prices is also erroneous, 'because the price changes [...] affect in the same degree the capitalist's product and his capital advances' (1906/07, III: 458). Von Bortkiewicz's algebraic argument, which he presents in terms of inequalities, basically anticipates the so-called 'Okishio theorem' on the choice of technique in linear production models.[31]

Von Bortkiewicz accordingly concluded that with regard to the theory of value and distribution Marx's contribution was devoid of any analytical advances over Ricardo.

6.2 Von Bortkiewicz on Rodbertus' and Marx's contributions to the theory of rent

In his paper entitled 'Die Rodbertus'sche Grundrententheorie und die Marx'sche Lehre von der absoluten Grundrente', published in two instalments in 1910/11, von Bortkiewicz critically examined the contributions of Rodbertus and Marx to the theory of ground-rent.[32] Again, he pursued several aims simultaneously in this essay: first, he wanted to provide a critical comparison of Rodbertus' and Marx's approach to the analysis of rent. Second, he critically examined the arguments that had been put forward by some German critics against Rodbertus' and Marx's analyses of rent. Third, von Bortkiewicz wanted to scrutinize Rodbertus' and Marx's critique of Ricardo's theory of rent. In the following, the attention will focus mainly on the last point.

The article opens with a summary account of Rodbertus' theory and a rejection of his claim that the value of the advanced capital in agriculture must necessarily be smaller than in industry. Von Bortkiewicz objects that the advanced capital must also comprise fixed capital, besides raw materials and intermediate inputs, and that Rodbertus wrongly reduces the production costs which emanate from the use of fixed capital to the charge for the annual wear and tear and disregards the interest payments which must accrue on the capital advances (1910/11, I: 3–4). Moreover, Rodbertus is scolded for having disregarded differences in the turnover periods of the circulating capitals. Most importantly, however, Rodbertus' claim that no raw materials or material inputs are required in agriculture, i.e., that there are no circular production relations, is rejected on the ground that 'these do in fact exist in the form of seed-corn, fodder for the cattle, and fertilizer' (1910/11, I: 6).

However, according to von Bortkiewicz, 'the Archilles' heel of Rodbertus's theory of ground rent' is that he operates with the 'original law of value' and disregards the 'law of the equalization of profits' (1910/11, I: 37), i.e., that he operates with labour values rather than production prices. As von Bortkiewicz stresses, this was noted by several critics, including Lexis. But unlike most of Rodbertus' earlier critics, von Bortkiewicz does not content himself with merely pointing out that Rodbertus' argument was based on the labour theory of value. In his view it is also necessary to scrutinize the reasons which led Rodbertus to his adoption of the 'original law of value' in his explanation of the 'rents' of land and capital – given that Rodbertus was perfectly clear about the fact that prices will in general deviate from labour values. The first part of von Bortkiewicz's article is accordingly devoted to a critical discussion of six reasons that could be invoked for operating with the 'original law of value'. As von Bortkiewicz demonstrates none of these reasons stands up to close scrutiny.

The first reason (which had in fact been advanced by Rodbertus) is that Ricardo, whose theory of rent he sought to disprove, had himself also operated with the 'original law of value', so that he felt justified in adopting it as well. This reason is of course emphatically rejected by von Bortkiewicz, who argues that Ricardo by no means adhered to the original law of value, but 'on the contrary had put forward in unequivocal form the view that under the regime of capitalism the original law of value is subject to considerable modifications' (1910/11, I: 13). Rodbertus' second reason for operating with the original law of value is that different planes of theoretical analysis require different sets of hypotheses and that it is legitimate to adopt the labour value theory when the concern is with the *origin* of the 'rent of land and capital' and its division among the landowners and the capitalists. Von Bortkiewicz commented:

> This would only be convincing, if […] it could be demonstrated […] that the competition for the most advantageous employment of capital takes place separately for the two branches (agriculture and industry). Only then would it be correct to disregard the law of profit equalization when the division of the 'rent' into the rent of land and the rent of capital is at issue. (1910/11, I: 25)

The third reason advanced by Rodbertus is that there is some 'theoretical advantage' in operating with the original law of value, because values are independent of the distribution of income, whereas the inter-relatedness of prices of production and income distribution gives rise to the problem of circular reasoning. As against this, von Bortkiewicz points out (with reference to his articles of 1906/07 and 1907) that a *simultaneous* determination of prices and income distribution is both necessary and possible. Von Bortkiewicz then discusses three further reasons, which are of little interest to us. The three reasons are: first, that historically the original law of value has prevailed before the introduction of capitalistic production relations; second, that labour values can be conceived as centres of gravitation, around which market prices oscillate; and third, that at any moment of time the supply of capital is limited and that therefore the competition among capitals is limited as well. Von Bortkiewicz dismissed all three arguments, and accordingly concluded that 'none of the six reasons stands up to close scrutiny' (1910/11, I: 36–7).

In the final paragraph of Part I of his essay, von Bortkiewicz noted that Karl Marx, in his economic manuscript of 1861–63, which had first been made accessible by Kautsky in his edition of 1905–10,

> has anticipated the contemporary critics of Rodbertus' theory of ground-rent in all essential points. He has also discussed in considerable detail, and strongly criticized, that Rodbertus inadmissibly adopted the original law of value in his explanation of ground-rent. It is therefore most surprising that Marx deduces his own theory of ground-rent, insofar as he assumes the existence of an 'absolute ground-rent' alongside with Ricardo's theory of differential rent, from the original law of value, and that in this way he basically commits the same error as Rodbertus. (1910/11, I: 40)

In Part II of his 1910/11 essay von Bortkiewicz then turned to the critique of Marx's theory of ground-rent. The essential elements of his painstaking critique will be discussed in the following section. Here it suffices to note two points. First, von Bortkiewicz firmly rejects Marx's claim that in his analysis of ground-rent Ricardo had erroneously 'identified values and cost-prices'. Von Bortkiewicz comments: 'Against Ricardo, the accusation of a mixing-up of value and price of production is completely groundless, because he was very clear about the deviations from the original law of value which are caused by the law of profit equalization' (1910/11, II: 406). As will be shown below, von Bortkiewicz's rejection of Marx's 'accusation' involves a misunderstanding of the precise nature of Marx's criticism, which concerns Ricardo's adoption of the labour theory of value *in his analysis of the wage–profit–rent relationship.* The second point to be noted here is von Bortkiewicz's interpretation of the differences between Marx's and Rodbertus' explanations of 'absolute rent':

> The question is whether the process of profit equalization by means of the transformation of values into prices of production encompasses also the agricultural sphere of production (what Ricardo takes for granted) or whether this production sphere is excluded from it (as Rodbertus presumes). The answer which Marx gives to this question is that this process encounters a hindrance or a 'barrier', namely private property in land. (1910/11, II: 407)

According to Marx, the property rights associated with private ownership of land confer to the landowners the power to set limits to the rule of capital; or in other words, to inhibit that agricultural products are drawn into the process by means of which values are transformed into prices of production. This implies higher prices of agricultural products, because their values systematically exceed their production prices due to the fact that the agricultural sector exhibits a relatively low organic composition of capital.

6.3 Von Bortkiewicz on Marx's critique of Ricardo's analysis of the wage–profit–rent relationship

In this section it will be shown that von Bortkiewicz's criticism of Marx's construction, by means of which the latter sought to elaborate on Ricardo's analysis of prices and income distribution, does not do justice to Marx's analytical achievements. It briefly summarizes some arguments which have been presented in much greater detail in Gehrke and Kurz (2006) and in Gehrke (2012).

The starting point of the following discussion is the observation that von Bortkiewicz, because of his adoption of the simplifying assumption of unidirectional production processes in his 1906/07 paper, failed to notice that Marx had detected an important error in Ricardo's argument on the wage–profit relationship. Marx had approved of Ricardo's novel concept of 'proportional wages'[33] and had translated it into his own concept of 'rate of surplus value', S/V, with S as the labour value of the social surplus and V as that of the social variable capital.[34] Accordingly, Ricardo's 'fundamental proposition' that the general rate of profits falls (rises) *if and only if* proportional wages rise (fall) is equivalent to the statement that its fall or rise is conditional on a fall or rise in the (aggregate) rate of surplus value (S/V). Marx had objected to this reasoning that Ricardo had erroneously identified the rate of profit with the rate of surplus value, and had overlooked a second determinant of the former: the technical conditions of production as they are reflected in the 'organic composition of capital' of the system as a whole. Ricardo had been led to this erroneous identification, Marx had suggested, because in his analysis of the wage–profit relationship he had argued *as if* all capital consisted only of wages, or could be reduced to wages in a finite number of steps. As Marx put it:

> In his observations on profit and wages, Ricardo […] abstracts from the constant part of capital, which is not laid out in wages. He treats the matter as though the entire capital were laid out directly in wages. ([1861–63] 1989b: 10)

Ricardo's simplifying assumption of unidirectional production processes and his associated neglect of 'constant capital' meant that he had not taken into account the existence of circular production relations, and had thus overlooked that the rate of profits depends not only on proportional wages (or the 'rate of surplus value') but also on the *maximum rate of profits* (or the 'organic composition of capital' of the system as a whole). To render this clear, let us turn to Marx's expression for the 'rate of profit',

$$r = \frac{S}{C+V} = \frac{S/L}{C/L+V/L} = \frac{1-\omega}{1/R+\omega} = \frac{R(1-\omega)}{1+R\omega},$$

with C as the labour value of constant capital, L as the amount of living labour expended during the year, ω as the wage share (V/L, or the rate of surplus value, $(1-\omega)\omega^{-1}$) and R as the inverse of the organic composition of capital (C/L). It is then obvious that the rate of profits depends on two magnitudes instead of only one: R and ω. In Marx's conceptualization, $L/C = R$ gives the maximum rate of profits that corresponds to zero wages. If the maximum rate of profits happens to fall (rise) in the course of economic development, and proportional wages remain constant, the rate of profits is bound to fall (rise). (Of course, with technical change and associated increases in labour productivity, constant proportional wages must be associated with rising real wages in commodity terms.) To have spotted and rectified Ricardo's blunder was perhaps one of Marx's most important *analytical contributions* to the development of the surplus approach to value and distribution.

It needs to be emphasized, however, that in the above formula for r, with the *entire* surplus value S in the numerator, the 'rate of profits' is defined in such a way as to include (in the numerator) all of the three components into which, according to Marx, surplus value is being transformed: (industrial) profit, interest, and ground-rent. This peculiar definition of the 'rate of profit'[35] was indeed the one which Marx used in Part III of vol. III of *Capital* – and it was *this* definition to which his famous 'law of the tendency of the rate of profits to fall' was meant to refer, as Marx made perfectly clear in the opening paragraphs of Chapter 13 ('The Law as such'):

> We intentionally present this law before going on to the division of profit into different independent categories. The fact that this analysis is made independently of the division of profit into different parts, which fall to the share of different categories of people, shows from the outset that this law is, in its entirety, independent of this division, and just as independent of the mutual relations of the resultant categories of profit. The profit to which we are here referring is but another name for surplus-value itself, which is presented only in its relation to total capital rather than variable capital, from which it arises.
>
> The drop in the rate of profit, therefore, expresses the falling relation of surplus-value to advanced total capital, and is for this reason independent of any division whatsoever of this surplus-value among the various categories. ([1894] 1959: 214)[36]

The above passage was clearly formulated as a critique of Ricardo's explanation of the falling rate of profit (of which Marx had provided a summary account in the paragraph immediately preceding it), and when Marx says that he 'intentionally' presents the law in this form he wants to impress the point on his readers' minds that the tendency of the rate of profit to fall is independent of any inverse movements of the shares (and rates) of profit and rent. Marx particularly stressed this point because he believed – erroneously – that

Ricardo had envisaged the two distributive shares, and also the *rates* of profit and rent, each defined as a percentage of the total social capital, as being inversely related to one another.[37]

However, apart from the 'didactical' reason which Marx gives in the above passage as justification for his peculiar definition of the rate of profit, there is also a more substantial, 'analytical' reason for it. In Marx's understanding, the proportional wage must be defined in relation to the annual net social product, which includes wages, profits, *and* rents. For Marx, the value of the annual *gross* produce is of course given by $C + V + S$, i.e., by the total amount of living labour, L, *plus* the value of the constant capital, C – and not by L alone, as Ricardo had erroneously maintained *with regard to manufacturing*.[38] But the total amount of living labour which has been annually expended, $L = V + S$, gives, for Marx, the value of the *net* social product which can be shared out among workers, capitalists, and landlords, and the two ratios V/L and S/L accordingly give, respectively, the 'proportional wages' (i.e., the wage share) and the 'proportional profits *plus* proportional rents', *jointly* (i.e., the 'profit *and* rent share'). In Marx's formulation of the r (ω)-relationship the proportional wage, V/L, is thus determined by the *average* amount of socially necessary labour for producing the wage goods, while the rent (or rather the part of surplus value that goes to rent) is confounded with the profit. On the contrary, in Ricardo's alternative formulation, where the proportional wage is taken to be determined by the amount of labour which is required at the agricultural margin, rent is instead confounded with, or 'hidden in', the proportional wage – which thus includes elements of (what in Marx's view properly belongs to) surplus value. In Marx's formulation, unlike Ricardo's, *intra*-marginal production methods are thus involved in the determination of ω, and the rent share is conceptualized as a proportion of the total annual labour.

Let us turn, then, to Marx's criticism of Ricardo's analysis of the wage–profit–rent relationship (in the following, the terms 'profit' and 'rate of profit' refer to the common usage). In Marx's reading, Ricardo's propositions on income distribution entailed not only the statement 'that wages and profit are related *inversely*', but also 'that profit and rent have an inverse relation' ([1861–63] 1989a: 308). More specifically, Marx interpreted Ricardo as having asserted that the same cause, namely the deterioration of the productivity of labour in agriculture, was bound up with a *fall* in the rate of profit and a *rise* in the rate of rent. Now, from an analytical point of view, Marx made two main objections to Ricardo's 'fundamental proposition': first, he sought to disprove it by showing that the 'rate of profits' (defined as the ratio of total surplus value to total advanced capital) depends not only on proportional wages, but also on the maximum rate of profits, R. An implication of this was that 'the *rate of profit* can fall without any rise in the *rate of interest* and *rate of rent*' ([1861–63] 1989b: 100). Secondly, Marx also sought to demonstrate that the rate of profit (where the term is now meant to refer to common usage, that is, to Marx's notion of the 'industrial rate of profit') can be affected not only by changes in the proportional wage, but also by variations in the rate of ground-rent:

> The rate of profit can rise as a result of a fall *or rise* in rent, independently of any change in the value of labour. ([1861–63] 1989a: 60; emphasis added)

In his *Grundrisse* manuscript, Marx provided a very concise statement of his understanding of Ricardo's (and A. Smith's) argument regarding the tendency of the rate of profit to fall:

> A. Smith explained the fall of the rate of profit, as capital grows, by the competition among capitals. To which Ricardo replied that competition can indeed reduce profits in the various branches to an average level, can equalize the rate, but cannot depress this average rate itself. […] Ricardo, for his part, says: 'No accumulation of capitals can permanently reduce profits unless an equally permanent cause raises wages.' […] He finds this cause in the growing, or rather in the *relatively* growing, unproductiveness of agriculture, that is, in 'the growing difficulty of increasing the quantity of subsistence', i.e., in the growth of proportional wages, so that the labourer's real wage is no greater, but is the product of more labour; in a word, a greater portion of necessary labour is required for the production of agricultural products. The falling rate of profit hence corresponds, with him, to a nominal increase of the wage rate and a real increase of ground rent. ([1857–58] 1974: 637–8)

Marx put forward (but less concisely) essentially the same interpretation in his economic manuscript of 1861–63, where he also spelled out the relationship which – in his reading – Ricardo had assumed to exist between the *rates* of profit and of ground-rent (each defined as a percentage of the total social capital):

> Ricardo thinks that rent gradually swallows up the rate of profit. […] The continuous fall in profits is thus bound up with the continuous rise in the rate of rent. I have already shown that Ricardo's view of rent is wrong. This then cuts out one of the grounds for his explanation of the fall in the rate of profits. ([1861–3] 1989a: 73 and 74)

Considerable portions of Marx's writings on rent are in fact devoted to showing, against Ricardo, that the tendency of the rate of profit to fall is first and foremost caused by a rising organic composition of capital in the economic system as a whole (that is, by a fall in R), and that it is unrelated to any tendency of the rate of ground-rent to rise. With his typical penchant for contrariness, Marx even went so far as to assert, in Chapter 15 of vol. III of *Capital*, that the latter tends to *fall* – rather than rise – over time:

> But the rate of ground-rent likewise has a tendency to fall, although its absolute mass increases, and may also increase proportionately more than industrial profit. (Marx [1894] 1959: 242)

How did he justify this claim? According to Marx, the rate of ground-rent falls because the organic composition of capital in the economic system as a whole tends to rise, so that the ratio of ground-rent to the total social capital will tend to fall, even if the amount of ground-rent increases in absolute terms. Marx conceded that the latter indeed exhibits a rising trend, but denied that this was caused by the deterioration of agricultural productivity. He rather suggested that in agriculture the increase in the organic composition of capital is notoriously lagging behind the one in industry, so that the labour productivity in agriculture, although absolutely increasing, declines in relation to the productivity in industry: agriculture becomes *relatively* more unproductive, so that the value of the agricultural product in relation to the industrial product, and thus also ground-rent, increases. The prices of agricultural products are therefore bound to rise relative to those of industrial commodities, just as Ricardo had maintained, but only because agriculture becomes *relatively* – not absolutely – less productive.[39] According to Marx, this implies that rents may rise at the expense of wages rather than profits, even if commodity wages are held constant, 'for the average wage is not determined by the relative but by the absolute value of the products which enter into it' ([1861–63] 1989a: 119). With a *relatively* declining productivity in agriculture, the commodity wage could remain constant, leaving profits the same or even greater, with increased rents in commodity or value terms.

It needs to be emphasized that Marx's reasoning constitutes no valid criticism of Ricardo's argument. First of all, Marx was tilting at windmills when he tried to show that the rates of profit and rent need not be related inversely to one another, because this was not a proposition to which Ricardo had meant to subscribe. More importantly, however, in his argument Marx allowed for the introduction of agricultural improvements which raise the productivity of labour. But in a regime of absolute increases in productivity it is clear that constant real wages (in commodities) must correspond to falling proportional wages: Marx's result therefore cannot be considered as a disproof of Ricardo's argument.

To sum up, Marx was justified in criticizing Ricardo for his neglect of non-wage capital in the analysis of the wage–profit–rent relationship, and he rightly insisted that this had misled Ricardo into failing to notice the importance of the maximum rate of profits. However, he was mistaken in his belief that Ricardo had focused attention on the relationship between ω and the rates of profit and rent, each defined as a percentage of the total social capital, and that he had envisaged all three distributive variables as being inversely related to one another in his 'natural course' scenario: in the *Principles*, Ricardo did not attach any specific analytical significance to the 'rate of rent' as a percentage of the total social capital.

Let us turn, then, to Marx's own treatment of the wage–profit–rent relationship and his misconceived attempt to elaborate on Ricardo's analysis by means of his concept of 'absolute rent'. One of the main objectives Marx sought to pursue with his concept of 'absolute rent' was to show that in Ricardo's determination of the rent share a specific rent component, which emerges from the deviations of production prices from labour values, had not been taken into account. This is plainly evident in Marx's correspondence with Engels from the summer of 1862, when he first adopted this concept. In a letter of 2 August 1862, in which he also provided Engels with a condensed version of his purported solution to the transformation problem, Marx wrote:

> Ricardo confuses value and cost price. He therefore believes that, if there were such a thing as absolute rent (i.e., rent independent of variations in the fertility of the soil), *agricultural produce*, etc., would be constantly sold for more than its value, because at more than cost price (*the advanced capital + the average profit*). That would demolish the fundamental law. Hence he denies absolute rent and assumes only differential rent. But his identification of *values of commodities* and *cost prices of commodities* is totally wrong. ([1860–64] 1985: 394)

And in a further letter to Engels of 9 August 1862, Marx asserted:

> All I have to prove theoretically is the possibility of absolute rent, without infringing the law of value. This is the point round which the theoretical controversy has revolved from the time of the physiocrats until the present day. Ricardo denies that possibility; I maintain it. I likewise maintain that his denial rests on a theoretically false dogma deriving from A. Smith – the supposed identity of *cost prices* and *values of commodities.* ([1860–64] 1985: 403)

Marx then explained that whether absolute rent exists is not a question that can be decided on theoretical grounds, but rather something which must be ascertained empirically. On the marginal land, absolute rent may, but need not necessarily exist:

> I demonstrate that, even presupposing the existence of absolute rent, it by no means follows that the worst cultivated land […] pays rent *under all circumstances*; rather, these will, in all likelihood, have to sell their products at market value, but at less than their individual value. In order to prove the opposite, Ricardo invariably supposes – which is theoretically false – that, *under all conditions of the market*, it is the commodity produced in the most unfavourable circumstances which determines the market value. ([1860–64] 1985: 403)

On the assumption that the *market value* of the agricultural produce is determined by the production conditions on the marginal land, absolute rent is the excess of the *individual values* of agricultural products over their *individual prices of production*: the former are given by the labour values on the various lands, while the latter are calculated on the basis of the cost prices on the different types of land (i.e., the advanced capital plus the industrial rate of profit on the various types of land). Marx supposed that the individual production prices are systematically lower than the corresponding values, because the agricultural sector exhibits below-average organic composition of capital (in relation to the economic system as a whole). Differential rent is the excess of the *market value* over the individual value, where the market value is in principle (but not always; see below) supposed to be determined by the labour value on the marginal land. Accordingly, total ground-rent (that is, the sum of absolute rent plus differential rent) is equal to the difference between the market value and the individual prices of production, which correspond to the cost prices on the various lands plus the 'industrial rate of profit'. Absolute rent therefore exists on the worst cultivated land if and only if the market value is above the price of production on this type of land. In Marx's view, this may but need not be the case.

Now, Marx's claim was that Ricardo, because of his identification of values with cost prices, had not only erroneously denied the possibility of the existence of 'absolute rent' on the worst cultivated land, but had also, and more importantly, omitted to take into account a part of the surplus value that is appropriated by the landowners as rent (even if the worst cultivated land pays no rent). Put differently, Marx's claim was that Ricardo's differential rent, which according to Marx consists only of the excess of the market value (which is identical with the individual value on the worst cultivated land) over the individual values on the superior lands, does not include that part of surplus value which arises from the differences between individual values and the individual prices of production on the various lands. As von Bortkiewicz pointed out, Marx's concept of 'absolute rent' was not meant to apply to single agricultural commodities, but only at the aggregate level:

> When Marx says that absolute ground-rent corresponds to the excess of the value of the agricultural produce over its price of production, reference is to the value and price of the entire agricultural produce and not to individual units of agricultural products, and accordingly also to the aggregate amount of rent and not to the quantum of rent which is contained, for instance, in the price of a quarter of corn. (1910–11: 409)

Von Bortkiewicz's perceptive remark points to the analytical significance of Marx's concept of 'absolute rent': it forms an integral part of his critique and purported improvement of Ricardo's analysis of the wage–profit–rent relationship *at the aggregate level*. What Marx insisted on was that Ricardo had only been able to determine the rate of profit on the marginal land, given proportional wages, because of his identification of values and production prices. The problem, however, was to determine the general rate of profits when Ricardo's simplifying assumption was dispensed with. This is the essential point of Marx's criticism of Ricardo's theory of rent, as becomes evident in his comment on Ricardo's famous statement that 'profits depend on the quantity of labour requisite to provide necessaries for the labourers, on that land or with that capital which yields no rent'. On this statement Marx commented as follows:

> According to this, the profit of the farmer on that land – the worst land, which according to Ricardo pays no rent – regulates *the general rate of profit*. The reasoning is this: the product of the worst land is sold at its *value* and pays no rent. We see here exactly, therefore, how much surplus value remains for the capitalist after deduction of the value of that part of the product which is merely an equivalent for the worker. And this surplus value is the profit. This is based on the assumption that *cost price* and *value* are identical, that this product, because it is sold at its cost price, is sold at its value.
>
> This is incorrect, historically and theoretically. I have shown that, where there is capitalist production and where landed property exists, the land or mine of the worst type cannot pay a rent, because its produce is sold *below its value* if it is sold at the market value of corn (which is not regulated by it). For the market value only covers its *cost price*. But what regulates this cost price? The rate of profit of the *non-agricultural capital*, into whose determination the price of corn naturally enters as well, however far removed the latter may be from being its sole determinant. Ricardo's assertion would only be correct if *values* and *cost prices* were identical. Historically too, as the capitalist mode of production appears later in agriculture than in industry, *agricultural profit* is determined by *industrial*, and not the other way about. ([1861–63] 1989b: 100)

In Marx's understanding, then, the formation of a general rate of profits and the associated transformation of values into prices of production must be studied by focusing attention on the 'industrial branches' only (although agricultural production methods are involved via the prices of raw materials and subsistence commodities) – hence Marx's use of the term 'industrial rate of profit'.

It will be evident that in Marx's overall theoretical construction the concept of 'absolute rent' properly belongs to, and indeed forms an integral part of, his analysis of the transformation of values into prices of production and the associated transformation of surplus value into (industrial and commercial) profit, interest, and ground-rent. In this regard it is highly significant that in Marx's original manuscripts of 1861–63 the section on 'Absolute rent' was drafted by the author *immediately after* the part on the transformation problem and *before* the parts on the theory of differential rent. Moreover, in

Marx's plan of January 1863 (for vol. III of *Capital*) the subsection 'Ground rent (illustration about the differences between value and price of production)', which was rewritten in 1865 and now forms Chapter 45 of vol. III of *Capital*, was still meant to be inserted between the two subsections 'Transformation of value into price of production' and 'Law of the tendency of the rate of profit to fall' (see Takenaga 2010: 5–6).[40]

Von Bortkiewicz (1910/11) clearly spelt out the major flaws of Marx's construction and showed that his analysis of 'absolute rent' cannot be sustained (even if we are prepared to disregard the problems associated with Marx's fallacious transformation algorithm).[41] Von Bortkiewicz's first criticism concerns Marx's identification of the general rate of profit with the 'industrial rate of profit'. As von Bortkiewicz rightly pointed out,

> it is a somewhat crude and contrived idea that *first* a particular rate of surplus value is established on the basis of the production conditions in both agriculture and industry, and that *thereafter* a definitive rate of profit is formed within industry alone, which is then transmitted to agriculture by conferring to it the ability to regulate agricultural profit. (1910/11: 409)

Von Bortkiewicz's reading obviously assumes that the 'average rate of profit' which Marx sought to determine in Part II of vol. III of *Capital* by means of his transformation algorithm is formed within industry alone (i.e., that it is identical with what Marx then called, in Chapter 15 in part III of *Capital*, the 'industrial rate of profit'). If one wants to make sense of Marx's reasoning, this interpretation seems indeed to be the only possible one: if agriculture were supposed to be involved in the transformation by which a uniform rate of profits on the total capital advanced in the various 'branches' is accomplished, Marx would have to determine, and deduct, the amount of surplus value which is turned into 'absolute rent' on the worst cultivated land before applying his transformation algorithm.

Von Bortkiewicz's second main criticism concerns the lack of any compelling argument by Marx in support of his idea that the *value* of the agricultural produce forms the upper limit for the amount of absolute rent:

> Marx claims that in a state in which all spheres of production are subject to competition, and accordingly the industrial products are sold at their prices of production, the agricultural products will be sold at a price (under certain conditions concerning the organic composition of capital) which is above their production price, but not above their value. […] But why should landed property, if it has the power to oppose the laws of capitalistic price formation, be bounded by the limit of value? (1919: 254)

Von Bortkiewicz's objection points to a conceptual problem associated with Marx's notion of competition. In the secondary literature,[42] Marx's concept of 'absolute rent' has sometimes been identified with a 'monopoly rent' in the sense of Smith and Ricardo, because Marx repeatedly uses the word 'monopoly' in connection with absolute rent. However, such a reading would seem to miss Marx's intended meaning, who had discussed this type of rent explicitly, arguing that 'monopoly price […] is determined neither by price of production nor by value of commodities, but by the buyers' needs and ability to pay' (Marx [1894] 1959: 764). On the other hand, there is a serious problem with Marx's notion of 'absolute rent' if it is interpreted as referring to competitive conditions – as indeed seems to be warranted in view of the following definition:

> Just as it is the *monopoly* of capital alone that enables the capitalist to squeeze surplus labour out of the worker, so the monopoly of landownership enables the landed proprietor to squeeze that part of surplus labour from the capitalist, which would form a constant *excess profit*. ([1861–63] 1989a: 326)

As Negishi has noted, the word 'monopoly' should be interpreted here, not in the modern sense that capitalists or landowners act jointly so as to maximize common gains, but in the classical or Marxian sense of an exclusive access to means of production by some specific class:

> The monopoly of capital […] does not exclude competition among capitalists. Otherwise, there would be no equality of the rate of profit. Similarly, the monopoly of landownership does not exclude the possibility that each landowner acts independently. Though Marx made some confusing statements […], it is clear that he did not have joint action of all the landowners in mind. (1985: 97)

But if the owners of uncultivated plots of marginal land are supposed to act independently, each one of them will seek to obtain some rent by inviting additional investment on his land, thus bidding down rent, until it has completely disappeared on the marginal land.

6.4 The contributions of Georg von Charasoff (1909, 1910)

In 1909 and 1910, Georg von Charasoff[43] published two books, entitled *Karl Marx über die menschliche und kapitalistische Wirtschaft* (1909) and *Das System des Marxismus. Darstellung und Kritik* (1910),[44] in which he critically examined Marx's contribution to the further development of the Ricardian theory of value and anticipated several results of the modern reformulation of the classical approach to the theory of value and distribution. During his lifetime, von Charasoff's outstanding contributions went almost unnoticed, and it was only after their 'rediscovery' in the 1980s that they were properly appreciated.

As opposed to von Bortkiewicz, Charasoff developed his main argument within the framework of an interdependent system of production, which exhibits all the properties of the later input–output model and which is fully specified in terms of the amounts of material inputs and labour needed per unit of output. The central concept of Charasoff's analysis is that of a 'series of production' (*Produktionsreihe*): it consists of a sequence, starting with an arbitrary (semi-positive) net output vector (where net output is defined exclusive of wage goods), followed by the vector of the means of production and the means of subsistence in the support of workers needed to produce this net output vector, then the vector of the means of production and the means of subsistence needed to produce the previous vector of inputs, and so on. Charasoff called the first input vector 'capital of the first degree' (*Kapital erster Ordnung*), the second input vector 'capital of the second degree' (*Kapital zweiter Ordnung*), and so on. The production series 'has the remarkable property that each element of it is both the product of the following and the capital of the preceding element. Its investigation is indispensable to the study of all the theoretical questions in political economy' (Charasoff 1910: 120).[45]

Let **y** denote the *n*-dimensional vector of net outputs and **A** the *nxn* matrix of augmented input coefficients, i.e., each coefficient represents the sum of the respective material and wage good inputs per unit of output (in this regard Charasoff followed the classical economists and Marx in reckoning the wages as capital advances). Then the 'production series' is given by

$$\mathbf{y}^{\mathrm{T}}, \mathbf{y}^{\mathrm{T}}\mathbf{A}, \mathbf{y}^{\mathrm{T}}\mathbf{A}^{2},\dots, \mathbf{y}^{\mathrm{T}}\mathbf{A}^{\mathrm{k}},\dots$$

With circular production relations this series is infinite. Tracing it backward, first all commodities that are luxury goods disappear from view; next, all commodities that are specific means of production in the production of luxuries; then, the specific means of production needed to produce those means of production, etc., etc. On the implicit assumption (which Charasoff failed to make explicit) that none of the commodities mentioned enters into its own production,

> it is clear that from a certain finite point onwards no further exclusions have to be made, and all the remaining elements of the series of production will always be made up of the self-same means of production, which in the final instance are indispensable in the production of all the different products and which therefore will be called *basic products* [*Grundprodukte*]. (Charasoff 1910: 120–21)

Charasoff added: 'The whole problem of price boils down […] to the determination of the prices of these basic products. Once they are known, the prices of the means of production used in the production of luxuries, and finally also the prices of the latter, can be derived'. (Charasoff 1910: 121)

A further property of the 'series of production' deserves to be stressed. The 'capital of the second degree' ($\mathbf{y}^T\mathbf{A}^2$) is obtained by multiplying the 'capital of the first degree' ($\mathbf{y}^T\mathbf{A}$) by $\mathbf{A}$: 'Yet since the physical composition of a sum of capitals is obviously always a medium between the physical compositions of the summands, it follows that capitals of the second degree deviate from one another to a smaller extent than is the case with the capitals of the first degree' (1910: 123). Accordingly, the farther one goes back in the series, the more equal the compositions of the capitals become, i.e., capitals of a sufficiently high degree 'may practically be seen as different quantities of one and the same capital: the *original* or *prime capital* [*Urkapital*]' (1910: 124). As Charasoff stressed, this finding is of the utmost importance for determining the general rate of profit. For it turns out that 'this original type, to which all capitals of lower degree converge, possesses the property of growing in the course of the process of production without any qualitative change, and that the rate of its growth gives the general rate of profit' (1910: 124). The rate of profit can thus be ascertained in terms of relating to one another two quantities of the same composite commodity: the 'original capital'.

Let $\mathbf{u}$ designate the n-dimensional vector of an elementary unit of the 'original capital', $\mathbf{u} \geq \mathbf{0}$, then $\mathbf{u}^T\mathbf{A}$ is the (original) capital corresponding to $\mathbf{u}^T$, and we have

$$\mathbf{u}^T = (1 + r)\mathbf{u}^T\mathbf{A},$$

with r as the general rate of profit. Von Charasoff emphasized: 'The original capital expresses the idea of a surplus-value yielding, growing capital in its purest form, and the rate of its growth appears in fact as the general capitalist profit rate' (1910: 112). These considerations also provide the key to a solution of the problem of price. For, if the various capitals can be conceived 'as different amounts of the self-same capital […], then prices must be proportional to the dimensions of these, and the problem of price thus finds its solution in this law-like relationship' (1910: 123). Let $\mathbf{p}$ designate the n-dimensional vector of prices, $\mathbf{p} \geq \mathbf{0}$, then we have the following system of price equations:

$$\mathbf{p} = (1 + r)\mathbf{A}\mathbf{p}.$$

Thus, while $\mathbf{u}$ equals the left-hand eigenvector of $\mathbf{A}$, $\mathbf{p}$ equals its right-hand eigenvector; and $1/(1 + r)$ is the dominant eigenvalue of matrix $\mathbf{A}$. The solution to the price problem can therefore be cast in a form, in which 'the notion of labour is almost entirely by-passed' (1910: 112). When the technical conditions of production and the real wage rate are taken as given, the general rate of profits and the prices of commodities can be determined without having recourse to labour values. However, von Charasoff by no means concluded from this finding that the labour theory of value must be jettisoned.

According to von Charasoff, the main task of political economy consists in providing a theory of capitalist development, with technical progress as a main driving force. The classical economists, that is, Smith, Ricardo and Marx, are credited with having put forward such a theory. Their emphasis on labour values is justified by von Charasoff in terms of the fact that human progress must inevitably involve a (partial) liberation of mankind from the struggle for the procurement of its material needs, so that ultimately technical progress must always involve a saving of labour time:

> This is the fundamental law underlying the classical law of value. By abandoning this objective basis of the determination of value, the modern subjective theorists have rejected the only possible explanation of technical progress and therefore they are without any theory of the technical development of the capitalist economy. (1910: xv-xvi)

According to von Charasoff, it was one of Ricardo's most important achievements to have focused attention on the development of the productive forces of labour and on technical progress, and also to have forged tools for its analysis. Characteristically, von Charasoff chose as a motto for his first book the following statement by Marx (in Chap. XV of vol. 3 of *Capital*, p. 259) on Ricardo:

> It is precisely that which is held against him, it is his unconcern for 'human beings', and his having an eye solely for the development of the productive forces, whatever the cost in human beings and capital-values – it is precisely that which is the important thing about him. (Charasoff 1909: ii)

Notes

1 Of course, when I refer to the German-speaking countries, I mainly have in view Germany (the German Reich) and Austria. However, since in the nineteenth century German was still a main language in economics, there were also contributions from authors who used the German language in their writings but were subjects of neither the German Reich nor the Hapsburg Empire.
2 Unless otherwise stated, all translations from German sources are mine.
3 On the disagreements between Ricardo and Say, see Gehrke and Kurz (2001).
4 See Mill (1824), McCulloch (1831), Marcet (1820), and Martineau (1834); see also Anon. (1824).
5 See McCulloch (1819).
6 On the meaning and significance of Ricardo's concept of 'proportional wages', see Gehrke (2011).
7 Early on, there were also German translations of Jean-Baptiste Say's treatises; cf. Say (1818) and Say (1829–30).
8 For a comprehensive analysis of the debates between the advocates of marginalism and socialism in the German-speaking countries, see Kurz (1995).
9 This simplifying device was also adopted by Ricardo in his analysis of the wage-profit relationship, as Marx rightly pointed out (see Section 6 below).

10 Roscher added: 'More alarming is that Ricardo was a progressive nature, at a time when the English nation was already on the decline and every speed-up of the development process must have accelerated the decline. It is from this that the capitalistic flavor of his writings derives, which in the hands of many of his followers became almost a leering for filthy lucre.' (1874: 652)
11 According to Brentano, Ricardo's statement (in a letter to Malthus in the context of a discussion of possible remedies for a general glut) that 'If a superior genius had all the capital of the country in his hand, he would soon make industry flourish as before' can be interpreted as an anticipation of the social democrats' demand for centrally planned production (1888: 31).
12 Hermann was clear about the necessity to render the notions of 'demand' and 'supply' *analytical* categories, and made some efforts in this regard; for a more detailed discussion, see Kurz (1998b: 95–6).
13 On Whewell's analysis of the choice of technique problem, see Gehrke (2003: 151–3).
14 See Gehrke (2003, pp. 149–52).
15 Apart from his textbook, Rau also contributed to the dissemination of economic ideas by founding and editing the first German periodical in economics, entitled *Archiv der Politischen Ökonomie und Polizeywissenschaft*, in 1835. Roscher tellingly characterized him as 'the economics teacher of the well-reigned German middle states from 1815 to 1848' (1874: 856).
16 Rodbertus (1805–1875) came from a wealthy and intellectual family. His father was a professor of law and his mother was a daughter of the well-known German physiocrat Schlettwein, from whom his family inherited large estates in northern Germany. He studied law at the Universities of Göttingen and Berlin, and afterwards entered the Prussian civil service. He retired from his post after a brief period of service in 1832, and embarked on a 'continental tour' for several years. He first took residence in Dresden and Heidelberg, where he 'absorbed [him]self completely in the study of political economy' (Rodbertus [1842] 1972: xviii). He then moved on to Switzerland, France and Holland. In 1836 he settled down at his newly acquired landed estate in Jagetzow in Pomerania, where he concentrated on the study of social and economic issues. In 1848 Rodbertus was elected to the Prussian National Assembly and, for two weeks, he became the Minister of Culture and Education. In 1849 he retired from the Assembly and returned to writing and study, spending most of his time on his estate in Jagetzow.
17 Gide and Rist also draw attention to the French sources of some of Rodbertus' ideas in the writings of Proudhon and Sismondi.
18 These manuscripts were later incorporated into Part II of Marx's *Theories of Surplus Value*; see Marx ([1905–10] 1968: 7–157).
19 See Böhm-Bawerk ([1884] 1921: 330–66).
20 The treatise was indeed published only in 1872 (in parts), and it was first published in full length only in 1885.
21 Rodbertus' assessment of Say's role in the corruption and gradual abandonment of the surplus approach in Germany and France is one of the few points on which Marx agreed with him. On the disagreements between Say and Ricardo with regard to the theory of value and distribution, see Gehrke and Kurz (2001).
22 The *Sociale Briefe an von Kirchmann* were published (in three parts) in the period from 1850–1854: *Erster Brief an von Kirchmann. Die Sociale Bedeutung der Staatswirtschaft* (1850), *Zweiter und Dritter Brief an von Kirchmann. Zur Beleuchtung der socialen Frage* (1850–1), and *Das Kapital. Vierter socialer Brief an von Kirchmann* (1854).
23 Rodbertus' other writings from the period under consideration seem to contain no substantial revisions or additions to the assessment of Ricardo's theory of value and distribution given in Rodbertus (1842). These writings are: *Die Preussische Geldkrisis* (1845), *Entwurf zu den neuesten landwirtschaftlichen Taxprinzipien für*

die Provinz Altpommern (1846), *Die neuesten Grundtaxen des Herrn von Bülow-Cummerow* (1847), and *Für den Kredit der Grundbesitzer* (1847). The essay *Die Handelskrisen und die Hypothekennot der Grundbesitzer*, in which Rodbertus developed his famous crisis theory, was first published in 1858.

24 See Rodbertus's *Dritter Brief* for an explicit statement of this assumption: 'Agriculture needs no products of a preceding sector as material input, but rather forms the starting point of the production process' (1854: 97–8).

25 See Rodbertus ([1842] 1972: 49, 110–11, 130–31); see also Rodbertus ([1851] 1972: 167, 171, 174, 180–81, 280–81).

26 In a letter he wrote to von Thünen on 29 September 1840, shortly after they had first met in Marienbad, Rodbertus expressed the hope that Thünen would soon recover so as to be able to continue his earlier work on the theory of rent, which, 'the more often I read it, the more invaluable it seems to me to be' (Rodbertus [1840] 1972: 3).

27 Ladislaus von Bortkiewicz (1868–1931) was born in Saint Petersburg into a family of Polish origin. He obtained his doctorate at the University of Strasbourg under the supervision of Wilhelm Lexis and became an Associate Professor at the University of Berlin in 1901. He published widely in mathematics, statistics, physics, and economics.

28 For a summary assessment of Dmitriev's contribution, see Gehrke (1998).

29 In von Bortkiewicz's view there can be no doubt that Marx's explanation of the *origin* of profits is essentially identical with Ricardo's: 'Both take the view that profit, or speaking more generally, the returns of capital, originate in a withholding of some of the produce of labour. All efforts of the opponents of the 'theory of withholding' to show that Ricardo does not base himself on this theory rest on an untenable interpretation of occasional remarks by him or on arbitrary additions to his ideas. We must, however, admit that the theory of withholding was not expressed by Ricardo as clearly as one might wish, whilst Marx succeeded in giving a clear and unequivocal expression to the view of the origin of profit which lies at the basis of this theory' (1906/07, III: 472–3).

30 On the meaning and significance of Ricardo's concept of proportional wages, see Gehrke (2011).

31 See Okishio (1961).

32 For a more detailed discussion of von Bortkiewicz's essays, see Gehrke (2012). Von Bortkiewicz later also published a short rejoinder to a critical comment on his 1910/11 paper; see von Bortkiewicz (1919).

33 See Marx ([1861–63] 1989b: 53–4).

34 See Marx ([1861–63] 1989b: 226–7 and 419).

35 In the section 'Theories of Surplus Value. Adam Smith' in his economic manuscript of 1861–63, Marx explained his peculiar use of the term 'profit on capital' in the following terms: 'When I speak of surplus value, in relation to the total sum of capital advanced, as *profit on capital*, this is because the capitalist directly engaged in production *directly* appropriates the surplus labour, no matter under what categories he has subsequently to share this surplus value with the landowner or the lender of capital' ([1861–63] 1988: 392).

36 Marx also stressed this point (which nevertheless seems to have been generally ignored in discussions of his infamous 'law') in his economic manuscript of 1861–63: 'Incidentally, when speaking of the law of the falling rate of profit in the course of the development of capitalist production, we mean by profit the total sum of surplus value which is seized in the first place by the industrial capitalist, [irrespective of] how he may have to share this later with the money-lending capitalist (in the form of interest) and the landlord (in the form of rent). Thus here the rate of profit = $\frac{\text{Surplus value}}{\text{Capital advanced}}$' ([1861–63] 1989: 94). Compare also Marx's discussion of the

components into which the 'profit on capital' can be split up in section 1 of chapter 15 in vol. III of *Capital* ([1894] 1959: 241–6).

37 Some textual evidence for this claim is provided below. When discussing income distribution at the aggregate level, Marx always calculated the 'rate of ground-rent' *as a percentage of the total social capital* – in the same way as Ricardo had done in the famous table of the *Essay on Profits.*

38 As Marx pointed out, 'Ricardo's statement that "the labour of a million men in manufactures will always produce the *same value*" (…) is only right in the *one* case, where the total capital = the variable capital' ([1861–63] 1989a: 49). Note that Ricardo, in the passage quoted by Marx, explicitly refers to 'manufactures': according to Ricardo, the labour of a million men in agriculture will *not* always produce the same value, because the value of 'corn' is determined by the amount of labour which is needed at the agricultural margin.

39 See Marx [1861–63] 1989a: 254).

40 However, when Engels later changed the order of presentation in vol. III of *Capital*, he did so by following Marx's written advice from 1865; see Takenaga (2010: 8).

41 'One need not be of the opinion that there is a contradiction between the first two volumes and the third volume of *Capital*, and one does not even need to consider Marx's transformation of values into prices of production to have been erroneous, in order to arrive at the conclusion that Marx's theory of absolute ground-rent must be rejected' (von Bortkiewicz 1919: 255–6).

42 See, for instance, Samuelson (1992).

43 Georg von Charasoff (1877–1931) was born in Tbilisi, Georgia, into a wealthy family of Armenian origin. He first studied medicine in Moscow from 1895 to 1896, and then mathematics and theoretical physics in Heidelberg from 1896 to 1902, when he obtained a doctorate in mathematics. He then lived as an independent private scholar in Zurich and Lausanne from 1902 to 1915. From 1910 to 1912 he studied political economy with Heinrich Sieveking at the University of Zurich. In 1915, he returned to Tbilisi, where his intellectual fascinations turned away from economic theory to avant-garde poetry, psychoanalysis, and theoretical physics. Because he lost his property in the Russian revolution, he then earned his living as a professor of physics, first at the newly founded National University of Georgia in Tbilisi, and then in Baku (Azerbaidjan). He died in 1931 in an accident. For further biographical details, see Gehrke (2013).

44 In the preface to his second book, Charasoff informed his readers that he intended to supplement the two books with a third one, which was to bear the title 'Die Probleme der Produktion und der Verteilung', and which was to contain 'a thorough criticism of the subjective theory of value' (Charasoff 1910: XIV n.). Alas, this book was never published.

45 In the preface to his second book, Charasoff emphasized: 'With regard to the theory of the production equations and the production series developed by me I would like to point out that in this regard priority claims could be made for the contributions of K. Menger, Böhm Bawerk, Walras and others. I nevertheless regard the entire theory of production stages as my own, since I developed it entirely on my own already several years ago (when I had not yet any knowledge at all of the similar theories of the founders of the subjective method)' (1910: xiv).

References

Anon (1821) Review of D. Ricardo: On the Principles of Political Economy and Taxation, *Hermes oder kritisches Jahrbuch der Literatur*, No. XI, pp. 156–75. (C.E.M.).

Anon (1821) Review of D. Ricardo: On the Principles of Political Economy and Taxation, *Leipziger Literatur-Zeitung*, 1821, columns 2275–95.

Anon (1824) Review of J. Mill: Elemens [*sic*] d'économie politique, Paris 1823, *Leipziger Literatur-Zeitung*, 1824, columns 1077ff.

Baumstark, Eduard (ed.) (1837) *David Ricardo's Grundsätze der Volkswirthschaft und der Besteuerung*. Trans. Dr Edward Baumstark. Leipzig: Verlag von Wilhelm Engelmann. [German translation of 2nd English edn (1819)].

Baumstark, Edward (1838) *Volkswirtschaftliche Erläuterungen, vorzüglich über David Ricardo's System*. Leipzig: Verlag von Wilhelm Engelmann.

Blaug, M. (1987) Hermann, Friedrich Benedikt Wilhelm von. In J. Eatwell, M. Milgate and P. Newman (eds), *The New Palgrave. A Dictionary of Economics*, London, vol. 2, 639–640.

Böhm-Bawerk, Eugen von ([1884] 1921) *Kapital und Kapitalzins. I. Geschichte und Kritik der Kapitalzinstheorien*, 4th edn. Jena: Gustav Fischer.

——(1886/87) Grundzüge der Theorie des wirtschaftlichen Güterwerts, *Jahrbücher für Nationalökonomie und Statistik*, two instalments: 47, 1–82; 48, 477–541.

——(1890) Ein Zwischenwort zur Werttheorie, *Jahrbücher für Nationalökonomie und Statistik*, 21, 519–522.

——(1892) Wert, Kosten, und Grenznutzen, *Jahrbücher für Nationalökonomie und Statistik*, 3rd Series, 3, 321–367.

——(1896) Zum Abschluß des Marxschen Systems. In O. v. Boenigk (ed.), *Staatswirtschaftliche Arbeiten. Festgaben für Karl Knies*. Berlin: Haering.

Bortkiewicz, Ladislaus von (1906/1907) Wertrechnung und Preisrechnung im Marxschen System, *Archiv für Sozialwissenschaft und Sozialpolitik*, in three parts: vol. 23 (1906), pp. 1–50, vol. 25 (1907), pp. 10–51 and pp. 445–488. English translation of parts II and III as Bortkiewicz, L. (1952), Value and Price in the Marxian System, *International Economic Papers*, 2, 5–60.

——(1907) Zur Berichtigung der grundlegenden theoretischen Konstruktion von Marx im 3. Band des 'Kapital', *Jahrbücher für Nationalökonomie und Statistik*, 34, 319–335.

Bortkiewicz, L. von (1910–11) Die Rodbertus'sche Grundrententheorie und die Marx'sche Lehre von der absoluten Grundrente, *Archiv für die Geschichte des Sozialismus und der Arbeiterbewegung*, I, 1–40; II, 391–434.

——(1919) Zu den Grundrententheorien von Rodbertus und Marx, *Archiv für die Geschichte des Sozialismus und der Arbeiterbewegung*, 8, 248–257.

Brandt, Karl (1992) *Geschichte der deutschen Volkswirtschaftslehre. Band 1: Von der Scholastik bis zur klassischen Nationalökonomie*, Freiburg: Rudolf Haufe Verlag.

Brentano, Lujo (1888) *Die klassische Nationalökonomie*, Vortrag gehalten beim Antritt des Lehramts an der Universität Wien am 17. April 1888, Leipzig.

Charasoff, Georg von (1909) *Karl Marx über die menschliche und kapitalistische Wirtschaft: eine neue Darstellung seiner Lehre*, Berlin: H. Bondy.

——(1910) *Das System des Marxismus. Darstellung und Kritik*, Berlin: H. Bondy.

Diehl, Karl (1905) *Sozialwissenschaftliche Erläuterungen zu David Ricardos Grundgesetzen der Volkswirtschaft und Besteuerung*, 2 vols, Leipzig.

——(1908) Entwicklung der Wert- und Preistheorie im 19. Jahrhundert. In G. P. Altmann et al. (eds), *Die Entwicklung der deutschen Volkswirtschaftslehre im neunzehnten Jahrhundert. Gustav Schmoller zur siebzigsten Wiederkehr seines Geburtstags*, Part I. Leipzig: Duncker & Humblot.

Dietzel, Heinrich (1890) Die klassische Werttheorie und die Theorie vom Grenznutzen, *Jahrbücher für Nationalökonomie und Statistik*, New Series, 20, 561–606.

——(1891) Zur klassischen Wert- und Preistheorie, *Jahrbücher für Nationalökonomie und Statistik*, 3rd Series, 1, 685–707.

Dmitriev, Vladimir Karpovich ([1898] 1974) David Ricardo's theory of value. An attempt at a rigorous analysis. In V. K. Dmitriev, *Economic Essays on Value, Competition and Utility*, 1974. Cambridge: Cambridge University Press.

Gehrke, Christian (1998) Dmitriev, Vladimir Karpovich. In H. D. Kurz and N. Salvadori (eds), *The Elgar Companion to Classical Economics*, vol. I, 222–226.

——(2003) The Ricardo Effect: Its Meaning and Validity, *Economica*, 70, 143–158.

——(2011) 'Price of Wages': A Curious Phrase. In R. Ciccone, C. Gehrke and G. Mongiovi (eds), *Sraffa and Modern Economics*, vol. 1, London and New York: Routledge, pp. 405–422.

——(2012) Marx's critique of Ricardo's theory of rent: a re-assessment. In C. Gehrke, N. Salvadori, I. Steedman and R. Sturn (eds), *Classical Political Economy and Modern Theory. Essays in honour of Heinz D. Kurz*, London and New York: Routledge, pp. 51–84.

——(2013) Traces of the Life of a Georgian Intellectual: Georg von Charasoff in Heidelberg, Zurich and Lausanne, Paper presented at the International Conference 'The Pioneers of Linear Models of Production', 17–18 January 2013, University of Paris-Nanterre.

Gehrke, Christian and Heinz D. Kurz (2001) Say and Ricardo on Value and Distribution, *The European Journal of the History of Economic Thought*, 8(4), 449–486.

——(2006) Sraffa on von Bortkiewicz, *History of Political Economy*, 38(1), 91–149.

Gide, Charles and Charles Rist (1923) *Geschichte der volkswirtschaftlichen Lehrmeinungen*, Franz Oppenheimer (ed.), 3rd edn. Jena: Verlag von Gustav Fischer.

Hayek, Friedrich August von (1968) Introduction. In Carl Menger, *Grundsätze der Volkswirtschaftslehre*, first edn 1871, reprinted in C. Menger, *Gesammelte Werke*, vol. 1, second edn, edited and introduced by F. A. Hayek. Tübingen: J.C.B. Mohr.

Hennings, Klaus H. (1997) *The Austrian Theory of Value and Capital. Studies in the Life and Work of Eugen von Böhm-Bawerk*. Cheltenham: Edward Elgar.

Hermann, F.B.W. (1832) *Staatswirthschaftliche Untersuchungen*, Munich: Anton Weber.

——(1837) Review of J. Dutens: Philosophie d'economie politique (Paris 1835). *Gelehrte Anzeigen*, 5 (1837), columns 345–351 and 358–360.

——(1838) Review of 'Trades, Unions and Strikes', *Gelehrte Anzeigen*, 7 (1838), columns 199f., 201–8, and 215f.

Kautsky, Karl (1905) 'Einleitung' zu Karl Marx, *Theorien über den Mehrwert*, vol. 1. Stuttgart: Dietz Verlag.

Kudler, Joseph (1846) *Die Grundlehren der Volkswirtschaftslehre*, 2 vols. Vienna: Braumüller & Seidel.

Kurz, Heinz D. (1989) Die deutsche theoretische Nationalökonomie zu Beginn des 20. Jahrhunderts zwischen Klassik und Neoklassik. In B. Schefold (ed.), *Studien zur Entwicklung der ökonomischen Theorie*, vol. VIII. Berlin: Duncker & Humblot.

——(1995) Marginalism, Classicism and Socialism in the German-speaking Countries, 1871–1932. In I. Steedman (ed.), *Socialism and Marginalism in Economics 1870–1930*. London and New York: Routledge.

——(1998a) Classical Economics in German-speaking Countries. In H. D. Kurz and N. Salvadori (eds), *The Elgar Companion to Classical Economics*, vol. I, pp. 128–135.

——(1998b) Friedrich Benedikt Wilhelm Hermann on capital and profits, *The European Journal of the History of Economic Thought*, 5, 85–119.

McCulloch, John R. (1819) Review of D. Ricardo: On the Principles of Political Economy and Taxation, *Hermes oder kritisches Jahrbuch der Literatur*, No. I (1819), pp. LIff.

——(1831) *Grundsätze der Politischen Oekonomie nebst kurzer Darstellung des Ursprungs und Fortschrittes dieser Wissenschaft*, trans. G. M. von Weber. Stuttgart: Hallberger.

Marcet, Jane (1820) *Unterhaltungen über die National-Oeconomie, worin die Grundsätze dieser Wissenschaft vertraulich erklärt werden von der Verfasserin der Unterhaltungen über die Chemie*. Ulm: Ebner.

Martineau, Harriet (1834) *Erläuterungen der Staatswirthschaftslehre durch allgemein verständliche Erzählungen*. Leipzig: Baumgärtner.

Marx, Karl ([1905–10] 1968) *Theorien über den Mehrwert*, Karl Kautsky (ed.), MEW, Bd. 26 (1–3), Berlin.

——([1894] 1959) *Capital*, vol. III, Moscow: Progress Publishers. English translation of *Das Kapital*, vol. III, Hamburg, 1894: Meissner.

——([1857–58] 1974) *Grundrisse der Kritik der Politischen Ökonomie (Rohentwurf)*, 2nd edn (1st edn 1953). Berlin: Dietz Verlag.

——([1861–63] 1988) *Economic Manuscript of 1861–63. A Contribution to the Critique of Political Economy ['Theories of Surplus Value']*, in Karl Marx, Frederick Engels: *Collected Works*, vol. 30. New York: International Publishers.

——([1861–63] 1989a) *Economic Manuscript of 1861–63. A Contribution to the Critique of Political Economy ['Theories of Surplus Value']*, in Karl Marx, Frederick Engels: *Collected Works*, vol. 31, New York: International Publishers.

——([1861–63] 1989b) *Economic Manuscript of 1861–63. A Contribution to the Critique of Political Economy ['Theories of Surplus Value']*, in Karl Marx, Frederick Engels: *Collected Works*, vol. 32, New York: International Publishers.

Marx, Karl and Frederick Engels ([1860–64] 1985) Letters 1860–1864, in Karl Marx, Frederick Engels: *Collected Works*, vol. 42, New York: International Publishers.

Mill, James (1824) *Elemente der Nationalökonomie*, übersetzt von A. L. Jakob. Mit Zusätzen vom Staatsrathe [Ludwig Heinrich] von Jakob. Halle: Kümmel.

Mombert, Paul (1919) *Soziale und wirtschaftspolitische Anschauungen in Deutschland von Beginn des 19. Jahrhunderts bis zur Gegenwart*. Leipzig: Quelle and Mayer.

Negishi, Takashi (1985) *Economic Theories in Non-Walrasian Tradition*, Cambridge: Cambridge University Press.

Okishio, Nobuo (1961) Technical Change and the Rate of Profit, *Kobe University Economic Review*, 7, 86–96.

Rau, Karl-Heinrich (1826–32) *Lehrbuch der Politischen Ökonomie*. Vol. I: *Grundsätze der Volkswirtschaftslehre*, Heidelberg 1826; Vol. II: *Grundsätze der Volkswirtschaftspflege*, Heidelberg 1828, Vol. III: *Grundsätze der Finanzwissenschaft*, Heidelberg 1832.

——(1837) *Lehrbuch der Politischen Ökonomie*. Vol. I: *Grundsätze der Volkswirtschaftslehre*, 3rd edn, Heidelberg.

——(1847) *Lehrbuch der Politischen Ökonomie*. Vol. I: *Grundsätze der Volkswirtschaftslehre*, 5th edn, Heidelberg.

Ricardo, David (1819a) *On the Principles of Political Economy and Taxation*, 2nd edn. London: John Murray.

——(1819b) *Des Principes de l'Économie politique, et de l'impôt*, traduit de l'anglais par F.S. Constâncio, D.M., etc.; avec des notes explicatives et critiques, par M. Jean-Baptiste Say. Paris: J.P. Aillaud. [French translation of 1st English edn (1817)].

——(1821) *Die Grundsätze der Politischen Ökonomie oder der Staatswirtschaft und der Besteuerung*. Weimar: Verlag des Gr.H.S. priv. Landes-Industrie-Comptoirs. [German translation of 1st English edition (1817).]

——(1837) *David Ricardo's Grundsätze der Volkswirthschaft und der Besteuerung*. Trans. Dr Edward Baumstark. Leipzig: Verlag von Wilhelm Engelmann. [German translation of 2nd English edn (1819)].

——(1877) *David Ricardo's Grundgesetze der Volkswirtschaft und Besteuerung*. Trans. Dr Edward Baumstark. Leipzig: Verlag von Wilhelm Engelmann. [German translation of 3rd English edn (1821)].

——(1905) *Grundsätze der Volkswirtschaft und Besteuerung*, aus dem englischen Original, und zwar nach der Ausgabe letzter Hand (3. Auflage 1821), ins Deutsche übertragen von Dr. Ottomar Thiele und eingeleitet von Professor Dr. Heinrich Waentig, Jena: Verlag von Gustav Fischer.

——([1821] 1951–73) *On the Principles of Political Economy and Taxation*. First edn 1817, 2nd edn 1819, 3rd edn 1821. Vol. I of *The Works and Correspondence of David Ricardo*. Piero Sraffa (ed.) in collaboration with M. H. Dobb. Cambridge: Cambridge University Press.

Rodbertus, Carl ([1837] 1972) *Die Forderungen der arbeitenden Klassen*. In C. Rodbertus (1972), *Gesammelte Werke und Briefe*, Abteilung I, Osnabrück.

——([1840] 1972) Brief an J.H. von Thünen vom 29.9.1840. In C. Rodbertus (1972), *Gesammelte Werke und Briefe*, Abteilung IV, Osnabrück, pp. 3–4.

——([1842] 1972) *Zur Erkenntnis unserer staatswirtschaftlichen Zustände. Heft 1: Fünf Theoreme*. In C. Rodbertus (1972), *Gesammelte Werke und Briefe*, Abteilung I, Osnabrück.

——(1851) *Soziale Briefe an v. Kirchmann. Dritter Brief: Widerlegung der Ricardo'schen Lehre von der Grundrente und Begründung einer neuen Rententheorie*. Berlin: Allgemeine Deutsche Verlagsanstalt.

Roscher, Wilhelm (1874) *Geschichte der National-Oekonomik in Deutschland*, Munich and Berlin: Oldenbourg.

——(1878) Review of the second edition of Baumstark's German translation of Ricardo's *Principles*, *Literarisches Centralblatt*, 19–22.

Samuelson, Paul A. (1992) Marx on Rent: A Failure to Transform Correctly, *Journal of the History of Economic Thought*, 14, 143–167.

Sartorius, Georg (1820) Review of 'D. Ricardo: On the Principles of Political Economy and Taxation', *Göttingische gelehrte Anzeigen*, Jg. 1820, pp. 681ff.

Say, Jean-Baptiste (1818) *Darstellung der Nationalökonomie und der Staatswirtschaft*, 2 vols, Heidelberg.

——(1819) Notes explicatives et critiques. In Ricardo, David (1819), *Des Principes de l'Économie politique, et de l'impôt*. Paris: J.P. Aillaud.

——(1829–30) *Vollständiges Handbuch der Nationalökonomie*, 6 vols, Stuttgart.

Schachtschabel, Hans Georg (1971) *Geschichte der volkswirtschaftlichen Lehrmeinungen*. Stuttgart and Düsseldorf: Kohlhammer.

Scherf, Harald (ed.) (1986) *Deutsche Nationalökonomie zu Beginn des 19. Jahrhunderts, Studien zur ökonomischen Theorie* V. Berlin: Duncker & Humblot.

Schmoller, Gustav (1900/1904) *Grundriss der Allgemeinen Volkswirtschaftslehre*, 2 vols, Munich and Leipzig.

Schumpeter, Joseph A. (1914) Epochen der Dogmen- und Methodengeschichte. In M. Weber et al. (eds), *Grundriß der Sozialökonomik*, I. Abteilung, Tübingen, pp. 19–124.

——(1954) *History of Economic Analysis*. London: Allen & Unwin.

Takenaga, Susumu (2010) Marx's theory on the ground-rent in the mid-1860s. A comparative study of excerpt notes, letters, manuscripts of 1861–63 and Part VI of Book III of *Capital*. Paper presented at the 14th Annual Conference of the European Society for the History of Economic Thought at the University of Amsterdam, Amsterdam, the Netherlands, 25–28 March 2010.

Thünen, Johann Heinrich von (1826/1850) *Der isolirte Staat in Beziehung auf Landwirtschaft und Nationalökonomie*, Theil 1 (Hamburg, 1826) and Theil 2 (Rostock, 1850), Jena.

Torrens, Robert ([1820] 1826) *An Essay on the Influence of the External Corn Trade upon the Production and Distribution of National Wealth*, 3rd edn. London: Hatchard.

Waentig, Heinrich (1905) Ricardo. In David Ricardo, *Grundsätze der Volkswirtschaft und Besteuerung*, aus dem englischen Original, und zwar nach der Ausgabe letzter Hand (3. Auflage 1821), ins Deutsche übertragen von Dr. Ottomar Thiele und eingeleitet von Professor Dr. Heinrich Waentig. Jena: Verlag von Gustav Fischer.

——(1921) Einleitung. In David Ricardo, *Grundsätze der Volkswirtschaft und Besteuerung*, aus dem englischen Original, und zwar nach der Ausgabe letzter Hand (3. Auflage 1821), ins Deutsche übertragen von Dr. Ottomar Thiele und eingeleitet von Professor Dr. Heinrich Waentig. Jena: Verlag von Gustav Fischer.

Weinberger, Otto (1925) Friedrich Benedikt Wilhelm Hermann, *Zeitschrift für die gesamte Staatswissenschaft*, 79, 464–519.

Whewell, William (1831) Mathematical Exposition of some of the Leading Doctrines in Mr. Ricardo's 'Principles of Political Economy and Taxation', *Transactions of the Cambridge Philosophical Society*, 1–44.

Wicksell, Knut ([1893] 1954) *Value, Capital and Rent*, English translation of *Über Wert, Kapital und Rente nach den neueren nationalökonomischen Theorien*. London: George Allen & Unwin (Reprint by A. M. Kelley, New York 1970).

——([1901] 1934) *Lectures on Political Economy*, vol. I, English translation of the Swedish original (1901). London: Routledge & Sons.

3 The diffusion of Ricardo and classical political economy in Portugal

José Luís Cardoso

1. Introduction

It is commonly acknowledged that Adam Smith and Jean-Baptiste Say were the most influent authors in the formation and institutionalization of political economy in Portugal throughout the period 1776 to 1848. When compared with these two big names, the influence of David Ricardo seems almost vanished. This predominance of both Smith and Say notwithstanding, it is nevertheless worth studying how Ricardo was directly or indirectly read and commented upon by Portuguese contemporary authors.

This paper aims at presenting and discussing the signs of the limited diffusion and appropriation of Ricardo's thought in Portugal throughout the first half of the nineteenth century. It also tries to explain the reasons for such a reduced influence. Though the paper does not cover the development of economic discourse after 1850, it should be pointed out that, having lost the opportunity to be influential during the period of the hegemony of classical economics, Ricardo's thought and Ricardian economics alike have not gained ground for later diffusion and assimilation among Portuguese economists in other recent periods.

The paper begins with a brief summary of Smith's and Say's influences in Portugal and follows with a descriptive account of the reading of Ricardo during the period under analysis. Given the relevance usually granted to the work of Solano Constâncio, the paper devotes a privileged focus on the contributions of this author to the development of a critical view concerning the alleged universal and abstract principles of political economy usually associated to Ricardo and Ricardian economics.

2. Smithian antecedents

At the very beginning of the emergence and development of political economy in Portugal, the work of Adam Smith receives special consideration from his contemporaries. Smith's influence occurs in the enlightened scenario of the last decades of the eighteenth century and provides both appropriate and useful arguments to reinforce the ongoing reforms designed to overcome some inefficiencies stemming from the Portuguese ancien regime economy and society. The novelty of political economy discourse provided by Smith notwithstanding, it is worth noting that the reading and assessment of the *Wealth of Nations* goes hand in hand with other simultaneous influences, namely the French physiocrats and some kind of late heterodox mercantilists.

The mercantile type of economic actions and policies, directed by the Marquis of Pombal between 1750 and 1777, gave a keen stimulus to commercial and industrial growth and therefore represented a legacy that could not easily be dismissed. A prudent, wise strategy assuring the success of a challenging programme of reforms implied that they should be accomplished on the basis of the previous policies undertaken. The new issue was the defence of a greater freedom of action for economic agents by repealing the prevailing regulatory policies, though without questioning the established political system of enlightened despotism.

Adam Smith was thus used in Portugal as an authority argument to illustrate the need for, and to emphasise the urgency of, some economic reforms. The main authors receptive to Smith's message over the period 1776–1808 – especially Rodrigo Souza Coutinho, Joaquim Rodrigues de Brito and José da Silva Lisboa – played important roles and functions within the economic and financial public administration. They paved the way towards an institutional awareness of how political economy could help to implement an economic, as well as political, process of modernization. The fight against the entail of land property, the defence of free competition in the grain market, the revocation of monopolist practices and exclusive privileges in both commerce and manufactures, and the overcoming of all kinds of obstacles to efficient resource allocation – namely those arising from the chaotic ancien regime tax system – represent the leading subjects under discussion for which the reading of the *Wealth of Nations* could be useful.

The diffusion and assimilation of Smith's ideas was particularly relevant in Brazil, where the first Portuguese translation was published in 1811–12 (with the omission of Book V and half of Books I and IV). It was not by chance that the publication took place in Rio de Janeiro, because it is clear from the translator's preface that the acknowledged reason for the translation and study of the *Wealth of Nations* was its doctrinal blueprint, encouraging the liberalization of economic relations between Portugal and her most important colony, thus fostering an autonomous development of the Brazilian economy and closer trade relations between Brazil and Great Britain.

Nevertheless, Smith's direct influence was challenged when the work of Jean-Baptiste Say became known in the intellectual and political milieu. One of the reasons for his remarkable impact was Say's attitude towards the role played by industry in economic development, an aspect that was especially grasped by the Portuguese Acúrsio das Neves in the early 1820s. But the reception of Say's work has primarily served the purpose for transforming political economy into a language that could be spoken to a broader audience, as a powerful instrument that could become an important element in general education, as well as a scientific, persuasive argument fostering economic and political reforms.

Say's work was abridged and very closely followed by Forjaz de Sampaio in 1839, the author of one of the first textbooks on political economy taught at the Faculty of Law at the University of Coimbra. The diffusion of J.-B. Say's work has very often been merged with the French edition – promoted by Say himself in 1824 – of the *Cours d'Économie Politique* by Heinrich Storch. An explanation for the active sympathy that the Portuguese authors ascribed to this German-Russian political economist may be found in the permanent search for the historical relativization and the national contextualization of abstract principles of political economy.

The concern with observable, concrete circumstances, and the rejection of general laws designed in and for different social, economic and historical conditions, have also been corresponded by other contemporary schools diverging from mainstream classical political economy, as regards the obedience to a rigid theoretical framework. Bearing this in mind, it is easy to understand two main features of the development of classical political economy in Portugal up to 1860: the reduced influence of Ricardian economics, and the affinity with heterodox, critical currents of economic thought.[1]

3. Ricardo's influence

The name and work of David Ricardo immediately suggest two allusions or reminiscences associating him to Portugal: his descent from a Jewish family of Portuguese origin, and the fact that he used Portugal as an illustration for the famous comparative advantage cloth-and-wine trade model between Portugal and England.

As for the first point, Ricardo's Jewish descendency has been definitely established and can be traced back and documented up to five generations of his family. After leaving Portugal by the end of the sixteenth century, Ricardo's ancestors lived in Livorno and Amsterdam. His father Abraham Israel Ricardo was the first member of the family to establish a business activity in London, where he pursued a successful career as a stockbroker.[2]

As far as the international trade example is concerned, it is more than obvious that Portugal is a mere element serving an abstract model conceived to argue in favour of the advantages resulting from productive specialization in a context of free trade operating in accordance to the rules of the international division of labour. Portugal as a country could well have a place in Ricardo's heart. However, in the present case it is likely that the Portuguese example was taken to keep in line with the example given by Adam Smith when discussing the trade relations between Portugal and England ruled by the mercantilist Methuen Treaty of 1703, which established the privileged conditions that each of the countries had in order to place their main products in each other's markets (Portuguese wine in England and English cloth in Portugal).

It is therefore apparent that none of these features associated with Ricardo's name and fame implied any special appeal – in a positive or negative way – to the study and dissemination of Ricardo's thought in Portugal. Ricardo's *Principles* of *Political Economy and Taxation* would only be translated in Portugal in 1975.[3] Before that, the single contact of Portuguese readers with Ricardo's own writings was the publication of the chapters on value and on rent, extracted from the *Principles* with a brief biographic note and the translation of the preface by Edward Carter K. Gonner to the 1919 edition (Ricardo 1938a and Ricardo 1938b). The first Portuguese translation of these two chapters also includes the notes by Gonner and the original notes by J.-B. Say to the first French translation of the *Principles* (Ricardo 1819).

This late and scarce diffusion of Ricardo's work does not mean, however, that he was not respected or acknowledged by his Portuguese contemporaries. In what follows, a brief description will be made of the main references to Ricardo that can be found in Portuguese economic literature of the first half of the nineteenth century.

The first reference to Ricardo is by José da Silva Lisboa in 1819. At the very beginning of his book, this Portuguese author born in Brazil acknowledges and accepts the notion put forward by Ricardo in the preface to the *Principles*, according to which the principal problem in political economy is to determine the laws which regulate the distribution of the produce of earth in three different shares under the form of rent, profit and wages (Lisboa 1819–1820, 7). One can also find scattered references to Ricardo's admiration of Smith, which did not prevent Ricardo from criticizing several aspects of Smith's work, namely in what refers to the concept of wealth and to the notion of labour as the source of value (ibid., 62, 94, 138 and 155). There is no further theoretical discussion and Ricardo is only quoted en passant with regard to the fertility of the soil as a basic condition to increase production (ibid., 117). Finally, it should be noted that Silva Lisboa is also aware of the debates that began around Ricardo's contributions as they were subject to discussion by Sismondi and Malthus (ibid., 79, 250 and 268).

One interesting reference to Ricardo is also given by Manuel de Almeida in 1821 when referring to the advantages and benefits of the use of paper money in monetary circulation. This is the first and very last time that Ricardo's monetary ideas are given full consideration by a Portuguese reader of his time, who praises Ricardo in the following terms:

> Mr. David Ricardo, who is considered throughout Europe as the man who better understands the theory and practice of money, has shown in a brochure entitled *Proposals for an Economical and Secure Currency*, London, 1816, that the all entire currency of a country could without any inconvenience (provided that there could be a sufficient guarantee of good administration of that country) be replaced by paper-money, and therefore a commodity with no value (as the paper itself is) could in its turn achieve the task of a costly and uneasy metal whose

metallic properties are useless when the metal is used as currency. (Almeida 1821, 46)

Manuel de Almeida was a priest and a member of the first Portuguese Parliament which was set up in the aftermath of the liberal revolution of 1820. One of the proposals he brought to the Parliament was the launching of a course in political economy, a science that could help the modernization of Portuguese economy and society. In 1828 a political revolt took over the liberal movement and the absolutist regime was restored. It was only at the end of the political turmoil and civil war (between 1832 and 1834), that the course of political economy was to be established at the Faculty of Law at the University of Coimbra in 1836.

One of the authors who exerted a strong influence in the structuring of this course on political economy was José Ferreira Borges, who had published two important books on political economy and on taxation and public finance during his exile in London on the occasion of the absolutist counter-revolution (Borges 1831 and Borges 1834). Until 1839 these two books were the main reading list for University students, together with the translation of J.-B. Say's *Catéchisme d'économie politique* (Say 1822), which had also a French print at Coimbra (Say 1837). Borges provides clear evidence of his reading of Ricardo, though his greatest praise was reserved for Smith and Say. The main references to Ricardo concern the general approval of the theory of differential rent and the implicit acceptance of a principle of diminishing returns in agriculture (Borges 1831–34, 17–20, 93, 231). The plea for technical progress in agriculture and for freedom in international trade relations are also important aspects of Ricardo's contributions explicitly supported by Borges (ibid., 93, 96–97). Trying to argue in favour of low prices in wage goods, Borges reveals special care when dealing with the taxation principles that should be designed in order to prevent price increases. In this context he fights against ancient regime taxes and calls for the authority of Ricardo to argue in defence of a fiscal policy aiming at not jeopardizing the process of capital accumulation (ibid., 101–102). He was also in favour of a firm control of public debt and quotes Ricardo in this regard (ibid., 123). Finally, it is worth mentioning Borges's discussion of some Ricardian themes on value theory, namely the search for an invariable measure of value and the notion of the relative value of money (ibid., 177–178, 262, 269). However, his critical appraisal of Ricardo's contribution is also disclosed when Borges regrets the fact that Ricardo did not take into account the role of utility in the determination of value (ibid., 169).

The institutionalization of the teaching of political economy at the University of Coimbra was largely due to the efforts of the holder of the *catedra* between 1839 and 1871, Adrião Forjaz de Sampaio, an author already mentioned above to illustrate the appropriation of Smith's and Say's thought in Portugal. The references of Sampaio to Ricardo are indeed quite scarce and focused on minor aspects of taxation policy (Sampaio 1839, 65). In one of his later textbooks, however, Sampaio develops a more critical stance and points out what he considers to be the incomplete theory of prices and cost of production elaborated by Ricardo (Sampaio 1853, 224). Another proof of his dissociation from Ricardo is the global assessment of the works of the English political economists Ricardo, Mill and McCullock which 'differ substantially on its abstraction and dryness from the humanity, interest with the fate of the working classes and sweetness of the writings of Droz, Sismondi, Rossi, Bargemont, Chevalier, etc.' (ibid., 152).

The little attention afforded to Ricardo had its counterpart in the attractiveness of the authors of the so-called French liberal school. But the key point to be emphasized is the difficulty in accepting the abstract and dry principles of political economy that were a hallmark of Ricardo's work. Incidentally, it was precisely one of the key features of his Portuguese-Jewish intellectual background, i.e., the special attraction towards abstract reasoning and deductive method that caused a reaction against the diffusion of his thought among contemporary Portuguese political economists.[4] I shall turn to this point later on.

From these short notes we may conclude that the most consistent analytical reference to Ricardo in Portuguese economic literature during the first half of the nineteenth century is provided by Ferreira Borges, who had lived in London where he certainly had an opportunity to become acquainted with political economy debates, at both the theoretical and policy levels. Another Portuguese émigré deserving attention is Silvestre Pinheiro Ferreira, who edited an abridged version of McCulloch's *Principles of Political Economy* in 1839 for teaching purposes in intermediate schools. This abridged compendium was published jointly with a Portuguese translation that was explicitly meant to address Portuguese and Spanish students of a private college in Paris.

While abroad, these Portuguese émigrés acted as sort of foreign correspondents in cultural and scientific matters, either by writing books, providing private information to their Portuguese friends, or plainly by editing journals aimed at the cultural enlightening of an enlarged Portuguese audience. Their interest on political economy issues was by and large much greater than the interest shown by authors living and writing in their own country. This rule is again made obvious when we look at the example provided by Francisco Solano Constâncio, undoubtedly the author who deserves a greater consideration when one discusses the spread of classical political economy within the Portuguese- speaking community.[5]

4. The case of Constâncio

Constâncio (1777–1846) is well known as the author of the translations of Ricardo's *Principles* and of Malthus's *Principles* into French (Ricardo 1819; Malthus 1820).[6] Readers acquainted with Portuguese and attracted by the theoretical debates and economic policy controversies of the early 1820s may also have noticed that Constâncio published some interesting articles concerning the so-called Say's law of markets and the debates on over-production and general gluts (Constâncio 1820 and Constâncio 1821a). These articles appeared in a bi-monthly journal written in Portuguese, co-edited by Constâncio and published in Paris. The main purpose of this journal was twofold: on the one hand, it tried to respond to the intellectual curiosity of the knowledgeable Portuguese public, which was looking forward to discovering the innovations and advances in knowledge in a variety of fields of scientific inquiry; on the other hand, it was designed to meet the practical needs of the common reader hoping to benefit from the application of science in the solution of everyday problems. In this regard, the role played by political economy was particularly noteworthy.[7]

A personal contact between Constâncio and Say is likely to have occurred for the preparation of the French translation of Ricardo's *Principles*, which included several notes by Say. The publication would have not been possible without the collaboration between the Portuguese and the French authors, even admitting that the collaboration was endorsed by the publisher J. P. Aillaud. However, there are no traces of any correspondence between them and Say has never referred to Constâncio in his writings. The presumption that there was a friendly relationship between them is testified by Constâncio himself when he explicitly refers to Say as his 'estimable et savant ami' in the foreword to the French translation of Malthus' *Principles* (Malthus 1820, 2). Some years later, when reviewing a book by Louis Say – Jean-Baptiste's brother – Constâncio tells us that 'I was a friend of J.-B. Say and I have always highly considered his character, reasoning and patriotism' (in Constâncio 1995, 283).

In a letter to Mill dated of 12 December 1818, Ricardo implicitly refers to the connection between the translator and the author of the notes:

> Murray writes to me that he has received a copy of a translation of my book into French, with copious notes – he would have sent it to me, but he thought I should receive a copy through the means of Say. I fear that Say is not quite friendly towards me, but I am sure he is not just if he is otherwise. (Ricardo, *Works*, Vol. VII, 361)

Malthus would also have the opportunity to refer to the French translator of his *Principles*, in not quite happy terms, in a letter to Ricardo dated of 28 August 1820:

> Generally speaking the French read but little political economy […]. The bookseller who undertook the translation of your work [J.P. Aillaud] told me that he had sold 900 copies, which under all the circumstances is I think a favourable report. My book was translating. I saw a few sheets, and fear it will not be very well done. (Ricardo, *Works*, Vol. VIII, 225)

The alleged affable liaison between Constâncio and Say may explain why it seems to have been so important for Constâncio to emphasize his disagreement with both Ricardo and Malthus, even when his line of reasoning seemed not to be so distant from Malthus's vision on the status of political economy as a field of scientific inquiry.

In the foreword to the translation of Malthus' book, Constâncio refers to the notes by his friend J.-B. Say as conveying a deliberate distance from Ricardo's work, in particular with regard to the theories of value and rent. Though acknowledging the importance of Ricardo's *Principles* that had greatly contributed to the advance of knowledge in political economy, Constâncio also stressed that Ricardo's theories had prompted some controversy. Therefore, by translating Malthus' *Principles*, he was above all attempting to present fresh arguments to overturn the predominant Ricardian system. However, in doing so, Constâncio could not avoid attacking Malthus as well. This attitude towards Malthus was quite usual at that time, due to the animosity generated either by his frequently misunderstood theory of population, or by his wholehearted defence of the economic, social and political interests of those social classes with high revenues, especially landlords.

The appeal to taking into account the distinctive nature of national realities is a permanent feature of his critique of the abstract principles of political economy. Constâncio was not motivated by a strict nationalist approach, nor was he interested in promoting conceptual principles of national identity. Yet he tried to elucidate that there is an obvious interaction between ideas related to the functioning of economic life and the very nature of institutions and social arrangements that shape national realities and their distinctiveness. In other terms, he could not overlook the specific environment to which general assumptions and principles about both the interpretation of economic phenomena and the implementation of economic policies could be applied.

This does not mean that Constâncio was against theoretical approaches to political economy. His translations of Ricardo's and Malthus's *Principles*, as well as his articles on the Malthus–Say debate on the *loi des débouchés*, provide robust evidence of both his keen interest and firm knowledge of the theoretical toolbox of the science he was dealing with. However, it was precisely this activity as translator and reviewer that made it possible for Constâncio to develop a new awareness of the limits to the application of general abstract principles of political economy. In this sense, Constâncio's methodological position on the limitations of scientific discourse could even be validated through an approval of Malthus's considerations on the scope and shortcomings of political economy:

> His [Malthus's] purpose is to show that those wishing to use science in a practical way should never adopt any general rules without consulting the relevant experience, nor should they use these rules without taking into account the particular circumstances of the case in mind. All his work is an attempt to prove that political economy is a science of proportions, and that it does not embody absolute truths (Constâncio 1820) [in Constâncio 1995, 152].

The gradual withdrawal of Constâncio from the abstract, allegedly universal principles of political economy, and the consequent acceptance of political economy as a 'science of proportions', was considerably reinforced during his stay in the United States between 1823 and 1826. In fact, the close contact with the American economic literature of this period – as well as the opportunity to follow economic policy debates on the system of tariffs, incentives and protection to industry, taxes and contributions, public debt and economic development – has acted as an essential tonic to stimulate Constâncio's vision on the instruments and conditions that the government should handle in order to promote the progress of the nation.

Constâncio paid tribute and acknowledged the intellectual legacy received from Franklin, Hamilton and Carey, namely in the articles that he published after his return to Europe. In one of these articles, concerning the topic of the balance of trade, Constâncio has jointly presented lengthy quotations from early eighteenth-century Portuguese mercantilists and from Mathew Carey – one of the champions of American protectionism in the 1820s and the 1830s – establishing a link and a convergence of opinions regarding the need to protect infant industries and the necessity to embrace all the economic sectors with the wise mission of the enlightened legislator. For Constâncio, the important issue was to implement economic policies that would contribute to the development of a national economy. With this purpose in mind any author could be quoted, provided that the reader would be served with sound reasons to understand that protection was a powerful means of advancing the interests of all members of the community.

The historical reconstitution of these influences in Constâncio's thought allows for the acknowledgement of an interesting similarity between the Portuguese author and Friedrich List, who has undoubtedly played a major role with his critique of the cosmopolitan nature of classical political economy and as a wholehearted defender of a national system of political economy. List himself had also spent a few years of his life on American soil, between 1825 and 1832. Besides this similar journey, both authors have explicitly shown their debt to the American protectionist literature in the formation of their system of thought, especially as regards the development of arguments in favour of industrial protection. While List's work has known a widespread diffusion and influence in many European circles, there is no doubt that Constâncio firstly drew attention to the same issues that were to place List as a central figure in the critical appraisal of the shortcomings of classical political economy.

If it is clear that the strengthening of nationalist and protectionist arguments was largely favoured by contact with American economic literature, the rise of Constâncio's social consciousness and his concern with the issues of social justice, inequity and social imbalance, came through the reading of Sismondi.

For Constâncio, whose views on these issues were clearly borrowed from Sismondi, the social and institutional structure inherent to the industrial system of capitalism had innumerable shortcomings – the most important being the growing differences and conflicts between social groups – which could only be relieved through a better, more equitable distribution of property. He therefore considers that 'the least possible inequality resulting from individuals sharing goods as well as sacrifices is or should be the aim of all political institutions right from their very foundation' (1820, 151); or even that 'a State is all the happier and wealthier the greater the number of property owners, or, which is exactly the same, the lower the concentration of property in the hands of a few' (1821a, 170). From this line of thought, we can easily detect a consistent argument in favour of a model of society founded on a system of small-scale property ownership; and we can also realise how far Constâncio was now moving from the mainstream, canonical discourse of classical political economy.

Sismondi was particularly helpful in offering Constâncio a general interpretation of the problems arising from the unequal distribution of income and from the undesirable consequences of the division of labour. From 1838 onwards, one may notice the growing importance of Sismondi's influence, especially in a couple of articles on the causes of the commercial crisis and the increasing poverty and helplessness of a vast section of industrial workers. As far as alternative, concrete solutions are concerned, two main issues have to be taken into account. First, Constâncio does not hesitate to recommend an economic policy based on raising taxes on luxury goods and inherited wealth, with a consequent attack on entails and primogeniture rights. Second, he recommends the formation of cooperative associations of industrial capital and labour, intentionally conceived to effect a real redistribution of capital amongst a large number of people. Such associations would also promote a better distribution of profits and economic surplus, which in turn would check the trend towards the formation of an all-powerful industrial and financial elite and would encourage 'equality of means, ownership, social conditions and rights' (Constâncio 1838, 294).

In keeping with these ideas, he praises the association experiences promoted by Robert Owen and generously favours the creation of a model of social organisation capable of providing absolute human happiness. Nevertheless, while propounding these beliefs, he also demonstrates how difficult it is to implement them in practical terms, and he sometimes denotes a certain preference for more radical solutions which would imply a process of social revolution (Constâncio 1838, 296).

These issues relating to the social conditions of the lower classes were already present in his writings of the 1820s. However, renewed attention was given in the last two periodicals he edited (Constâncio 1841a; 1841b), taking into account both the qualitative and quantitative data available about the economic and social situation in England, which was actually the country that provided most opportunities for such studies.

When discussing the deeper causes of the social unrest inherent to the development of industrial societies, Constâncio is coherent in blaming the unequal distribution of property, capital and revenue. This attitude contradicts prevailing contemporary opinion, according to which misery and poverty were partially or largely the consequence of technological unemployment resulting from the substitution of machinery for labour. It is most certain that Constâncio also believed that the growth in productive power as a result of technological progress would give rise to an expansion of output that would ultimately lead to an increase in the value and remuneration of fixed capital. Despite this, Constâncio saw no reason to condemn machinery itself and therefore criticised Sismondi – and implicitly the Barton–Ricardian tradition on the machinery question – for

> considering that the wretched situation of workers results from the introduction of machinery, which saves labour and works with great perfection. This is a dreadful error, and the suppression of machines would surely be one of the greatest disasters facing the nations that use them. (Constâncio 1838, 316)

In summing up this overall presentation of the writings of the Portuguese author Constâncio, we may now conclude that – despite having first started to reflect upon social and economic issues as a result of his close contact with some of the most relevant authors and books in the classical canon of political economy – he never revealed any form of unconditional adherence to this school of thought. Despite his important role as a translator into French and publicist of classical economics, Constâncio gradually moved away from a theoretical and doctrinal model that had difficulties in incorporating two important elements that were to become the essential ingredients of his economic and social reasoning: i) the specific problems pertaining to concrete national economic realities; and ii) the social consequences resulting from economic growth in general and from industrial growth in particular.

The way in which Constâncio carefully contextualises the adoption of abstract principles is a very distinctive and coherent feature of all his writings. In this respect, Constâncio does not agree with the approach provided by Say's heirs and disciples, who have insisted of the need for a clear separation between political economy as a science and as an art of government. In fact, Constâncio's conceptualisation of political economy as a science of proportions, as a practical science, implied that it could not be reduced to mere guiding principles, as far as policy prescriptions were concerned. On the contrary, political economy was conceived as a means to overcome the practical problems of the time. According to his view, the necessary contextualisation of political economy essentially meant that there are neither abstract paths nor any perfectly and unanimously agreed routes to be followed in building up our knowledge about economic life. In his own words:

> political economy is a science, not one that is made up of abstractions, but rather a practical science, whose principles cannot be judged on an

> absolute basis, but only by comparing the situation of each nation with the situation of the others. (Constâncio 1821b, 208)

This process of relativization – applied to the level of knowledge reached by the new science of political economy – is clearly revealed by his deliberate eclecticism, which leads him to the selective reading and application of the message transmitted by the authors who most helped to shape his economic thought: Ricardo, Malthus, Say and Sismondi are either acclaimed or opposed and Constâncio establishes a non-exclusive and cooperative relationship with their writings, depending on the particular aims of an economic discourse that is supposed to serve as an instrument for innovation and modernisation. After all, Constâncio does no more than interpret this changeable, erratic geometry of alliances and divergences – both on theoretical and political grounds – between protagonists belonging to the same school of thought.

In conjunction with his clear intuition and accurate perception of those problems that require careful analysis and eventual solutions, Constâncio's attitude against conventional orthodoxy encouraged him to adopt innovative approaches to social and economic issues. His critical reading frequently developed along lines which undoubtedly went far beyond his interest in the original message contained in his sources. This was the case, for example, with Sismondi and Owen, whose influence was supplanted by Constâncio's belief in the ability of the lower, oppressed classes to overcome the prevailing status quo.

His contribution to the critical spread and assimilation of political economy at a European level was outstanding – both through his translations and participation in seminal debates – especially if we remember that political economy was just one of the many fields of his intellectual inquiry. In that respect, the scope of his work stretches far beyond the narrow limits of Portuguese economic thought. It clearly belongs to the wider realm of contributions made towards the development of classical political economy and its criticism, a field of research where the conventional approach has almost always overlooked the extent of its own theoretical impact in different geographical and linguistic areas.

5. Concluding remarks

As explained in the previous section, the main features of Constâncio's work consist of his gradual breaking-up with mainstream classical, Ricardian economics, and of his increasing support of heterodox political economy. This brings us to one crucial tenet characterizing the development and diffusion of classical political economy in Portugal. In fact, the narrow and fragmentary acceptance of Ricardian economics should not be merely seen as the result of a low propensity to analytical, deductive thought. It should rather be interpreted as a consequence of the simultaneous influence of several European authors and schools, differing from each other on fundamental doctrinal or political issues, but converging on the acceptance of a 'general rule': the difficulty of establishing general rules indifferently applicable to each and every country, with the consequent attention paid to the appraisal of a national, historical perspective in studies of political economy. Among those influential authors and schools, one should consider Sismondi, List, the first German historical school, the cameralist and the philosophy of law traditions renewed by Karl Rau and Krause, as well as Say's disciples like Blanqui, Rossi, Garnier and the French liberal group around Coquelin and Guillaumin – the editors of the *Dictionnaire d'Économie Politique* published in 1852/53 – and around the *Journal des Économistes*. The downturn of the English influences is more than evident, with John Stuart Mill as its principal victim.

Most of these German and French authors have been translated into Spanish and have found national followers and disciples in both Iberian countries, but especially in Spain. Their influence has served two fundamental objectives: to speed up the process of institutionalization of political economy through teaching at university level; and to improve the theoretical and doctrinal debates concerning the main economic issues in discussion at the time. They were aware of the risks of an almost permanent increase of the impoverished population; they have stressed the need for protecting 'infant industry'; and they have rejected the possibility of the free issue of money. In some cases, they have used Storch's ideas on collective welfare as a means to develop a modest, applied analysis of social betterment. However, their influence in the academic milieu began declining in the 1850s and onwards, at a time when the strong influence of the French liberal group around the *Journal des Économistes* was growing faster. In contrast with this influence, it should be pointed out that the diffusion of the system of thought of John Stuart Mill was very late (from 1870 onwards) and scarce, appearing above all in the colourful Parliament debates on fiscal policy and taxation principles.

A pragmatic, instrumental attitude towards economic discourse was thus kept alive and developed, following lines similar to those observed in the case of the use and abuse of Smith's and Say's work. The raison d'être for this attitude was twofold: the reinforcement of the institutional procedures that could help the public administration to implement and accomplish lasting reforms, and the strengthening of the arguments and choices available to a public opinion which became increasingly aware of the scope and aim associated with the science of political economy, conceived as a 'science of proportions', not as a science of abstract principles.

Notes

1 For further details on the diffusion of the work of Smith and Say in Portugal cf. Almodovar and Cardoso 1998, chapters 2 and 3; and Cardoso and Reeder 2002.

2 For a detailed account of Ricardo's Jewish origins see Heertje 2004.

3 Ricardo 1975 is a translation of the Everyman's Library, London 1965, edited by Michael Fogarty.

4 On the influence of the Jewish background in Ricardo's thought see Heertje 2004, 289–92.
5 For a lengthy discussion of the process of institutionalization of classical political economy in Portugal see Almodovar 1995.
6 This section offers a summary of arguments presented in Cardoso 1999, Almodovar & Cardoso 2004 and Cardoso 2009.
7 *Anais das Ciências, das Artes e das Letras* (The Annals of Sciences, Arts and Lettres), 16 volumes, each one containing approximately 350 pages, published between 1818 and 1822. Constâncio was one of the four editors of this journal, and he was the most enterprising of them all. The journal was devoted to the dissemination of scientific knowledge in a variety of fields, such as medicine, chemistry, physics, botany, natural history, mathematics, astronomy and political economy. History, language, literature, poetry and the humanities in general were also covered in the pages of the journal. The journal was aimed at reaching the readership of the Portuguese elite of intellectual émigrés spread throughout several European countries, though it also circulated in academic and intellectual circles in Portugal.

References

Almeida, Manuel (1821) *Compêndio de Economia Política* (New edition, Lisbon: Banco de Portugal, 1993, Series of Portuguese Economic Classics, edited with an introduction by M. Fátima Brandão).

Almodovar, António (1995) *A Institucionalização da Economia Política Clássica em Portugal*. Porto: Edições Afrontamento.

Almodovar, António and José Luís Cardoso (1998) *A History of Portuguese Economic Thought*. London and New York: Routledge.

——(2004) Neo-Smithian political economy in Portugal, 1803–1848. *Économies et Societés, Série Oeconomia,* PE, no. 34(2), 299–324.

Cardoso, José Luís (1998) Classical economics in Spain and Portugal. In Heinz D. Kurz and Neri Salvadori (eds), *The Elgar Companion to Classical Economics*, Vol. 1, 149–154.

——(1999) The road to heterodoxy: F. S. Constâncio and the critical acceptance of classical political economy. *History of Political Economy,* 31(3), 473–492.

——(2009) F. Solano Constâncio on political economy: a 'science of proportions'. *History of European Ideas*, 35(3), 227–235.

Cardoso, José Luís and John Reeder (2002) Adam Smith in the Spanish and Portuguese Speaking World. In Tribe, Keith and Mizuta, Hiroshi (eds), *A Critical Bibliography of Adam Smith*. London: Pickering & Chatto, 184–197.

Borges, José Ferreira (1831) *Princípios de Sintelologia*. London: Bingham. (New edition, Lisbon: Banco de Portugal, 1995, Series of Portuguese Economic Classics, edited with an introduction by A. Sousa Franco).

——(1834) *Instituições de Economia Política*. Lisbon: Imprensa Nacional. (New edition, Lisbon: Banco de Portugal (1995), Series of Portuguese Economic Classics, edited with an introduction by A. Sousa Franco).

Constâncio, Francisco S. (1995) *Leituras e Ensaios de Economia Política*. Lisbon: Banco de Portugal (Series of Portuguese Economic Classics, edited with an introduction by J.L. Cardoso).

——(1820) Reflexões acerca de algumas questões relativas à economia política, e sobre a obra recente de M. Malthus. *Anais das Ciências, das Artes e das Letras*, Vol. X, Part I, 72–88 [reprinted in Constâncio 1995].

——(1821a) Lettres à M. Malthus, etc. ou Cartas a M. Malthus sobre diversos assuntos de economia política, e particularmente, sobre as causas da estagnação do comércio. J.-B. Say et al., Paris, 1820. *Anais das Ciências, das Artes e das Letras*, Vol. XII, Part I, 28–51 [reprinted in Constâncio 1995].

——(1821b) An inquiry concerning population, etc. ou Investigação acerca da população e da faculdade de multiplicação da espécie humana; obra destinada a refutar a doutrina do Ensaio de M. Malthus sobre este assunto. W. Godwin, Londres, 1820. *Anais das Ciências, das Artes e das Letras*, Vol. XII, Part I, 63–104 [reprinted in Constâncio 1995].

——(1838) *Armazém de Conhecimentos Úteis, nas Artes e Ofícios.* Paris: J.-P. Aillaud [reprinted in Constâncio 1995].

——(1841a) *Esprit des Revues Anglaises. Analyse Critique des Revues Trimestrielles d'Edimbourgh et de Londres, Paraissant Tous les Mois.* Paris: Charpentier Libraire [reprinted in Constâncio 1995].

——(1841b) *La Grande-Bretagne en 1840, ou Annuaire Financier, Commercial et Statistique du Royaume-Uni.* Paris: Charpentier Libraire [reprinted in Constâncio 1995].

Heertje, Arnold (2004) The Dutch and Portuguese-Jewish Background of David Ricardo. *The European Journal of the History of Economic Thought*, 11(2), 281–294.

Lisboa, José da Silva (1819–1820) *Estudos do Bem Comum e Economia Política.* Rio de Janeiro: Impressão Régia, Vol. I (1819) and Vol. II (1820) (New edition, *Escritos Económicos Escolhidos, II*, Lisbon: Banco de Portugal, 1993, Series of Portuguese Economic Classics, edited with an introduction by António Almodovar).

Malthus, Tomas R. (1820) *Principes d'Économie Politique Considérés sous le Rapport de leur Application Pratique, par T.R. Malthus*, trans. F.S. Constâncio. Paris: J.-P. Aillaud Libraire, Vols. I and II.

Ricardo, David (1819) *Des Principes de l'Économie Politique et de l'Impôt*, trans. F. S. Constâncio. Paris: J.P. Aillaud Libraire, Tomes I et II.

——(1938a) *Sobre a Teoria do Valor.* Lisbon: Editorial Inquérito [trans. Eduardo Salgueiro from Gonner's edition 1919].

——(1938b) *Sobre a Teoria da Renda.* Lisbon: Editorial Inquérito [trans. Eduardo Salgueiro from Gonner's edition 1919].

——(1975) *Princípios de Economia Política e de Tributação.* Lisbon: Fundação Calouste Gulbenkian [translated by Maria Adelaide Fereira from Fogarty's edition 1965].

——(1951–1973) *Works and Correspondence*, P. Sraffa (ed.). Cambridge: Cambridge University Press.

Sampaio, A. Forjaz (1839) *Elementos de Economia Política. Tradução Livre do Catecismo de Economia Política de J.-B. Say.* Coimbra: Imprensa da Universidade (New edition, *Estudos e Elementos de Economia Política 1839–1874*). Lisbon: Banco de Portugal, Vol. I, Series of Portuguese Economic Classics, edited with an introduction by Alcino Pedrosa.

——(1853) *Estudos de Economia Política, ou breve explicação dos elementos desta ciência* (New edition, *Estudos e Elementos de Economia Política (1839–1874)*. Lisbon: Banco de Portugal, Vol. I, Series of Portuguese Economic Classics, edited with an introduction by Alcino Pedrosa.

Say, Jean-Baptiste (1822) *Cathecismo de Economia Política.* Lisbon: Impressão Liberal.

——(1837) *Catéchisme d'Économie Politique, ou Instructio Familière qui montre de quelle façon les richesses sont produites, distribuées et consomées dans la société.* Coimbra: Imprimerie de l'Université.

4 The reception and dissemination of Ricardo's ideas in Spain

Salvador Almenar

To date, the reception and dissemination of David Ricardo's economic ideas in Spain (and more broadly, in Spanish) has not had the benefit of an entire monographic article. The most directly related precedents are the pioneering studies by Robert Sidney Smith on the influence of classical economists in Spain (1957; 1968; 1969), some papers on Álvaro Flórez Estrada (Almenar 1980; 2000), a controversy over the Spanish translation of Ricardo's *Principles* in 1848 (Cabrillo 1977; Frías Hernández 1993) and some later studies on classical economics in Spain (Lluch and Almenar 2000, 2004).

This chapter analyzes different formal and substantive levels of the direct and indirect transfer of Ricardo's economic ideas. Internationally, these ideas were accessed, selected and interpreted in different ways. As a result, Spanish readers also received them differently, accepting his ideas, adapting them, criticising them, expressly rejecting them, deliberately not commenting on them or ignoring them.

The rest of the chapter examines the variety of ways in which Ricardo was received in Spanish, partly in chronological order. The first section covers the period up to 1834 (which coincides with the end of absolute monarchy), the second is devoted exclusively to Flórez Estrada and the third encompasses the period from 1834 to 1868.

1. Echoes and reflections: the arrival of David Ricardo in Spain (1818–1834)

Spain's preference for French as the leading foreign language for the learned community had consolidated since the middle of the eighteenth century, although universities almost exclusively used textbooks in Spanish. The first textbooks on political economy that were most used at the end of the eighteenth century (Danvila, Genovesi, Condorcet-Smith) were progressively replaced from 1807 onwards by *Traité d'économie politique* by Say. Six translations of *Traité* were published in Spain between 1804 and 1840 and a further six of *Cathéchisme* (not to mention other translations published in France and Mexico). Spanish economists also adopted Smith's and Say's approaches, albeit to rectify them in some issues (Almenar 2012b).

In a context where publishing rights were periodically suppressed and Say's work was pre-eminent among the publications available, Ricardo's texts and ideas were initially received cautiously and half-heartedly in three ways: i) directly, by reading the French translation by Francisco Solano Constâncio, contaminated by notes from Say; ii) indirectly, through texts considered closely related to Ricardo (Mill and McCulloch); and iii) by means of texts by other authors that reflect, comment, criticise or even seek to refute some of Ricardo's ideas.

As far as this author is aware, there are no contemporary mentions of Ricardo's texts any earlier than 1817. Ricardo's *Principles* was not widely disseminated, judging by the few news items and advertisements in the press. The number of editions of *Principles* that are currently available in the main Spanish libraries gives the same impression, although these data must be taken cautiously, as a *relative* indicator of dissemination. There is only one copy of each of the three first English editions, while there are a total of 37 copies of the four French translations published between 1819 and 1847. In contrast, 35 copies remain of the 1831 Spanish translation of *Elements of political economy* by James Mill, together with 130 copies of the three pre-1823 Spanish translations of Say's *Traité*.[1] The first Spanish translation of Ricardo's *Principles* appeared in 1848, three decades after it was first published in English.

The first news of Ricardo is a brief presentation or advertising prospectus of the French translation of *Principles* by Constâncio (Gaceta 1818), which reproduces that published in the *Moniteur universel*. The prospectus praises the merit of Ricardo's monetary ideas and highlights the singularity of his theory regarding rent and taxes. However, the news item includes an entire critical comment by Say on Ricardo's abstract method and his inappropriate deduction of 'foolproof' general principles in political economy.

One of the few authorised journals, *Crónica científica y literaria*, published an anonymous review of the aforementioned French translation in 1819, written by José Joaquín de Mora, the editor of the journal (1819). The author states that it was very difficult to add any new knowledge in political economy to that already expounded by Smith and Say. The danger of this science is 'metaphysical speculation', which converts it into 'an aerial science' with no practical application in terms of government intervention or business. Ricardo is 'an occasionally overly deep thinker', who bases his ideas on 'safe principles' and practical experience acquired on the stock market, although these ideas are occasionally cast in 'unintelligible and inapplicable theories', as is the case, for example, in the initial chapters of the book that address value, rent, wages and profits. However, Ricardo 'descends from those mysterious heights' in other chapters on taxes, banks and the exchange rate, making useful contributions to the 'public-minded and the capitalist'.

Mora had been a professor of logic and, when giving his opinion about Ricardo, he did not hide his preference for an empirical approach to scientific development, in the tradition of Bacon. And it is worth noting that Mora drew inspiration from one review or another on Ricardo published in the French journals that he read frequently. His final comment emphasises that the 'main adornment of the work [of Ricardo] are the notes' by J. B. Say, characterised by 'excellent logic', 'depth' and 'vigour'. By way of example, he included the text from two critical notes by Say in his comment.

In the 1820s, Ricardo began to receive mentions as a prominent economist, although many of these references came from indirect and occasional sources. One translator of *Lettres á Mr. Malthus* by J. B. Say (Anonymous 1820a) states that the *scientific* progress of political economy after Smith is due to 'a small number of highly distinguished writers' (Malthus, Ricardo, Say and Sismondi), but in another comment regrets the theoretical discussions and praises the members of parliament who voted against import prohibitions and some protectionist duties (Anonymous 1820b). Another translator stated in 1821 that he was pleased by the *political* dissemination of economic knowledge among Spanish members of parliament and highlighted the positive influence of the ideas of 'Say, Smith, Ricardo, Steuard [*sic*], Filanghieri, Beccaria and other famous writers' on the recent liberal legislation (Sánchez Rivera 1821). The parliamentary committee on the half tithe in 1821 referred to Ricardo as an authority in support of its proposals (Martín Rodríguez 2009: 128). In these statements, the 'utility' of political economy is usually determined by the 'application' of theories in economic policy, paying less attention to analytical development and contemporary theoretical discrepancies.

In 1825, a government journal entitled *Mercurio de España*, directed by engineer and economist Juan López de Peñalver, published the Spanish translation of the debate between Sismondi and Say in *Révue Britannique* over general gluts (Say 1825; Sismondi 1825). The critical allusions to Ricardo are numerous and precise, albeit indirect. In contrast, the translation of the work by François Ferrier *Du gouvernement* (1826) contains the most vigorous criticism of 'economists', expressly including Ricardo, for becoming involved in sterile disputes.

The main Spanish economic works of the period fall into the intellectual orbit of J. B. Say, although they express marked deviation from and even outright criticism of Say himself in crucial aspects such as the freedom of foreign trade. This was the case for the books by the Marquis of Valle Santoro (1829) and José Espinosa de los Monteros (1831), who completely ignore Ricardo. The translations of the works by Bergery, Ganilh and Babbage, published in the early 1830s, are not directly or closely related to Ricardo either. It would once again be Sismondi, with a late translation of the first edition of *Nouveaux principes* (1834), who criticised Ricardo for his method of political economy, the theory of rent and the equilibrium between production and expenditure.

The *Catecismo de economía política* (Catechism of political economy), published in London in 1825 by José Joaquín de Mora in exile, once again displays a pragmatic attitude to political economy and the need for implementation in response to a wide variety of social circumstances (Mora 1825: 81–102). *Catecismo* is deliberately simple and mentions Mill and McCulloch, but not Ricardo. Generally speaking, it is not even Ricardian in analytical terms (value, rent, capital, taxes, foreign trade, public debt), or in numerous economic policy prescriptions.[2]

Nor is there any trace of Ricardo in the works of other exiled authors such as José Canga Argüelles or Andrés Borrego. The volume by Pablo Pebrer on the British Empire mentions Ricardo and McCulloch accurately when discussing the settlement of public debt (Pebrer 1833: 483–4, 495n).

Ricardo in James Mill's mirror

In 1822, an advertisement appeared for the publication in Madrid of a translation by Reinaldo Mackinnon of *Elements of political economy* by James Mill. The book was presented as a 'revolution' in economic science of similar proportions to that of Bentham in legislation. But it was not published in its entirety due to a lack of subscriptions.[3]

A translation of Mill's *Elements* appeared in Argentina in 1823, and minister B. Rivadavia planned to use it as a political economy textbook at the new university in Buenos Aires. Professor Fernández suggests that this initiative failed in 1825 due to a lack of students and the inconsistent dedication of the professor in charge, P. J. Agrelo, but also as a result of the distance between Mill's scenario and the Argentine economy: 'there was neither a lack of land nor diminishing returns […] there was no conflict between landowners and the rest of society, or fear of the stationary state' (Fernández López 2000).

Another Spanish translation of *Elements* by Mill (1827) was published in Paris in 1827, based on the French version by J. Parissot in 1823 and more than likely with the Latin American market in mind.

Mill's work was finally published in Spain in 1831, translated and with a prologue by Manuel María Gutiérrez, with a laudatory dedication to the Minister of Public Finance (Mill 1831). Gutiérrez had translated Say's treatise (in 1816 and 1817) and Destutt de Tracy's treatise (in 1817) and was a political economy professor in Malaga from 1818 to 1824 (Grice-Hutchinson 1993). Working in the Department of Trade, he abandoned the free trade theories but translated Mill's book (from the French translation by J. Parissot) as a possible textbook because it was shorter than Say's *Traité*.

Gutiérrez included a prologue in which, in a neutral manner, he summarises Mill's main arguments, such as the labour theory of value, the differential rent theory, the ratio between wages and profits in different proportions or intensities of capital, the theory of capital population and accumulation, the analysis of comparative advantages in trade (in the version of the first edition of *Elements*), the advantages of convertible paper money, international trade and money flows and the impact of different types of taxes (Gutiérrez 1831). Gutiérrez relegated his discrepancies with Mill to notes that contain a protectionist response to free trade theories (pp. 217–9, 230), colonial policy (pp. 227–8, 231–2) and the distinction between productive and unproductive consumption (pp. 241–4, 264). Mill's book can be considered the main substantive example of the indirect reception of Ricardian ideas in Spain up to 1834, despite the paradox of this initiative coming from a protectionist economist like Gutiérrez.

2. Flórez Estrada's singular reception of Ricardo

Alvaro Flórez Estrada (1766–1853) published *Curso de economía política* (Course of political economy) in London in 1828. It contains a singular approach to classical economics. In exile for the second time in England, he was then known for his extensive career as the author of several constitutional papers, a supporter of the first liberal patriotic committee in response to French occupation in 1808, and as a radical liberal member of parliament.[4]

His political texts reveal a convergence, not exempt of tension, between the traditions of civic republicanism from the Enlightenment and Smithian economic liberalism. He endeavoured to reconcile 'safety, freedom and equality' and civic virtues with individual economic initiative, 'public happiness' with 'prosperity'. Flórez adapted some of the ideas of Hume, Condillac and Smith to denounce the effects of absolute monarchy and mercantilism, proposing economic growth based on export agriculture in small and medium-sized farms (to benefit the 'middle classes') and free trade for all Spanish, European and American regions governed by the parliamentary monarchy established in the Spanish Constitution of 1812 (Almenar 2010; Flórez Estrada 1812).

Seven editions of *Curso* were published between 1828 and 1852, representing a noticeable change from his previous economic ideas, particularly in regard to his perception of industrialization. As the book was banned in Spain, the first two editions published in London (Flórez Estrada 1828) and Paris (Flórez Estrada 1831) targeted the Latin American market, while the third edition, *Cours éclectique d'économie politique* (Flórez Estrada 1833) was published for the European continent.

Following the death of the king and the amnesty, Flórez was elected a member of parliament from 1834 to 1840, and his prestige as an economist grew with the publication of the fourth edition in Madrid (1835), his speeches in parliament and articles in the press.

A singular reception of classical political economy

Flórez conceived *Curso* as a 'complete treatise' of political economy (two volumes, 850 pages) to disseminate 'the great advances made in this science over the last twenty years' across Spain and America (Flórez Estrada 1828: I, 5). The author did not intend 'to discover a new system' but rather to include

> all the truths already discovered in such an important science. I have attempted to consult the classical authors from the most advanced

> nations and take the ideas that, in my opinion, have best addressed each of the points […] Similarly, I have also tried to present their doctrine as clearly as possible, rectifying it and filtering out any errors I believe it contains. (Flórez Estrada 1828: I, 5–6)

As the book was written to diffuse ideas, Flórez did not consider it important to provide a detailed acknowledgement of the original texts included in his work, perhaps following authors such as Heinrich Storch (who was nevertheless accused of plagiarism by J.-B. Say).

Following the proposal by Professor Ernest Lluch (1964), I performed a comparative textual analysis and detected three forms of intellectual sources: (i) full translations and extracts from translations, (ii) more or less accurate summaries and (iii) direct and indirect references to the work of various contemporary economists. In 1980, I published a critical edition of this book in order to shed light on the hidden intellectual sources and variations in the text between the different editions (Flórez Estrada 1980).[5]

However, that formal analysis is not conclusive because Flórez sometimes accepted the content of the texts he incorporated, but other times was in either total or partial disagreement or even considered theoretical or doctrinal alternatives. For these reasons, *Curso* must be considered a complex and extensive *collage* that has a different overall meaning to the simple sum of its individual components.

In writing the first edition, Flórez Estrada most frequently used the already recognised books by John McCulloch (1824; 1825b), James Mill (1821), David Ricardo (1821), Heinrich von Storch (1823), Jean-Baptiste Say (1823; 1826), Jean Simonde de Sismondi (1827) and Count Destutt de Tracy (1823), which had recently been either published or re-edited. Apart from this highly heterogeneous series of books, it is worth adding further works, such as the volume by William Thompson (1824), the inclusion of texts by Adam Smith and Thomas Malthus and, after 1828, the recent contributions by Robert Torrens (1829) and Richard Jones (1831).[6] This choice reveals a remarkable knowledge of the contemporary economic literature and a special appreciation of the scientific reputation of the authors and the theoretical and political relevance of their ideas.

John McCulloch, James Mill and David Ricardo himself were the most important intellectual contributions, in terms of both the number of texts incorporated into *Curso* and the nature of the ideas included and accepted. According to Flórez Estrada, these three authors formed a group or school under the intellectual authority of Ricardo, although he also recognised their differences and specific personal contributions.

The second group of doctrinal influence comprises Heinrich von Storch and Jean-Baptiste Say. Their contributions can be detected in the analysis of the influence of demand on economic growth, collective welfare, monetary theory and bank organization.

The third group, albeit less important than the aforementioned group in terms of the number of texts included in *Curso*, comprises Sismondi and Jones, but their historicist influence can be considered strategic, particularly their perception that product distribution is influenced by the type of institutional organization of land ownership and tenure.

In subsequent reviews of the book, the author refined some juxtapositions and contradictions between these three doctrinal groups, thereby reinforcing his own global view with each step he took.

Flórez Estrada and Ricardian political economy

Flórez's *Curso* is divided into four parts, following the criteria of James Mill (production, distribution, interchange, consumption) and is preceded by a 'preliminary discourse' that reproduces the discourse by McCulloch with various rectifications. According to Flórez, political economy is not separate from the rest of knowledge about society. Unlike Say or McCulloch, he always upheld a unitary conception of politics and political economy as separate but related parts of the 'science of government', that of 'organising society' (1980: 68–9, 11–5).

The initial comment on Ricardo is full of praise (1828: I, 56) and exempt from objections, very similar to the panegyric made by McCulloch (1825a: 68–75). The texts and references from Ricardo's *Principles* included in the first edition address: (1) the difference between total and net product (1980: 188–94); (2) land rent (pp. 331, 337–41, 353–9); (3) mines rent (pp. 427–9); (4) wages (pp. 452–5); (5) wealth, value and utility (pp. 553–6); (6) trade with the colonies (pp. 756–60); (7) public consumptions (pp. 819–21); (8) rent tax (pp. 867–8); (9) farm land-tax (pp. 877–81); (10) wage tax (p. 908); (11) tax on the sale of land ownership (pp. 938–9); and (12) public debt (pp. 1021–3).

These texts by Ricardo are usually literal translations, extracts from texts that are not revealed to the reader and which Flórez either implicitly or expressly agrees with, barring some secondary exceptions. In terms of proportion, Ricardo's texts account for close to 7 per cent of the entire text of the first edition of *Curso*. But it is worth adding that Ricardo's influence indirectly affects the book as a whole through the frequent and abundant texts by McCulloch and Mill.

Subsequent editions summarised some original texts by Ricardo, McCulloch and Mill (without losing their original meaning), while removing others without leaving any trace of disagreement with their ideas. Other texts were accompanied or replaced by critiques or corrections and, finally, many others remained in the book with slight changes in style.

Discrepancies appear in the second edition, with a generic reference to the existence of 'some inaccuracies and contradictions' in the work of Ricardo and praise for Thomas Tooke's criticism of the 'abstractions of the Ricardo school' (1831: I, 49–51). Let us examine the main details.

Production

Flórez incorporates a discussion on the definition of production and wealth that is similar to Torrens. He understands wealth as 'anything that is the product of people's work and which they desire'. Flórez uses these two conditions to categorically separate utility exchange value and rejects the requirement posed by Say and McCulloch that wealth must necessarily have exchange value (Flórez Estrada 1980: 71–86; Torrens 1821: 1–17). In the third part, he ties this approach in with Ricardo's stance, which is detailed in Chapter xx ('Value and Riches') of *Principles*, more than half of which Flórez included in *Curso*, adding a criticism of Louis Say (1980: 543–56; Ricardo 1951: 273–81).

Another related topic is the difference between gross and net product. Flórez transferred practically the entire chapter on this topic in Ricardo's *Principles* to his book, including the criticism of Smith and Say, and immediately explains the 'effects of Machinery'. Here Flórez completely ignores Chapter xxxi of *Principles* (3rd edn), following McCulloch's reasoning very closely. The expansion of production has no limits in terms of demand and, at most, can cause frictional unemployment that will be relocated in other sectors (Flórez Estrada 1828: I, 196–208; McCulloch 1825b: 167–72, 181–92). In subsequent editions, Flórez supported that reasoning with examples of the positive effects of technical progress (1980: 197–206).

Finally, Flórez adapted Heinrich von Storch's notion of productive labour (1824: 25–37), due to the direct or *indirect* contribution of material wealth to the productivity of workers (1980: 305–21), without relating his analysis to the Ricardian distinction between gross and net product, more than likely considering that the two perspectives were not contradictory.

Distribution

Indeed, Flórez delimited a theory on 'the *primitive* distribution of wealth' among landlords, capitalists and workers, excluding those who 'contribute indirectly to producing wealth' (1980: 324).

Flórez's theory on land (and mine) rent is initially Ricardian and is partly explained using texts by Ricardo himself and McCulloch, and despite adopting a definition of rent borrowed from Malthus (1827), as the difference between gross product and the cost of production. Flórez believes that Ricardo's definition ('the portion[…] paid to the landlord') is a special case as 'there can be no rent without tenure' (1828: 285–6). Furthermore, he upholds that when *all* land is 'owned', landlords have 'a type of monopoly', literally echoing Thomas Perronet Thompson (1830).

In the second edition, a striking discrepancy with Ricardo emerges regarding the *process* of how rent emerges. According to Flórez, it is sufficient for all the first-class land to be owned, even if second-class lands are not cultivated (1831: I, 301–2). He also deduces that, in this case, subsequent farming of lower quality land would not increase the rent, but consolidate it (1831: I, 314–17). This approach is intended to contradict the Ricardian theory that lower quality land under cultivation never pays rent. In reality, Flórez's criticism reproduces the objections raised by Robert Torrens (1829: 132–5, 142–6), which are based on the emergence of non-differential rent associated with the divergence between the market and the natural price of wheat. From this point of view, the criticism of Torrens and Flórez is conceptual in nature and focuses on the *transition* between two natural equilibriums, although the intention is to highlight that the increase in rent precedes the cultivation of lower quality lands.

Moreover, Flórez added two new chapters to *Curso* (1831: I, 318–25, 410–15) on the effects of corn trade prohibitions and an increase in the 'value' of raw materials on the rate of profit, literally following Torrens (1829: 153–73, 110–17). His explanation uses a model of two sectors in physical terms ('bread and cloth'), which simultaneously determines the rate of profit and the relative price, such that the 'value of raw materials must rise as the cost of production is greater' and then the general rate of profit decreases (natural equilibrium). But in this case, an increase in the price of raw materials first benefits 'the tenant farmers who cultivate more fertile land […], but this advantage will only last as long as their previous leasing agreement'. The new contracts will see that advantage transformed into an increase in rent. In summary, now the *transition* does not determine a temporary increase in the rent of the most fertile land, but rather a temporary increase in the rate of profit in agriculture.

Flórez did not realise the possible contradiction between the two perspectives. But his explanation in other chapters suggests that he considered both arguments with different analytical and political functions. The first contains an isolated conceptual criticism, while the second, in keeping with Ricardo, provides further support for the diminishing trend in the rate of profits and grounds for free trade.

Further discrepancies appeared in the fourth edition in 1835. Flórez now described Richard Jones as 'the author that has best addressed the theory of rent […] he discovers two capital errors in which Malthus, Ricardo, Mill and McCulloch concurred', and extols Jones' analysis of the effects of the different systems for 'leasing property' on distribution, but reproaches 'his partiality in favour of the landlord class' (1980: 59–60). Flórez adopted Jones' theory, which attributes growth in rent to the increase in capital invested in land that is already farmed, under the assumption of constant historical returns at each level of fertility. However, he clarified Jones' analysis of the effects of 'greater capital efficiency' on rent in grain and money using Ricardian arguments. Nevertheless, Ricardo's theory (reduced to the supposition of diminishing fertility) became a special case (1980: 342–45; Jones 1831: 189–94, 236). Parallel to this, some paragraphs from Ricardo's *Principles* were summarised or removed.

Even so, the Ricardian process of differential rent with an extensive margin remains dominant throughout the work, both in the dynamic analysis of trends in rent and the rate of profit and also in the political scope of the conflict between land owners and the rest of society.

One of Flórez Estrada's analytical differences from the Ricardian literature is the attention he paid to the influence of land ownership and contracting systems on the distribution of production. Flórez redefined the theory of rent in history using contributions by Sismondi and Jones. He defended modern emphyteusis on the grounds that long-term contracts encourage ongoing improvements, dynamically neutralising diminishing returns and bringing the process closer to a potential long-run trend of constant returns (1980: 361–81).

The explanation regarding wages is drawn from to McCulloch, with his simple wage-fund doctrine, the tendency to equality within the framework of occupations and the establishment of real and 'necessary' wages. Flórez included a few paragraphs from Ricardo's *Principles* (1951: 97–102) to complete the real wage tendencies (1980: 452–5). Flórez's analysis of the rate of profit also follows McCulloch's *Principles* very closely, within the canonical framework of diminishing fertility and increasing differential rent.

Interchange

Once again, the chapters addressing the theory of value are very faithfully based on the singular position of McCulloch in first edition of *Principles*, interpreted as an incoherent transition (O'Brien 1970: 138–40). In the third edition of *Curso*, Flórez modified the confusing initial order and the topic was explained using the following sequence: real value (which is identified with the 'cost of production'), exchange value and the effects of changes in wages and profits on the exchange value, depending on the duration of capital and the ratio between 'immediate' labour and capital. Ricardo appears as an indirect theoretical reference. Flórez accepted that it is impossible to find a measure of invariable value and concluded that 'the labour necessary for production […] is the least uncertain measure […] of a great number' of products (1980: 541).

Flórez's approach to monetary theory and bank organisation is drawn from Mill, Storch and McCulloch. However, the extensive chapter on paper money levels systematic criticism at the fact that paper money was legal tender and above all that it was not convertible, due to the unfair effects stemming from the 'unavoidable' depreciation of the paper. The price of paper money depends on the 'confidence' in being reimbursed, not on legal tender (1980: 654–8) as McCulloch states (1828: 230). Therefore, even in a system in which paper money could be converted into ingots, such as that proposed by 'Ricardo, Mill and McCulloch', controlling 'the amount of paper money […] that is strictly indispensable for circulation' would not guarantee the stability of the value of money (1980: 671). According to Flórez, calculating that amount is impossible and only a limited amount of metallic money can be actually replaced by paper money, as Ricardo himself says, due to 'the value of the standard for which it is exchangeable' (1951: 195). As issuing paper money does not imply a decrease in the total amount of gold used as reserves, the supposed advantages of paper money do not exist. As 'Tooke justly states', those limited advantages do not compensate their 'grave disadvantages' (1980: 670–4).

Finally, Flórez accepted the analysis of comparative cost in the primitive version of the first edition of *Elements* by James Mill, and transferred to his book a selection of Chapter xxv from *Principles* by Ricardo on the effects of colonial trade as a monopoly (1980: 753–61).

Consumption

The author distinguishes between productive and unproductive consumption according to their direct or *indirect* contribution to production, inspired by Storch and McCulloch. Flórez attempts to establish a rather weak link with Ricardo by accepting Destutt's distinction between active and idle capitalists (1980: 763–822).

His ideas regarding taxes are based on texts by McCulloch (1824) and Ricardo. In particular, Flórez literally accepted Ricardo's general criteria (Chapter viii) on the tax burden for income or capital and the need to analyse the effective or final incidence of taxes (1980: 819–21). Flórez also follows Ricardo's text literally in the case of land tax (1980: 877–81).

In the third edition, Flórez completely rewrote and reworded the chapters on land tax and rent 'from a new point of view', providing a detailed analysis of five tax bases in agriculture: (i) land area, (ii) profit, (iii) net product, (iv) total product and (v) rent. In order to systemise Ricardo's analysis, Flórez studied thirteen alternative cases using numerical examples under similar general assumptions: three categories of land and extensive margin (1833, III: 221–75; 1980: 833–66).

Flórez indicated with unusual and exaggerated condescension that 'even though Ricardo may not have examined the different bases […] or applied the land rent doctrine […], he has made a discovery in this subject matter, albeit incomplete, of some importance' (1980: 845). There is a prominent difference between the two. Flórez merely established the primary or initial incidence on the three categories of agricultural income (which he calls 'the isolated effect'), whereas Ricardo also addressed the complex effects on the rest of the economic system.

Flórez accepted Smith's four general criteria on taxes and Ricardo's analysis of tithes, but did not consider tithes an equitable tax ('an equal tax', Ricardo says) because consumers have unequal capacities to pay and because it does not tax wealth but consumption (1980: 887–8). His analysis of taxes on profits and wages also follows Ricardian logic, through McCulloch, as is the case with an extensive study of indirect taxes.

Flórez repeatedly underlined the negative effects of increasing rent on accumulation and growth and the passive nature of landlords. He also repeats his defence of rent tax, arguing that it is:

> the contribution system that is least incompatible with the progress of industry and which [makes] the sacrifices demanded of the nation more bearable […] In a word; all other contributions […] should be considered supplementary, as all other taxes cause greater damage to the progress of wealth. (1980: 859)

Finally, Flórez analysed the unfavourable effects of public debt following Sismondi and Ricardo, but expressly criticised Ricardo's 'serious mistakes' caused by treating an extraordinary contribution and a public loan plus interest as equivalents. According to Flórez, 'equivalence' is based on unreal suppositions regarding the interest rate, tax collection expenditure and debt management expenses, and it also omits other factors such as asymmetry in the financial market and the diversion of resources due to 'idle capitalists'. He created a catalogue of eighteen 'evils that the public loan system causes' (1980: 999–1020), taking into account the enormous amount of Spanish debt.

Apart from explaining his ongoing preference for rent tax, despite the difficulties of administrative estimation, Flórez discarded the possibility of a single proportional tax on income and accepted tax plurality with the restriction that indirect taxes do not fall on the wage basket. He also adapted a suggestion by James Mill regarding India, to use the rent from state-owned land, leased to peasants, as income to reduce the tax burden.

This last point confirmed his prior convictions and conveyed a political strategy developed by Flórez in Spain between 1835 and 1839, in parliament and the press. The government should not sell church land (convents) to pay off inherited public debt or to contract new public loans. The government should lease those lands to the existing farmers, using new emphyteusis contracts to encourage improvements, pay debt interest and consolidate the constitutional system (Almenar 2012a).

The influence of Flórez Estrada. The social question

The influence in Latin America appears to be confirmed by various relationships and initiatives, although no overall study is available. The first two editions of *Curso* were financed by the ambassador of Mexico (Vicente Rocafuerte) and politician José Cecilio del Valle attempted to disseminate the book in Guatemala and throughout Central America. The fourth edition of *Curso* was republished, maybe pirated, in Caracas in 1840. Professor Antonio Bachiller used and recommended it in the 1840s as a textbook in the chair of political economy in Havana.

In Spain, *Curso* became a university textbook also in an abridged version entitled *Elementos de economía política* (1841) and was an omnipresent reference in Spanish economic literature from 1835 onwards. However, its social influence diminished gradually after 1839, probably because that year Flórez Estrada rejected the legitimacy of the natural right to the private ownership of land, because it is a non-reproducible good. Instead, he proposed a gradual process of conversion into collective property managed by the State (which appears to be a precedent set by Stuart Mill and Henry George). These ideas, formulated in the 1839 pamphlet entitled *La cuestión social* (The Social Question), were included in subsequent editions of *Curso* published in Madrid in 1840 and 1848, and in Oviedo in 1852 (1980: 104–6, 383–422). This doctrinal U-turn received a great deal of criticism and generated deep-rooted mistrust of his ideas, which were considered socialist. In 1850 *Curso* by Flórez was no longer officially 'recommended' as a textbook for university education, but remained an intellectual reference for other economists.

3. Ricardo ignored, rectified and refuted (1834–1868)

Following the end of absolute monarchy in 1834, the resurgence of economic literature was focused mainly on textbooks for educational purposes and dissemination, studies on Spanish public finances and the controversial issue of free trade.

Economic growth and trade: some paradoxes

One sector of Spanish economic literature over the period 1834–1842 neglected Ricardo's ideas. Examples include the books published by José Soto in 1834, Benito Amor and Ramón de La Sagra in 1840 and Nicolás Paso in 1841, or the translation of Say's *Traité* with comments by José Antonio Ponzoa in 1838. It is not easy to discern whether this neglect was due to ignorance, differences of opinion or convenience of explanation, but these authors are all very close to Say, or the new 'social economy' (La Sagra).

Translations were a means of disseminating Ricardo's ideas, albeit not always neutral. *Histoire de l'économie politique* by Blanqui presents a brief comment on Ricardo filled with objections to his 'abstract' method (Blanqui 1839: 356–60). His *Précis élémentaire*, translated in 1840 and 1843, does not cover Ricardo, while Joseph Droz only makes a few comments about him in *Economie politique.* The translations of these three books were also used to teach political economy in Spain during the final period of Say's predominance.

In contrast, the translation of *Conversations* by Jane Marcet, wrongly attributed to Mrs Lowry (1835), reflects some basic 'Ricardian' proposals in a simple manner, as well as providing numerous political economy recommendations. The translation of the first volume of *Cours* by Pellegrino Rossi (1840) also contributed towards the indirect dissemination of Ricardo's ideas regarding rent. The notes written by translator Pedro de Madrazo, a student of Rossi in Paris, contain some clarifications quoting Ricardo's *Principles.*

Other authors occasionally mentioned Ricardo, although their knowledge was indirect. The extensive treatise by Mariano Torrente, *Revista general de economía política* (1835), presents a broad scenario of doctrines and information, albeit showing a preference for Melchiorre Gioia. Torrente was not aware of Ricardo's work, but mentioned his ideas through *Curso* by Flórez Estrada. He rejected Ricardo's theory of rent, but accepted that public debt reduces individual frugality and that it should be settled by selling public properties.

Professor Eudaldo Jaumeandreu published *Curso de economía política* (1836) as a protectionist response to Flórez Estrada's work and as an indirect confrontation with Ricardo. Jaumeandreu proposed a theory of growth in terms of economic stages: 'A backward nation […] must successively improve its rankings to reach the top.' He upheld that free trade has a *negative* effect on the rate of profit and an inverted 'Say's law': effective domestic demand is the main stimulus for growth (Lluch 2009: ch. xiii).

Entrepreneur and Catalonian member of parliament Guillermo Oliver (1834: 37–8) presented a summary of Ricardo's comparative cost theory, but disagreed with specialization when caused by initial conditions. Prohibitions and tariffs 'compensate the people for the disadvantages they would be condemned to suffer by the initial situation' of natural resources, capital and labour endowments.

Manuel M. Gutiérrez, considered a champion of protectionism in Madrid, gave a protectionist interpretation to a suggestion by Ricardo, justifying a tariff on wheat to offset the effects of the tithe (Gutiérrez 1837: 64–66). In a different context, he questioned Ricardo's preference for net product because it does not value the level of collective welfare (employment) accordingly. He reproduced the example of trade between England and Portugal and confronts comparative advantage with a growth sequence based on learning and domestic competition equivalent to the infant industry argument (Gutiérrez 1839: 276–82).

Oliver had sarcastically shown surprise that his free-trade adversaries had no knowledge of Ricardo. In fact, Ricardo's theory of international trade would remain absent from the work of almost all Spanish free-trade advocates, with the exception of Flórez Estrada, from 1830 to 1868.

Ricardo and the 'eclectic' economists

During the 1840s, the work by Eusebio María del Valle, Manuel Colmeiro (both professors at the University of Madrid) and Andrés Borrego figured prominently. They shared both a rejection of the new socialist currents and a fear of the adverse social effects of unlimited competition, supported by the 'chrematistic school'. Their eclecticism entailed separating political economy principles from their *application* to specific national conditions, in keeping with Karl H. Rau.

Curso de economía política by Valle (1842) is mainly based on Say, Sismondi and Storch. Ricardo remained in the background. After identifying value with the 'degree of utility', Valle considered Ricardo's assumption regarding value proportional to the 'amount of labour' inappropriate (1842: 80). Valle also maintained that it is 'impossible to accurately determine the equilibrium between production and consumption […], it is rash to uphold absolute principles in this subject matter' and discredits the position of 'Ricardo and his disciples' (pp. 118–9). In response to the Ricardian dilemma between taxes and debt, he suggested the possibility of landowner mortgages (p. 342). Valle presented a discussion on land tax and accepted the *possibility* explained by Ricardo of the tax falling on consumers and even benefiting the landowner, as Flórez stated (pp. 484–5). The author also criticised the 'unlimited' freedom of foreign trade (which had converted Portugal into an English 'colony') and defended the protection of 'incipient' industries. His book was published again, unchanged, in 1848.

Professor Manuel Colmeiro, who had translated *Economie politique* by Joseph Droz, defended a critical analysis of theories in the light of experience in his *Tratado elemental de economía política ecléctica* and proposed 'rejecting Ricardo's austere dogmatism', as Say had suggested (1845: I, xxii, 12–13). Colmeiro understood 'eclecticism' as a halfway point between extreme positions. For example, in response to Sismondi and Ricardo, he accepted convertible paper money as a supplementary means, without circulation 'reaching the labourers' (1845: I, 206–7). He upheld that Ricardo's 'mathematical' method, ignoring wage structure, leads to the error of predicting an exact equilibrium of the natural wage, without any influence on the part of changes in domestic prices or taxes (1845: I, 254–5, 266, II, 385–6).

The book by journalist and politician Andrés Borrego entitled *Principios de economía política* (1844) was devoted to the debate over economic policy, with criteria borrowed from Sismondi and the new German 'nationalökonomie'. He disagreed with Ricardo over the theory of value (which is similar to Say's), the theory of rent and the natural wage. Borrego presented a Ricardian model of diminishing fertility, based on Flórez Estrada, but reformulated as a process of increasing average cost. This is the point where his disagreement begins, as population growth 'subjects grain price rises to demand, instead of making them depend entirely and absolutely on the cost of production […] in accordance with the doctrine of Flórez Estrada and Ricardo', because both have 'confused effect with cause' (p. 297); this criticism is in keeping with Thompson's Smithian approach (1830). The next step was to reject the Ricardian analysis of the tithe, because the increase in the cost of production cannot be passed on to consumers and it reduces rent (pp. 298–9). This coincides with Italian economist Antonio Scialoja's criticism of Flórez Estrada (Scialoja 1844: 153–6, 303–11). His main objection to the classical theory of natural wage is empirical: 'blind competition' for foreign markets lowers the wage rate below the natural rate, but there is no automatic correction because when poverty increases, the population does not decrease (Borrego 1844: 335–43).

Other more accurate interpretations also emerged. In the parliamentary discussion of the tax reform of 1845, member of parliament and former professor of political economy Claudio Moyano unsuccessfully attempted to warn the rest of parliament about the difference between agricultural net product and rent, formulated by Ricardo and Flórez Estrada. However, his attempts fell on deaf ears as the majority of them were followers of Say (Martín Rodríguez 2009: 218).

Two belated translations: Ricardo (1848) and McCulloch (1855)

The Spanish translation of *Principles* by Ricardo in 1848 was ignored and forgotten for a century until Piero Sraffa recovered a reference made by L. Cossa in 1895, although 'no copy of such a translation has been traced, and its existence is extremely doubtful' (1955: 355–6). After subsequent and equally unsuccessful searches, Cossa's reference was deemed erroneous (Cabrillo 1977). However, Frías (1993) finally located a translation that covered the first seven chapters of the third English edition of *Principles*, with notes made by translator Juan Antonio Seoane. It was published in 1848 in instalments to subscribers of the journal *El Amigo del País*, directed by Seoane and published by the Real Sociedad Económica de Madrid. According to Frías, the extensive critical notes made by Seoane reveal that the latter had not understood Ricardo's ideas on value and distribution and his ignorance of political economy was an indication of the economic and cultural backwardness of Spain.

Further information leads to two observations. In the first place, I located a 'second part' of the translation that spans Chapter viii to the beginning of Chapter xx of *Principles*, written by Fernando Cos-Gayón (writer at the aforementioned journal) and which raises the percentage of the book that has been translated to two thirds. This 'second part' does not contain any comments and was interrupted because the journal stopped publishing in 1850 due to financial problems; hence *Principios* was never sold as a book and only very few collections of the instalments received by journal subscribers remain. It was not widely disseminated and did not make a lasting impression.[7]

In the second place, the nine notations made by Seoane (1848) propose a doctrinal alternative to Ricardo, albeit crudely formulated. Seoane defended a price theory based on utility (Say) and 'labour saving' (Smith) for consumers as opportunity cost. Seoane also formulated the hypothesis of considering wages as remuneration for the 'labourer's sum of productive faculties, which are nothing more than a fixed capital', such that the inverse relationship between wages and profits becomes diluted. Finally, he proposed an alternative to Ricardo: 'the productive faculties [of land] […] are destructible', which confirms the *active* role of the right to land ownership and its moral and productive importance and remuneration as rent (pp. 52–9).

Seoane's notes, despite his analytical clumsiness, suggest that his main goal as editor and translator of Ricardo was not to disseminate *Principles* in Spain, but rather to refute the Ricardian viewpoint of the economic and social process on different theoretical and moral grounds and to replace it with a perspective that highlighted the competition between individuals (not between classes) and a less conflictive functional approach to the relationship between labour, capital and land ownership (p. 50).

And Seoane's criticism was not an isolated case. Around 1846–1850, new analytical and doctrinal approaches emerged in the economic literature published in Spain, making it more plural. These approaches included the translations of works by Joseph Garnier, Friedrich List, and Auguste Walras, but this was mainly due to success of Frédéric Bastiat's works both in academic circles and among the general public.

Reports of a substantive use of Ricardo's ideas (beyond rhetorical mentions) were increasingly rare, although they reappeared in the monetary debates during the financial crisis of 1848. An anonymous 'Ricardist' (who intentionally used the pseudonym *Ricardista*) defended the temporary suspension of the convertibility of the notes issued by the Banco de San Fernando and the replenishment of its metal reserves, arguing for a monetary system that appears to be based on Ricardian ideas (Ricardista 1848). Two members of parliament, Fermín Gonzalo Morón and Andrés Borrego, mentioned Ricardo during the parliamentary debate on the bank act of 1949, albeit without following his ideas accurately (Martín Rodríguez 2009: 447–8, 453–4). A short time later, Luís M. Pastor (Pastor 1850) made an outright defence of 'free banking', inspired by Charles Coquelin and apart from Ricardo.

The engineer Cipriano Montesino published a translation of the third edition of *Principles* by McCulloch in 1855 that can be considered one of the last contemporary manifestations of Ricardian economics in Spain, although the original text from 1843 has an orientation that is far from Ricardo in various subject areas. The book contains extensive notes from the translator (and from another collaborator) that discuss theoretical and political aspects alluded to by McCulloch. Montesino used numerical examples to explain Ricardo's analysis in *Principles* of the effects of wage variations on relative prices in the cases of different ratios between fixed and total capital, differing durability of capital and production periods, but he did not analyze the invariable measure of value (Montesino 1855: 338–41). Other notes on McCulloch used a dynamic wage-fund theory (pp. 346–8), but criticised the Ricardian assumption of perfect mobility of capital in agriculture (pp. 356–8) and only accepted convertible paper money (p. 307).

Ricardo and the 'economist school'

A new doctrinal approach became established in 1856 following the constitution of a group of economists known as the Sociedad de Economía Politica de Madrid, the foundation of a free trade association and the publication of several journals, all of which replicated the French group Chez Guillaumin and the *Journal des Economistes*. The Spanish 'economist school' included several professors of political economy, lawyers, politicians and business people. One of the common features they all shared was that Ricardo remained a background figure in their works, references being confined almost exclusively to criticizing the theory of rent, while the authors moved away from or abandoned Malthus' population theory.

The lengthy *Curso de economía política* by Benigno Carballo (1855–1856) is to a great extent constructed using texts and ideas borrowed from the *Dictionaire d'économie politique* (Coquelin and Guillaumin) and other complementary material. Carballo examined Ricardo's theory of rent in detail, questioned the criticism made by Molinari, Carey and Bastiat, but finally adopted the position of Passy because 'we see the origin of rent in the fertility of land', although 'primitive' fertility is continuously changed by the crop, the accumulation of capital and agronomical improvements (1855–1856: I, 381–409). This rectification of the Ricardian theory was not reflected in his static analysis of the impact of taxes (1855–1856: II, 39–47).

Manuel Colmeiro abandoned the 'eclectic' approach in a subsequent book (Colmeiro 1859) that closely followed some authors from the French economist school, particularly Henri Baudrillart. His position in regard to Ricardo was similar to that of Carballo. He accepted that rent is the effect and not the cause of the increase in the 'cost of production', but immediately maintained that the diminishing fertility trend is offset by the use of 'machines', 'new methods' and the reduction in transport costs (pp. 304–10).

Mariano Carreras' (1865) criticism of Ricardo's theory of rent is much more profound and vehement, fully accepting the reasoning of Carey, Bastiat and Molinari. Ricardo's mistakes are the 'natural productivity' of land and the order of the farming process by fertility, which should be replaced by a more general capitalisation theory. 'Hence, there is not one word of truth in Ricardo's theory of rent' (p. 296) and the upward tendency of the price of agricultural products is 'the dream of a pessimist' (p. 310).

Epilogue: translations of David Ricardo into Spanish

More than 80 years elapsed between the first translation of *Principles* (Ricardo 1848–49), which was incomplete, commented and restricted, and the next. The interest in Ricardo's work waned over that period until the end of the nineteenth century, when *Progress and Poverty* by Henry George became widely known (up until the 1930s). Although the 'Georgist movement' emerged in the shape of non-academic reformist groups, heterodox economist Germán Bernácer used the ideas of Turgot, Ricardo and George to criticise the marginal theory of interest and to formulate a theory of economic crises caused by a lack of effective demand (Almenar 1999; Bernácer 1925).

Three full translations of the *Principles* were published within the space of very few years (see the bracket references in the Appendix): the first two in Spain (1932, 1936) and the third in Argentina (1937), coinciding with the discussion on agricultural reform in Spain and the revival of classical economists prompted by the crisis. All three translations were reprinted or re-edited on numerous occasions throughout the rest of the twentieth century.

However, the largest editorial project was the translation undertaken in Mexico of the Sraffa and Dobb edition *The Works and Correspondence of David Ricardo* (1958–65), which did not include the last two volumes of biography and index. Manuel Sánchez Sarto, a Spanish economist in exile since the civil war who was specialized in economic history and the history of economic thought, appears to have been behind this project. The first volume (*Principles*) achieved long-lasting publishing success in Latin America and Spain despite some shortcomings in the translation (Rodríguez Braun 1982).

4. Concluding remarks

The reception of Ricardo's economic thought in Spain was influenced by factors 'external' to economic analysis, such as the persecution of liberals, the restrictions on publishing rights up to 1834 and the predominance of the French language and French publications among the learned public. The references to Ricardo made by Spanish political economy writers indicate this was the case, as these references were largely indirect or dependent on either the French translation by F. S. Constâncio or the views of authors such as Say and Sismondi. In contrast, the exile of some liberal thinkers in England facilitated their contact with British economic culture, as in the case of Álvaro Flórez Estrada, José Joaquín de Mora, Pablo Pebrer and, indirectly, José Antonio Seoane and Cipriano Montesino (whose parents had been exiled). However, these circumstances do not appear to have been (sufficiently) decisive in the reception of Ricardo's ideas, as the diversity of positions adopted by these exiles indicates. Meanwhile, the close relationship with French economic culture intensified further after 1834, reaching a high point with the emergence of the 'economist school'.

How can we explain the problems with disseminating Ricardian innovations? Nassau Senior considered that the differences between Ricardo's work and continental European currents stemmed from disagreements over the scientific method and the epistemological position with regard to political economy. 'The modern economists of France, Germany, Spain, Italy, and America, so far as I am acquainted with their works, all treat Political Economy as an art' (Senior 1852: 46). Senior's 'hasty sketch', notwithstanding his simplification, appears to be true in the case of the Spanish authors who disagreed with Ricardo, particularly if those differences are studied as part of the various individual intellectual itineraries and national economic traditions. For a large majority of Spanish economists, the economic backwardness of Spain (especially after the fall of the empire in America) prompted the need to adapt the 'universal' approaches to political economy, to include specific criteria to interpret and remedy that backwardness. Why did Spanish economists show a preference for Say? *Traité* allowed for an easier adaptation to the 'facts' (compared with Ricardo's compact model) and exalted functional and general industrialism, while the centralised institutionalization of political economy in education favoured Say. After the new liberal society had stabilized in the 1840s, there was a clearer reception of the new political economy, optimistic and harmonious, on behalf of a new generation that imitated the French 'economist school'.

The influence of Ricardo, McCulloch and Mill on *Curso de economía política* by Flórez Estrada was substantial in the case of the theory of distribution (rent, profits and wages), the theory of economic growth, the theory of value and prices, in some aspects of the monetary theory and international trade, and his position on taxation and public debt. From this point of view, Flórez Estrada was the most prominent receiver, disseminator and reformulator of Ricardian economics in Spain and Latin America. This conclusion supports the interpretation of two contemporary economists, namely Théodore Fix (1833) and Antonio Scialoja (1844: 153–6), and suggests that the label of 'eclectic economist' applied by Blanqui (1837: II, 288–302) to Flórez and Storch should be rejected.

The singular nature of Flórez's book within Spanish economic literature could be naïvely interpreted as a rare case of acceptance, albeit not exclusive, of the deductive method in political economy (1980: 67). However, his intellectual evolution also shows that Flórez perceived the Ricardian model of distribution and growth as a tool of analysis and radical critique of traditional Spanish society, where landowners predominated in economic and political life. But his approach to Ricardian economics and his adaptation can also be seen as a new attempt to reconcile his deeply-rooted social principles of civic republicanism with the features that are typical of a modern society.

Appendix. Twentieth century translations of David Ricardo into Spanish

(1932). *Principios de economía política e imposición fiscal*, Introd., notes and app. by Sir E.C.K. Gonner, trans. by E. Hazera; 2 vols. Barcelona: El Consultor Bibliográfico (*Biblioteca de Cultura Económica*, 13).

(1936). *Principios de economía política y de tributación*, Prologue and trans. by V. A. Álvarez. Madrid: Aguilar. (Dated from 'Últimos libros publicados', *Gaceta del libro* May–June 1936, III(19–20): 24).

(1937). *Principios de economía política y de tributación*, Introd. by F. W. Kolthammer, trans. by Dr E. Pepe. Buenos Aires: Claridad.

(1942). *Principios de economía política y de tributación* [1937 2nd reprint]. Buenos Aires: Claridad. (Dated from US Library of Congress in 1941.)

(1955). *Principios de economía política y de tributación* [1936 new edn]. Madrid: Aguilar (*Biblioteca de Ciencias Sociales, Economía*).

(1958–1965). *Obras y correspondencia de David Ricardo*, ed. by P. Sraffa and M. H. Dobb. México: Fondo de Cultura Económica (*Las obras maestras de la economía*).

I. 1959. *Principios de economía política y tributación*, trans. by J. Broc, N. Wolff and J. Estrada, revision by M. Sánchez Sarto.

II. 1958. *Notas a los principios de economía política de Malthus*, trans. by F. M. Torner.

III. 1959. *Folletos y artículos, 1809–1811*, trans. by F. M. Torner.

IV. 1960. *Folletos y artículos, 1815–1823*, trans. by F. M. Torner.
V. 1961. *Discursos y testimonios : 1819–1823*, trans. by F. M. Torner.
VI. 1962. *Cartas, 1810–1815*, trans. by N. Wolff.
VII. 1963. *Cartas, 1816–1818*, trans. by J. Broc and M. Álvarez Franco.
VIII. 1964. *Cartas, 1819–junio 1921*, trans. by F. M. Torner.
IX. 1965. *Cartas, julio 1821–1823*, trans. by Carlos Villegas.
X. 'Miscelánea biográfica' [announced but not published].

(1959) *Principios de economía política y de tributación* [1955 2nd reprint]. Madrid: Aguilar (*Biblioteca de Ciencias Sociales, Economía*).

(1973a). *Principios de economía política y tributación*, Introd. by M. Román, trans. by E. Hazera [1932]. Madrid: Ayuso.

(1973b). *Principios de economía política y de tributación*, New prologue and trans. by V. A. Álvarez [1936]. Madrid: Seminarios y Ediciones.

(1973c). *Principios de economía política y de tributación* [1958–65 vol. I, 2nd reprint]. México: Fondo de Cultura Económica.

(1974). 'Dos escritos de Ricardo' ('Ensayo sobre la influencia del bajo precio del grano sobre los beneficios del capital', trans. by V. Llombart; 'Valor absoluto y valor de cambio') in C. Napoleoni, *Fisiocracia, Smith, Ricardo, Marx*. Vilassar de Mar, Barcelona: Oikos-tau.

(1985a). *Principios de economía política y tributación* [1973a new ed. 2 vols]. Barcelona: Orbis (*Biblioteca de política, economía y sociología*).

(1985b). *Principios de economía política* [1973a new ed.]. Madrid: Sarpe (*Los grandes pensadores*, 74).

(1985c). *Principios de economía política y tributación (selección)*, Intro. and selection by A. Barceló, trans. by E. Hazera. Barcelona: Orbis & Buenos Aires: Hyspamérica.

(1985d). *Principios de economía política y de tributación* [1958–65 vol. I 3rd reprint]. México: Fondo de Cultura Económica.

(1986). *Principios de economía política y tributación (selección)* [1985c reprint]. Barcelona: Orbis.

(1993). *Principios de economía política y de tributación* [1958–65 vol. I reprint]. Colombia: Fondo de Cultura Económica.

(1994). *Principios de economía política y de tributación* [1958–65 vol. I 5th reprint]. México: Fondo de Cultura Económica.

(1996). *Valor, distribución y paro* [Selection from *Principles*], Introd., selection and trans. by C. Rodríguez Braun. Madrid: Pirámide.

(1998). *Principios de economía política y de tributación* [1958–65 vol. I 6th reprint]. México: Fondo de Cultura Económica.

(2003). *Principios de economía política y tributación*, Introd. by J. Reeder, trans. P. de la Nuez y C. Rodríguez Braun. Madrid: Pirámide.

Notes

1 *Nuevo diario de Madrid* (Nuevo 1822), advertisement of the sale of the French translation of Ricardo in the liberal club Fontana de Oro. The online catalogues of

university libraries (Rebium), the Biblioteca Nacional and the Catálogo Colectivo del Patrimonio Bibliográfico provide the data for the quantitative estimation.

2 Three editions were published in London (1825, 182? 1828) for the market in Latin America, 4,000 copies being printed. It was published in secret in Spain in 1827 under the title *Lecciones de economía política*.

3 Advertisements appeared in March and July 1822 for a four-instalment subscription (Gaceta 1822a; 1822b), but the book was not advertised further. The first instalment might have been published.

4 Almost all of Flórez's books were included in the Spanish edition of his works (Flórez Estrada 1958). Some were translated into English between 1810 and 1826. For an up-to-date biography and numerous expert studies on Flórez, see Varela (2004).

5 The critical edition of 1980 reproduces the fourth edition as the main text (Flórez Estrada 1835).

6 In addition, it is worth mentioning other works used to provide further reasoning or information, such as Thomas Tooke, Fréderic Gentz, William Jacob, Henry Parnell, Giuseppe Pecchio, *Cours d'économie politique* by Say and a contribution by M. de Jovellanos and José Canga Argüelles on the Spanish economy.

7 The copy with both parts of the translation (Ricardo 1848–49) that belongs to the Real Academia de la Historia library (Madrid) was untrimmed until 2012. The copy that remains at the Biblioteca Nacional de España (Madrid) only contains the first part.

References

Almenar, S. (1980) Estudio preliminar. El pensamiento económico de A. Flórez Estrada. Economía ricardiana y reformismo radical. In Á. Flórez Estrada, *Curso de Economía Política*. Madrid: Instituto de Estudios Fiscales, vol. I: xxxv–cxxiii.

——(1999) Keynes's economic ideas in Spain before the *General Theory*: spread, 'anticipations' and parallels. In L. L. Pasinetti and B. Schefold (eds), *The Impact of Keynes on Economics in the 20th Century*. Cheltenham: Edward Elgar: 99–116.

——(2000) Álvaro Flórez Estrada y la economía política clásica. In E. Fuentes Quintana (ed.), *Economía y economistas españoles. 4. La economía clásica*, Barcelona: Galaxia Gutenberg - Funcas, vol. 4: 369–411.

——(2010) Estudio preliminar. Álvaro Flórez Estrada: revolución y Constitución, economía política y cuestión social. In Á. Flórez Estrada, *Curso de economía política (1852)*. Gijón: Ediciones Trea: lxiii–cxlix.

——(2012a) Propiedad, igualdad y prosperidad. Flórez Estrada y la desamortización. In S. de Dios, J. Infante, R. Robledo, et al. (eds), *Historia de la propiedad: la expropiación. VII Encuentro interdisciplinar*. Salamanca: Eds. Universidad de Salamanca, 241–316.

——(2012b) Teaching, spreading and preaching: textbooks of political economy in Spain 1779–1936. In M. M. Augello and M. E. L. Guidi (eds), *The Economic Reader: Textbooks, Manuals and the Dissemination of the Economic Sciences during the 19th and Early 20th Centuries*. London: Routledge, 158–88.

Anon (1820a) Prólogo del traductor. In J.-B. Say, *Cartas de M. Jn. Bta. Say á M. Malthus sobre varios puntos de economía política*. Madrid: Imp. de El Censor, iii–vii.

——(1820b) Review of Cartas de J. B. Say a M. Malthus, *El Censor* (14) 4 November: 147–56.

Bernácer, G. (1925) *Interés del capital. El problema de su orígenes*. Alicante: Lucentum.

Blanqui, A.-J. (1837) *Histoire de l'économie politique en Europe depuis les anciens jusqu'à nos jours, suivie d'une bibliographie raisonnée des principaux ouvrages d'économie politique*, 2 vols. Paris: Guillaumin.

Blanqui, A.-J. (1839) *Historia de la economia política en Europa*, trans. J. Carasa. Madrid: Imp. de Nicolas Arias.

Borrego, A. (1844) *Principios de economía política con aplicación a la reforma de aranceles de aduana, a la situación de la industria fabril de Cataluña, y al mayor y más rápido incremento de la riqueza nacional*. Madrid: Imprenta de la Sociedad de Operarios del mismo Arte.

Cabrillo, F. (1977) Una controvertida traducción al español de los Principios de David Ricardo, *Moneda y Crédito* (143): 187–191.

Carballo, Wangüemert B. (1855–1856) *Curso de Economía Política*, 2 vols. Madrid: Imp. de Pedro Montero.

Carreras, y González M. (1865) *Filosofía del interés personal. Tratado didáctico de economía política*, 1st edn. Madrid: Imprenta y Librería de M. Guijarro.

Colmeiro, M. (1845) *Tratado elemental de Economia política ecléctica*, 2 vols. Madrid: Viuda e hijos de D. Antonio Calleja.

——(1859) *Principios de economía política*. Madrid, Valparaiso: Librerias de Angel Calleja; Libreria española de Calleja.

Destutt de Tracy, A.-L.-C. C. (1823) *Traité d'économie politique (Élémens d'idéologie, IV Partie)*. Paris: M. Bouguet et Lévy.

Espinosa de los Monteros, J. (1831) *Tratado de economía politica aplicada á España*. Madrid: Imprenta de Eusebio Aguado.

Fernández López, M. (2000) Enseñar Economía en un país nuevo, *El Economista* 19 May.

Ferrier, F. L. A. (1826) *Del gobierno considerado en sus relaciones con el comercio, ó de la administracion comercial en oposicion con los economistas del siglo XIX*, 2 vols. Madrid: Repullés.

Fix, T. (1833) Review of Alvaro Flórez Estrada, *Cours éclectique d'économie politique*, *Revue mensuelle d'économie politique* 1: 281–297.

Flórez Estrada, Á. (1812) *Examen imparcial de las disensiones de la América con la España, de los medios de su reconciliacion y de la prosperidad de todas las naciones*. 2nd edn, Cádiz: Imp. Ximenez Carreño.

——(1828) *Curso de economía política*, 2 vols. London: D. M. Calero.

——(1831) *Curso de economía política. Segunda edición corregida y aumentada considerablemente*, 2 vols. Paris: Imp. de Gaultier-Laguionie.

——(1833) *Cours Éclectique d'Économie Politique, écrit en espagnol … et traduit sur les manuscrits originaux de l'auteur par L. Galibert*, trans. L. Galibert, 3 vols, Paris: Treuttel et Würtz, 1833.

——(1835) *Curso de economía política. Cuarta edición corregida*, 2 vols. Madrid: Imprenta de D. Miguel de Burgos.

——(1839) *La cuestión social o sea orijen, latitud i efectos del derecho de propiedad.- Indicaciones acerca de la cuestión social que actualmente se ventila con empeño por los economistas europeos, sometidas á la discusión de los sabios*. Madrid: Miguel de Burgos.

——(1841) *Elementos de economía política*. Madrid: Miguel de Burgos.

——(1958) *Obras*, M. Artola and L. A. Martínez Cachero (eds), Biblioteca de Autores Españoles, 2 vols, Madrid: Ediciones Atlas.

——(1980) *Curso de economía política*, S. Almenar (ed.), 2 vols. Madrid: Instituto de Estudios Fiscales.

Frías Hernández, J. C. (1993) Atraso económico y cultura de élites. A propósito de la traducción castellana en 1848 de los Principios de Economía Política y Tributación de David Ricardo, *Revista de Historia Económica* 11(3): 541–562.

Gaceta (1818) Paris, 30 (Nov.) En el Monitor se anuncia (...) Principios de economia politica y de los impuestos, *Gaceta de Madrid* 15 December: 1251–4.

——(1822a) Anuncios, *Gaceta de Madrid* 24 March: 460.

——(1822b) Anuncios, *Gaceta de Madrid* 7 July: 1058.

Grice-Hutchinson, M. (1993) The Vicissitudes of an Economist: Manuel María Gutiérrez. In L. S. Moss and C. K. Ryan (eds), *Economic Thought in Spain: Selected Essays of Marjorie Grice-Hutchinson*. Aldershot: Edward Elgar: 100–25.

Gutiérrez, M. M. (1831) Prólogo del traductor ó análisis de la obra. In J. Mill, *Elementos de economía política*. Madrid: Imp. de D. Miguel de Burgos: xix–xlv.

——(1837) *Impugnación a las cinco proposiciones de Pebrer*. Madrid: Marcelino Calero.

——(1839) *Nuevas consideraciones sobre libertad absoluta de comercio y puertos francos*. Madrid: Vda. de M. Calero.

Jaumeandreu, E. (1836) *Curso elemental de Economia política: con aplicación á la legislacion económica de España*, 2 vols. Barcelona: Imp. de Gaspar.

Jones, R. (1831) *An essay on the distribution of wealth and on the sources of taxation. Part I. Rent*. London: John Murray.

Lowry, J. [J. Marcet] (1835) *Conversaciones sobre la economía política: en las cuales se esplican [sic] de un modo simple y familiar los elementos de esta ciencia*, trans. G. Escosura, 2 vols. Madrid: Imprenta de Repullés.

Lluch, E. (1964) Notas a la edición de la obra de Álvaro Flórez Estrada, *Anales de Economía, segunda época* (8): 813–819.

——(2009) *El pensament econòmic a Catalunya (1760–1840)*, 2nd edn. Barcelona: Edicions 62.

Lluch, E. and Almenar, S. (2000) Difusión e influencia de los economistas clásicos en España (1776–1870). In E. Fuentes Quintana (ed.), *Economía y economistas españoles. 4. La economía clásica*, Barcelona: Fundación FIES – Galaxia Gutenberg, vol. 4, 93–170.

——(2004) The Itineraries of Neo-Smithian Political Economy in Spain (1800–1848), *Economies et Sociétés* 34: 267–297.

McCulloch, J. R. (1824) Taxation, *Supplement to the fourth, fifth, and sixth editions of Encyclopaedia Britannica*. Edinburgh: A. Constable, vol. 6, 608–645.

——(1825a) *A Discourse on the Rise, Progress, Peculiar Objects, and Importance, of Political Economy*, 2nd edn. Edinburgh: Archibald Constable.

——(1825b) *Principles of Political Economy with a Sketch of the Rise and Progress of the Science*. Edinburgh: William & Charles Tait.

——(1828) Supplemental notes and dissertations. In A. Smith, *An Inquiry Into the Nature and Causes of the Wealth of Nations*. Edinburgh: Adam Black & William Tait, vol. 4, 71–580.

Malthus, T. R. (1827) *Definitions of Political Economy*. London: John Murray.

Martín Rodríguez, M. (2009) *Análisis económico y revolución liberal en España. Economistas académicos en las Cortes liberales, 1834–1874*. Madrid: Civitas.

Mill, J. (1821) *Elements of Political Economy*, 1 edn. London: Baldwin, Cradock & Joy.

——(1827) *Elementos de economía política*, 2 vols. Paris: Imp. de J. Smith.

——(1831) *Elementos de economía política*, trans. M. M. Gutiérrez. Madrid: Imprenta de D. Miguel de Burgos.

Montesino, C. S. (1855) Notas del traductor y de Pedro Gómez de Laserna. In J. R. McCulloch, *Principios de economía política.* Madrid: Imp. de M. Sanz y Gómez: 295–366.

Mora, J. J. (1819) Economía política. De los principios de la economía política y del impuesto, por Mr. David Ricardo ... Juicio de esta obra, *Crónica científica y literaria* (213) 13 April: 2–3.

——(1825) *Catecismo de economía política.* London: R. Ackermann.

Nuevo (1822) Anuncios, *Nuevo diario de Madrid* 5 July.

O'Brien, D. P. (1970) *J. R. McCulloch. A Study in Classical Economics.* London: George Allen & Unwin.

Oliver, G. A. (1834) *Vindicación de la industria de Cataluña.* Barcelona: H. de Agustín Roca.

Pastor, L. M. (1850) *Filosofía del crédito*, 1st edn. Madrid: Imp. D. W. Ayguals de Izco.

Pebrer, P. (1833) *Taxation, revenue, expenditure, power, statistics, and debt of the whole British Empire; their origin, progress, and present state.* London: Baldwin & Cradock.

Ricardista (1848) Cartas económicas, *La España* (126, 162) 13 September, 25 October.

Ricardo, D. (1821) *On the principles of political economy, and taxation*, 3rd edn. London: John Murray.

——(1848–1849) *Principios de economía political y fiscal*, trans. J. A. Seoane and F. Cos-Gayón. Madrid: Imp. del Colegio de Sordomudos y Ciegos.

——(1951) *On the Principles of Political Economy and Taxation*, Piero Sraffa (ed.), The Works and Correspondence of David Ricardo, vol. 1. Cambridge: Cambridge University Press.

Rodríguez Braun, C. (1982) Debilidades en la edición del Fondo de Cultura Económica de los Principios de Ricardo, *Investigaciones económicas* 18: 201–209.

Rossi, P. (1840) *Curso de Economía Política: año escolar de 1836–1837*, trans. P. d. Madrazo. Madrid: Boix.

Sánchez Rivera, J. (1821) Prólogo del traductor. In J.-B. Say, *Tratado de Economia Politica: ó exposición sencilla del modo con que se forman, se distribuyen y conservan las riquezas.* Madrid: Imp. de Fermin Villalpando, vol. 1, vii–viii.

Say, J.-B. (1823) Notes explicatives et critiques. In H. v. Storch, *Cours d'économie politique.* Paris: Aillaud, Bossange, Rey et Gravier.

——(1825) Sobre la balanza de los consumos y las producciones, *Mercurio de España* II (March): 209–218.

——(1826) *Traité d'économie politique, ou simple exposition de la manière dont se forment, se distribuent et se consomment les richessses*, 5th edn, 3 vols. Paris: Chez Rapilly.

Scialoja, A. (1844) *Les principes de l'économie sociale*, 2nd edn, trans. H. Devillers. Paris: Guillaumin.

Senior, N. W. (1852) *Four Introductory Lectures on Political Economy Delivered before the University of Oxford.* London: Longman, Brown, Green, and Longmans.

Seoane, J. A. (1848) Notas. In D. Ricardo, *Principios de economía política y fiscal.* Madrid: Imp. del Colegio de Sordomudos y Ciegos, 7–11, 30–40, 52–57.

Sismondi, J.-C. L. Simonde de (1825) Disertación del Sr. Sismondi sobre la balanza de los consumos y las producciones, *Mercurio de España* II (January, February): 41–54, 125–137.

——(1827) *Nouveaux principes d'économie politique, ou de la richesse dans ses rapports avec la population*, 2nd edn, 2 vols. Paris: Delaunay.

——(1834) *Nuevos principios de economía política o de la riqueza en sus relaciones con la población*, 1st edition, trans. F. Xerez y Barona, 2 vols. Granada: Imp. de Benavides.

Smith, R. S. (1957) The Wealth of Nations in Spain and Latin America, 1780–1830, *Journal of Political Economy* 65: 104–125.

——(1968) English economic thought in Spain, 1776–1848. In C. D. W. Goodwin and I. B. Holley (eds), *The transfer of ideas: historical essays.* Durham: The South Atlantic Quarterly, 106–137.

——(1969) The reception of Malthus's Essay on population in Spain, *Rivista Internazionale di Scienze Economiche e Commerciali* 16(6): 550–565.

Sraffa, P. (1955) Bibliography of Ricardo's Works, in Piero Sraffa (ed.), *The Works and Correspondance of David Ricardo.* Cambridge: Cambridge University Press, 10: 355–385.

Storch, H. v. (1823) *Cours d'économie politique, ou exposition des principes que determinent la prosperité des nations, avec des notes explicatives et critiques pas J.-B. Say.* Paris: J.P. Aillaud, Bossange, Rey et Gravier.

——(1824) *Considérations sur la nature du revenu national.* Paris: Bossange.

Thompson, T. P. (1830) *The true theory of rent, in opposition to Mr. Ricardo and others*, 7th edn. London: Robert Heward.

Thompson, W. (1824) *An inquiry into the principles of the distribution of wealth most conducive to human happiness; applied to the newly proposed system of voluntary equality of wealth.* London: Longman.

Torrens, R. (1821) *An Essay on the Production of Wealth.* London: Longman.

——(1829) *An essay on external corn trade*, 4th edn. London: Longman.

Torrente, M. (1835) *Revista general de la economía política*, 3 vols. La Habana: Imp. de Jordan.

Valle, E. M. del (1842) *Curso de economía política.* Madrid: Imprenta del Colegio Nacional de Sordo-Mudos.

Valle Santoro, M. del (1829) *Elementos de economía política con aplicación particular a España.* Madrid: Imprenta de Ramón Vergés.

Varela, J. (ed.) (2004) *Álvaro Flórez Estrada (1766–1853). Política, economía, sociedad.* Oviedo: Junta General del Principado de Asturias.

5 The influence of Ricardo on the monetary debate in Italy

Anna La Bruna and Annalisa Rosselli

1. Introduction

It may appear unusual that, on being asked to discuss the reception of Ricardo in Italy, we decided to focus this chapter on his influence on the monetary debates of the nineteenth century, instead of dealing with his more famous contribution to the theory of value and distribution. The reason is that, as far as these latter issues are concerned, a general consensus has already been reached that Ricardo's theory had limited influence on the development of Italian economic thought (Faucci, 2000) for the greater part of the nineteenth century. Indeed, none of the major economists then enjoying academic power and prestige in Italy were strict followers of Ricardo, with interest in building on his ideas regarding these issues being confined to isolated scholars such as Francesco Fuoco, or lesser-known economists such as Emilio Nazzani, only recently rediscovered (Perri 2003). The diffusion of Marx's ideas and those of the German Historical School stimulated renewed interest in Ricardo at the end of the century through the works of Achille Loria, Giuseppe Ricca Salerno and Augusto Graziani,[1] but it was by far and away the marginalist approach, in a Marshallian or Austrian version, that dominated the development of Italian economics well into the twentieth century.

Several reasons have been put forward to explain why Ricardo's theory of value failed to appeal to Italian economists, some being connected with developments in the political and social situation in Italy. Culturally speaking, Italy was very much under the influence of France, and the French approach *à la* Say was more in keeping with the utilitarian stream in Italian economic thought of the previous century. Say's optimistic vision of harmonious progress sounded more encouraging for economists engaged in building a new nation than the dismal predictions of Ricardianism. However, British classical political economy was not ignored: it has been said (La Bruna 2007a: 29–30; Perri 2003: 107) that every Italian economist attempted his own reconciliation between the subjective and objective elements in the theory of value, giving rise to an eclectic approach which mixed cost of production and utility in various combinations as determinants of value. The theory of the 'cost of reproduction', adopted and spread by Francesco Ferrara, the most famous

Italian economist of the second half of the nineteenth century, is an eloquent example of these endeavours (Minnelli et al. 2004; Bonaccorsi di Patti 2001), even if his markedly subjectivist and anti-Ricardian approach situates him at the end of the spectrum of these attempts at reconciliation.

Political motivations added to the discredit of Ricardo. The main tenets of Ricardo's theory of distribution – the inverse relation between wages and profits and, above all, the theory of rent which showed how the increase of rents caused a fall in the rate of profit and in the general prosperity of the country – were perceived as lending support to socialist sentiments against private ownership of land (Ferrara 1860: 159–160). Since the 1830s concern for social stability had begun to prevail over any other consideration and Italian political economy inclined towards moderation and conservatism (Faucci 2000: 131). After the social and political upheaval of 1848, which alarmed the ruling classes, Ricardo's theory of rent was superseded by that of Carey and Bastiat, while the labour theory of value came in for strong criticism.

The delay in publication of Ricardo's works in Italian constituted a further stumbling block in the way of direct knowledge and appreciation of the author.[2] The first translation of the *Principles* came out in 1856 as a volume of the *Biblioteca dell'economista*, with an Introduction by the editor of the series, Francesco Ferrara, which, unsurprisingly, contains severe criticism of Ricardo's theory of labour-value (Ferrara 1856a). A selection of Ricardo's writings[3] on money was published the following year, as volume six in the second series of the *Biblioteca dell'economista,* together with essays on banking by writers, mainly French, such as Coquelin, Chevalier, Carey and Du Puynode (Ferrara 1857). It is to be noted, however, that educated people in Italy generally had a knowledge of French. The first French translation of the *Principles* became available in 1819, with explanatory notes by Say which inspired Ferrara's criticism of Ricardo. The French translation of the *Works of David Ricardo* by McCulloch appeared in 1847. As Sraffa notes with reference to this translation in his edition of Ricardo's works, '[it] has provided for nearly a century the standard introduction to Ricardo for a large part of the non-English speaking world' (*Works and Correspondence of David Ricardo*, X, 375).[4]

Be as it may, even if we cannot say that the Ricardian theory of value and distribution became the foundation of the prevailing approach to the subject in Italy, generally speaking it did not even give rise to overt anti-Ricardianism, Francesco Ferrara being somewhat an exception. Although prestigious, his teaching, inspired by optimism, harmony and ultra-liberalism, remained a minority view. Most of his contemporaries persisted in the Italian tradition of economic thought, although innovated, to varying degrees, through the influence of the British classical school.

We have several examples of this eclectic moderatism which was expected to contribute to and not exalt social conflict. The economist most representative of the scene at the end of the 1870s was in fact Gerolamo Boccardo, an eminent academic, senator and editor of the third series of the *Biblioteca dell'economista*, with his interdisciplinary pragmatism, of positivist mould, and his 'political economy of social conciliation' (Macchioro 2006: 179). Boccardo drew inspiration more from Smith than Ricardo, but his rival and interlocutor Salvatore Majorana would look to Ricardo while attempting a synthesis of utility and labour, cost of production and reproduction. On the eve of 1848, he had become a supporter of the Ricardian theory of rent which was widely debated in those years by economists from southern Italy. Later, in his work as Minister of Agriculture, Industry and Commerce of the Kingdom of Italy, he would again be looking to Ricardo when proposing a monetary reform, as we will see below.[5]

In conclusion, Italian economists pursued a synthesis of principles apparently irreconcilable, often with great originality, mixing historical and analytical approaches, combining naturalism and historicism, liberalism and interventionism, integrating Ricardian-Marxian elements with neo-classical features to address particular problems (such as explanation of the surplus). If Ricardo had no real followers, nor did the pure marginalist or the pure Austrian School.

Having acknowledged that there is strong evidence that Ricardo failed to constitute (or soon ceased to) a starting point for the developments of the theory of value and distribution in Italy, it is natural to inquire whether the same fortune was shared by the rest of his theory. Unlike Francesco Ferrara, who said of the *Principles* that 'if you destroy that key concept [the labour theory of value], it is hard to believe that more than 10 pages of his book will be left standing' (Ferrara 1856b: 298, *our translation*), it can be maintained that theories such as the theory of rent, comparative costs, taxation and the positions taken by Ricardo in the monetary controversies, gained attention or support even in theoretical contexts that did not include acceptance of the theory of value.

Such is the route followed by this chapter, which inquires as to whether Ricardo's monetary thought and theory of value met with different fortunes. It is legitimate, indeed, to separate the destiny of Ricardo's ideas on money from that of his ideas on value and distribution for the following reasons:

i) Ricardo's analysis of the problems of the British monetary system and his proposals for remedying them were presented with few modifications over the years, while his theory of value was undergoing considerable changes, as attested by the various different justifications for the invariability of the value of gold put forward in his works (see below). Hence, the same monetary theory is compatible with different foundations for the value of commodities. Rejection of Ricardo's value theory did not logically and *necessarily* imply rejection of his monetary thought.[6]
ii) In nineteenth-century Italy there was great interest in some of the issues which prompted Ricardo's intervention in the Bullionist controversy: the causes of the high price of gold and depreciation of the rate of exchange; the consequences of the use of paper money; and the choice of the standard.

iii) Ricardo advanced actual detailed proposals for the organization of the monetary and banking system and discussed extensively who – a private or a public institution – should be entrusted with the power of issuing paper money. This issue, and the ensuing harmonization of the local banking systems, came to the fore after the unification of Italy in 1861.

iv) The political and economic interests which could have been threatened by adoption of Ricardo's proposals were not the same as had stirred up antagonism towards his theory of value and distribution; hence Ricardo's monetary ideas might have been accorded a less chilly reception.

Indeed, we will demonstrate that Ricardo's views on money enjoyed a wider and more favourable reception than those on value and distribution, but ultimately they were no better understood or endorsed since neither the historical situation nor the approach to economics favoured their acceptance.

In order to prove this conclusion we will firstly outline the main monetary issues that were under discussion in Italy subsequent to independence in 1861 (Section 2), the major laws proposed or approved to solve them, and the protagonists of the debates they entailed (Section 3). We will then proceed to summarize the main conclusions of Ricardo's theory which are relevant to the issues debated in Italy (Section 4). The influence of Ricardo on the monetary debates in Italy in the nineteenth century is discussed in Section 5, with particular focus on the controversy in the late 1870s.

2. Monetary questions in the newborn Italian state

The political unification of Italy under the sovereignty of the Piedmontese dynasty in the nineteenth century was accompanied by extensive economic and monetary reforms. The transformation of the whole of Italy into one free-trade area entailed monetary unification, but the latter was much more difficult to accomplish than the former. The seven states that gave birth to Italy in 1861 had monetary systems which differed in many respects. Some had a bimetallic decimal system and others a monometallic non-decimal system based on a silver standard, the fineness of the metal varying from place to place. Moreover, none of the pre-unification states was large enough to have a completely independent currency. Coins of neighbouring states circulated together with old coins of previous regimes. Definition as a 'monetary babel' was all too apt for a circulation on the national territory that counted at least ninety-two different types of coins which were legal tender in addition to more than 100 which were not, all of which had to be brought to the mints and re-coined into the new Italian *lira* (Omiccioli 2011).

Obviously, the first monetary question to be debated by the newborn state was the choice of the standard. There were two alternatives, which reflected the current division of Europe into two areas. The first was extension to the rest of Italy of the monetary system of Kingdom of Sardinia, which was a near-perfect replica of the French one: bimetallic, decimal, with a gold/silver ratio fixed at 15.5, and silver with 900/1000 fineness. The second alternative was the move towards the gold standard which prevailed in Great Britain and which was perceived as 'the system of the future', appropriate for a modern country (De Cecco 2007: 65). Technical considerations were involved in this debate,[7] although ultimately the final decision was driven mainly by political considerations. The mixture of political and scientific arguments, after all, was not unusual for Italy in the first decades of its life, when many economists had a seat in Parliament.[8] In spite of many arguments in favour of a monometallic gold standard, Italy adopted the bimetallic system in 1862,[9] in conformity with the system in France, which had supported Italy in her wars for independence and was her main commercial partner. Political alliance and the hope of receiving from France the capital Italy badly needed to modernize the country prevailed over any other consideration.[10] In 1866, however, Italy suspended convertibility of the banknotes of the main bank of issue, the Banca Nazionale nel Regno d'Italia, in return for a large loan from the Bank. It should have been a temporary measure to cope with the cost of a war against Austria. Instead, inconvertibility was to become permanent, with the exception of a short period between 1883 and 1885. The second big monetary question became if, when and how to return to convertibility.

The third monetary question is closely connected to the other two and concerns the issue of banknotes. At the time of unification paper money constituted only a small part of the currency in a country where the population was poor, and 80 per cent of it illiterate. The suspension of convertibility in 1866 forced the use of paper money on the population but exacerbated a problem that the new Italian state had not been able to solve. Faced with the choice between adopting the British system of one single bank endowed with the monopoly of issuing paper money, and the system of free banking adopted by the United States and advocated by the most liberal economists, on its foundation the new Italian state opted for a compromise to protect the local interests. Five (later six) of the issuing banks of the pre-unification states survived, but one of them only, the bank of the Kingdom of Sardinia named Banca Nazionale degli Stati Sardi (and Banca Nazionale nel Regno d'Italia from 1866 onwards), had branches in all regions. This privileged position became even stronger after the suspension of convertibility, when its banknotes had to be accepted throughout the national territory, while those of the other banks were confined to local circulation. It soon became clear that such an uneven situation was untenable and that reform was needed before the return to convertibility. It was necessary either to put all the establishments on the same footing or to move definitively towards a centralized system. Again, the debate raged over several years.

The similarities between the monetary problems of Italy in the years after unification and those of England at the time when Ricardo was writing are remarkable: in both cases the problems under discussion were the return to convertibility and the role of a bank which was much bigger than the others and that – thanks to its special relations with the government – enjoyed a privileged position. However, the institutional and cultural environment was different and this had an impact on how the debate developed and the role that Ricardo's ideas played in it.

3. The protagonists in monetary debate after the unification of Italy

The three major questions – the choice of standard and composition of the currency, the system of issue and return to convertibility – were intertwined and often discussed together. The occasion for debate was always discussion of a new law in Parliament. In particular, after the adoption of the bimetallic system, three legislative acts raised the most heated controversies: i) the decree which suspended the convertibility of banknotes into coins in 1866; ii) the banking law of 1874, which had the aim of regulating the issue of banknotes in preparation for the return to convertibility;[11] and iii) the proposal of a law for reorganization of the banks of issue advanced in 1879 (the law was approved but never became effective).

The debate over the suspension of convertibility was wide-ranging and focused on the causes which had determined it and the remedies to its least desirable consequences. Several proposals to put an end to inconvertibility were advanced, one by Francesco Ferrara himself who presented two different plans, in 1867 and 1873 respectively. All the proposals advanced by him and others started from analysis of the causes of the high price of gold on the market, which became one of the central issues.[12]

The law of 1874 represented an attempt to reorganize the banking system, abolishing the privileges of the Banca Nazionale in preparation for the return to convertibility. It marked a setback in the process towards the monopoly of issue that some advocated, but also dissatisfied those who were in favour of free banking. The law introduced a new kind of banknote, issued by a consortium of all six pre-existing banks of issue, to which the debt of the state to the Banca Nazionale was transferred. The six banks of the consortium were able to issue the banknotes, which were inconvertible, on behalf of the state up to a fixed amount. They were also able to issue their own banknotes, of larger denomination, up to a limit determined by their reserves and capital. These banknotes were legal tender (*corso legale*) and the banks were obliged to convert them into banknotes of the consortium or coins.

This law – the *Legge Minghetti* – was named after the Prime Minister of the time, Marco Minghetti, but it was drafted with the substantial contribution of two economists, Luigi Luzzatti and Isacco Maurogonato, belonging to the 'statist' school of thought, centred on the Universities of Pavia and Padua in northern Italy. The debate on this law can be said to have marked the division of Italian economists into two schools. On one side free-market positions prevailed, even on the subject of money and banking, rejecting any control over the issue of banknotes. In order to assert his beliefs, Francesco Ferrara, the most prominent member of this school, founded the Società Adamo Smith (Adam Smith Society) and summoned all the economists who shared with him the laissez-faire tradition of classical political economy. On the other side another society was founded, the Associazione per il progresso degli studi economici (Society for the progress of economic studies) inspired by the doctrines of the German school. An intermediate, moderate position was taken by a few economists, such as Salvatore Majorana,[13] who considered the law of 1874 a step forward to a solution to the time-honoured problem of the banks of issue and an important measure to prepare for the resumption of convertibility (La Bruna 2007a: 143–148).

Majorana himself, as Minister of Agriculture, Industry and Commerce, prepared a modification of the law in 1879. His proposals inflamed debate once again. Majorana wanted to break monopolistic privileges in the banking sector, and favoured the cautious introduction of freedom for any bank, subject to the authorization of the central government, to issue banknotes with the 100 per cent backing of government bonds and up to a given overall limit.[14] His moderate stance in favour of competition, albeit subject to strict regulation, was opposed by those who favoured private monopoly of issue. Among these a crucial role was played by Boccardo (Boccardo 1879), who enjoyed close connections with the Banca Nazionale.[15] Criticism also came from the opposite front where ultra-liberal views prevailed, the exponents including one of Ferrara's pupils, Tullio Martello (Martello 1877).

4. Ricardo on the high price of gold and the power of issue

From the above account it is clear that different policy proposals were founded on different responses to the main theoretical question underlying the whole debate: what are the effects of variations in the quantity of money? It was the same problem that Ricardo addressed in many of his writings. Therefore, before reconstructing the Italian debates on monetary questions with the aim of assessing Ricardo's influence on them, it may be useful to recall some of the main conclusions of Ricardo's theory which are relevant to the issues under discussion.

The very foundations of Ricardo's theory of money clearly include the distinction between depreciation and changes in the value of money. Depreciation is a matter of the gold/money relation when gold is chosen as standard of money. It is defined and measured by the price of the gold on the market, or in other words the value of gold in terms of money. It answers the question: how many pounds and shillings per ounce of gold? The Mint price defines what this value ought to be and deviations of the market price of gold from its Mint price signal and measure depreciation (more rarely appreciation). The value of money, on the other hand, is the value of gold in terms of commodities. It answers the question: how much corn, or beer, or cloth or any other commodity can be bought with an ounce of gold bullion? It is a vaguer concept which cannot be translated into one single number for measurement (IV, 59).

Ricardo sees confusion between the two concepts as a source of many mistakes and misunderstandings (see, for example, IV, 330; V, 166), which loom large when the need arises to analyze the causes behind variations in prices. Indeed, variations in the purchasing power of the money over commodities are the result of two combined effects: variation in the purchasing power of the money over gold and variation in the purchasing power of gold over commodities. We can express the same concept by saying that the price of commodities has two components: the price of gold and the value of gold in terms of commodities. The former depends entirely and exclusively on the quantity of money. In Ricardo's opinion, there is one and only one explanation for an increase in the price of gold and this is an increase in the amount of money above the needs of trade. Similarly, there is only one way to correct it and that is a contraction in the quantity of money.

On the contrary, the value of gold in terms of commodities may change either because the value of gold has changed due to changing conditions of supply and demand for the metal, or for some general cause which has affected all the commodities in general. Ricardo clarified these propositions over the years while developing his theory of value up to its final form as a fully fledged labour theory of value. In doing so, he added consistency to his arguments without changing their substance (see Marcuzzo and Rosselli 1991: 45–7).

The distinction between depreciation and changes in the value of money has important policy implications, since it offers a tool to distinguish between rises in prices of monetary origin – which can be corrected – and rises in prices due to real causes, which cannot be prevented. The distinction recurs in Ricardo's works, starting from his early endeavours.[16]

However, nowhere is this distinction clearer than in his last works and speeches, when Ricardo defended himself against the accusation of promoting serious deflation in 1819 by supporting return to convertibility at the pre-war parity. In *Protection to Agriculture*, written in 1822, Ricardo explains that the deflation was the effect of two different causes. One was the appreciation of the Sterling, as proven by the return of the price of gold to its Mint level; the other was the increase in the value of gold due to the mistakes of the Bank of England, which had imported and bought huge amounts of gold bullion in preparation for the return to convertibility:

> Such a demand for gold could not fail to elevate its value, compared with the value of commodities. Not only, then, had we to elevate the value of our currency 5 per cent, the amount of the difference between the value of paper and of gold before these operations commenced, but we had still further to elevate it to the new value to which gold itself was raised, by the injudicious purchases which the Bank made of that metal. (V, 225)

All Ricardo's proposals for reform of the monetary system are based on the assumption that the difference between the market and Mint price of gold marks and *measures* depreciation. This difference constitutes a signal that must be followed by the monetary authority – whichever it may be – for correct management of the currency. Ricardo's plans for reform of the monetary system in England underwent several changes from the first proposal in the Appendix to the fourth edition of *High price of Bullion* in 1811 to the *Plan for a National Bank* posthumously published in 1824. The plans were pragmatically adjusted to the changing historical and political circumstances, but they all shared the fundamental feature[17] that the quantity of money must be regulated by a price signal (the price of gold bullion on the market) and not adjusted to a pre-established amount, since it cannot be judged whether the quantity of money is excessive or insufficient simply by looking at the variations in the quantity of banknotes in circulation. As Ricardo said: 'regulating their issues by the price of gold the commissioners could never err' (IV, 293).

The role of gold was that of standard of the currency. Coins should not be part of the circulation, since a 'currency may be considered perfect, of which the standard is invariable, which always conforms to that standard, and in the use of which the utmost economy is practised' (IV, 55).

Although adopting the rule of keeping the price of gold at its Mint parity would have constituted the correct behaviour for the Bank of England, Ricardo favoured a plan in which issue of paper money was not left to a 'company of merchants' who were 'allowed to regulate the value of money as they might think proper' (V, 223); the power to issue money should have been given to a public institution, independent of the government, forbidden to lend money either to the government or to the public. The Bank of England would have become a bank like all the others; country banks should be required to hold reserves in a definite proportion to their issues, since the public could not be entrusted to assess the soundness of every bank whose banknotes were in circulation.

We will now proceed to examine which of these ideas of Ricardo's – the interpretation of a premium on bullion, the plan for a circulation entirely made of paper, the rules for the issue of banknotes – entered into the debate in Italy.

5. Anti-Ricardians and quasi-Ricardians

Choice of the standard, the consequences of inconvertibility and reform of the issue system were the problems at the core of Italian debate in the early decades subsequent to unification, as pointed out in the previous sections, and, as they were matters on which Ricardo had made important contributions, we would have expected to find some influence of his ideas, well known in Italy at the time. However, as far as the first question is concerned, this influence, if any, was only at a theoretical level. We have already recalled how debate on the choice of the standard concluded. It is well represented by the words of Gioacchino Pepoli, Minister of Agriculture, Industry and Commerce, in the report which accompanied the adoption of bimetallism in 1862:

> A system with one standard is, in my view, the most logical and perfect; it is the one that early Italian thinkers suggested in the past to avoid the ills resulting from the changing values of gold and silver; it is the one recommended by most modern economists. But it cannot be put into practice all at once and certainly not on the occasion of the present reform. Not to mention the disagreements among the economists, some preferring the gold standard, others the silver, while science and empirical evidence have yet to come up with their final judgment […] I think […] that this question, by its very nature, must be solved by mutual agreement among the main nations of Europe.[18]

Subsequently, Italy and its economists failed to play a leading role in the debate on bimetallism of the 1860s and 1870s: the country, burdened with a large national debt, was in too weak a position to exert any power on the international scene. In any case, there was a general consensus that the role for the metal chosen as standard included being also a component of the currency itself. As in many other countries including his homeland, Ricardo's proposal for a currency made exclusively of paper with transactions in gold reduced to a minimum was rejected and forgotten.

It was a different matter when attention was focused on the consequences of the suspension of convertibility in 1866. The causes of the increase in the price of gold, which rapidly rose to a level above the Mint price, became an object of debate, as it had in England over fifty years before. References to Ricardo and his followers and to his positions in the Bullionist controversy became frequent and explicit. Those who put the blame primarily on the behaviour of the Banca Nazionale echoed the accusations made against the Bank of England by Ricardo and the Bullionists of having exploited the suspension of convertibility to increase its profits abnormally. Those who had closer links with the Banca Nazionale defended the conduct of the bank, claiming that the issue of banknotes was neither a sufficient nor a necessary condition for the increase in the price of gold.[19]

This contrast is well represented by the conflict between the main exponents of the two parties, and in particular by Majorana, one of the staunchest critics of the Banca Nazionale, and Boccardo. They wrangled both in their writings and in Parliament.[20] In his work Boccardo explicitly attacked Ricardo and the connection he had established between variations in the issue of banknotes by the country's main bank and the price of gold. Boccardo argued that other reasons could equally well account for the fluctuations in the price of gold:

> Ricardo […] forgot that putting the brake on the issue of banknotes does not prevent the appreciation of gold when it is affected by more powerful causes, such as disturbances on the foreign exchange market, gold outflows and balance of trade deficit. (Boccardo 1879:51)

In the same treatise, in order to disprove Ricardo's theory, Boccardo assembled data on the amount of banknotes in circulation and the corresponding market price of gold in the United States, England, Austria and Italy. Having shown that there was no correlation between the two variables, he triumphantly concluded that:

> We could not wish for better evidence that the impact on the premium on bullion of the issue of banknotes – when the issue is not exorbitant – is very low, compared to that of the government deficit or trade balance. (Boccardo 1879: 58)

The same conclusion had been reached some decades earlier by Bosanquet (III, 166) and the Directors of the Bank of England. They, too, tried to rebut Ricardo's thesis along the same lines, setting out the data on the amount of banknotes in circulation, as if Ricardo had argued that any variation in the quantity of money implied a proportional variation in the price of gold, no matter what other circumstances there might be. Ricardo's reply had been that the fact that the quantity of money is increasing, decreasing or remaining stationary does not tell us anything about its adequacy to the needs of the economy; the adequacy can be ascertained only by observing deviations of the price of gold from the Mint price or of the rate of exchange from par (see IV, 67; IV, 232).

In opposition to Boccardo's anti-Ricardianism, the Italian economists who disapproved of the behaviour of the Banca Nazionale and other banks of issue were more inclined to accept Ricardo's thesis, at least partially. Among them, Majorana argued repeatedly and vehemently that the quantity of money had an impact on the market price of gold. He wrote:

> We may disagree on minor points of economic science, but it is a gross and unforgivable error to deny the influence of the amount of the medium of exchange over its value. The war with the East, or the bad harvests may have had some effect on the depreciation of paper money, but the continuing increase in its mass […], from 1876 on, for the sole interest of the Bank, has been the cause of the permanent and growing premium on bullion. (quoted in La Bruna 2007b: 63–4)

It is to be noted that Majorana does not embrace the extreme views of Ricardo, retaining a moderate position.[21] He does not share Ricardo's conviction that abuse of the power to issue money was a sufficient and necessary cause of any increase in the price of gold. He did not deny that abuse of the power to issue money was a sufficient cause for increases in the price of gold, but he did not accept that it was also a necessary cause. A temporary premium on bullion might occur for reasons related to a balance of trade deficit due to a bad harvest, or to the expenses of a war, as pointed out in the quotation above.

However, this is not the main difference between the Italian 'Ricardian' and Ricardo. When we reconstruct the route by which the quantity of paper money might have an impact on its value, we find a completely different approach. When Ricardo says that 'overissue' determines the depreciation of money, he has in mind a sequence of steps by which an increase in the money supply determines the profitability of the exportation of gold through its impact on the rate of exchange and consequently an increase in the demand for gold and its price. At each step of the sequence there is a price which plays the role of signal and there are specific agents (bullion merchants, foreign exchange dealers) on specific markets who react to the signal. The sequence may not always have been spelled out without a touch of ambiguity (see Rosselli 2008), but it can be reconstructed in its general terms and the macroeconomic picture emerges with clarity.

Instead, Majorana focuses attention on the individual agent who chooses among the different forms of money according to his preferences and the confidence he has in them. The public prefers gold but is ready to accept paper as long as it is confident that it is – or will soon be – convertible into gold. The quantity of money affects the relative prices between gold and paper money through its impact on the confidence the public has that convertibility will be resumed. The greater the quantity of banknotes, the lower the confidence that a return to convertibility may be in the offing:

> if the opinion prevails that the inconvertible paper money may shortly be exchanged for gold, even though it may now be in a quantity much greater than in the past, provided it is not even greater than necessary, not only will the premium on gold not become higher, but it will be slowly decreasing, eventually approaching zero when it is clear that the expectations hopefully conceived will certainly be fulfilled in the near future. (quoted in La Bruna 2007b: 123)

And again:

> But if there is no confidence in paper, i.e. no confidence that inconvertibility would soon be abolished, and it is believed that government, Parliament, public opinion will continue to rely on this *extremely bad institution*, then, […] the scarcity of paper money does not prevent a high premium on bullion; and by driving true money out of circulation it aggravates the crisis and is seriously damaging; then, under these circumstances, the fear of excessive issue depreciates paper money even more than the actual issue. If the fears even prove only partially grounded, the premium on bullion can become immense. (quoted in La Bruna 2007b: 124; *italics added*)

Boccardo shares the same approach. He argues that when the currency is made of inconvertible paper the premium on gold can be anything between zero and infinite. It depends exclusively on the confidence the public holds in the possibility of conversion. It may even be zero, if the confidence is great enough.

The debate between Majorana and Boccardo is developed at this micro-economic level, the differences between them concerning the factors that affect the preferences of individual agents for one kind of banknote or the other. Boccardo is convinced that the banks, above all the Banca Nazionale, could not be blamed for the rise in the price of gold. He maintains that the public trusted the soundness of the banks; if anything, it was the banknotes issued by the consortium on behalf of the state that could have weakened the confidence of the public, alarmed by the Government debt. Majorana holds the opposite view, and the policy recommendations of the two reflect this disagreement. Boccardo wants to limit the paper issued by the State, while Majorana tries to set a limit to the paper issued by the banks.

In this context the premium on bullion still measures the depreciation of the currency relatively to gold as it had done for Ricardo, but it reflects only the subjective assessment of the probability of a return to convertibility.[22] Having lost a direct relation with the quantity of money, the price of gold cannot – in this theoretical approach – be conceived as the market signal which guides monetary policy. It is not a reliable signal since it can be influenced by a number of factors, not necessarily of an economic nature, not embedded in the structure of the economy, but subject to the changing mood of the public.

For Ricardo the preference accorded to gold by the public pertains to exceptional times of uncontrolled panic and runs on the banks, while in normal times the use of coins and the urge to hoard them were to be discouraged by any means available, as belonging to a 'less enlightened period' (IV,65). Instead, for Majorana and Boccardo the use of species alongside paper currency represented the optimal condition for the payment system. Moreover, having abandoned Ricardo's approach, the monetary authority is left with no way to regulate the quantity of money. The only solution open to Majorana and Boccardo is to rely on the mechanism of convertibility. When this is not at work, to avoid the risks of an excess of issue, Majorana proposes fighting the de facto monopoly of the Banca Nazionale by boosting competition in the banking sector, and fighting the forces of all the banks together by putting a constraint on their power to issue paper money. Boccardo, on the other hand, while defending the monopoly of the Banca Nazionale, does not put forward any rule of issue because his theory does not contemplate any. Nothing could be more distant from Ricardo's ideal monetary system, 'which always conforms to that standard, and in the use of which the utmost economy is practised'.

In conclusion, what clearly distinguished the opposing parties in the debate over the 1879 law were the policy recommendations, which were profoundly different: Boccardo set firmly against any constraint on the freedom of the banks; Majorana favouring some form of limitation. And yet the theoretical framework from which they drew their proposals was very similar. Schumpeter's observation on the debate between Currency and Banking School at the time of the Peel Act seems equally applicable to the division between so-called Ricardians (perhaps we should call them 'quasi-Ricardians') and anti-Ricardians in Italy in the 1870s: 'the difference between the two positions remains no doubt of practical importance. But it involves none but minor disagreements as regards analysis' (Schumpeter 1954: 728).

Notes

1 Emerging in Italy from the interest in Ricardian theory at the end of the nineteenth century and Loria's reconsideration of it was an approach to capital theory in which the value of capital goods depended on the distribution of income (Ricca Salerno) and the capital theory of Böhm-Bawerk was combined with the comparative costs of Ricardo (Graziani). After World War II these themes came to occupy a central position in the neo-Ricardian Italian school which advocated a return to Classical Political Economy (Perri 2003: 126–128).

2 Ricardo's ideas reached the Italian public through the intermediation of James Mill, whose *Elements of Political Economy* were translated into Italian in 1826, perhaps by Francesco Fuoco himself, and had an important influence in shaping the views on Ricardo in Italy, according to Cossa (Cossa 1892: 509).

3 The selection included four works only: *Dell'alto prezzo dei metalli preziosi* (High price of bullion); *Risposta alle osservazioni pratiche del signor Bosanquet* (Reply to Bosanquet); *Proposta di una circolazione monetaria economica e sicura* (Proposal for an economic and secure currency); and *Disegno della istituzione di un banco nazionale* (Plan for a National Bank).

4 From now on references to Sraffa's edition of Ricardo's works (Ricardo 1951–73) will be in the following form: the Roman numeral indicates the volume, the Arabic numeral the pages. The title is omitted. Sraffa also notes that the translation of the *Principles* was little more than a pastiche of the first and third edition. It is doubtful, however, that this lack of clarity lay behind rejection of Ricardo's theory of value.

5 For biographical and bibliographical information about Majorana and Boccardo, see fn. 13 and 15 respectively below.

6 Although this was case of Francesco Ferrara who, in his introduction to the volume containing Ricardo's pamphlets on money, seemed to reject the whole monetary Ricardian theory because he did not accept cost of production as determinant of the value of gold (Ferrara 1857b: 260–265).

7 After the discoveries of gold in California, the silver/gold ratio had moved away from the French ratio of 15.5 to a lower value on the international market. If bimetallism was to be introduced to Italy, there was a risk that the undervalued silver coins could be exported, leaving the country, which already had a large supply of gold, depleted of silver – a more convenient metal for small transactions.

8 Many economists of the Risorgimento, as members of Parliament, played an active role in building the new state and its economic policy. When this initial period came to an end, there was also renewed interest in pure theory with the works of Pantaleoni and Pareto. (See Augello and Guidi 2003).

9 The only ploy adopted to prevent the outflow of silver was a decrease in the silver content of the divisional coins.

10 The links with France were further tightened when, in 1865, Italy together with some other countries formed with France the Latin Monetary Union (LMU), which lasted formally until 1927. The members of the LMU sought a common

solution to the demonetization of silver and the fall in its (gold) price, which started in the early 1870s with the discovery of new mines and extracting techniques and with the adoption of the Gold Standard by the United States and Germany.

11 The law should have held only until the end of inconvertibility, but was still in force in 1893 when the Bank of Italy was established.

12 The literature, old and new, on this aspect of the debate is extensive. See Ferrara 1873, Romanelli 1874–75, Stringher 1879, Ferraris 1879, Piperno 1880, Corbino 1931, Supino 1929, Di Nardi 1953, Spinelli and Fratianni 1991, De Mattia 1990.

13 Salvatore Majorana Calatabiano (1825–97), professor of political economy at University of Catania, was a leader of the political Left in southern Italy. In 1874 his political group named 'Sinistra Giovane' was characterized by a pragmatic and reformist attitude. He was Minister of Agriculture, Industry and Commerce in the first governments of the Left (1876–79). After proposing a liberal reform of the banking regulation in 1879, he clashed with the Banca Nazionale and its supporters. This conflict marked the beginning of his progressive isolation in Parliament and in politics (see La Bruna 2003).

14 Majorana's project was clearly inspired by the National Banking System introduced by Salmon Chase in the US in 1864 at the end of the Civil War (see La Bruna 2007b: 116–120).

15 Gerolamo Boccardo (1829–1904), professor of political economy at the University of Genoa, member of the Senate, belonged to the political Right. His views on the monetary and banking system changed over the years. From laissez-faire positions, he ended up supporting the *de facto* monopoly of issue of the Banca Nazionale (see La Bruna 2005).

16 For example, in the *Reply to Bosanquet* we read: 'The effect produced on prices by the depreciation has been most accurately defined, and amounts to the difference between the market and mint price of gold. An ounce of gold coin cannot be of less value […]than an ounce of gold bullion of the same standard; a purchaser of corn therefore is entitled to as much of that commodity for an ounce of gold coin, or 3l. 17s. 10 1/2d., as can be obtained for an ounce of gold bullion. Now, as 4l. 12s. of paper currency is of no more value than an ounce of gold bullion, prices are actually raised to the purchaser 18 per cent, in consequence of his purchase being made with paper instead of coin of its bullion value. Eighteen per cent is, therefore, equal to the rise in the price of commodities, occasioned by the depreciation of paper. All above such rise maybe either traced to the effects of taxation, to the increased scarcity of the commodity, or to any other cause which may appear satisfactory to those who take pleasure in such enquiries' (III, 239).

17 For a detailed analysis of Ricardo's plans see Deleplace 2008 and Diatkine 2008.

18 The translations of the passages by Boccardo and Majorana in this section are ours.

19 The Government inquiry into the inconvertibility of banknotes confirmed that the Banca Nazionale had abused its power of issue. See *Relazione sul corso forzoso dei biglietti di banca*, Atti Parlamentari, Camera dei Deputati, 1867–68, 3 voll.

20 The contrasting positions of Majorana and Boccardo have been reconstructed by La Bruna 2005. For the opinions of Majorana and his approach to monetary questions, see La Bruna 2007b, which is based on the correspondence of the minister and other unpublished or little-known material.

21 The same 'moderate' position was taken, for example, by Malthus in Ricardo's time.

22 Like Ricardo, Majorana distinguishes between the purchasing power of the currency over gold and over commodities, denying that a given premium on bullion always implies the same increase in prices.

References

Augello, M. and M. Guidi (eds) (2003) *Gli economisti in Parlamento, 1861–1922*, vol. II. Milan: Franco Angeli.

Banca d'Italia (2011) *La moneta dell'Italia unita dalla lira all'euro*, Codice Edizioni.

Boccardo, G. (1879) *Le banche e il corso forzato*. Rome: Tipografia del Senato.

Bonaccorsi di Patti, E. (2001) Francesco Ferrara and subjective value theory, *History of political economy*, 33: 315–344.

Corbino, E. (1931) *Annali dell'economia italiana*, vol. II. Castello: Tipografia Leonardo da Vinci.

Cossa, L. (1892) *Introduzione allo studio dell'economia politica*. Milan: Hoepli.

De Cecco, M. (2007) The Latin Monetary Union revisited once again. In P. Cottrell, G. Notaras and G. Tortella (eds), *From the Atenian tetradrachm to the Euro*. Aldershot: Ashgate.

Deleplace, G. (2008) Le deux plans monétaires de Ricardo, *Cahiers d'économie politique*, 55: 13–31.

De Mattia, R. (1990) *Gli istituti di emissione in Italia*. Rome and Bari: Editori Laterza.

Diatkine, S. (2008) La politique monétaire selon Ricardo, *Cahiers d'économie politique*, 55: 35–46.

Di Nardi, G. (1953) *Le banche di emissione in Italia nel XIX*. Turin: Utet.

Faucci, R. (2000) *L'economia politica in Italia*. Turin: Utet Università.

Ferrara, F. (ed.) (1856a) *Biblioteca dell'economista*, 1st Series, vol. XI. Turin: Unione Tipografico-Editrice.

Ferrara, F. (1856b, 1956) Prefazione a David Ricardo. In Id. *Opere Complete*, vol. III, *Prefazioni alla Biblioteca dell'Economista*. Rome: Associazione Bancaria Italiana.

Ferrara, F. (ed.) (1857a) *Biblioteca dell'Economista*, 2nd Series, vol. VI. Turin: Unione Tipografico-Editrice.

Ferrara, F. (1857b, 1961) Della moneta e dei suoi surrogati. In Id. *Opere Complete*, vol. V, *Prefazioni alla Biblioteca dell'Economista*. Rome: Associazione Bancaria Italiana.

——(1860, 1956) Agricoltura e questioni economiche che la riguardano, in Id. *Opere Complete*, vol. IV *Prefazioni alla Biblioteca dell'Economista*, Parte terza. Rome: Associazione Bancaria Italiana.

——(1873) La questione dei banchi in Italia, *Nuova Antologia* 3: 883–913.

Ferraris, C. F. (1879) *Moneta e corso forzoso*. Milan: U. Hoepli.

La Bruna, A. (2003) Un economista liberal-democratico: Salvatore Majorana Calatabiano tra visione, teoria e politica economica. In M. Augello and M. Guidi (eds), *Gli economisti in Parlamento 1861–1922*, vol. II. Milan: Franco Angeli.

——(2005) Boccardo e Majorana a confronto: teoria monetaria e carteggi. In M. Augello and G. Pavanelli (eds), *Tra economia, politica e impegno civile: Gerolamo Boccardo e il suo tempo(1829–1904)*. Genoa: Brigati.

——(2007a) *Salvatore Majorana Calatabiano, economista politico*, Caltanissetta and Rome: Sciascia editore.

——(2007b) *Il governo della moneta nelle carte di un ministro. L'Italia e la questione bancaria 1876–1879*. Caltanissetta and Rome: Sciascia editore.

Macchioro, A. (2006) *Studi di storia del pensiero economico italiano*. Milan: Franco Angeli.

Marcuzzo, M. C. and Rosselli, A. (1991) *Ricardo and the Gold Standard. The Foundations of the International Monetary Order*. London: Macmillan.

Martello, T. (1877) *La questione dei banchi in Italia*. Florence: Tipografia della gazzetta d'Italia.

Minnelli, E., M. Guidi and A. Guccione (2004) A note on Francesco Ferrara's cost of reproduction, *Journal of the history of economic thought*, 26: 107–114.

Omiccioli, M. (2011) Dalla babele all'unità monetaria. In Banca d'Italia, *La moneta dell'Italia unita dalla lira all'euro*, Codice Edizioni.

Perri, S. (2003) La diffusione dell'economia ricardiana in Italia: riflessioni sul rapporto tra bisogni-lavoro-utilità e teoria del sovrappiù (1825–1900). In P. Barucci (ed.), *Le frontiere dell'economia politica. Gli economisti stranieri in Italia: dai mercantilisti fino a Keynes*. Florence: Edizioni Polistampa.

Piperno, S. (1880) Le cagioni dell'aggio, *Archivio di statistica* 5: 299–347.

Ricardo, D. (1951–1973) *The works and correspondence of David Ricardo*, Piero Sraffa (ed.), with the collaboration of M. H. Dobb. Cambridge, Cambridge University Press.

——(1819) *Des Principes de l'économie politique et de l'impôt*. Paris, Aillaud.

Romanelli, A. (1874–1875) *L'aggio dell'oro e le sue vicende in relazione con la quantità di carta, colle condizioni del credito pubblico e colla bilancia dei pagamenti internazionali*, Acts of Parliament, Chamber of Deputies, Document 94, Attachments, Part One.

Rosselli, A. (2008) Ricardo and Thornton on an ' unfavourable' balance of trade, *Cahiers d'économie politique*, 55: 65–79.

Schumpeter, J. (1954) *History of Economic Analysis*. New York: Oxford University Press.

Spinelli, F. and M. Fratianni (1991) *Storia monetaria d'Italia*. Milan: Arnoldo Mondadori editore.

Stringher, B. (1879) Sull'estinzione del corso forzoso negli Stati Uniti, *Annali dell'industria e del commercio*, 8.

Supino, C. (1929) *Storia della circolazione cartacea in Italia dal 1860 al 1928*. Milan: Società editrice libraria.

6 The diffusion of Ricardo's theories in Russia

Denis Melnik

1. Introduction

Ricardo's theories entered Russia relatively late. In 1871 Nikolai Sieber, the first Russian translator and editor of Ricardo's *Principles*, observed that in the Russian economic literature of the time, the essence of the Ricardian approach – the theory of value and distribution – remained overshadowed by elements of secondary importance: the theory of rent, 'one of the least original parts of his doctrine', and Ricardo's alleged adherence to the Malthusian theory of population (Sieber 1871: xiii). But even afterwards, the diffusion of Ricardo's theory in Russia was far from being an uninterrupted, one-way process. Later theoretical approaches cast their shadows on the analytical essence of this theory. Different interpretations of the Ricardian legacy competed with and contradicted each other. With a few notable exceptions, Ricardo's theory was regarded in Russian economic literature as a prior stage in the development of any given approach, rather than an element of the current theoretical context. In other words, it had entered Russia already a part of history.

The history of economic thought as a discipline only emerged after the economic science itself had reached a fairly advanced level of development, and by now it has acquired its own and interesting history. Since the 1960s and 1970s, some important questions have been raised as to the scope and methodology of the history of economic thought. The idea that its task is nothing more than the depiction of progress in economics and of specific mistakes and deviations made along the way was challenged by comparing different approaches in economics, each possessing its own view of the history of the preceding stages of economic reasoning. The traditional understanding of the object to be studied by the historians of economic thought has been called into question. It is not that the idea of the history of analysis ought to be rejected, but there is obviously a need to synthesize the facts accumulated and the methodologies developed up to now. In this respect, a broad vision of what may be defined as 'the history of the history of economic thought' would be useful.

The inevitable problem is that such a vision would entail the relativization of knowledge, as we need to deal with different histories, instead of one fixed 'truth' about the development of economics. By a 'history' in this sense we mean an established canon in describing the path made by economic science as an ascension towards a certain 'modern' theoretical approach, of which this history is a part. This canon is represented in the authoritative sources (textbooks, entries in encyclopedias etc.), and in pieces of research that contribute to the making and perpetuation of that history. But even though a history of economic thought cannot be regarded as 'objective', the very process of comparison between the different versions (or 'visions') of history could elucidate the milestones and turning points in the development of economics.

The aim of this contribution is to provide an overview of the development of economics in nineteenth- and twentieth-century Russia by focusing on the interpretations of Ricardo's theory that prevailed during this period. The choice of a reference point will make the overview somewhat selective, but it is not an arbitrary one. In Russian economic literature since the 1870s, several versions of the history of economic thought have been developed, of which the Marxist, the Marshallian (or the neoclassical), and the Sraffian are the most influential. The interpretation of the Ricardian legacy plays an important analytical part in each of them.

The contribution consists of four parts. The second section provides a brief outline of the period when the need to discuss pressing economic issues was met mainly by the selective import of the ideas of Western economists. As we shall see, the analytical system of Ricardo simply did not match that context. The third section deals with the period of the formation of a national economic science in Russia. Apart from the adoption of Western theoretical approaches (and as a result of it), that period saw the development of original interpretations of Ricardo, intended to adapt his legacy to the new context. These were the interpretations provided by Zhukovsky, Sieber, Dmitriev. The last section deals with Soviet economic science. Attention is focused on Rubin as one of the most original Soviet Marxists and a (if not the) founder of the Soviet version of the history of economic thought. It provides a basis for the comparison between the paths of development of the classical approach in Russia (within the framework of Soviet Marxism) and in 'the West', where the revival of this approach was closely related to the reassessment and updating of the analytical content of Ricardo's theory by Sraffa.

2. Ricardo in the 'prehistory' of economic science in Russia

Unlike Smith's *Wealth of Nations*, first translated and published in Russian relatively early, in 1802–1806, Ricardo's works were not translated until the 1870s. This did not prevent his name and ideas from being known, as was exemplified, for instance, in the first textbook on political economy written in Russian (Butovsky 1847). But Ricardo was seen mainly through French economists' eyes. Since the ideas of the Enlightenment first entered Russia in the middle of the eighteenth century, French culture had remained a synonym for culture itself; the French language was used as the principle means of communication among the Russian elite and educated circles well into the 1840s–60s. Consequently, it was French economists – Jean-Baptist Say, Charles Ganilh, Jean-Gustave Courcelle-Seneuil, Barthélemy-Charles Dunoyer, Jérôme-Adolphe Blanqui, Joseph Garnier and Michel Chevalier – who exerted the most significant impact on both the liberal and the conservative parts of the Russian elite (at least until the 1860s), while the ideas of Henri de Saint-Simon, Auguste Comte, Charles Fourier, Victor Considerant and Louis Blanc had had a great impact on the radical stance of the nascent Russian intelligentsia since the 1830s.

From the French economists, their Russian counterparts adopted a respectfully critical attitude towards Ricardian economics. But it was not merely a question of language and cultural preferences: for instance, this factor did not prevent Adam Smith from being popular, even fashionable, at the beginning of the nineteenth century. Ricardo's rigorous (and sophisticated) analysis of value and distribution did not match the aspirations of the Russian reader, who expected to acquire from foreign sources a comprehensive set of political recommendations or concepts that could be used in discussions about current affairs. References to Western economists were widely used to lend authoritative support, to legitimize a certain opinion or proposal. For example, a reference to 'Smith's system of natural liberty' allowed a wide range of issues to be discussed: from tariffs and taxes to the problem of serfdom (and to overcome censorship at the same time). Perhaps the only element of the Ricardian system that could be used for such kinds of reference was his theory of rent. Characteristically, it is precisely this theory that was presented as Ricardo's main contribution to political economy in the first Russian textbook[1] on the history of economic thought, although this contribution was described as outmoded due to the critique by Frédéric Bastiat and Henry Charles Carey (Vernadsky 1858: 155). Although the author[2] asserted that this textbook was just a comprehensive bibliographical account of the literature of political economy, it demonstrated a keen knowledge of the developments in economic science. For example, Vernadsky cited Hermann Gossen's *Die Entwicklung der Gesetze des menschlichen Verkehrs …* published in 1854, and highly praised this work (Vernadsky 1858: 162). It is interesting to note that he expressed the view that it was precisely the Ricardian theory of rent, when properly generalized, that could provide a proper foundation for the theory of value:

> It is not land [as a factor of production] and its fertility [rate of return], but […] the right of ownership and the hardship of acquiring it that constitute the main element in price formation of a commodity. Rent thereby obtains another, more general, significance. (Vernadsky 1858: 155)

Thus we may observe that the grounds for a 'neoclassical' interpretation of Ricardo's theory had been laid well before the marginalist revolution and the Marshallian synthesis – in the works, well known at the time, of Bastiat,

Carey, Henry Macleod and other representatives of 'bourgeois political economy'. Vernadsky's work also signified that by the 1860s, the period of dominance of the French authors as intermediaries between Russian and Western economic thought was about to end, as the literature in other European languages came into circulation.

3. Ricardo and the development of Russian economics (1860s–1910s)

The second half of the nineteenth century was the period when Russian economics developed into a system of knowledge with its own institutional structure. But the problems posed at the centre of the discussions during that period differed from those that were relevant for the founders of the classical political economy. Russian economists were concerned above all with the choice, or the construction, of the most suitable model of social and economic development for Russia. In short, it was not a context favorable for adopting the analytical essence of the value theory developed by Ricardo.

Many academic economists (university teachers, middle- and high-ranking state officials) took into account certain elements of the classical approach. But in general they tended to follow an analysis and methodology not dissimilar to that of the German historical school. Accordingly, they criticized the classical approach for what they perceived as an extremely abstract way of reasoning. Ricardo became a symbol of such a reasoning. Towards the end of the period under consideration, marginalism had gained considerably in importance in academia.

As for non-academic economists (journalists, local community officers) who represented the intelligentsia and predominantly belonged to the Narodniks (Populist) movement, they developed a homegrown version of socialism, into which in due time they incorporated those elements of Marxism that strengthened their critique of capitalism. Only after the 1890s was the position of the Narodniks seriously undermined among the intelligentsia by the group of 'orthodox' Marxists (including Mikhail Tugan-Baranovsky, Peter Struve and Vladimir Lenin among others). But the rise of this group coincided with a crisis of Marxism in Europe, to which internal political and individual clashes were added, resulting in a split of the group. In Russia, unlike Western Europe, the classical approach was never the indisputable mainstream of economic science at any period of time before the October Revolution of 1917.

The institutionalization of economic science endorsed interest in the interpretations of the preceding economists. However, the attempts to update Ricardo's theory to the Russian context were made by outsiders: Nikolai Sieber, Yuli Zhukovsky and Vladimir Dmitriev (see also Bogomazov and Melnik 2014). These writers can be defined as 'outsiders' in terms of their positions vis-à-vis the academic community, the 'profession'. Formal as it is, this criterion allows us to understand why, despite the depth of their contributions and the influence they exerted on the diffusion of Ricardo, they did not leave a lasting 'institutional memory' (disciples, successors to chairs, 'schools', etc.): Zhukovsky (1833–1907) was a publisher, journalist, prolific writer and civil servant (being the Governor of the State Bank of the Russian Empire in 1889–94); Sieber (1844–88) started to teach political economy in 1873 at Kiev University, but resigned from the position in 1875; and Dmitriev (1868–1913) lived in a detached way (for instance, there is no known picture of him). Upon graduating from Moscow University he did not enter a career in academia (although there is a hypothesis that he taught at the Saint Petersburg Polytechnic Institute during his last years). All three were highly original thinkers, and their attempts to update Ricardo were greatly influenced by the impact of Marx. This is specifically characteristic of the works of Sieber and Zhukovsky, who were among the first in Russia to react to Marx's writings. Zhukovsky was critical of Marxism from the very beginning,[3] while Sieber would become renowned during the Soviet period as the 'first popularizer' of Marxism.

Zhukovsky's rejection of Marxism was rooted in his interpretation of the classical approach and of Ricardo in particular. Indeed, it was Zhukovsky (1864a; 1864b; 1864c; 1871) who presented the first extended interpretation of Ricardo's legacy in Russian literature. Even more remarkable, he made the first attempt in Russian literature to reformulate Ricardian theory in mathematical terms. Zhukovsky objected to what he perceived as an arbitrary division of different theoretical elements in the Ricardian approach (by isolating the theory of rent from the rest of his doctrine). He insisted, on the contrary, that it was the theory of value that constituted the focal point of the analysis; and that the theory of rent represented 'just a specific case of the general theory of value' (Zhukovsky 1871: 309). Starting from this proposition, Zhukovsky interpreted Ricardo in terms not dissimilar to the later neoclassical interpretation: he presented labour and capital as 'factors'; he argued that the notion of differential rent, while properly generalized, should not be restricted to agriculture and could be applied to price formation in general; he also introduced supply and demand into the analysis. The notions of marginal utility and maximizing behavior were obviously absent from his approach. According to Zhukovsky, an increase in demand leads to an increase in supply, inducing producers to switch to more costly methods of production, with a consequent rise in exchange value. So 'exchange value depends on demand and can be considered a function of demand' (Zhukovsky 1871: 350).

If Zhukovsky came to Marx from his understanding of the preceding stages in the development of economics, Sieber came to Ricardo from Marx. Like Zhukovsky, Sieber too understood the importance of Marx's theory. Unlike Zhukovsky, however, he saw this theory as a direct continuation of the preceding classical tradition. In Marx's own words:

> An excellent Russian translation of *Das Kapital* appeared in the spring of 1872. The edition of 3,000 copies is already nearly exhausted. As early as 1871, N. Sieber, Professor of Political Economy in the University of Kiev,

> in his work "David Ricardo's Theory of Value and of Capital," referred to my theory of value, of money and of capital, as in its fundamentals a necessary sequel to the teaching of Smith and Ricardo. That which astonishes the Western European in the reading of this excellent work, is the author's consistent and firm grasp of the purely theoretical position. (Marx, 1909 [1873]: 21)

Based on his reading of the history of economic thought, Sieber unambiguously rejected the approach to value and distribution that was alternative to the classical approach. He noted, for instance, that even William Petty 'had a better command of methodological techniques, than many modern economists (Bastiat, Macleod)' (Sieber 1871: 55). According to Sieber (1937 [1885]: 122), one of the main misunderstandings in studies of the price mechanism at that time resulted from 'predominant concern about the causes of fluctuation in prices; while it is of foremost importance to know the causes due to which prices are kept at a certain stable level'. Starting from such a methodological stance, he rejected attempts to establish a theory of value on the basis of utility or scarcity, as in case of the 'Senior – Walras school' (Sieber 1871: 101).

Zhukovsky had no immediate followers; it was only three decades later that Dmitriev paid due attention to the substance of his reasoning (Dmitriev 2001 [1904]; Dmitriev 2001 [1908]). Sieber's interpretation was more influential than Zhukovsky's, as he was also the first translator and editor of Ricardo's writings in Russia. His dissertation, in which he presented the development of economic theory from Ricardo to Marx (Sieber 1871), was followed in 1873 by the translation of the first volume of Ricardo's *Works* containing *Principles of Political Economy and Taxation*. Sieber had planned to publish the second volume containing Ricardo's pamphlets and Sieber's own extended commentaries. This plan, however, was not completed then – perhaps due to Sieber's resignation from Kiev University. Only ten years later did he publish an extended edition of Ricardo's *Works* (1882). In 1885 there followed a revised and extended edition of his dissertation (Sieber 1937 [1885]), the last work published during his lifetime. However, the analytical conjectures made by Sieber were in a sense inconclusive, as his severe illness and premature death (in 1888) prevented him from developing them over the course of the debates following the rise of the marginalist theory, and especially the publication of Volume III of *Das Kapital* with the subsequent critique by Böhm-Bawerk (1949 [1896]).

However, both Zhukovsky's and Sieber's attempts to update Ricardo felt short of their goal. For the majority of economists, Ricardo's theory was a part of history, rather than a kit of analytical tools at their disposal. While the diffusion of Marxism in Russia that started in the 1870s allowed the importance of Ricardo to be highlighted, it also overshadowed Ricardian theory. To cite one salient example, Zhukovsky and Sieber, regardless of all the differences in their interpretations, both started their analysis of the Ricardian approach from the notion of value, and clearly saw the analytical link between the theory of value and the theory of distribution. But as late as 1903 Tugan-Baranovsky found it necessary to remind the reader that Ricardo had established the 'inseparable connection' between these two theories (see Tugan-Baranovsky 1998 [1903]: 75). At the same time, Tugan-Baranovsky considered that for Ricardo, the labour theory of value was nothing more than a 'methodological assumption' (ibid.: 76). This clearly reflected a widely accepted thesis that the labour theory of value is but a hypothesis reflecting a certain vision of society (see Bernstein 1907 [1899], ch. II, part A). Such an idea reinforced the aspirations for a synthesis between classical and marginalist approaches:

> Both theories, contrary to the common opinion, are actually in full accord with each other. Both theories provide insights to the opposite sides of the process of economic evaluation. Marginal utility theory has elucidated the subjective factors of value; labor theory – the objective factors. (Tugan-Baranovsky 1911: 49)

It was precisely in this context that the last attempt to update Ricardo's theory to pre-revolutionary Russia was made. This attempt remained almost completely unnoticed, and Dmitriev's *Economic Essays* had to wait a long time before being rediscovered (Dmitriev 1968 [1904]; Dmitriev 1974 [1904]). In the historical context in which this analysis originated, Dmitriev's approach could not be seen as an isolated insight (as was often the case). It is true that in many aspects his approach surpassed the time; but it still conformed to the then influential tendencies in Russian economic literature. Originally *Economic Essays* had a subtitle 'An outline of an organic synthesis of the labour theory of value and the marginal utility theory'.[4] As Dmitriev himself stated:

> The journals at the end of the 1890s were overfilled with the polemical articles *pro et contra* the labor theory of value. The marginal utility theory played in this struggle, indeed, a relatively small role […] The fall of the labor theory made the acceptance of the 'subjective' theory of value practically unavoidable; the latter being thus a necessary addition to the cost of production theory (in its Ricardian version) to which economic theory naturally returned, after it had rejected the exclusive concentration on but one of the *factors of production* [that is, labour; our emphasis]. (Dmitriev 2001 [1908]: 477)

Thus a return to Ricardo was justified as a necessary step backwards to escape the alleged deadlock of Marxist theory and move into the mainstream.

By the beginning of the twentieth century the new tendencies had still not affected the consensus among economists concerning Ricardo. This was exemplified by an entry on Ricardo in the most authoritative Russian encyclopedia of the pre-revolutionary period – the voluminous *Brockhaus and*

Efron Encyclopedic Dictionary. The author [Sobolev 1899] provided a concise description of Ricardo's life and ideas, choosing the labour theory of value as a reference point. At the same time he criticized Ricardo's methodology and the practical relevance of his theory on the grounds of the German historical school. By the end of the pre-revolutionary period, however, the consensus seemed to have shifted towards the neoclassical interpretation. As a sign of this shift, in September 1917, at the session of the Russian Academy of Sciences on the eve of the October Revolution, Peter Struve[5] (who had been elected to the Academy only in May of that year) introduced a paper on the occasion of a centennial of publication of Ricardo's *Principles*. The author, Victor Stein,[6] acknowledging the outstanding place occupied by Ricardo in the history of economic thought, wrote: 'Ricardo gave to recent theory the notion of the decisive influence exerted on prices by marginal costs. He himself, however, limited this notion to land [as a factor of production] only' (Stein 1917: 1346).

We may assume that the neoclassical interpretation would have soon become dominant if the October Revolution of 1917 had not changed the course of Russian history.

4. Ricardo and the making of the Soviet history of economic thought

One of the outcomes of the debates on Marxism at the end of the nineteenth century was that the Russian social democratic movement split into two parties at the beginning of the next century: the Bolsheviks and the Mensheviks. The Bolsheviks proclaimed themselves truly 'orthodox' Marxists and postulated the illegitimacy of all alterations to the original teaching of Marx. They tended, however, to skip the analytical elements of the debates. The Bolsheviks – a rather secluded and small group within the revolutionary movement – had the primary task of gaining political influence. That is why they were not in favor of 'obscure' analytical conundrums. They took it for granted that they needed only to uncover the class essence of the critics of Marxism in order to reveal the inconsistency of their theories. Their first and foremost task was to popularize Marxist ideas among 'the masses', and not to defend Marxian theory in academic journals.

After the Bolsheviks had seized power in 1917 and secured it during the Civil War they faced the urgent need to create theory (again, not so much for the sake of theory but mainly for political and didactic reasons). Lacking their own 'cadre' capable of accomplishing the task, the Party leadership allowed the non-Bolshevik socialists to participate in teaching and research activities. Thus Isaak Rubin, a Menshevik, became one of the leading and most influential figures in the Soviet social sciences of the first post-revolutionary decade.

Like Sieber several decades before him, Rubin came to Ricardo from Marx. Rubin developed his approach, however, in the context of heated debates that challenged the very foundations of the classical approach.

In the aftermath of the Marginalist revolution of the 1870s to 1890s, the classical approach was becoming increasingly 'submerged and forgotten', while Marxism – the last stronghold of the classical political economy – faced serious external and internal challenges. Besides the attempts to 'close' Marx's system on the part of the marginalists, from within Marxism, just a few years after Friedrich Engels' death in 1895, Eduard Bernstein and other authors launched the 'revision' of its basic principles. But in addition to these theoretical and political assaults, the rapid economic and social changes also rendered it necessary to reassess the classical approach. As a result, a new generation of scholars working within the framework of the classical approach faced the task of its critical reconstruction rather than evolutionary development.

Here it is worth outlining the possible basis for comparison between Piero Sraffa (1898–1983) and Isaak Rubin (1886–1937). They were among the most influential contributors to the classical tradition in the twentieth century. Sraffa inspired the classical revival in the West. Rubin's reconstruction of Marx's theory of value had great impact – albeit, for political reasons, mostly in a covert way – on the Soviet political economy, as well as on the canonical version of the history of economic thought. (Since the 1970s, after the translations of some of his works, his approach has become widely known abroad as well). Despite their difference in age, they began publishing the results of their studies in the classical approach almost simultaneously. Sraffa's first contribution to the critique of the marginalist theory of value and distribution was published in Italian in 1925. In 1923 the first edition of Rubin's *Essays on Marx's Theory of Value* was published in Russian. For both authors, these contributions to a purely theoretical field appear, at first glance, to be a deviation from previous scholarly activity. Before his 1925 article, and starting with his dissertation of 1920, Sraffa prepared several publications on monetary and banking problems. Rubin started his publication activity in 1913, and published thereafter more than 30 entries in newspapers and journals – mainly commentaries on labour legislation, trade unions, etc. It was not until 1922 that he published 'purely' theoretical works – two reviews, including one on the most influential political economy textbook of the time, by A. Bogdanov and I. Stepanov (see Vasina 2011b). In both cases, the immediate cause of the 'deviation' was the beginning of a teaching activity. But the scope and degree of originality of the contributions revealed the fact that this was not a singular occurrence for either author. 'Sraffa's cultural project' (see Roncaglia 2006: 435) was based on his formation within the '*cultura positiva*' (see d'Orsi 2001: 3–6). On the contrary, Rubin's approach was developed within the specific 'anti-positivistic culture' that was a feature of Russian economic thought.

The Ricardian legacy played a remarkable role in the works of both Sraffa and Rubin. Not only did the latter present his interpretation of Ricardo in the *History of Political Economy*, but, in a striking coincidence with Sraffa, at the end of the 1920s he became one of the contributors to the project on the translation and editing of Ricardo's collected works in Russian. The project was initiated by David Ryazanov, director of the Marx–Engels Institute, but neither he nor Rubin were able to complete it.[7] Both were arrested: Rubin at the very end of 1930, and Ryazanov in February 1931 (see Vasina 2011a). As a sign of his interest in Ricardo, shortly before his last arrest and execution Rubin (having no access to libraries) was able to complete a short essay *Ricardo's Doctrine of Capital* published by L.L. Vasina and Ya.G. Rokityanskiy (Rubin 1992 [1936–7]).

It is the interpretation of Ricardo that provides the most transparent basis for the comparison of Sraffa's and Rubin's approaches to the reconstruction of the classical political economy. There is no need to repeat here the basic principles of Sraffa's seminal interpretation of Ricardian theory. In what follows, we shall briefly outline Rubin's interpretation. Its aim was to clarify ambiguities in the exposition of Marxian theory by applying the logic of Hegel's philosophical approach, from which this theory, according to Rubin, had originated. In doing so, Rubin sought to define the social essence of the concepts on which the Marxian theory of value was built: abstract labour, value, exchange value and money (see Rubin 1978 [1927]).

Rubin's approach contradicted both the neo-Kantian (or, broadly, 'ethical') revision of Marxism, and the positivistic responses to the revision (based on the attempts to define the 'real' essence of the Marxian concepts).[8] In many senses, it resembled later developments in Western Marxism based on the writings of the 'Frankfurt School' and the 'discovery of a young Marx'. Rubin insisted:

> According to Marx, value is not only a regulator of the distribution of social labor, but also an expression of the social production relations among people. From this point of view, value is a social form which is acquired by the products of labor in the context of determined production relations among people. From value seen as a quantitatively determined magnitude, we must pass to value which we treat as a qualitatively determined social form. In other words, from the theory of the 'magnitude of value' we must pass to the theory of the 'form of value'. (Rubin 1972 [1928]: Ch. 8)

From this followed his critique of the developments in the value theory of the classical economists before Marx:

> […] the attention of the classical economists and their epigones was drawn either to the content of value, mainly its quantitative aspect (amount of labor), or to relative exchange value, i.e., to the quantitative proportions of exchange […] Marx's predecessors […] paid attention to the content of value mainly from the quantitative aspect (labor and the magnitude of labor), and in the same way, the quantitative aspect of exchange value. They neglected the qualitative aspect of labor and value, the characteristic property of the commodity economy. Analysis of the

> 'form of value' is precisely what gives a sociological character and specific traits to the concept of value. (Rubin 1972 [1928]: Ch. 12)

According to Rubin, these economists were pursuing the wrong path, by trying:

> to find a standard of value which would make it possible in practice to compare and measure the quantity of various products in the act of market-exchange. It seemed to them that the labor theory of value emphasized labor precisely as this practical standard of value […] [They] could not free themselves from an erroneous idea which had built itself a nest in political economy and which attributed to the theory of value a task which was not its own, namely to find a practical standard of value. In reality the theory of value has a completely different task, theoretical and not practical. It is not necessary for us to seek a practical standard of value which would make possible the equalization of the products of labor on the market. This equalization takes place in reality every day in the process of market exchange. In this process, spontaneously, a standard of value is worked out, namely money, which is indispensable for this equalization. This market exchange does not need any type of standard which is thought up by economists. (Rubin 1972 [1928]: Ch. 13)

Following this line of argument, Rubin presumably contradicted the approach that Sraffa would define in his interpretation of Ricardo somewhat later. The contradiction becomes more apparent when we turn to Rubin's explicit evaluation of Ricardo's views concerning the problem of the standard measure: 'Ricardo firstly rejected any search for constant measure of value, and repeatedly returned to the proof of the impossibility of finding such a measure' (Rubin 1930: 232).

Rubin's reconstruction was developed in an atmosphere of heated theoretical discussions among Soviet economists that started at the beginning of the 1920s. By the end of the decade, however, the discussions were suppressed. The harsh ideological pressure promptly led economic science into dogmatism. The main task set before the history of economic thought was to prove and legitimize simple truths like this:

> The Marxist doctrine is omnipotent because it is true. It is comprehensive and harmonious, and provides men with an integral world outlook irreconcilable with any form of superstition, reaction, or defence of bourgeois oppression. […] Classical political economy, before Marx, evolved in England, the most developed of the capitalist countries. Adam Smith and David Ricardo, by their investigations of the economic system, laid the foundations of the labour theory of value. Marx continued their work; he provided a proof of the theory and developed it consistently. (Lenin, 1977 [1913]: 21)

Soviet scholars acknowledged the theoretical achievements of Ricardo with due reverence, but not without some condescension. The same applied to the depiction of the history of classical political economy in pre-revolutionary Russia. For instance, Sieber obtained a prominent position in the pantheon of Russian economists, but his merit was reduced to that of having popularized Ricardo's and Marx's writings in Russia. If the followers of the neoclassical approach considered Ricardian theory to be a precursor to the notion of marginal productivity, the Marxists considered it to be a precursor to Marxian theory. In both cases, to borrow an expression used by Gary Mongiovi (2002: 155) on a different occasion: 'Ricardo's economics was interpreted as a primitive form of a fundamentally strong orthodoxy.' In both cases, Ricardo's theory was bound to remain simply part of their respective histories of economic thought.

The most complete Russian edition of Ricardo's *Works* (1955–61) was the last sign of active interest in Ricardo in Soviet economic literature. It was in fact a much belated (due to the reasons outlined above) result of the project to create a Soviet history of economic thought started shortly after the Revolution, in the 1920s. The majority of researchers who had contributed their efforts to post-revolutionary economic studies did not survive into the 1950s, falling victim to the great terror (Maria Smith,[9] the editor of the *Works*, was among those who were able, or lucky enough, to survive). The new generations of economists did not see the development of the legacy left by the founders of the classical approach as a relevant task.

The Sraffian approach did not shake the foundations of the Soviet history of economic thought. In her notes, Maria Smith explicitly acknowledged the use of Sraffa's Cambridge edition. She used it, however, only for editorial work on Ricardo's letters, completely discarding the interpretation proposed by Sraffa. This was hardly the result of simple misunderstanding. Those Soviet scholars who studied the newest developments in Western economics acknowledged Sraffa's contribution (which was treated as part of the post-Keynesian approach), but they clearly perceived it as opposing to the Soviet version of Marxism. It was not an ideological, but a methodological refutation. In a book published in 1991, in the last months of the Soviet Union when the ideological pressure had been substantially relieved, it was written that:

> the post-Keynesians hope to escape marginalist apologetics and to overcome simultaneously Marxian metaphysics by revival of Ricardo's system. But its research potential had already been exhausted during the lifetime of a classic […] Therefore, reliance on Ricardo objectively opens the only two ways: either to the analysis of Marx or through vulgar Ricardianism to marginalism. (Otmahov 1991: 73)

The author argued that the 'post-Keynesian theory of value' formulated by Sraffa was focused solely on the analysis of quantitative relations and lacked the social and historical dimensions characteristic of Marxism (ibid.: 73–77).

That is, the return to Ricardo was considered a step backwards compared with Marx.

After the fall of the Soviet Union, the neoclassical interpretation of Ricardo promptly occupied an influential position in the history of economic thought. But it did not remain without a rival. In the late 1990s, the translation of Sraffa's *Production of Commodities* (Sraffa 1999) became a milestone in the diffusion of the Sraffian approach in Russia. This process contributed to a reappraisal of the preceding history of Russian economic thought, one of the salient results being the 'discovery' of Dmitriev in a volume scrupulously edited by Peter Klyukin (Dmitriev 2001 [1904]). But it also allowed Ricardo's theory to be updated, and in 2008 the new authoritative edition of Ricardo's works was published, edited by the same scholar (Ricardo 2008). A new chapter in the long history of the diffusion of Ricardo's theory in Russia has opened.

Notes

1 In 1869 the first translated textbook was published – a Russian translation of the 4th edition of two-volume *Histoire de l'économie politique en Europe depuis les anciens jusqu'à nos jours* by J.-A. Blanqui; three decades after the translation of his *Precis élementaire d'économie politique* in 1838.

2 Ivan Vernadsky (1821–84) was one of the most notable academic economists of that period. He was a professor of political economy and statistics consecutively in Kiev, Moscow and Saint Petersburg – the most important educational centres of the Russian Empire. But his influence also derived from his activity as a publisher. It was he who founded the first Russian periodical specializing in economic matters. In his writings Vernadsky energetically promoted the ideas of economic liberalism and opposed socialism. The history of Vernadsky's family illustrates the uneasy fate of Russian science in the twentieth century. His son, Vladimir Vernadsky (1863–1945), was a prominent scientist whose interests ranged from geology and mineralogy to biology. In 1912 he was elected a member of the Imperial Academy of Sciences. He was involved in pre-revolutionary politics, and following the liberal stance of his father he became one of the leaders of the liberal Constitutional Democratic Party. In 1918 he became the first President of the Ukrainian Academy of Sciences. Despite his critical attitude towards the Bolsheviks, he returned to the USSR in 1926 after a brief period of emigration and recovered all his positions. He made a contribution to the early stages of the Soviet atomic project and was awarded the Stalin prize in 1943, on the occasion of his jubilee. Unlike his father, George Vernadsky (1887–1973), a historian, he chose not to return from his emigration. He published an original concept of the history of his native country and eventually became a professor of Russian history at Yale University.

3 For instance in 1877 he published an article, *K. Marx and His Book on Capital*, that provoked heated debate among Russian writers and captured the attention of Marx himself, who sent a special letter on this occasion to a Russian journal (see Marx, 1968 [1877]). In a message to his Russian translator a year later, Marx referred to Zhukovsky as 'a crank who imagined himself an encyclopedist' (Marx, 1964 [1878], p. 277). The case was notable enough for F. Engels to remember 'a certain Mr. Zhukovsky' more than 15 years later (Engels 1894 [1989]).

4 This subtitle was reproduced in the French edition (Dmitriev 1968 [1904]), but disappeared from the English one (Dmitriev 1974 [1904]).

5 Peter Struve (1870–1944) started his scholarly and political career as a Marxist. At the turn of the twentieth century he was one of the leading representatives of a group of young Marxist intellectuals who sought to promote 'orthodox' Marxism. At that period he was on good terms with Vladimir Lenin, for instance organizing the publication of Lenin's book *The Development of Capitalism in Russia* (1899) while the author was in exile in Siberia. After a few years, however, he broke ties with Marxism and shifted towards liberalism. In 1905 he co-founded the Constitutional Democratic Party. After the Revolution and during the Civil War he was one of the political leaders of the counter-Bolshevik movement. Struve was sentenced to death in absentia by the Soviet court and after the defeat of the counter-Bolshevik forces he left the country. When German troops occupied Yugoslavia, where he lived, he was arrested as an alleged Bolshevik. Struve was released after some months, presumably due to the fact that he presented the official Soviet textbook on the history of the Bolshevik Party published in German in Moscow, which he discovered while in detention: his name was listed there among the worst enemies of the Revolution. In 1942 Struve and his wife managed to leave for Paris where their son was living at the time.

6 Victor Stein (1890–1964) started his postgraduate studies at the Saint Petersburg Polytechnic Institute in 1913 under Struve's supervision. He was a versatile scholar and journalist, and the history of economic thought was only one of his fields of research. He opposed the Bolsheviks but did not emigrate. Instead, in 1922 he was sentenced to exile from Soviet Russia along with a large group of 'alien' intellectuals. However, this sentence was revoked due to the intervention of another scholar close to the Bolsheviks at that time, who valued Stein's abilities highly. Consequently, Stein stayed in Russia and soon published two works on the history of classical political economy. He was then sent as an economic adviser to the Guomindang in China. Upon his return Stein became one of the leading experts on China (he would study Chinese later) and the Far East. He taught in Leningrad and in 1940, in addition to his other academic positions, joined the newly-founded Faculty of Political Economy at Leningrad University. During the war, while in evacuation, he resumed his longstanding interest in the history of economic thought, and in 1948 his book on the history of the Russian political economy was published. The choice soon proved to be an unhappy one. In 1948 the 'Leningrad Affair', the last big political purge of the Stalin era, was launched, and the Faculty of Political Economy was among the targets. The book was condemned, and in 1949 the author was sentenced to ten years in the Gulag. In 1955 he was released and resumed his Chinese studies at one of the academic institutions in Leningrad.

7 David Ryazanov (1870–1938) did not provide any extended interpretation of Ricardo, but his name stands out in the history of Ricardian studies in Russia. It was he who prepared and published the authoritative edition of *Principles* (1908) that replaced Siber's edition, which had become largely outmoded due to the changes in terminology and to overall progress in research standards. It was the 1908 edition that was used as a basis for the Ricardo project launched by Ryazanov twenty years later. As a part of this project, the 1908 edition was reprinted in 1929 (it attracted Sraffa's attention (see Klyukin 2008: 41)), and the forthcoming *Collected Writings* were announced. In 1935, the new edition of *Principles*, that was apparently the result of Ryazanov and his wife's efforts to refine the translation, was published as a second volume of Ricardo's *Works*. Any mention of the translators in this edition is notoriously absent. The next attempt to publish the *Collected Writings* was made in 1941, when the first two volumes appeared. This edition was interrupted by the war. At last, Ricardo's five-volume *Works* were published in 1955–61 (each volume being printed in 20,000 copies). On the history of Ricardo's editions in Russia see Klyukin 2008: 8; 37–41.

8 It was an approach pursued by A. Bogdanov and I. Stepanov. The debates of the 1920s between the followers of both approaches was one of the most interesting pages in the history of Soviet political economy.

9 Maria Smith (Falkner–Smith) (1878–1968), born in Taganrog, southern Russia, had been involved in revolutionary activity during the late 1890s. From 1901–05 she studied at the University of London (hence her British surname). In 1918 she joined the Bolshevik Party and in 1921 she became a professor.

References

Bernstein, E. (1907 [1899]) *Evolutionary Socialism*. Available online: www.marxists.org/reference/archive/bernstein/works/1899/evsoc/index.htm (accessed 30 January 2013). London: Independent Labour Party.

Bogomazov, G. and D. Melnik (2014) Ricardo's Writings in Russia: Influence and Interpretations. In E. S. Levrero, A. Palumbo and A. Stirati (eds), *Sraffa and the Reconstruction of Economic Theory*, vol. 3, *Sraffa's Legacy: Interpretations and Historical Perspectives*. London: Palgrave Macmillan.

Böhm-Bawerk, E. von (1949 [1896]) *Karl Marx and the Close of His System*, P. Sweezy (ed.). New York: Augustus M. Kelley.

Bukharin, N.I. (1927 [1919]) *The Economic Theory of the Leisure Class*. Available online: <http://www.marxists.org/archive/bukharin/works/1927/leisure-economics/index.htm> (accessed 30 January 2013). Moscow: International Publishers.

Butovsky, A.I. (1847) *Опыт о народном богатстве, или О началах политической экономи (An Essay in the National Wealth, or On the Elements of Political Economy)*, vols 1–3. St Petersburg: The Press of the 2nd Dept of H. I. M. Own Chancellery.

d'Orsi, A. (2001) A Child of *Cultura Positiva*. Turin and the education of Piero Sraffa, in *Piero Sraffa's Political Economy*, T. Cozzi and R. Marchionatti (eds). London: Routledge.

Dmitriev, V.K. (2001 [1904]) *Экономические очерки (Economic Essays)*, P.N. Klyukin (ed.). Moscow: Higher School of Economics.

——(2001 [1908]) Теория стоимости (обзор литературы на русском языке) (Theory of Value. A Review of Literature in Russian). In V.K. Dmitriev, *Экономические очерки* (Economic Essays). Moscow: Higher School of Economics.

——(1968 [1904]) *Essais économiques: esquisse de synthèse organique de la théorie de la valeur-travail et de la théorie de l'utilité marginale*. Paris: Editions of the National Centre for Scientific Research.

——(1974 [1904]) *Economic Essays on Value, Competition and Utility*, with an introduction by D. M. Nuti, Cambridge University Press.

Engels, F. (1894 [1989]) Afterword. In *Marx–Engels Collected Works (2nd edition)*, vol. 27. Available online: <http://www.marxists.org/archive/marx/works/1894/01/russia.htm> (accessed 30 January 2013).

Klyukin, P.N. (2008) Значение теоретического наследия Рикардо: П. Сраффа, российская аналитическая традиция и их синтетическое восприятие (On significance of Ricardo's theoretical legacy: P. Sraffa, the Russian analytical tradition and their synthetic understanding), in Ricardo, D. (2008).

Lenin, V.I. (1977 [1913]) Три источника и три составных части марксизма (The Three Sources and Three Component Parts of Marxism). In Lenin, V. I., *Collected Works*, vol. 19. Moscow: Progress Publishers.

Marx, K. (1909 [1873]) Preface to the Second Edition. In *Capital: A Critique of Political Economy*, vol. 1, trans. from the 3rd German edition by Samuel Moore and Edward Aveling, edited by F. Engels. Chicago: Charles H. Kerr and Co.

——(1964 [1878]) Письмо Н.Ф. Даниельсону, 15 ноября 1878 (Letter to N.F. Danielson, November 15, 1878). In K. Marx, F. Engels. *Collected Works (2nd edition)*, vol. 34. Moscow: Politizdat.

——(1968 [1877]) Letter from Marx to Editor of the *Otecestvenniye Zapisky*. Available online: <http://www.marxists.org/archive/marx/works/1877/11/russia.htm> (accessed 30 January 2013). Moscow: International Publishers.

Mongiovi, G. (2002) Some Reflections on Sraffa's Ricardo. In S. Nisticó, D. Tosato (eds), *Competing Economic Theories: Essays in memory of Giovanni Caravale*. London and New York: Routledge, 155–64.

Otmahov, P.A. (1991) *Современная американская политэкономия (вопросы методологии) (The modern American political economy. Methodological issues)*. Moscow University Press.

Roncaglia, A. (2006) *The Wealth of Ideas. A History of Economic Thought*. Cambridge University Press.

Ricardo, D. (1873) *Сочинения* (*Works*), vol. 1., trans. and ed. N. I. Sieber. Kiev University Press.

——(1882) *Сочинения* (*Works*), trans. and ed. N. I. Sieber. St. Petersburg: L. F. Panteleev.

——(1955–1961) *Сочинения* [*Works*], vol. 1–5, M. N. Smith (ed.). Moscow: Politizdat.

——(2008) *Начала политической экономии и налогообложения. Избранные работы (Principles of Political Economy and Taxation. Selected Works)*, ed. and with an introduction by P. N. Klyukin. Moscow: ECSMO.

Rubin, I. I. (1930) *A History of Economic Thought*. 4th edn. GiZ. (In Russian).

——(1972 [1928]). *Essays on Marx's Theory of Value*. Trans. M. Samardžija and F. Perlman. Available online: <http://marxists.org/archive/rubin/value/index.htm> (accessed 30 January 2013). Detroit: Black and Red.

——(1978 [1927]) Abstract Labour and Value in Marx's System, trans. K. Gilbert. In *Capital and Class* 5, Summer. Available online: <http://marxists.org/archive/rubin/abstract-labour.htm> (accessed 30 January 2013).

——(1992 [1936–37]) Ricardo's Doctrine of Capital. In *Herald of the Russian Academy of Sciences* 8: 144–152. Available online: <http://www.marxists.org/archive/rubin/ricardo-capital.htm> (accessed 30 January 2013).

Sieber, N. I. (1871) *Теория ценности и капитала Д. Рикардо* (*D. Ricardo's Theory of Value and of Capital*). Kiev University Press.

——(1937 [1885]) Давид Рикардо и Карл Маркс в их общественно-экономических исследованиях. (*David Ricardo and Karl Marx in their Socio-Economic Studies*). Moscow: The State Social and Economic Press.

Sobolev, M. (1899) Рикардо (Ricardo). In *Encyclopedical Dictionary*, 26a: 696–698. St Petersburg, Brockhaus–Efron Publishers.

Sraffa, P. (1999) *Производство товаров посредством товаров* (*Production of Commodities by Means of Commodities*), I. I. Eliseeva (ed.). Moscow: UNITI.

Stein, V. M. (1917) Давид Рикардо (David Ricardo). In *The Bulletin of the Russian Academy of Sciences*. Petrograd: Academy of Sciences.

Tugan-Baranovsky, M. I. (1911) *Основания политической экономии* (*Foundations of Political Economy*). St Petersburg: Pravo.

——(1998 [1903]) Очерки из новейшей истории политической экономии и социализма (Essays in the recent history of political economy and of socialism). In Tugan-Baranovsky, M. I. *Economic Essays.* Moscow: Rosspen.

Vasina, L. L. (2011a) И.И. Рубин и его рукопись 'Очерки по теории денег Маркса' (I.I. Rubin and His Manuscript 'Essays on Marx's Theory of Money'). In *Istoki*, Moscow: Higher School of Economics.

——(2011b) Библиография работ И.И. Рубина (I. I. Rubin's Works Bibliography). In *Istoki*, Moscow, Higher School of Economics.

Vernadsky, I. V. (1858) *Очерк истории политической экономии* (*An Outline of the History of Political Economy*). Saint Petersburg: Ekonomicheskiy Ukazatel.

Zhukovsky, Yu. G. (1864a) Смитовское направление и позитивизм в экономической науке (The Smithian approach and the positivism in the economic science – I), *Sovremennik* 104: 23–52.

——(1864b) Смитовское направление и позитивизм в экономической науке (The Smithian approach and the positivism in the economic science – II), *Sovremennik* 104: 135–170.

——(1864a) Смитовское направление и позитивизм в экономической науке (The Smithian approach and the positivism in the economic science – III), *Sovremennik* 105: 33–60.

——(1871) *История политической литературы XIX столетия (History of the Political Literature of the Nineteenth Century)*, vol. 1. Saint Petersburg: Polyakov.

7 The reception of Ricardo in Japan

Masashi Izumo and Shigemasa Sato

1. Introduction: Japanese economic thought and the Meiji Restoration*

Japan's first contact with Western economic ideas can be reasonably dated to the late eighteenth century. The theories of Western economics were likely to have first been introduced to Japan by Carl Peter Thunberg (1743–1828), a Swedish botanist, in 1776, the same year as the publication of Adam Smith's *The Wealth of Nations.*[1] During his short stay in Edo (now Tokyo) in May of that year, Thunberg taught agricultural economics along with physics, botany, and medicine to Japanese scholars of Dutch Learning.[2]

However, Japan's own economic thought was advancing in the face of the difficulties attendant to the development of a money economy under the feudal system of the Edo period shogunate (1603–1868). Japanese economic circumstances, and its models of economic growth based on increased agricultural productivity, expanded commerce, and price fluctuation, were not so vastly different from those in European countries; that is, Japanese scholars were confronting similar economic problems in the age during which 'political economy' emerged as an independent field of learning in Europe.[3] Some Japanese economists of this time were Confucian scholars, such as Kumazawa Banzan (1619–91) and Dazai Shundai (1680–1747), but others did not adhere to Confucianism, such as Honda Toshiaki (1743–1821), Kaiho Seiryō (1755–1817), and Satō Nobuhiro (1769–1850).[4] Although their economic thought cannot be bracketed simply – because it contains various elements and fragments of Buddhist, Confucian, and Western thought, among others – in the several decades preceding the Meiji Restoration, these scholars produced numerous impressive works that analysed the money economy, the pursuit of profits by merchants, the advantages and disadvantages of foreign trade, and the role of the government in formulating economic policy.[5]

When Western economic thought was widely introduced to Japan around the Meiji Restoration in 1868, its acceptance was largely facilitated by the rich traditions of economic thought that had already developed in Japan.[6]

* In this chapter, Japanese names are given in the customary Japanese order, i.e. surname first.

The industrialisation of Japanese society brought about by the Meiji Restoration nevertheless prompted an influx of a large number of Western writings. Therefore, the 'advanced' capitalist societies of the late nineteenth century became the models – both for the government and leading intellectuals – upon which to establish Japan's new political and economic systems.

The first translated work on Western economic thought was Kanda Takahira's (1830–98) *Keizai Shōgaku* (Elementary Economics) published a year before the Meiji Restoration in 1867. Kanda translated it not from William Ellis's original English work, *Outlines of Social Economy* (1846), but from the Dutch *Grondtrekken der Staatshuishoudkunde*, which was translated by H. Hooft Graafland in 1852.[7] However, this was not Kanda's first reference to Western economics. Prior to this time, in 1861, Kanda had written *Nōshōben* (An Exact Explanation of an Agrarian Nation and a Merchant Nation) which was the first Japanese work that explored Western economic thought.[8] Kanda was a scholar of Dutch Learning and a language teacher at an institute of Western learning and languages – initially Dutch, but later also English, French, and German – which had been opened by the government in the late Edo period to promote the study of foreign knowledge.[9]

Moreover, a great number of scholars and intellectuals were also sent by the government to Europe and the United States to study Western ideas, sciences, technologies, systems, and economics. Among them, those who had a particularly great influence on Japanese economic thought were Nishi Amane (1829–97), Tsuda Mamichi (1829–1903), and Fukuzawa Yukichi (1835–1901). Fukuzawa visited the United States in 1860 and 1867 and Europe in 1862, while Nishi and Tsuda lived in Leiden, the Netherlands, from 1862 to 1865 to study international law, philosophy and economics. Nishi and Tsuda studied the traditions of nineteenth-century European liberal thought at Leiden University under Simon Vissering (1818–88), a professor of economics, who taught political economy, statistics and diplomatic history.[10] Vissering was one of the most prominent Dutch economists of his day and was well known as an expert on British and French economic theories. In particular, he advocated the laissez-faire principle, influenced by Frédéric Bastiat and John Stuart Mill, and it is not difficult to find the reflection of this liberal approach to economics in the later writings of Nishi and Tsuda (Sugihara 1972: 5, Morris-Suzuki 1989: 49).

After their return to Japan, Fukuzawa, Nishi, and Tsuda were among the original 10 members of the Meirokusha (Meiji Six Society), along with Nakamura Masanao (1832–91) and Katō Hiroyuki (1836–1916). The Meirokusha was the brainchild of Mori Arinori (1847–89), a statesman and educator, and was founded in 1873 as the first modern academic society for enlightenment – six years after the Meiji Restoration. The group was a small but influential intellectual society whose extensively read main publication, the *Meiroku Zasshi* (Meiroku Journal), played a substantial role in introducing and popularising Western ideas, including economic thought, during the early Meiji period.[11] Earlier, in 1866, and again in 1868 and 1870, Fukuzawa had published *Seiyō Jijō* (Affairs in the Western Countries) in which he translated selected passages from Western economic writings by the likes of Francis Wayland and William Chambers. Fukuzawa used Wayland's *Elements of Political Economy* (1837) for his lectures at Keio Gijuku, the forerunner of Keio University, and this inspiration features strongly in his articles for the *Meiroku Zasshi*. Kanda also joined the Meirokusha when it expanded its membership and wrote nine articles for the journal. Mitsubashi points out that the notion that Japan should adopt Western capitalist principles was spread by the talk of Fukuzawa and diffused by the pen of Kanda (Mitsubashi [1928] 1987: 8).

By the 1870s, however, as the study of foreign languages other than Dutch gained ascendancy among Japanese scholars, economic texts began to be translated directly from English, French, and German, and the number of translations in circulation rapidly increased. According to Honjō (1957), a surprising 274 books on Western economic thought were translated into Japanese and published between 1867 and 1897. The great majority were translated works originally by British authors, followed by American, German, and French (see Figure 7.1).[12]

In particular, J. S. Mill's *Principle* was translated by Hayashi Tadasu (1850–1913) with Suzuki Shigetaka in 1875 and again in 1882, Thomas Robert Malthus's *Population* was translated by Ōshima Sadamasu (1845–1914) in 1877, and Adam Smith's *The Wealth of Nations* was translated by Ishikawa Eisaku (1858–86) and Saga Shōsaku (1853–90) and published in 1884. Friedrich List's *National System* was also translated by Ōshima Sadamasu in 1889, though as a retranslation from the English of the German original. Ōshima also translated William Stanley Jevons's *Money and the Mechanism of Exchange* in 1893, while Karl Marx's *Manifest der Kommunistischen Partei* was translated by Kōtoku Shūsui (1871–1911) and Sakai Toshihiko (1871–1933) in 1904, and *Das Kapital* was translated by Takabatake Motoyuki (1886–1928)

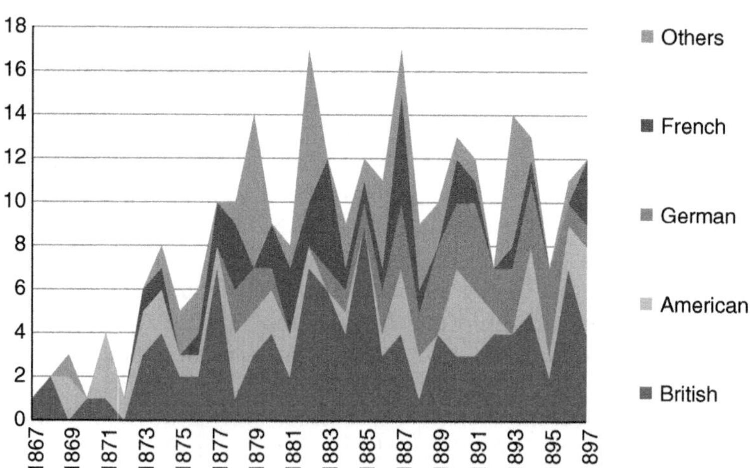

Figure 7.1 Number of Western economic writings translated in Japan: 1867–97
Source: Honjō (1957: 36–7).

in 1919. In addition, Jean-Baptiste Say's *Catéchisme d'économie politique* was translated in 1882, and Alfred Marshall's *The Economics of Industry* and Wilhelm Roscher's *Nationalökonomik des Ackerbaues* were translated in 1886. Furthermore, Frédéric Bastiat's *Harmonies économiques* was translated in 1888, and Luigi Cossa's *Primi Elementi di Scienza delle Finanze* was translated in 1889.[13]

Intriguingly, the first translation of Ricardo's *Principles* – separately by Wada Saichirō (1894–1944) and Hori Tsuneo (1896–1981), both professors of Tohoku Imperial University – did not appear until 1921.[14] Why was Ricardo introduced so late to Japan? Moreover, what features surrounded the acceptance and dissemination of Ricardo's writings, and how did the Japanese intellectuals receive and interpret his works? In this chapter, we consider these questions.[15]

This chapter traces the outline of the reception and diffusion of Ricardo's economics in Japan from 1869 to 2012. Although this task must unavoidably be selective, it singles out those studies that well illustrate the Japanese reception and diffusion of Ricardo's works and the main themes of Japanese Ricardo studies. The chapter also deals with two distinct periods, each of them starting with a major event that deeply influenced Japanese society: the Meiji Restoration and World War II. In particular, it describes the background to Ricardo's widespread acceptance in Japan during the first period (i.e. during the late nineteenth century and early twentieth century) and illustrates the hallmarks of Japanese Ricardo studies that would be passed on to later generations of scholars. In describing the second period (i.e. from 1945 to the present), particular attention is paid to those Japanese studies that offer controversial interpretations of Ricardo's thought in order to provide interesting comparisons with similar debates abroad.

2. The reception of Ricardo in Japan in the late nineteenth and early twentieth centuries

From the Meiji Restoration to the middle of the Meiji period

Ricardo's name and works had already been introduced to Japan by the late 1860s – the beginning of the Meiji period. Ricardo may have been first introduced in the government publication *Kanpan Keizaigenron* (The Principles of Economics), which was translated in 1869, the year after the Meiji Restoration, from Arthur Latham Perry's *Elements of Political Economy* by the bureaucrat Ogata Tadashi (later Wakayama Giichi, 1840–91). The translator was educated at Tekijuku, a school established in Osaka in 1838 by Ogata Kōan (1810–63), a famous doctor and Dutch scholar.

Ricardo first became the subject of a regular lecture during 1870–73, at a school called Ikueisha, founded by Nishi Amane, the aforementioned philosopher and bureaucrat who had studied economics at Leiden University. In Nishi's *Hyakugaku Renkan* (Encyclopaedia), Ricardo was regarded as one of the six British classical economists in the legacy of David Hume and a theorist of taxation, rent, and value (Hori 1948: 155–56). Nishi was responsible for coining many of the philosophical and scientific terms currently used in the Japanese language, such as 'tetsugaku' (philosophy), 'geijutsu' (art), 'kagaku' (science), and 'gijutsu' (technology).

It was not surprising that both Ogata (Wakayama) and Nishi had a 'Dutch connection' in this period, because Dutch Learning, as a systematised field of enquiry dedicated to the Western sciences, had huge draw for the Japanese intellectuals of the late eighteenth to mid-nineteenth centuries. Through Dutch Learning, the Japanese could acquire fundamental knowledge on language, medicine, astronomy, physics, art, chemistry, and military technology not to mention law, politics, and economics. This field was also particularly significant in helping intellectuals assess the existing systems in Japan in comparison with those used in the West.[16]

In 1876, the Research Department of the Bank of Japan translated Arthur Crump's *A Practical Treatise on Banking, Currency, and the Exchanges* (1866) and published it as *Ginkō Jikkenron* (A Practical Treaty on Banking), printed by the National Printing Bureau. This translated book first introduced Japan to the monetary and financial theory of Ricardo. Nagata Kensuke (1844–1909), a professor of Keio University, then translated Millicent Garrett Fawcett's *Political Economy for Beginners* and published it as *Hōshi Keizaigaku* (Fawcett's Economics) in 1877.[17] This translation was a great success and was reprinted over several editions. This book chiefly examined Ricardo's rent theory, and consequently the image of Ricardo as a representative rent theorist became widely known in Japan (Mazane 1962: 80).[18]

Also in 1877, Wakayama Giichi translated John Barnard Byles's *Sophisms of Free-Trade and Popular Political Economy Examined* into Japanese and criticised Ricardo's theory of comparative advantage from the standpoint of protectionism. Interestingly, Taguchi Ukichi (1855–1905), who was called the 'Japanese Smith', also criticised comparative advantage in his *Nihon Keizairon: Jiyū Kōekiron* (Japanese Economy: Free Trade) in 1878, although he based his arguments on the principle of free trade. In 1879, Taguchi began the publication of the fortnightly (later weekly) journal *Tokyo Keizai Zasshi* (Tokyo Economics Journal), the first economics journal in Japan, and wrote in favour of free trade. As mentioned above, one of the editors of this journal was Ishikawa Eisaku, who translated Smith's *The Wealth of Nations* into Japanese for the first time in Japan.[19] Inukai Tsuyoshi (1855–1932), later a prime minister, argued against the kind of free trade advocated by Taguchi in *Tokyo Keizai Zasshi* and instead lauded the value of protectionism in *Tōkai Keizai Shinpō* (East Sea Economics Courier), which he founded in 1880. Inukai gradually enjoyed strong support from the Japanese press and urban intellectuals. Notably, it would seem that Ricardo's theory of foreign trade did not play an important role in their controversy between free trade and protectionism here.[20]

In 1882, Suzuki Kentarō (1863–1939), a journalist, wrote 'Keizaigaku Shitaika Hyōden' (A Critical Biography of Four Great Economists) in *Tokyo*

Keizai Zasshi. This was the first biography of Ricardo, along with those of Thomas Robert Malthus, James Mill and Frédéric Bastiat, printed in Japan. Takata Sanae (1860–1938), a politician and later chancellor of Waseda University, published *Kahei Shinron* (The New Monetary Theory), a textbook based on Francis A. Walker's *Money* and W. S. Jevons's *Money and the Mechanism of Exchange*. Amano Tameyuki (1861–1938), president of Waseda University, penned 'Rishi Chidairon' (Ricardo's Theory of Rent) for *Chuō Gakujutsu Zasshi* (Central Scientific Journal) in 1885. He also published *Keizai Genron* (The Theory of Political Economy) in 1886, which sold a groundbreaking 30,000 copies as the first full textbook written by a Japanese. It went through 22 editions and was a best-seller in its time. Sakatani Yoshio (1863–1941) published the first textbook of the history of economic thought in Japan – *Keizaigakushi Kōgi* (Lecture of the History of Economic Thought) – in 1887. Moreover, Nakae Chōmin (1847–1901) – who was a creative writer in Meiji Japan and translated some of the works of Jean-Jacques Rousseau into Japanese – referred to Ricardo, along with Bastiat, as a liberalist in *Rikken Jiyū Shimbun* (Constitutional Liberal News) in 1891.[21]

From the Sino-Japanese War to Japan's annexation of Korea

Japanese industrialisation advanced rapidly after the war with China (1894–95) and Russia (1904–5). The military successes achieved in these wars and rising domestic industrialisation stabilised the authority of the Japanese state. At the same time, these achievements also emphasised Japan's expansionist tendencies with regard to other Asian countries and served to strengthen the official oppression of critics of the Meiji imperial bureaucratic system. Indeed, the government's nature and stance were revealed clearly in two events: Japan's annexation of Korea and the 'Taigyaku Jiken' (High Treason Incident) of 1910.

As farmers that lived in rural villages became poorer, large numbers relocated to urban areas and as migrants, they were forced to work in factories for low wages. Japan's rapid industrialisation heralded the rapid growth of major cities, such as Tokyo and Osaka, but also increased the number of urban poor. Consequently, various social and economic challenges emerged in Japan at the start of the twentieth century.

In 1894, Hamada Kenjirō (1860–1918) and Isemoto Ichirō published *Keizaigakushi* (History of Economics) based on John Kells Ingram's *A History of Political Economy*. Two years later, Abe Toranosuke translated Ingram's *A History of Political Economy* into Japanese, the first complete translation of a standard Western textbook on the history of economic thought. During this period, several textbooks were also written by professors of Japanese universities, with Ricardo introduced to students through such texts.

Kita Terujirō (another name for Kita Ikki, 1883–1937) – who was a famous national socialist, executed in 1937 for his involvement in the failed coup, '2.26 Jiken' (the 26 February Incident) – published *Kokutairon oyobi Junsei Shakaishugi* (National Polity Theory and Genuine Socialism) in 1906.

In this book, Kita mentions Ricardo's rent theory, and uses it to criticise the interests of landlords and the concept of rent itself in particular. In this sense, Kita references Ricardo to support socialist ends.

Shakai Seisaku Gakkai (Society for the Study of Social Policy) – the first academic society for economics and social sciences in Japan – was established in 1897, and its first conference was held in 1907. In the following year, 1908, Yoshida Kinosuke translated British economic historian Arnold J. Toynbee's *The Industrial Revolution in England.* In this book, Toynbee criticised the socialist interpretation of Ricardo's wage theory and pointed out that Henry George, an American writer and the most influential advocate of land value tax, was an absolute follower of Ricardo. This translation seems to be reflected in the foundation of Shakai Seisaku Gakkai in the face of the social problems that accompanied rapid industrialisation.

The sociologist Ōhara Kyūsui (another name for Ōhara Shōichi, 1877–1958) wrote 'Ricardo shi no Chingin oyobi Rijunron wo Hyōsu' (A Critical Comment on Ricardo's Theory of Wage and Profit) in *Tokyo Keizai Zasshi* in 1901, which found fault with Ricardo on the basis of the interpretation of his wage theory by the German socialist Ferdinand Lassalle, who referred to it as the 'Iron Law of Wages'. On this issue, in 1908, Fujimoto Kōtarō (1880–1967) wrote 'Iwayuru Ricardo no Rōgin Tessoku nitsuite' (On the So-called Iron Law of Wages of Ricardo) in *Nihon Hōsei Shinshi* (New Journal of Japanese Law and Politics) and rejected the Iron Law of Wages' socialistic interpretation of Ricardo's wage theory. In the next year, 1909, Matsumura Kōzō wrote 'Chingin Gakusetsu' (Theory of Wages) in *Kokumin Keizai Zasshi* (Journal of Political Economy and Commercial Science). This is but one of the many journal articles that debated Ricardo's wage theory in an age marked by urbanisation, low wages, high poverty rates, and poor living conditions in Japan.

From World War I to World War II

The Liberty and People's Rights Movement was suppressed in the middle Meiji period. When the 'Taigyaku Jiken' was concocted by the government, many socialists and anarchists were arrested and twelve suspects were executed. After this incident, although socialist and democratic movements rapidly declined, and the so-called 'winter time' of socialism deepened, academic freedom and university autonomy remained strong, even in the face of official policies of oppression.

Fukuda Tokuzō (1874–1930), a prominent economist and advocate of the right to life, liberty, and security, rigorously studied Ricardo on the basis of 'textual principles'. Fukuda became a professor of the Tokyo Higher Commercial School (later Hitotsubashi University) after studying in Germany from 1897 to 1900. His 1908 lecture at Chuo University, titled 'Ricardo no Chidairon kara Marx he' (From the Rent Theory of Ricardo to Marx), published in 1915, pointed out that Marx's theory of exploitation was amplified by Ricardo's rent theory, in which the landlord was viewed as an enemy, and that Ricardian socialists held a position midway between Ricardo and Marx (Fukuda [1908] 1925: 1259–64). Fukuda also wrote 'Kachi no Gen-in to Shakudo tonikansuru Malthus to Ricardo tono Ronsō' (Controversy on the Cause and Measure of Value between Malthus and Ricardo) in 1912 and 'Ricardo Keizaigenron no Chūshin Mondai' (The Fundamental Issues of Ricardo's Theory of Economics) in 1913 in *Kokumin Keizai Zasshi.* In these articles, he used the standpoint of Marshallian economics to explain that Smith's labour theory of value had two separate successors – namely, Malthus's labour command theory of value and Ricardo's labour-bestowed theory of value – and that these theories should be integrated with J. S. Mill's cost of the production theory of value (Fukuda [1908] 1925: 1234–40).

Kawakami Hajime (1879–1946), one of the most influential economists in early twentieth-century Japan, began to introduce Ruskin's economic and social ideas in 1916. These ideas were popularised in the country through his articles and books. One of his students, Mikimoto Ryūzō (1894–1971), whose father was Mikimoto Kōkichi, the founder of the Mikimoto Pearl Company, said about Kawakami that 'the greatest Marxian teacher in Japan has once been so Ruskinian that he was called the Japanese Ruskin by his colleagues' (Mikimoto 1931: 40). Kawakami, a professor of economics at Kyoto Imperial University first became well known through the publication of *Binbō Monogatari* (Tale of Poverty) which acquired popularity around 1916–17. Ruskin is conjured in the preface thus:

> Ruskin says in his famous words, 'There is no wealth, but life'. Wealth is the purpose of life – that is, the only purpose of life is to quest the way, wealth is significant simply as a means of achieving this purpose. Therefore I hope to eradicate poverty from human society because poverty obstructs the way of life human beings pursue. (Kawakami [1916] 1982: 4)

Kawakami expressed his deep sympathy with Ruskin's concept of wealth and criticism of 'individualist economics', in line with the critiques of J. S. Mill and Thomas Carlyle, in his article, 'Ruskin no *Kono Saigo no Mono nimo*' (Ruskin's *Unto This Last*) (Kawakami [1918a] 1982: 159). Moreover, in his preface to Ishida Kenji's translation of *Unto This Last* in 1918, Kawakami, probably for the first time, classified economics into three streams: 'individualist economics', which is characterised by selfishness and the pursuit of profits; 'socialist economics', which seeks to reform the economic system; and 'humanitarian economics', which demands the reformation of the human mind. Kawakami typecasts Smith, Bentham, J. Mill, Malthus, and Ricardo as leading economists of 'individualist economics', Marx, of course, as a leader of 'socialist economics', and 'our John Ruskin' as a great figure of 'humanitarian economics' (Kawakami [1918b] 1982: 509–10).[22] He then repeats the same sentiments in the preface to Ruskin's *Unto This Last*, which he added when he published *Shakai Mondai Kanken* (My Views on Social Problems), including this article with others in 1918 (Kawakami [1918c] 1982: 158).

In the same year, the Rice Riots broke out at the instigation of housewives in the small fishing village of Toyama and subsequently spread across Japan. These events followed just a year after the start of the Russian Revolution. Yet, it was not until the 1920s that Marxism came to be widely known among Japanese intellectuals. The notion of anti-industrialisation, such as that advocated by John Ruskin and William Morris, became the handiest intellectual tool for criticising the system prevalent at that time. From the late 1910s to the 1920s, many translations of Ruskin's works were published in Japan. Ironically, Kawakami ultimately became a Marxist after his 'humanitarianism' economics were strongly challenged in 1924 by Kushida Tamizō (1885–1934), a noted Marxian economist and disciple of Kawakami. Thus, although Kawakami introduced the Marxian strain of scholarship to Ricardo studies, it seems as though Kawakami maintained his humanitarian point of view, which differed from the Marxian stance, throughout his life.[23]

The general field of Ricardo studies, from both the Marshallian and the Marxian perspectives, was continued by the next generation of Ricardo scholars such as Koizumi Shinzō (1888–1966), president of Keio University, Hori Tsuneo (1896–1981), later president of Kwansei Gakuin University, Mori Kōjirō (1895–1962), professor of Kyushu Imperial University, and Maide Chōgorō (1891–1964), professor of Tokyo Imperial University. Koizumi, a disciple of Fukuda, energetically published several books and articles on Ricardo in the 1920s that concurred with Marshallian thought. On the contrary, Mori and Hori, both disciples of Kawakami, based their arguments on Marx's interpretation of Ricardian theories. Indeed, the complete Japanese translation of Ricardo's *Principles* was published by Koizumi and Hori separately in 1928 and various studies of Ricardo were additionally published during the 1930s, but the number of works declined gradually following the onset of World War II (see Figure 7.2).[24]

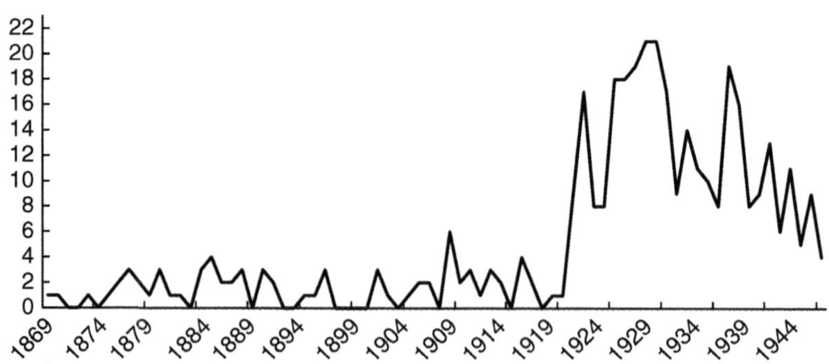

Figure 7.2 Number of Ricardo studies in Japan: 1869–1944

3. Japanese studies of Ricardo after World War II

Japanese studies of Ricardo

Numerous Japanese works published after World War II have reviewed previous studies of Ricardo. For example, Takagi and Nakamura (1966) review the literature on the theory of money and credit from 1950 to 1965, while Hatori (1966) examines articles on the theory of capital accumulation written between 1963 and 1966. Mazane and Mizokawa (1968) focus on the reception of classical economics in Japan from the Meiji period onwards, and Nakamura (1972) researches monographs that refer to Ricardo written between 1966 and 1972. Furthermore, Nakamura and Aramaki (1982) survey studies of the theory of money and credit written between 1966 and 1981.

Similarly, Mizuta (1985) classifies studies written between 1972 and 1984 into four genres: 1) early Ricardo, 2) the structure of Ricardo's theory, 3) the theory of value, and 4) the theory of distribution and capital accumulation. In addition, Nakamura's (2007) work offers a broad perspective of Japanese studies of Ricardo's *Principles* since the 1920s, while Fukuda (2008) summarises the Japanese controversy over Ricardo's early theory of value and profit. Finally, Sato (2008) surveys articles that focus on the theory of money from 1982 to 2007, while Sato (2013) outlines Japanese studies of Ricardo after World War II.

Based on the above-mentioned works, in this section we describe and discuss Japanese studies of Ricardo after World War II and underline some of the controversies Japanese authors identified in the early works of Ricardo, especially concerning the theory of value and capital accumulation.

Specifically, the section is divided into three periods: 1) the postwar period to the 1960s; 2) the 1970s and 1980s; and 3) the 1990s to date. The reason for this periodisation is the gradual publication of *The Works and Correspondence of David Ricardo* edited by Piero Sraffa between 1951 and 1973. The project of translating these works into Japanese began in 1955, with volume III appearing in 1969, and nearly all volumes appearing by the early 1970s. This series of publications allowed Japanese scholars not only to access Ricardo's original texts in order to gain a broad overview of his theories but also to return to the original texts once more. It could thus be said that Japanese studies of Ricardo entered a second 'reception period' in the 1970s and 1980s – repeating the first full-scale 'reception period' of the 1920s – with each followed by a 'diffusion period' (i.e. the 1950s and 1960s and the 1990s to date, respectively).

The theory of value and capital accumulation between the 1950s and 1960s

Immediately after the end of the Second World War, many books on Ricardo's theory were published at the same time (their respective authors most likely worked on these texts during the wartime period). For instance, Ide (1948) discusses Ricardo's theory of public debt and Nawa (1949) the theory of international value, while Hori's work from 1929 on Ricardo's theory of value was reprinted in 1949 (Hori 1949). The primary theme of such postwar works was the theory of value and distribution in response to the massive reconstruction effort needed in Japan after the war. In this period, however, Ricardo was regarded as only a minor theorist relative to Smith and Marx, the giants of economics. Nevertheless, it was also during this period that Tamanoi (1954) tackled theoretical questions about the history of value from Ricardo to Marx, and Hori (1958) traced the ideas discussed in the *Principles* by examining British economic thought from Smith to J. S. Mill.

From the 1950s, Japanese studies of Ricardo gradually shifted from the theory of value to the theory of capital accumulation in line with the corresponding development in Japanese capitalism from the restarting stage to the taking off stage. In response to his shifting emphasis, Yoshizawa (1953) analyses England's transition to capitalism after the Napoleonic War, characterising Ricardo as an 'anchorman' who perfected classical economics. This theme was developed by Yoshizawa (1970), whose concept of the 'advancing social state' opened up a new theoretical vista in Japanese studies of Ricardo.

Many texts accused capitalism of bringing about such evils as unemployment, an unstable economy, and economic crises. In line with Ricardo's changing views on the topic, Mazane (1959) questions whether the adoption of machinery could offset unemployment, while Toyokura (1959) links Ricardian and Malthusian values in order to investigate the theory of crisis. Similarly, Hatori (1963) analyses Ricardo's two views on employment, namely whether labour demand depends on circulating capital or on gross production, arguing that if the former were true, unemployment would increase following capital accumulation. Tomizuka (1965) also discusses the structure of accumulation in Ricardo's theory with regard to the theory of crisis and advocates the concept of the 'equilibrium orbit of accumulation'.

During this period, a number of Japanese authors also drew comparisons between Ricardo and other pre-eminent economists. For example, Mizokawa (1966) identifies differences between J.-B. Say and Ricardo, explaining that Ricardo based his theories on the capital market rather than on the goods market. Kobayashi (1966), by comparing Ricardo's writings with those by Malthus, concludes that Ricardo's understanding of the theory of money allowed him to construct his theory of falling profit. Nakano (1969) traces the theory of crisis in Ricardo's speeches in Parliament and, in contrast with the findings presented by J.-B. Say, insists that Ricardo properly identified the general depression in capitalism. Finally, Ebihara (1974) discusses the causal relations between capital accumulation and the working class, especially in connection with the theories of crises and unemployment by classical economists such as Smith, Ricardo, and Ricardian socialists.

Based on these studies of capital accumulation, some books attempted to grasp Ricardo's theory as a whole. In this regard, Onishi (1969) presents a broad-spectrum view of *Principles*, Tsutsui (1973) discusses Ricardo's theory of distribution from both static and dynamic points of view, and Mazane

(1975) skilfully arranges Ricardo's life and theories in order to refine *Principles* for Japanese academics. Moreover, Hishiyama (1979), one of the Japanese translators of Sraffa's *Production of Commodities by Means of Commodities*, interprets Ricardo's theory of accumulation, distribution, and value in connection with Sraffa, emphasising the need to re-estimate his labour theory of value by comparing it with the views of Walras and Marshall as well as those advocated by Post Keynesians.

At the same time, some Japanese scholars started to reread *The Works of Ricardo* edited by Sraffa, and their efforts were gradually reaching publication as early as the 1950s. Hatori's (1972) seminal work analyses the fundamental differences between Smith, Malthus, and Ricardo in the constitutions of accumulation theory. A decade later, Hatori (1982) deepens our understanding of Ricardo's theory of value and distribution based on his last manuscript, *Absolute Value*. Nakamura (1975) also offers a close reading of Ricardo's principal writings and letters from the *Bullion Controversy* to *Absolute Value* and observes Ricardo's departure from Smith's monetary theory. These elaborate studies of Ricardo that offered an original Japanese interpretation served to challenge Sraffa's 'corn ratio theory'.

Criticisms of Sraffa's 'corn ratio' theory in the 1970s and 1980s

Japanese postwar studies of Ricardo produced numerous theoretical results, especially concerning his early profit theory. These results originated in the deep and thoughtful analysis of Ricardo's texts and thus they surely deserve our attention. We herein outline how this original interpretation was born in Japan by referring to the findings of Fukuda (2008) and Senga (2011).

Sraffa advocated his corn ratio theory in the 'Introduction' to volume I of *The Works of Ricardo* in 1951, resulting in intense debate among Western scholars. Many Japanese scholars, who tended to hold Sraffa's theory in high regard, explored Ricardo's original texts, not only *Principles* but also *Notes on Malthus* and *Correspondence*, when they became available after the publication of Sraffa's *Works*. Eventually their views converged, resulting in so-called 'dual sector theory', which argued that Ricardo's early works offered two contrasting interpretations for how the profit rate is regulated.

For instance, Hatori (1965) declares that he could not fully agree with Sraffa's interpretation. Based on Ricardo's letter to Malthus (26 June 1814) and Malthus's letter to Ricardo (5 August 1814) and on *Essay on Profits,* Hatori shows that Sraffa's corn ratio theory is misleading, because Ricardo only adopted corn as a measure of value under the influence of Smith's commanded labour theory of value. Furthermore, Hatori (1972) suggests that late Ricardo thought helped him successfully develop his distribution theory-based on the labour theory of value – through his discussions with Malthus.

Thereafter, Nakamura (1968), by analysing Ricardo's letters to Malthus (26 June 1814 and 11 August 1814), asserts that Sraffa's corn ratio theory is incorrect. This paper shows that Ricardo's early writings grasped the basic idea behind inverse proportion theory, which states that wages and profit vary in inverse proportion to each other. At the same time, he also defends Ricardo's dual explanations for the determination of the profit rate: one is in real terms, which is tied to the agricultural sector, and the other is in nominal terms, which is tied to the manufacturing sector. Subsequently Nakamura (1974) criticises Sraffa again, by examining *Essay on Profits* in 1815, suggesting that such inconsistencies can be explained by Ricardo's immaturity and that focus should be placed on his later theoretical progress, which supports his labour theory. However, by examining Ricardo's letters to Malthus (25 July 1814 and 11 August 1814) and *Essay* in 1815, Senga (1972) also demonstrates that Ricardo's inconsistencies in profit rate originate in the yet theoretical incompletion of his value theory.

Nakamura (1972) immediately criticises Senga by quoting Ricardo's letter to Malthus (26 June 1814). Hatori ([1977], 1982), however, supports Senga's position, after which Nakamura (1982) accepts Hatori's interpretation and ultimately agrees with Senga. Eventually there was scholarly consensus in Japan that Ricardo, in his early writings, offered two contradictory explanations of profit rates owing to the immaturity of his labour theory of value. Consequently, Senga's interpretation was approved by many Japanese scholars and by the early 1980s, it had become the de facto standard interpretation of early Ricardian thought in Japan.

Subsequent studies of Ricardo followed two main directions. One aimed to clarify the theoretical progress of Ricardo's value theory, while the other attempted to extract from *Principles* the essence of Ricardo's theory.

As for the former direction, Mizuta (1981), by analysing distribution theory, identifies different theoretical stages in Ricardo's work. He argues that first, in 1814, Ricardo established his profit rate determination theory; second, in *Essay* (1815), Ricardo developed value theory with the assistance of rent theory; and third, in *Principles* (1817), he completed his distribution theory. Hatori (1995) then examines how value and distribution rates are determined, by exploring Ricardo's theory of rent, wages, machinery, and bounties. In the same vein, Nakamura (1996) focuses on the changing processes of Ricardo's theory, while Fukuda (2006) re-emphasises the earlier criticism of dual sector theory by insisting that early ambiguity in the definition of profits should be understood as an evolutionary process in Ricardo's price theory.

As for the latter direction, scholars concentrated on Ricardo's theory itself and aimed to purify it by refining idealistic models. At the same time, they also attempted to put aside their reservations of capitalism and overlook the inconsistencies of Ricardo's early writings. For example, Negishi (1983) discusses Ricardo in an historical context – from classical economics to Keynes – and strives to rebuild his theory mathematically by focusing on the field of foreign trade (see also Negishi 2008). Morishima (1989) analyses Ricardo's economics from the perspective of general equilibrium theory, looking at prices, revenues, economic growth, and theoretical paradigms. Finally, Mori (1992) explores the classical theories of economic growth proposed by Smith, Malthus, Ricardo and J. S. Mill.

Thus, Japanese studies of Ricardo began by critically examining Sraffa's corn ratio theory and ended up discussing dual sector theory. However, this did not necessarily mean that Japanese scholars denied Sraffa's interpretation in entirely, because their principal problem was not only connecting Ricardo's visible surface categories, but also understanding the latent method implied in his texts. Thus, the problem of Sraffa's 'corn ratio' theory, which could lead us to the material arrangement in economy, remained unsolved.

Disputes over monetary theory from the 1990s

In the late 1990s, when the second diffusion period started, Japanese studies of Ricardo opened up many new theoretical frontiers in numerous fields, such as the theory of value and distribution, profits, rents, wages, money and banking, machinery, supply and demand, foreign trade, and taxation. Outstanding advances were particularly made with regard to the theory of money (see Sato 2008). Indeed, the revival of scholarly interest in the theory of money and foreign trade, a popular topic in Japan since the 1950s (Nakamura 1972), may reflect the recent crises in international money markets.

Studies published in the late 1990s differ markedly from those of the 1950s. The most remarkable difference is that scholars do not take Ricardo's monetary theory in isolation, but rather compare it with other contemporary theories. Below, we discuss this trend by focusing on the works of three scholars, Nakamura Hiroji, Senga Shigeyoshi, and Sato Yuji, who have written extensively about Ricardo's monetary theory.

First, Nakamura (1996) insists that Ricardo's quantity theory of money played an important role in the completion of his labour theory of value. Smith states that a rise in corn price brought about a rise of wages, while a rise in wages increased the price of all commodities, whereas a fall in gold value raised the price of all commodities (i.e. the 'linking theory' of wages and prices). Ricardo opposed this causal mechanism and instead proffered the 'production difficulties theory', which explained that the price of commodities was defined by production difficulties. Nakamura (1996) emphasises the need to differentiate these two causalities in the linking theory between the price of corn and the value of gold and insists that the theory of money might play an important role in the completion of Ricardo's value theory.

Nakamura (1999) studies the theory of gold bullion in Ricardo's *Price of Gold* and, by additionally reading the speeches he made in Parliament, concludes that Ricardo's theory of money offered an original explanation of the international system of the gold standard. Furthermore, Nakamura (2000), by examining from Marx's perspective the money theories of Smith, Malthus, Ricardo, Fullarton and J. S. Mill, points out Ricardo's originality in distinguishing between the dip in gold value and depreciation of bank notes.

Senga (1989) emphasises Ricardo's insistence about an unvaried gold standard in relation to the fixed measure of value. Senga had already paid attention to the great possibilities of Ricardo's monetary theory when he analysed the controversy between Ricardo and Malthus in 1815 and *Economical and Secure Currency*. Senga, like Nakamura, argued that Ricardo had already noted the difference in the price-rippling processes between corn and gold when he established his inverse proportion theory, which, he argued, showed a close connection to Marx's theory of absolute price level.

Furthermore, Senga (1993a) explores why Ricardo presupposed a fixed standard contrary to Keynes and emphasises that Ricardo's money control theory never meant the abolition of the standard. Senga (1993b), by contrasting the work of Jevons with that of Ricardo, finds that the latter derived his idea about the negative effects of the over-issue of bank notes from Jevons's fixed measure of value and uses this point in order to identify the missing link between Ricardo's value theory and monetary theory. Later, Senga (1996), by referring to the findings of Marcuzzo and Rosselli (1991), Hollander (1979), and Mason (1963), argues in favour of a link between Ricardo's early monetary theory and capital accumulation theory in his later writings, suggesting the possibility of tracing Ricardo's theoretical maturation processes from gold standard theory to inverse proportion theory.

Sato (1999) advocates that Ricardo's monetary theory is tightly connected with his theory of politics, which reflects the political dynamic of his day. The author explains that Ricardo's emphasis on the economic significance of the money standard might have lead him to promote the idea of 'well-regulated money', which he consistently proposed since his *Plan for National Bank* and which might have eventually lead to his appeal for the Bank of England to initiate a disclosure system.

Furthermore, Sato (2003) subsequently challenges the prevailing paradigm about the international adjustment of money (which was called the 'monetary approach to the balance of payments'). By investigating the quantity theory of money from Hume to Smith and Ricardo, he concludes that Ricardo's theory was not a naïve quantity theory of money at all. Indeed, he analyses the barometer function of prices from Ricardo's financial policies and asserts that the split paradigm of 'rule or discretion' is actually nonsense.

Japanese studies of Ricardo have advanced greatly thanks to the excellent articles of these three Ricardo scholars. On the quantity theory of money, Sato (2002) re-emphasises that Ricardo tended to depart from the classical quantity theory of money. Nakamura (2000), however, criticises Sato's work, insisting that Ricardo continued to adhere to classical money theory. Arai (1998) and Otomo (2001) added to the literature in this regard by exploring Ricardo's theoretical progress of the theory of money from *The Price of Gold* to *The Plan for a National Bank* and tracing Ricardo's departure from the classical quantity theory of money. Similarly, Senga's discussion about the invariability of the standard carved a theoretical path toward the cognition of money as a nominal substance. In addition, Mizuta (1994) and Okada (1994) argued that Ricardo's money theory offered a theoretical starting point for Wicksell's cumulative process.

Ricardo's topic of the relationship between economics and politics raised by Sato (1999) was taken up by Masunaga (1997) and Takenaga (2000) based on the problem of 'market or state'. The study of Senga (1989) had already investigated how the relation between politics and economics should be understood in Ricardo's political economy. In this regard, Senga proposes an original interpretation, arguing that in his late works Ricardo began to speak about absolute value after having modified his concept of relative value. This topic is also discussed by Noguchi (1993) and Mizuta (2004) in their works on what is 'rule or discretion' in Ricardo's writings.

It might be worth pointing out, in brief, two promising research areas on which future Ricardo studies should concentrate.

First, authors should broaden their research areas to scrutinise Ricardo's contemporaries, not only Smith and Malthus but also, for example, Bentham, J. Mill, Torrens, McCulloch, Thornton, Baring, Barton, Tooke, Sismondi, Say, Marcet, and Martineau. Understanding Ricardo's social network with his contemporaries might offer interdisciplinary approaches that comprise a promising and potentially fruitful field for future study (see Appendix).

Second, future works concentrate on topics such as value and distribution, wages, profits, rent, capital accumulation, machinery, foreign trade, finance and politics, poor laws, and money. In the past decade or so, some researchers have already started along this path. For example, Takenaga (2000) examines Ricardo's theories of value and money and concludes, based on his analysis of both *Principles* and *Absolute Value*, that Ricardo's value theory centres on cost production theory rather than the labour theory of value. Furthermore, by investigating original texts since *The Price of Gold*, he argues against Marx's interpretations of Ricardo's quantity theory of money.

Likewise, Dome (2004) argues that Ricardo's theories of government expenditure, taxation, and public debt have influenced public finance in Britain. Ebihara (2004) examines capital accumulation theory by focusing on the theory of machinery in connection with Sismondi and Barton. Sato (2006) reads closely chapters 8–18 in *Principles* on taxation as well as some controversial later chapters (i.e. 19–23, and 25) in order to outline Ricardo's price theory, taking particular note of his references to J.-B. Say. Fukuda (2006) analyses *Principles* and *An Essay on Profits* and, by distinguishing the differences in presuppositions, shows that Ricardo's economic theory can be characterised as the analysis of distribution and growth. Other studies in this regard include Nakamura (2009) who, based on his long research interest, offers an extensive and generous description of Ricardo's life, birth, religion, business, writings, activities in Parliament, and death. Finally, Ishii (2012) assesses the problem of poverty in capitalism by examining texts on machinery by Ricardo, Barton, and Marx. Further interpretative studies along these lines would expand Japanese studies of Ricardo and keep it a dynamically evolving field of study in Japan.

4. Concluding remarks

Various elements beyond the reception and diffusion of Ricardo can be recognised as holding sway in Japan from the late nineteenth to early twenty-first centuries. How was Ricardo's economics received during this period in Japan? We can distinguish five crucial points. First, in the late nineteenth and early twentieth centuries, the Japanese interest in Ricardo can be said to have peaked in the 1920s, judging by the number of scholarly works on Ricardo published in that decade (see Figure 7.2).[25] Two periods of crises engulfed Japan – 1920 and 1927 – before the worldwide depression of 1929–1932, and the sense of social ruin palpable in Japan at this time implied – for Japanese nationalists, in particular – the demise of the home country in both the material and the spiritual senses. Under such circumstances, there arose a strong interest in the theories of Ricardo among Japanese intellectuals.

Second, the translation of Western economic writings played a significant role in advancing and expanding the field of Ricardo studies in Japan particularly between the Meiji Restoration and World War II. As can be seen from Figure 7.3, translations account for 112 of the 396 total publications related to Ricardian thought.

Third, Japanese scholars focused their attention on Ricardo's theories of rent, value, and money in the late nineteenth and early twentieth centuries (see Figure 7.3).[26] They were particularly interested in confronting the real challenges of their day and age, such as the reform of the land and banking systems, low wages, unemployment, and so on. It should also be emphasised that

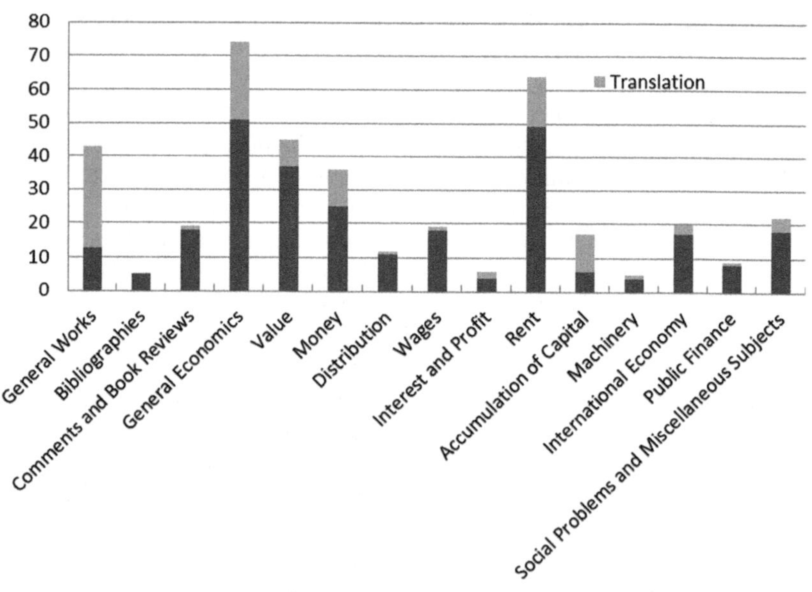

Figure 7.3 Field of Ricardo studies in Japan: 1869–1944

some intellectuals even attempted to use Ricardo's differential rent theory to support their ideas of 'socialism'.

Fourth, careful consideration is required as to the reason for Ricardo's delayed introduction in Japan. 'Political economy' in the broad sense, including social philosophy, morals, policy study, and state theory, but not 'economics' in the narrow sense, was seemingly viewed as more pressing for intellectuals at that time. This finding is supported by the fact that translations of J. S. Mill, Smith, Malthus, Say, Marshall, and Marx appeared much earlier than those of Ricardo in Japan. However, why economic thought, in a broad sense, did not spread its roots in Japanese society remains unclear.[27]

Fifth, after World War II, it seems as though Japanese studies of Ricardo did not result in antagonistic conflict, as it did in the West between Sraffians and neoclassical economists. However, this declaration does not imply an absence of controversy among Japanese scholars. On the contrary, as mentioned above, heated discussions were frequent. However, Japanese scholars rather tended to mention their own theories clearly to each other, dispute and examine differences or coincidences, and bring discussions to meaningful consensus. In this respect, the publication of the *Works* of Ricardo provided a turning point for establishing such studying styles. After the 1970s at the latest, Japanese studies were forced to be grounded in Ricardo's original sources, suggesting that mere ideological assertions spoken only by gathering Ricardo's partial words or sentences were repelled by his full texts. Such an academic atmosphere made – and continues to make – scholars more associative and active.

Notes

1 In August 1775, Thunberg (1743–1828) arrived at Dejima in the Bay of Nagasaki as the head surgeon of the Dutch factory of the V.O.C. (Verenigde Oost-Indische Compagnie). He left Japan in November 1776, stopped off at Java and Dutch Ceylon, and returned to Sweden in 1779. In 1781, he was appointed president of Uppsala University and he published *Flora Japonica* three years later.

2 See Mitsubashi ([1928], 1986: 6–7). Mitsubashi (1976) informs our understanding of economic and social thought in nineteenth-century Japan, as do the findings of Kada (1934, 1937) and Hori (1935). Yoshio Kōgyū (1724–1800), Katsuragawa Hoshū (1751–1809) and Nakagawa Jun'an (1739–86), the foremost Dutch scholars in Edo, were taught by Thunberg. Intriguingly, Miura Baien (1723–89), an original nature philosopher and the author of *The Origin of Price* (1773), which was an outstanding work among other economic writings at the time, was acquainted with Yoshio.

3 It has been widely held that the Japanese feudal government took up its national isolation policy in the Edo period, so there was limited contact with foreign countries during this time. However, various cultural exchanges with China and the Netherlands continued throughout Nagasaki. Shitsuki Tadao (1760–1806), a scholar of Dutch Learning, first used the term 'Sakoku' (national isolation) in his translated book *Sakoku-ron* (Theory of National Isolation) in 1801. This translation was from the last chapter of the appendix to the second Dutch edition of *De*

Beschryving Van Japan written by Engelbert Kaempfer, a German naturalist and physician, in 1773. In 1772, the original text *History of Japan* was published in two volumes in London, as the English translation from Kaempfer's unpublished manuscripts. Kaempfer stayed in Dejima, Nagasaki, as a doctor working at the Dutch trading house between 1690 and 1692.

4 Kaiho's attitude to overcoming traditional Confucianism can be considered to have been influenced by his close friend Katsuragawa, who was taught by Thunberg. For further details regarding their economic ideas, see, for example, Honjō (1957), Tamanoi (1971), Sugihara (1972), and Morris-Suzuki (1989).

5 For further details, see, for example, Morris-Suzuki (1989) and Komuro (1998).

6 However, it must be noted that the translation of Western economic writings involved much more than the simple replacement of Western words and phrases with their Japanese equivalents. Significant concepts inherent to Western societies and cultures, such as 'society', 'liberty', 'individual', 'nature', 'supply', and 'demand' did not exist in the Japanese language. Translators at the end of the Edo period and early Meiji period faced the almost unimaginable difficulty of creating totally new Japanese words and phrases.

7 This Dutch translation was from the second edition of the English original published in 1850. This was the first and last retranslation of the Dutch translation of Western economic writings.

8 For further details, see Minamimori (2008).

9 These schools were the origins of Japan's first university – Tokyo Imperial University, established in 1877. The first professor of economics at Tokyo Imperial University was Ernest Fenollosa (1853–1908) who is rather famous today as an eminent American art historian of Japanese art. It is said that he used the writings of J. S. Mill, J. E. Cairnes, W. G. Sumner, F. A. Walker, and others as the text books for his students, and they studied the economic theories of J. S. Mill, W. S. Jevons, H. D. Macleod, F. List, and W. Roscher, among others (Sugihara 1972: 10). Many foreign advisors like Fenollosa were hired by the Japanese government for their specialised knowledge, to encourage and support the industrialisation of Japan. Among them were Gustave Emile Boissonade de Fontarabie (1825–1910), Uda Eggert (1846–93), Dwight Whitney Learned (1848–1943), Karl Rathgen (1855–1921), George Victor Appert (1850–1934), and Adolf von Wenckstern (1862–1917). For further details of their contributions, see Sumiya (1948), Honjō (1957, 1966), and Sugihara (1980).

10 Tsuda translated Vissering's lecture on statistics into Japanese and published it in 1874. Although neither Tsuda nor Nishi translated his lecture on economics, Vissering's ideas were reflected in their articles concerning economy for the *Meiroku Zasshi* (Shimode [1929] 1992: 19–24, Honjō 1957: 5–6).

11 Nakamura translated Samuel Smiles's *Self-Help* and J. S. Mill's *On Liberty* into Japanese in 1871 and 1872, respectively. Both works proved to be extremely popular. The translation of *Self-Help* is said to have sold a million copies. Katō was a president of Tokyo Imperial University, and later became an advocator of social Darwinism.

12 These works can be categorised according to the nationality of the original authors, as follows: British, 103; American, 48; German, 40; French, 37; Austrian, 7; Belgian, 3; Dutch, 2; Italian, 2; unknown, 32.

13 In 1893, Soyeda refers to the fact that Western economic writings such as the works of J. S. Mill, Fawcett, Jevons, Marshall, Walker, and Roscher were taught in Japanese universities and colleges as text-books. In addition, the works of Wayland, Perry, Smith, J. S. Mill, and Fawcett became popular, while the translation of the works of these authors as well as of Carey, List, Jevons, and Marshall gradually emerged (Soyeda 1893: 334–35). There is no mention of Ricardo here.

14 Wada translated chapters 1–6, 21, and 30 of *Principles* from both editions of McCulloch's and Gonner's. Hori translated chapters 1–7, 19–21, 24, and 30–32 from Gonner's edition of *Principles* (Mazane 1975: 176).

15 Apart from the studies by Mazane (1962, 1965, 1975), only a few attempts have been made to analyse the reception of Ricardo's writings in the late nineteenth and early twentieth centuries in Japan. Mazane pointed out the following peculiarities of the reception: 1) it was unrelated to contemporary opinion; 2) Ricardo was indirectly introduced to Japan, through Marx; 3) the introduction of Ricardo's writings was late compared with those of J. S. Mill, Malthus, and Smith. While we are particularly indebted to these studies, we would like to reconsider a further, different possibility.

16 Christianity was also one of the thought systems imported from the West and had the greatest effect on the Japanese intellectuals of the late nineteenth and early twentieth centuries by making it possible to mount a fundamental critique of the existing systems in Japan.

17 Hayashi Masaaki and Suzuki Shigetaka also translated this book in 1873 and 1905, respectively.

18 This book also had a strong effect on the introduction in Japan of a co-operative idea.

19 Ishikawa Eisaku engaged in the sake brewing business in Nishi-Aizu, Fukushima. The Sakaegawa Shuzō still produces sake called 'Fukokuron' (*The Wealth of Nations*) in his memory.

20 Soyeda classified 26 Japanese economists into the following three schools: free trade, 8; protection, 6; state socialism, 6; neutral, 6, and says that 'Hitherto the University views have been more or less on the side of Free Trade, but now are tending towards State Socialism'. He also suggested that protectionists and state socialists were going to combine against free traders just before the Sino-Japanese War (Soyeda 1893: 336–38).

21 Kōtoku Shūsui, one of Nakae's students and a famous socialist and anarchist, was executed in early 1911 for being involved in 'Taigyaku Jiken' (The High Treason Incident). Kōtoku translated Marx's *Manifest der Kommunistischen Partei* together with Sakai Toshihiko, who was an Esperantist.

22 Kawakami also refers to these three groups in his 1919 article, 'Marx no Shakaishugi no Rironteki Taikei' (A Theoretical System of Marxist Socialism); however, he simply mentions *Atarashiki Mura* (New Village) published by Mushanokōji Saneatsu (1885–1976) as a leading publication of humanitarianism, with no discussion of Ruskin here (Kawakami [1919] 1982: 238–43). However, Kawakami again refers to Ruskin as a humanitarian economist in his book *Shihonshugi Keizaigaku no Shiteki Hatten* (Historical Development of Capitalist Economics) in 1923 (Kawakami [1923] 1982: ch.5). In this book, Kawakami re-describes the mainstream justification of self-interest by Mandeville, Smith, Bentham, Malthus, and Ricardo in the history of economic thought and the opposite development following J. S. Mill, Carlyle, Ruskin, and Marx's socialist economics.

23 Kimura points out the significance of the phrasing, 'from Ruskin to Marx', not 'Ruskin or Marx', and the positive evaluation of Ruskin as the father of the 'revival of socialism' (Kimura 1982: 3–4).

24 While Marxism was severely repressed by the government after the 1920s, the studies on Ruskin, Smith, and List escaped official sanction. In another paper, we aim to consider studies of Ricardo during the war.

25 The number of studies includes both direct and indirect studies on Ricardo. We cite the figure 396 here, but it must certainly be even greater than this. Some works were excluded because of unknown dates of publication.

26 It must be noted that Amano (1962) classifies each publication into 15 fields: General Works, Bibliographies, Comments and Book Reviews, General

Economics, Value, Money, Distribution, Wages, Interest and Profit, Rent, Accumulation of Capital, Machinery, International Economy, Public Finance, Social Problems, and Miscellaneous Subjects. However, it is difficult to verify the basis for Amano's classifications. We fundamentally follow his approach, but we have attempted to revise his classification and to count the number of publications based on Amano (1962) and some articles, and calculated each publication as one item. The period of greatest activity falls between 1924 and 1929.

27 The fact that 'political economy' took intellectual precedence over 'economics' will lead us to further consider this interesting question. However, to provide a satisfactory answer, more thorough research is needed to examine the full, complicated process of the general dissemination of Western thought in Japan. See Hayasaka (1971: 88–93).

References (for sections 1 and 2)

Abe, T. (1896) *Tetsuri Keizaigakushi* (Philosophical History of Economic Thought: a translation from *A History of Political Economy* written by J. K. Ingram). Tokyo: Keizai Zasshi-sha.

Amano, K. (1962) *Bibliography of the Classical Economics: vol.2, part 3, David Ricardo*. Tokyo: Science Council of Japan.

Amano, T. (1885) Rishi Chidairon (Ricardo's Theory of Rent), *Chuō Gakujutsu Zasshi* (Central Scientific Journal), 1, 2.

—— (1886) *Keizai Genron* (The Theory of Political Economy). Tokyo: Fuzanbo.

Bank of Japan (1876) *Ginkō Jikkenron* (A Practical Treaty on Banking: a translation from *A Practical Treatise on Banking, Currency, and the Exchanges* written by A. Crump). Tokyo: National Printing Bureau.

Fujimoto, K. (1908) Iwayuru Ricardo no Rōgin Tessoku nitsuite (On the So-called Iron Law of Wages of Ricardo), *Nihon Hōsei Shinshi* (New Journal of Japanese Law and Politics), 12(12).

Fukuda, T. ([1908] 1925) Ricardo no Chidairon kara Marx he (From the Rent Theory of Ricardo to Marx), *Keizaigaku Zenshū* (The Complete Works of Fukuda Tokuzō, 6 vols.), vol. 3. Tokyo: Dobunkan.

——([1912] 1925) Kachi no Gen-in to Shakudo tonikansuru Malthus to Ricardo tono Ronsō (Controversy on the Cause and Measure of Value between Malthus and Ricardo), *Keizaigaku Zenshū*, vol. 3. Tokyo: Dobunkan.

—— ([1913] 1925) Ricardo Keizaigenron no Chūshin Mondai (The Fundamental Issues of Ricardo's Theory of Economics), *Keizaigaku Zenshū*, vol. 3. Tokyo: Dobunkan.

Fukuzawa, Y. (1866) *Seiyō Jijō* (Affairs in the Western Countries). Tokyo: Shokodo.

Hamada, K. and I. Isemoto (1894) *Keizaigakushi* (History of Economics). Tokyo: Yao Shinsuke.

Hayasaka, T. (1971) Nihonkeizaigakushi no Shodanmen (1): Keizaigaku tono Sesshoku (Some Aspects of Japanese History of Economic Thought (1): Contact with Western Economics), *Keizai Seminar*, 193. Tokyo: Nippon Hyoron-sha.

Honjō, E. (1957) *Nihon no Keizaigaku* (Japanese Economics). Tokyo: Nippon Hyoron--sha.

—— (1966) *Nihon Keizai Shisōshi Kenkyū*, Jō (A Study on History of Japanese Economic Thought, 1st volume). Tokyo: Nippon Hyoron-sha.

Hori, T. (1929) *Ricardo no Kachiron oyobi sono Hihanshi* (Ricardo's Theory of Value and the History of its Criticism). Tokyo: Hyoron-sha.

—— (1935) *Meiji Keizaigakushi* (History of Economic Thought in the Meiji Period). Kyoto: Kobundo Shobo.

—— (1948) *Shinshū Meiji Keizaigakushi*, Jō (New edition: The History of Economic Thought in Meiji, 1st volume). Tokyo: Takashimaya Shuppanbu.

Inukai, T. (1880) Hogo Nan no Ii (What is Protectionism), *Tōkai Keizai Shinpō*, 1.

Ishikawa, E. (1884) *Fukokuron* (a translation from *The Wealth of Nations* written by Adam Smith). Tokyo: Keizai Zasshi-sha.

Kada, T. (1934) *Ishin Igo no Shakai Keizai Shisō Gairon* (Outlines of Social and Economic Thought after the Meiji Restoration). Tokyo: Nippon Hyoron-sha.

—— (1937) *Meiji Shoki Shakai Keizai Shisōshi* (History of Social and Economic Thought in the Early Meiji Period). Tokyo: Iwanami Shoten.

Kanda, T. (1867) *Keizai Shōgaku* (Elementary Economics). Tokyo: Kinokuniya Genbei.

—— ([1861] 1879) *Nōshōben* (An Exact Explanation of an Agrarian Nation and a Merchant Nation). In Doi, K. (ed.) *Keisei Yoron: Hyōten* (Supplementary Essay on Governing a Nation). Tokyo: Seieido.

Kawakami, H. ([1916] 1982) Jo (Preface to *Binbō Monogatari*), *Kawakami Hajime Zenshū* (The Complete Works of Kawakami Hajime, 36 vols.), vol. 9. Tokyo: Iwanami Shoten.

—— ([1918a] 1982) Ruskin no Kono Saigo no Mono nimo (Ruskin's *Unto This Last*), *Kawakami Hajime Zenshū*, vol. 9. Tokyo: Iwanami Shoten.

—— ([1918b] 1982) Jo (Preface to Ishida Kenji's translation of *Unto This Last*), *Kawakami Hajime Zenshū*, vol. 9. Tokyo: Iwanami Shoten.

—— ([1918c] 1982) Jo (Preface to Ruskin's *Unto This Last*), *Kawakami Hajime Zenshū*, vol. 9. Tokyo: Iwanami Shoten.

—— ([1919] 1982) Marx no Shakaishugi no Rironteki Taikei (A Theoretical System of Marxist Socialism), *Kawakami Hajime Zenshū*, vol. 10. Tokyo: Iwanami Shoten.

—— ([1923] 1982) *Shihonshugi Keizaigaku no Shiteki Hatten* (Historical Development of the Capitalist Economics), *Kawakami Hajime Zenshū*, vol. 13. Tokyo: Iwanami Shoten.

Kimura, M. (1982) Kawakami Hajime to Ruskin (Kawakami Hajime and Ruskin), *Kawakami Hajime Zenshū Geppō* (The Monthly Newsletter for *The Complete Works of Kawakami Hajime*), no. 3. Tokyo: Iwanami Shoten.

Kita, T. (1906) *Kokutairon oyobi Junsei Shakaishugi* (National Polity Theory and Genuine Socialism). Niigata: Kita Tetsujiro (self published).

Koizumi, S. (1929) *Ricardo Kenkyū* (Study on Ricardo). Tokyo: Tettoshoin.

Komuro, M. (1998) Trends in Economic Thought in the Tokugawa Period. In Sugihara, S. (ed.) *Economic Thought and Modernization in Japan*. Cheltenham: Edward Elgar.

Kushida, T. (1924) Shakaishugi wa Yami ni Mensuruka Hikari ni Mensuruka (Is Socialism Facing the Darkness or the Light: a book review on Professor Kawakami's *Shihonshugi Keizaigaku no Shiteki Hatten*), *Kaizō*, 6(7).

Maide, C. (1937) *Keizaigakushi Gaiyō*, Jō (Outline of the History of Economic Thought, 1st volume). Tokyo: Iwanami Shoten.

Matsumura, K. (1909) Chingin Gakusetsu (Theory of Wages), *Kokumin Keizai Zasshi*, 7(4).

Mazane, K. (1962) Meiji oyobi Taishō Zenki niokeru Ricardo Dōnyūshi (The Reception History of Ricardo in the Meiji Period and Early Taishō Period), *Keizaigaku Nenpo* (Osaka City University), 16.

—— (1965) Taishō Kōki yori Senzen madeno Ricardo Dōnyūshi (The Reception History of Ricardo from the late Taishō Period to Prewar Period), *Keizaigaku Nenpo* (Osaka City University), 22.

—— (1975) *Ricardo Keizaigaku Nyūmon* (Introduction to the Economics of Ricardo). Tokyo: Shin Hyoron.

Mikimoto, R. (1931) *What is Ruskin in Japan*. Tokyo: Shimei-sha.

Minamimori, S. (2008) Agrarian Taxes and Commercial Profits in Nōshōben: A Study of *An Exact Explanation of an Agrarian Nation and a Merchant Nation*, *The History of Economic Thought* (Japanese Society for the History of Economic Thought), 50 (1).

Mitsubashi, T. ([1928] 1986) Meiji Keizai Shisōshi Shiryō Kaidai (A Bibliographical Introduction to the History of Economic Thought in the Meiji Period), *Zatsubunshū, Furuhon to Furuhonya* (Miscellaneous Essays on Used Books and Used Bookstores). Tokyo: Nihon Koshotsushin-sha.

—— (1976) *Meiji Zenki Shisōshi Bunken* (Literature on the History of Ideas in the Early Meiji Period). Tokyo: Meijido Shoten.

Mori, K. (1926) *Ricardo Kachiron no Kenkyū* (Study on Ricardo's Theory of Value). Tokyo: Iwanami Shoten.

Morris-Suzuki, T. (1989) *A History of Japanese Economic Thought*. London: Routledge.

Nagata, K. (1877) *Hōshi Keizaigaku* (Fawcett's Economics: a translation from *Political Economy for Beginners* written by Millicent Garrett Fawcett). Tokyo: Nagata Kensuke.

Nakae, C. (1891) Seifukoku (The National Government), *Rikken Jiyū Shimbun* (Constitutional Liberal News), January 28. In Matsumoto, S., et al. (eds) *Nakae Chōmin Zenshū* (The Complete Works of Nakae Chōmin, 17 vols with 1 supplement), vol. 12. Tokyo: Iwanami Shoten.

Nakamura, M. (1871) *Saigoku Risshihen* (Stories of Self-made Men in the West: a translation from *Self-Help* written by Samuel Smiles). Tokyo: Kimura Aiji.

Nishi, A. ([1870] 1981) *Hyakugaku Renkan* (Encyclopaedia). In Okubo, T. (ed.) *Nishi Amane Zenshū* (The Complete Works of Nishi Amane, 4 vols), vol. 4. Tokyo: Munetaka Shobo.

Ogata, T. (1869) *Kanpan Keizaigenron* (The Principles of Economics: a translation from *Elements of Political Economy* written by A. L. Perry). Tokyo: Kaisei Gakko.

Ōhara, K. (1901) Ricardo shi no Chingin oyobi Rijunron wo Hyōsu (A Critical Comment on Ricardo's Theory of Wage and Profit), *Tokyo Keizai Zasshi* (Tokyo Economics Journal), 1065.

Sakatani, Y. (1887) *Keizaigakushi Kōgi* (Lecture of the History of Economic Thought). Tokyo: Tetsugaku Shoin.

Shimode, S. ([1929] 1992) Hyōki Teikō Kaidai (A Bibliographical Introduction to Statistics lectured by Simon Vissering), *Meiji Bunka Zenshū* (The Complete Works of Culture of the Meiji Period, [1927–29, 24 vols.], 1992, 32 vols.), [vol. 9], vol. 12. Tokyo: Nippon Hyoron-sha.

Soyeda, J. (1893) The Study of Political Economy in Japan, *The Economic Journal* (British Economic Association), 3. London: Macmillan.

Sugihara, S. (1972) *Seiō Keizaigaku to Kindai Nihon* (Western Economics and Modern Japan). Osaka: Kansai University Press.

—— (1980) *Nihon Keizai Shisōshi Ronshū* (Collection of Essays on History of Japanese Economic Thought). Tokyo: Mirai-sha.

—— (1992) *Nihon no Keizaigakushi* (History of Japanese Economic Thought). Tokyo: Mirai-sha.

—— (1998) Introduction Modernization and the Development of Economic Thought in Japan. In Sugihara, S. (ed.) *Economic Thought and Modernization in Japan*. Cheltenham: Edward Elgar.

Sumiya, E. (1948) *Nihon Keizaigakushi no Hitokoma* (A Page of History of Japanese Economic Thought). Tokyo: Nippon Hyoron-sha.

Suzuki, K. (1882) Keizaigaku Shitaika Hyōden (A Critical Biography of Four Great Economists), *Tokyo Keizai Zasshi*, 99.

Taguchi, U. (1878) *Nihon Keizairon: Jiyū Kōekiron* (Japanese Economy: Free Trade). Tokyo: Keizai Zasshi-sha.

Takata, S. (1884) *Kahei Shinron* (The New Monetary Theory). Tokyo: Toyokan.

Tamanoi, Y. (1971) *Nihon no Keizaigaku* (Japanese Economics). Tokyo: Chuokoron-sha.

Tsuda, M. ([1874] 1992) *Hyōki Teikō* (Introduction to Statistics lectured by Simon Vissering), *Meiji Bunka Zenshū* (The Complete Works of Culture of the Meiji Period, [1927–29, 24 vols.], 1992, 32 vols.), [vol. 9], vol. 12. Tokyo: Nippon Hyoron-sha.

Yoshida, K. (1908) *Eikoku Sangyō Kakushinron* (Industrial Innovation in England: a translation from *The Industrial Revolution in England* written by A. J. Toynbee). Tokyo: Dainihon Bunmei Kyokai.

Wakayama. G. (1877) *Jiyū Kōeki Anasagashi* (Finding Faults in Free Trade: a translation from *Sophisms of Free-Trade and Popular Political Economy Examined* written by J. B. Byles). Tokyo: Wakayama Giichi (self published).

References (for section 3)

Arai, E. (1998) Ricardo niokeru Rōdō Kachiron to Kahei Sūryōsetsu (Theory of Value and Quantity theory of Money on Ricardo), *Shakaikagakuronshu* (Saitama University), 93.

Dome, T. (2004) *The Political Economy of Public Finance in Britain 1767–1873*. London: Routledge.

Ebihara, R. (1974) *Kotenha Shihon Chikusekiron no Hatten to Rōdōshakaikyū* (Theory of Accumulation of Capital in Classical Economics and Working Class). Tokyo: Hoseidaigaku Shuppankyoku.

—— (2004) *Shihonchikuseki to Shitsugyō, Kyōkō* (Accumulation of Capital, Unemployment, and Crisis). Tokyo: Hoseidaigaku Shuppankyoku.

Fukuda, S. (2006) *Ricardo no Keizai Riron* (Economic Theories of Ricardo). Tokyo: Nihon Keizai Hyoron-sha.

—— (2008) Nihon no Shoki Ricardo Kenkyū (Japanese Studies on Early Ricardo), *Hirosakidaigaku Jinbunshakai Ronso* (Hirosaki University), 20.

Hatori, T. (1963) *Kotenha Shihonchikusekiron no Kenkyū* (Studies on Accumulation of capital in Classical Economics). Tokyo: Mirai-sha.

—— (1965) Shoki Ricardo no Kachi to Bunpai no Riron (The theory of Value and Distribution in Early Ricardo), *Shogakuronshu* (Fukushima University), 34(3).

—— (1966) Kotenha Chikusekiron no Keisei to Hatten (History of Studies on Capital Accumulation in Classical Economics in Japan), *The Annual Bulletin of Japan Society for the History of Economic and Social Thought*, 4.

—— (1972) *Kotenha Keizaigaku no Kihonmondai* (Fundamental Issues in Classical Political Economy). Tokyo: Mirai-sha.

—— (1977) Shoki Ricardo no Rijunritsu Teikaron I, II (Early Ricardo on the Falling Rate of Profit), *Keizaigakkaizasshi* (Okayama University), 9(1), 9(2).

—— (1982) *Ricardo Kenkyū* (Studies on Ricardo). Tokyo: Mirai-sha.

—— (1995) *Ricardo no Rironken* (Theoretical Sphere of Ricardo). Tokyo: Sekai-shoin.

Hishiyama, I. (1979) *Ricardo* (Ricardo). Tokyo: Nihonkeizai Shinbun-sha.

Hollander, S. (1979) *The Economics of David Ricardo*. Toronto: Toronto University Press.
Hori, T. ([1929] 1949), *Ricardo no Kachiron oyobi sono Hihanshi* (Ricardo's Theory of Value and the History of its Critiques). Tokyo: Hyoron-sha.
—— (1958) *Rironkeizaigaku no Seiritsu* (Formation of Theoretical Economics). Tokyo: Kobundo.
Ide, F. (1948) *Ricardo Kosairon* (Public Debt in Ricardo). Tokyo: Hokuryukan.
Ishii, J. (2012) *Kotenha Keizaigaku niokeru Shihonchikuseki to Hinkon* (Accumulation of Capital and Poverty in Classical Economics). Tokyo: Aoki Shoten.
Kobayashi, T. (1966) *Kotengakuha no Kōsatsu* (Studies on Classical Economics). Tokyo: Mirai-sha.
Marcuzzo, M. C. and A. Rosselli (1991) *Ricardo and the Gold Standard*, trans. J. Hall. London: Macmillan.
Mason, W. (1963) *Clarification of the Monetary Standard*. Philadelphia: University of Pennsylvania Press.
Masunaga, A. (1997) D. Ricardo no Kokuritsu Ginkō Puran (Plan for a National Bank in D. Ricardo), *Chuodaigaku Daigakuin Kenkyunenpo* (Chuo University), 26.
Matsuura, H. (1982) *Ricardo Keizaigaku* (Ricardo's Economics). Tokyo: Oka Shobo.
Mazane, K. (1959) *Kikai to Shitsugyō* (Machinery and Unemployment). Tokyo: Riron-sha.
—— (1975) *Ricardo Keizaigaku Nyūmon* (Introduction to Ricardo's Economics). Tokyo: Shinhyoron.
Mazane, K. and K. Mizokawa (1968) Nihon Keizaishisōshi (Introduction and Development of Classical Economics in Japan), *The Annual Bulletin of Japan Society for the History of Economic and Social Thought*, 6.
Mizokawa, K. (1966) *Kotenhakeizaigaku to Hanrosetsu* (Classical Economics and the Law of Market). Kyoto: Minerva Shobo.
Mizuta, K. (1981) Shoki Ricardo niokeru Kachiron to Bunpairon no Kanren (Relations of the Theory of Value and Distribution in Early Ricardo), *Keizaigaku Nenshi* (Hosei University), 18.
—— (1985) Gakkaitenbō: Ricardo Kenkyū (Japanese Studies on Ricardo), *The Annual Bulletin of Japan Society for the History of Economic and Social Thought*, 23.
—— (1994) Kaheiteki Bunseki no Shosō to Henri Thornton (Some Aspects of Monetary Analysis and Henri Thornton), *The Annual Bulletin of Japan Society for the History of Economic and Social Thought*, 32.
—— (2004) Keizaiseisaku to Keizai Jiyūshugi (Economic Policy and Economic Liberalism), *Kenkyunenpo Keizaigaku* (Tohoku University), 65(3).
Mori, S. (1992) *Kotenha Keizai Seichōron no Kihonkōzō* (Fundamental Structures of Economic Growth in Classical Schools). Tokyo: Dobunkan.
Morishima, M. (1989) *Ricardo's Economics*, Cambridge: Cambridge University Press.
Nakamura, H. (1968) Ricardo Keizaigaku Genri no Seiseikatei (Formation Processes of Ricardo's *Principles*), *Keizaironshu* (Oita University), 20(1), reappeared in Nakamura (1975).
—— (1972) Ricardo Kenkyū (Studies on Ricardo in Japan), *The Annual Bulletin of Japan Society for the History of Economic and Social Thought*, 10.
—— (1974) Ricardo Shoki Rijunron no Kansei (Completion of Early Ricardo's Theory of Profits), *Keizaironshu* (Oita University), 25(5).
—— (1975) *Ricardo Taikei* (A System of Ricardo). Kyoto: Minerva Shobo.
—— (1982) Ricardo Shoki Rijun Riron no Kansei to Kachiron no Seisei (The Completion of Ricardo's Early Theory on Profits and the Formation of Value Theory), *Nenpo Keizaigaku* (Hiroshima University), 3.

—— (1996) *Ricardo Keizaigaku Kenkyū* (Studies on Ricardo's Economics). Fukuoka: Kyushudaigaku Shuppankai.

—— (1999) Ricardo 'Jikin-an' Kō (Observation on Ricardo's 'Ingot Plan'), *Kumamotogakuendaigaku Keizaironshu* (Kumamoto Gakuen University), 5 (3/4).

—— (2000) Kinkachikiteiron no Kotentekikeifu: Mondaishiteki Kanken (A View on the Definition of Gold Value in Classical Economics), *Economics* (Kyushusangyo Univerysity), 4 (3/4).

—— (2007) Wagakuni niokeru Ricardo Kenkyū (Ricardo Studies in Japan), *Shokeironso* (Kanagawa University), 43(1).

—— (2009) *Ricardo Hyōden* (Ricardo's Critical Biography). Kyoto: Showado.

Nakamura, T. and M. Aramaki (1982) Kahei Shinyō Gakusetsushi Kenkyū (Research of Japanese Studies on Money and Credit), *The Annual Bulletin of Japan Society for the History of Economic and Social Thought*, 20.

Nakano, T. (1969) *Koten Kyōkōron* (Crisis in Classical Economics). Tokyo: Yushodo.

Nawa, T. (1949) *Kokusaikachiron Kenkyū* (Studies on the Theory of International Value). Nippon Hyoron-sha.

Negishi, T. (1983) *Keizaigaku no Rekishi* (History of Economics). Tokyo: Toyokeizai Shinpo-sha.

—— (2008) *Keizaigaku no Riron to Hatten* (Development of Economic Theory). Kyoto: Minerva Shobo.

Noguchi, A. (1993) Ricardo Taikei niokeru Kinkō to Hendō (Equiribrium and Fluctuation in Ricardo's System). In Hirai, H and Y. Fukagai (eds) *Shijō Shakai no Kenshō* (Verification of Market Society). Kyoto: Minerva Shobo.

Okada, M. (1994) Kaheiteki Keizai Rironshi niokeru Ricardo to Wicksell (Ricardo and Wicksell in a History of Monetary Theory), *The Annual Bulletin of Japan Society for the History of Economic and Social Thought,* 32.

Onishi, N. (1969) *Ricardo Shin-kenkyū* (New Studies of Ricardo). Tokyo: Nippon Hyoron-sha.

Otomo, T. (2001) *Shinyō Rironshi* (Theoretical History on Credit). Tokyo: Keiogijukudaigaku Shuppan.

Ricardo, D. ([1809] 1951–73) The Price of Gold. In Sraffa, P. (ed.) with the collaboration of M. H. Dobb, *The Works and Correspondence of David Ricardo*, vol.3. Cambridge: Cambridge University Press.

—— ([1815] 1951–73) *An Essay on the Influence of a Low Price of Corn on the Profits of Stock*. In Sraffa, P. (ed.) *The Works and Correspondence of David Ricardo,* vol.4. Cambridge: Cambridge University Press.

—— ([1816] 1951–73) *Proposals for an Economical and Secure Currency; with Observations on the Profits of the Bank of England*, In Sraffa, P. (ed.) *The Works and Correspondence of David Ricardo*, vol.4. Cambridge: Cambridge University Press.

—— ([1817] 1951–73), *On the Principles of Political Economy and Taxation*, 1st edn, 1817, 2nd edn, 1819, 3rd edn, 1821. In Sraffa, P. (ed.) *The Works and Correspondence of David Ricard*, vol 1. Cambridge: Cambridge University Press.

—— ([1823] 1951–73) *Absolute Value and Exchangeable Value*. In Sraffa, P. (ed.) *The Works and Correspondence of David Ricardo*, vol 4. Cambridge: Cambridge University Press.

—— ([1824] 1951–73) *Plan for the Establishment of a National Bank*. In Sraffa, P. (ed.) *The Works and Correspondence of David Ricardo*, vol 4. Cambridge: Cambridge University Press.

Sato, S. (2006) *Ricardo Kakakuron no Kenkyū* (Studies on Ricardo's Theory of Price). Tokyo: Yachiyo Shuppan.

—— (2008) Nihon niokeru Saikin no Ricardo Tsūkaron Kenkyū (Recent Japanese Studies on Ricardo's Theory of Currency), *Onomichidaigaku Keizaijohoronshu* (Onomichi university), 8 (2).

—— (2013) Japanese Studies on Ricardo after World War II, *The History of Economic Thought* (Japanese Society for the History of Economic Thought), 54(2).

Sato, Y. (1999) Genkinshiharai Saikai no Seijigaku (The Politics of the Resumption of Cash Payment: Reconsidering Ricardo's Plans for Bullion Payment and for the Establishment the National Bank), *Study Series*, no. 41. Tokyo: Center for Historical Social Science Literature (Hitotsubashi University).

—— (2002) Adam Smith to Seika Ryūshutsunyū Mekanizumu (Adam Smith and the Specie Flow Mechanism). In Otomo, T., Y. Ikeda and Y. Sato (eds) *Keizaishisō nimiru Kahei to Kinyū* (Money and Finance in the History of Economic Thought). Tokyo: Sanrei Shobo.

—— (2003) Kotenha Kahei Riron: Furui Kaishaku to Atarashii Kaishaku (The Interpretation of Classical Monetary Theory: Old and New), *The History of Economic Thought* (Japanese Society for the History of Economic Thought), 44.

Senga, S. (1972) Shoki Ricardo niokeru Kachi to Kahei no Riron (The Theory of Value and Money in Early Ricardo), *Keizai Kagaku* (Nagoya University), 19 (3).

—— (1989) *Ricardo Seijikeizaigaku Kenkyū* (Studies on Ricardo's Political Economy). Tokyo: Sanrei Shobo.

—— (1993a) Kanri Kahei wo meguru Ricardo to Keynes (The Theory of Managed Money in Ricardo and Keynes), *Yokohamashiritsudaigaku Ronso* (Yokohama City University), 44 (1/2/3).

—— (1993b) Bukkaron niokeru Ricardo to Jevons (The Theory of Consumer Prices in Ricardo and Jevons), *Keizai to Boeki* (Yokohama City University), 163.

—— (1996) Ricardo no Kinhoniron (Ricardo's Theory of the Gold Standard), *Kagoshimakeidaironshu* (Kagoshimakeizai University), 36(4).

—— (2011) Early Ricardo's Theory of Profit: From Two-Sector Approach to Value Theory, *The History of Economic Thought* (Japanese Society for the History of Economic Thought), 52(2).

Takagi, N. and H. Nakamura (1966) Kahei Shinyō Gakusetsu no Kenkyū (History of Studies of Money and Credit in Japan), *The Annual Bulletin of Japan Society for the History of Economic and Social Thought*, 4.

Takenaga, S. (2000) *Ricardo Keizaigaku Kenkyū* (Studies on Ricardo's Economics). Tokyo: Ochanomizu Shobo.

—— (2011) Ricardo no Kaheiriron niokeru Kahei Kachiron to Kahei Sūryōsetsu (Value of Money and Quantity Theory on Ricardo's Theory of Money), *Daitobunkadaigaku Keizaironshu* (Daitobunka University), 96.

Tamanoi. Y. (1954) *Ricardo kara Marx he* (From Ricardo to Marx). Tokyo: Shinhyoron-sha.

Tamanoi. Y., et al. (1973) Ricardo Kenkyū niokeru Seiō to Nihon (Notes on the Ricardo Symposium: Europe and Japan on Ricardo Studies), *The Annual Bulletin of Japan Society for the History of Economic and Social Thought*, 11.

Tomizuka, R. (1965) *Chikusekiron Kenkyū* (Studies on Accumulation of Capital). Tokyo: Mirai-sha.

Toyokura, M. (1959) *Kotenha Kyōkōron* (Crises in Classical Economics). Tokyo: Kobundo.

Tsutsui, T. (1973) *Ricardo Kenkyū* (Studies on Ricardo). Tokyo: Chuokeizai-sha.

Yoshizawa, Y. (1953) Kotenkeizaigaku no Kansei (Completion of Classical Political Economy). In Deguchi, Y. (ed) *Keizaigakushi* (History of Economic Thought). Kyoto: Minerva Shobo.

—— (1970) Hattenteki Shakaihaaku niokeru Ricardo to Marx (Concept of Advancing Society in Ricardo and Marx). In Uchida, Y. (ed) *Keizaigakushi* (History of Economic Thought). Tokyo: Chikuma Shobo.

Appendix. Further references on Japanese Ricardo studies

1) *Japanese translations of Ricardo's writings (chronological order)*

Wada, S. (1921) *Keizaigaku Genri (On the Principles of Political Economy and Taxation)* abridged edn. Tokyo: Uchida Rokakuho.

Hori, T. (1921) *Keizai Genron (On the Principles of Political Economy and Taxation)* abridged edn. Tokyo: Iwanami Shoten.

Koizumi, S. (1928) *Keizaigaku oyobi Kazei no Genri (On the Principles of Political Economy and Taxation,* 3rd. edn*)*. Tokyo: Iwanami Shoten.

Hori, T. (1928) *Keizai Genron (On the Principles of Political Economy and Taxation)* variorum edn. Kyoto: Kobundo Shobo.

Koizumi, S. (1930) *Keizai oyobi Sozei Genron* (*On the Principles of Political Economy and Taxation, 3rd. edn*). Tokyo: Iwanami Shoten.

Obata, S. (1931) *Ricardo Kahei Ginkō Ronshū (The Price of Gold, Three Contributions to the Morning Chronicle; The High Price of Bullion, A Proof of the Depreciation of Bank Notes; Reply to Mr. Bosanquet's Practical Observations on the Report of the Bullion Committee; Proposals for an Economical and Secure Currency; Plan for the Establishment of a National Bank)*. Tokyo: Dobunkan.

Yoshida, H. (1932) *Keizaigaku oyobi Kazei no Sho-Genri, Kokumotsu no Hikuki Kakaku, Nōgyō Hogoron* (*Economic Essays* edited with Introductory Essay and Notes by E.C.K. Gonner). Tokyo: Shunju-sha.

Mitamura, I. and F. Ide (1937) *Ricardo Gunji Kōsairon (Funding System)*. Tokyo: Maruzen.

Okawa, K. (1938) *Nōgyō Hogo Seisaku Hihan, Chidairon (On Protection to Agriculture; An Essay on the Influence of a Low Price of Corn on the Profits of Stock)*. Tokyo: Iwanami Shoten.

Nakano, T. (1942–43) *Ricardo no Malthus heno Tegami (Letters of David Ricardo to Thomas Robert Malthus, 1810–1823* edited by James Bonar*)*, 2 vols. Tokyo: Iwanami Shoten.

Ide, F. (1948) *Kōsairon (Funding System)*. Tokyo: Hokuryukan.

Yoshida, H. (1948) *Nōgyō Hogo Seisaku Hihan (On Protection to Agriculture)*. Tokyo: Nippon Hyoron-sha.

Yoshida, H. (1948) *Keizaigaku oyobi Kazei no Sho-Genri* (*On the Principles of Political Economy and Taxation*: 3rd edn). Tokyo: Shunju-sha.

Hori, T. (1948) *Keizai Genron (On the Principles of Political Economy and Taxation:* 3rd edn*)*, 2 vols. Tokyo: Kaizo-sha.

Kato, S. (1949) *Keizaigaku to Kazei no Sho-Genri* (*On the Principles of Political Economy and Taxation*, 3rd edn, Chapters 1–6). Tokyo: Kenshin-sha.

Nakano, T. (1949) *Ricardo no McCulloch heno Tegami (Letters of David Ricardo to John Ramsay McCulloch, 1816–1823* edited by Jacob Harry Hollander*)*. Tokyo: Iwanami Shoten.

Hattori, K. (1950) *Nōgyō Keizai Ronshū (On Protection to Agriculture; An Essay on the Influence of a Low Price of Corn on the Profits of Stock)*. Tokyo: Shunju-sha.

Koizumi, S. (1952) *Keizaigaku oyobi Kazei no Genri* (*On the Principles of Political Economy and Taxation*, 3rd edn), 2 vols. Tokyo: Iwanami Shoten.

Nakano, T. (1955) *Ricardo no Trower heno Tegami (Letters of David Ricardo to Hutches Trower and Others* edited by J. Bonar and J. H. Hollander*)*. Tokyo: Iwanami Shoten.

Takeuchi, K. (1961) *Ricardo, Malthus, Mill kara* (Ricardo's *Principles;* Malthus's *Population;* J. S. Mill's *Principles*). Tokyo: Keiyu-sha.

Takeuchi, K. (1962) *Keizaigaku oyobi Kazei no Genri* (*On the Principles of Political Economy and Taxation*, 3rd edn), 2 vols. Tokyo: Keiyu-sha.

Hatori, T. and Y. Yoshizawa (1964) *Keizaigaku oyobi Kazei no Genri* (*On the Principles of Political Economy and Taxation*, 3rd edn). Tokyo: Kawade Shobo Shin-sha.

Hatori, T. (1966) Rijunron *(An Essay on the Influence of a Low Price of Corn on the Profits of Stock)*. In Mizuta, H. (ed.) *Igirisu no Kindai Shisō* (Modern Thought in Britain). Tokyo: Kawade Shobo Shin-sha.

Suenaga, S., et al. (1969) *Zenki Ronbunshū: 1809–1811* (*Pamphlets and Paper, 1809–1811.* In Sraffa, P. (ed.) *The Works and Correspondence of David Ricardo,* vol. 3. Cambridge: Cambridge University Press). Tokyo: Yushodo Shoten.

Tamanoi. Y., et al. (1970) *Kōki Ronbunshū: 1815–1823* (*Pamphlets and Paper, 1815–1823.* In Sraffa, P. (ed.) *The Works and Correspondence of David Ricardo,* vol. 4). Tokyo: Yushodo Shoten.

Hori, T. (1970) *Denki oyobi Tairiku Ryokōki* (*Biographical Miscellany.* In Sraffa, P. (ed.) *The Works and Correspondence of David Ricardo,* vol. 10). Tokyo: Yushodo Shoten.

Nakano, T., et al. (1970–75) *Shokanshū: 1810–1815, 1816–1818, 1819–1821, 1821–1823* (*Letters, 1810–1815; 1816–1818; 1819–June 1821; July 1821–1823.* In Sraffa, P. (ed.) *The Works and Correspondence of David Ricardo,* vols. 6–9). Tokyo: Yushodo Shoten.

Suzuki, K. (1971) *Malthus Keizaigaku Genri Hyōchū* (*Notes on Malthus.* In Sraffa, P. (ed.) *The Works and Correspondence of David Ricardo,* vol. 2). Tokyo: Yushodo Shoten.

Hori, T. (1972) *Keizaigaku oyobi Kazei no Genri* (*On the Principles of Political Economy and Taxation.* In Sraffa, P. (ed.) *The Works and Correspondence of David Ricardo,* vol. 1). Tokyo: Yushodo Shoten.

Takeuchi, K. (1973) *Keizaigaku oyobi Kazei no Genri* (*On the Principles of Political Economy and Taxation*, 3rd edn). Tokyo: University of Tokyo Press.

Sugimoto, T., et al. (1978) *Gikai no Enzetsu oyobi Shōgen* (*Speeches and Evidence.* In Sraffa, P. (ed.) *The Works and Correspondence of David Ricardo,* vol. 5). Tokyo: Yushodo Shoten.

Takeuchi, K (1981) *Keizaigaku oyobi Kazei no Genri* (*On the Principles of Political Economy and Taxation*, 3rd edn). Tokyo: Chikura Shobo.

Hatori, T. and Y. Yoshizawa (1987) *Keizaigaku oyobi Kazei no Genri* (*On the Principles of Political Economy and Taxation*: 2nd edn), 2 vols. Tokyo: Iwanami Shoten.

Sugimoto, T., T. Hori, T. Nakano, et al. (1999) *Sō-sakuin* (*General Index.* In Sraffa, P. (ed.) *The Works and Correspondence of David Ricardo,* vol. 11). Tokyo: Yushodo Shoten.

2) *Others*

Dazai, S. ([1729] 1894) *Keizairoku* (Essay on Economy). Tokyo: Keizai Zasshi-sha.

Endo, A. (2002) Ricardo Shin Kikairon niokeru Ichimondai (Ricardo's Revised Theory on Machinery), *Kyushukyoritsudaigaku Kiyo* (Kyushukyoritsu University), 90.
Fujitsuka, T. (1973) *Keizaigaku Kurabu* (Political Economy Club). Kyoto: Minerva Shobo.
Fukamachi, I. (1959) Ricardo no Kinyūseisakuron nitsuite (On Ricardo's Theory of Monetary Policy), *Banking*, 138.
Hirao, S. (1975) *Ricardo-ha Shakaishugi no Kenkyū* (Studies on Ricardian Socialist). Kyoto: Minerva Shobo.
Hisamatsu, T. (2009) Robert Torrens' Theory of Profit Reconsidered, *History of Economic Review*, 49.
Honda, T. ([1798] 1970) *Seiiki Monogatari* (A Story on the West). In Tsukatani, A. (ed.) *Nihon Shisō Taikei*, vol. 44. Tokyo: Iwanami Shoten.
Iida, H., M. Izumo, and Y. Yanagita (eds) (2006) *Malthus to Dōjidaijintachi* (Malthus and his Contemporaries). Tokyo: Nihon Keizai Hyoron-sha.
Izumo, M. (2006) Jane Marcet to Keizaigaku no Taishūka (Jane Marcet and Popularization of Economics). In Iida, H., M. Izumo, and Y. Yanagita (eds) *Malthus to Dōjidaijintachi* (Malthus and his Contemporaries). Tokyo: Nihon Keizai Hyoron-sha.
Kaiho S. ([1813] 1970) *Keikodan* (A Practical Essay). In Kuranami, S. (ed.) *Nihon Shisō Taikei*, vol. 44. Tokyo: Iwanami Shoten.
Kamata,T. (1968) *Kotenhakeizaigaku to Shoki Shakaishugi* (Classical Economics and Early Socialism). Tokyo: Mirai-sha.
Kitami, H. (2001) J.-B.Say to Geneva (J.-B.Say and Geneva), *Bulletin of the Center for Hitotsubashi Social Science Literature* (Hitotsubashi University), 21.
Kumazawa, B. ([1672] 1971) *Shūgi Washo* (Essays in Japanese), In Goto, Y. and R. Tomoeda (eds) *Nihon Shisō Taikei*, vol. 30. Tokyo: Iwanami Shoten.
Masunaga, A. (2004) 19 Seiki Shoki no Gikaikaikakumondai niokeru Konsuitchūshonron to D. Ricardo (Ricardo on Reform of Parliament and Constitution in the Early 19th Century), *Keizaigakuronshu* (Meikai University),16.
Mizuta, K. (1992) Smith to Ricardo toniokeru Kachi Bunpairon (Theory of Value and Distribution in Smith and Ricardo), *Keizaigakushi: Kadai to Tenbō* (Issues and Perspectives in the History of Economic Thought). Fukuoka: Kyushudaigaku Shuppankai.
Mori, K. (2008) *Koten Keizaigaku no Chihei* (Horison of Classical Economics). Kyoto: Minerva Shobo.
Moroizumi, S. (2008) Ricardo no Kikairon nitsuite (On Ricardo's Theory of Machinery), *Sagadaigaku Bunkakyoikugaku Kenkyu Ronbunshu* (Saga University),13(1).
Nagamine, A. (2008) James Mill to D. Ricardo (James Mill and D. Ricardo), *Seikeironso* (Meiji University), 77(1/2).
Nakamiya, T. (2004) Sismondi to Ricardo no Ichisetten (A Point of Contact between Sismondi and Ricardo), *Shin Sennenki no Paradaimu* (Paradigm of the New Millennium). Fukuoka: Kyushudaigaku Shuppankai.
Nakamura, H. (1983) Ricardo Shoki Rijun Riron no Kaitai to Kachiron no Kakuritsukatei (The Collapse of Ricardo's Early Theory on Profits and the Establishing Process of his Value Theory), *Nenpo Keizaigaku* (Hiroshima University), 4.
—— (1992) Malthus to Ricardo (Malthus and Ricardo), *Keizaigakushi: Kadai to Tenbō* (Issues and Perspectives in the History of Economic Thought). Fukuoka: Kyushudaigaku Shuppankai.
Onuma, S. (2011) *Keizaishisōshi* (History of Economic Thought). Tokyo: Sousei-sha.
Otonashi, M. (ed) (2007) *Kōrishugi to Shakai Kaikaku no Shoshisō* (Utaritarianism and Thoughts of Social Reform). Tokyo: Chuodaigaku Shuppanbu.

—— (ed) (2011) *Kōrishugi to Seisakushisō no Tenkai* (Utilitarianism and Development of Thought of Policy). Tokyo: Chuodaigaku Shuppanbu.

Satō, N. ([1827] 1876) *Keizaii Yōroku* (Ountline of Economics), 7 vols. Tokyo: Gyokuzando, et al.

Senga, S. (1992) Ricardo to Marx (Ricardo and Marx), *Keizaigakushi: Kadai to Tenbō* (Issues and Perspectives in the History of Economic Thought). Fukuoka: Kyushu-daigaku Shuppankai.

Shibata, K. (1935–36) *Riron Keizaigaku* (Theoretical Economics), 2 vols. Tokyo: Kobundo.

Shiozawa, Y. (2007) Ricardo Bōekiriron no Shinkōsei (Reconstitution of Ricardo's Theory of Trade), *Keizaigaku Zasshi* (Osaka City University), 107(4).

Shirasugi, T. (2005) *Sraffa Keizaigaku Kenkyū* (Study on Sraffa's Economics). Kyoto: Minerva Shobo.

Takamasu, A. (1991) *Neo-Ricardian no Bōeki Riron* (Theory of Foreign Trade in the Neo-Ricardians). Tokyo: Sobun-sha.

Watarai, K. (2000) David Ricardo no Kyūhinron to Chochikuginkō (David Ricardo on Poor Relief and Saving Banks), *Study Series*, no. 45. Tokyo: Center for Historical Social Science Literature (Hitotsubashi University).

Name index*

* The name of David Ricardo has been omitted.

For Product Safety Concerns and Information please contact our EU representative GPSR@taylorandfrancis.com Taylor & Francis Verlag GmbH, Kaufingerstraße 24, 80331 München, Germany

Batch number: 10725973

Printed by Printforce, the Netherlands